PELICAN BOOKS

Psychoanalysis and Women

JEAN BAKER MILLER earned her B.A. at Sarah
Lawrence College and her M.D. at Columbia.
Certified by the New York Medical College in
1958, she is today a practicing psychoanalyst
and psychiatrist as well as Clinical Assistant
Professor in the Department of Psychiatry at
Albert Einstein College of Medicine in New
York. She has served as Secretary of the American Academy of Psychoanalysis and in 1972
and 1973, spent a year at the Tavistock Institute and Clinic in London. Articles by Dr. Miller have appeared in numerous professional
journals. *Psychoanalysis and Women* is her first
book.

Psychoanalysis

AND

WOMEN

EDITED BY JEAN BAKER MILLER, M.D.

PENGUIN BOOKS

Penguin Books Ltd, Harmondsworth,
Middlesex, England
Penguin Books, 625 Madison Avenue,
New York, New York 10022, U.S.A.
Penguin Books Australia Ltd, Ringwood,
Victoria, Australia
Penguin Books Canada Limited, 2801 John Street,
Markham, Ontario, Canada L3R 1B4
Penguin Books (N.Z.) Ltd, 182–190 Wairau Road,
Auckland 10, New Zealand

First published 1973
Reprinted 1974, 1977

Library of Congress catalog card number: 72–95634

Printed in the United States of America by
Kingsport Press, Inc., Kingsport, Tennessee
Set in Monotype Bulmer

A hard-cover professional edition of this work is available from
Brunner/Mazel, Inc., 19 Union Square West, New York, New York 10003.

Acknowledgments

"The Flight from Womanhood: The Masculinity Complex in Women as Viewed by Men and by Women" reprinted in slightly abridged form from *International Journal of Psycho-Analysis* 7 (1926): 324–39 with the permission of the International Journal of Psycho-Analysis, the Karen Horney estate, and the Association for the Advancement of Psychoanalysis.

"The Problem of Feminine Masochism" reprinted in slightly abridged form from the *Psychoanalytic Review* 12, no. 3 (1935): 241–57 through the courtesy of the editors and the publisher of the National Psychological Association for Psychoanalysis, the Karen Horney estate, and the Association for the Advancement of Psychoanalysis. Copyright © 1935 by the *Psychoanalytic Review*.

"Sex" in an abridged form reprinted from *Understanding Human Nature* by Alfred Adler. Reprinted with the permission of Dr. Kurt A. Adler and George Allen & Unwin Ltd. Copyright © 1927, 1954 by Kurt A. Adler.

" 'Penis Envy' in Women" originally published in *Psychiatry* 6 (1943): 123–25 and reprinted with the special permission of the William Alanson White Psychiatric Foundation, Inc., and with the permission of Dr. Maurice R. Green, executor and editor of Clara Thompson's papers. Copyright © 1943 by the William Alanson White Psychiatric Foundation, Inc.

"Some Effects of the Derogatory Attitude Toward Female Sexuality" reprinted from *Psychiatry* 13 (1950): 349–54 with the special permission of the William Alanson White Psychiatric Foundation, Inc., and the permission of Dr. Maurice R. Green. Copyright © 1950 by the William Alanson White Psychiatric Foundation, Inc.

"Cultural Pressures in the Psychology of Women" reprinted in slightly abridged form from *Psychiatry* 5 (1942): 331–39 with the special permission of the William Alanson White Psychiatric Foundation, Inc., and with the permission of Dr. Maurice R. Green. Copyright © 1942 by the William Alanson White Psychiatric Foundation, Inc.

choanalysis. Copyright © 1970 by Ruth Moulton and Contemporary Psychoanalysis.

"The Sense of Femaleness" reprinted from the *Psychoanalytic Quarterly* 37 (1968): 42–55. Reprinted with permission of the Psychoanalytic Quarterly.

"The Bedrock of Masculinity and Femininity: Bisexuality" reprinted in an abridged form from the *Archives of General Psychiatry* 26 (1972): 207–12. Reprinted with permission of the Archives of General Psychiatry. Copyright © 1972 by the American Medical Association.

"Phobias after Marriage: Women's Declaration of Dependence" reprinted from the *American Journal of Psychoanalysis* 31, no. 2 (1971): 144–52 with the permission of the editor of the American Journal of Psychoanalysis.

"Is Anatomy Destiny?" and "For the Future—Equity?" reprinted in abridged form from *Marriage in Life and Literature*, by Robert Seidenberg, with the permission of Philosophical Library, Inc. Copyright © 1970 by Philosophical Library.

"The Trauma of Eventlessness" reprinted in an abridged form from the *Psychoanalytic Review* 59, no. 1 (1972): 95–109. Reprinted through the courtesy of the editors and the publisher of the National Psychological Association for Psychoanalysis, New York, N.Y.

"Masculinity-Femininity: A Study in Imposed Inequality" reprinted by permission of the author.

Contents

Introduction

WHAT DO WOMEN WANT—and need? For the first time the psychological and social sciences are being asked to establish a body of modern knowledge about women in answer to this and other related questions. Psychoanalytic ideas have, in the modern era, exerted the greatest weight on our outlook on the nature of femininity. They have prevailed throughout most of this century and dominated the conception of women portrayed in the professional and popular media.

But is psychoanalysis relevant to women today—either as therapy or as theory on the nature of women? Many women have raised this pertinent question.

The writings collected here, however, present a view of women that differs from the commonly known psychoanalytic formulations. They bring forward a new outlook on the psychology of women and provide a forum from which to reexamine the role that the suppression of women has played in the conscious and unconscious life of both sexes. In addition, the biological sciences have now given us new scientific information on women, which the contributors have incorporated into their thinking and used to advance their psychological formulations.

In view of the significance of these contributions, it is remarkable that many people—especially, but not only, young people—do not seem to know that psychoanalysts who offer alternative ideas did and do exist. This is particularly striking because many of these analysts are highly gifted, some quite prominent in the field. Their writing is germane to the changing situation of women today; to changes that are taking place amidst political and social conditions marked by new pressures for population control, the inverse relationship between women's growing participation in the labor force and the economic advancement available to them, the so-called sexual revolution, the crisis in the family, and other dilemmas that affect women but over which they have previously assumed little leadership.

Many women today are seeking to enlarge their vision of life. Perhaps the many recent complicated changes can be tentatively summarized by saying that women in large numbers are trying to *grow*. They are more openly questioning the meaning and consequences of all their activities and seeking out the challenge that personal growth can bring to their own lives and to the lives of others. This inquiry into past purposes and the search for self-definition is engaging women in totally new sets of decisions, implying even deeper responsibilities than the ones they have traditionally shouldered. Moreover, large numbers of women, not merely the great or exceptionally gifted, have embarked on this course. They seek to move from perceptions into action rather than resignation. They are doing so today, against a background of major national social and political issues that mark our time.

These contributions compose a significant body of fresh material from which to focus on the difficult questions that women now face. The papers were written at various times for various reasons, and therefore do not proceed from a single starting point. They have been selected because the specifics of the problems discussed lead to more generally applicable themes. None of these authors pretends to know the final truth; most caution against such claims, but all offer provocative, valuable, and sometimes quite unexpected formulations.

Very early in the development of the psychoanalytic movement, several psychoanalysts began to offer alternative ideas on the psychology of women. Gregory Zilboorg, in the paper included here, related that this issue was the main subject of contention within the psychoanalytic movement in the years between 1925 and 1935, and was also one of the underlying reasons for the first major schism within the field in the United States in the late 1930s and '40s. Many of these early writings are still pertinent today. Although some material has been superseded by new knowledge, it is impressive to see how many of the early ideas have been substantiated by subsequent scientific data. A brief sampling of this material is included in the hope that it will spark a renewed interest in, and recognition of, that body of work.

A few preliminary observations require comment. It is striking to realize that in the psychoanalytic writings on the *psychology* of women, the greatest amount of material is on their *sexuality*. This finding is a comment in itself. To some extent it is attributable to some of the authors' grounding in the classical psychoanalytic tradition. The authors here, in most cases, present material on women as total people. In an effort to avoid undue emphasis on sexuality, some valuable papers have been omitted. Conversely, other papers have been chosen which offer a different view of sexuality in relation to both sexes because the implications are especially cogent for women.

In order to make the material more accessible to the general reader, a few papers have been edited, especially those that were written some time ago. Editorial comments, when pertinent, are provided in brackets or as footnotes for explanatory purposes. Since several authors review portions of Freud's theories before presenting their own material, some articles have been condensed to avoid repetition.

For those less familiar with psychoanalysis it seemed important to place the earlier writers into perspective in the history of the field. The shortness of introductory notes on more recent authors should not be interpreted as an evaluation of importance; on the contrary, it should indicate the lack of necessity to comment on people whose contemporary stature is self-evident. For a truly valid appreciation of the material, the reader is urged to use this collection as a guide and to consult the original papers and the additional references.

I believe each paper offers something of value, often great value, yet there are portions—sometimes only words or phrases—that convey attitudes I do not share. In some cases these points of difference are made obvious in the concluding chapter. Equally, the authors' kind permission to reprint their work in no way indicates that they endorse my outlook. Clearly, then, I do not look upon this book as a statement of final knowledge. I trust that none of it is. If we are truly serious in thinking that an understanding of women will be greatly enlarged and developed, then we must also believe that all this material will soon be seen within a new, fuller context.

Like most psychoanalytic writing, the material is marked by the refinements of a highly trained discipline, with ideas grown out of intensive work with troubled people. This background offers the advantage of carefulness and, in some cases, imaginativeness. But it does not tend to produce visionaries; with a few notable exceptions, psychoanalysts do not leap too freely into what might be—and that is the issue for many women today. This book is, however, an assemblage of some of the history and the present state of knowledge among psychoanalysts who have worked at developing new starting points for a more valid understanding of women.

I should like to thank those who have referred me to papers of which I was unaware. Several people have done so at various times in the past—long before I started this collection. Unfortunately, I do not remember all their names, but I should like to acknowledge their contribution along with that of Ruth Moulton, Esther Greenbaum, Marianne Echardt, Robert Seidenberg, Jack Schmiel, Samuel M. Seitz, and my husband, Mike (S. M.) Miller.

Special thanks go to Margit Winckler and Valerie Greer, who both made major contributions to the formulations of the ideas expressed in the editorial portions and to assembling the material. Most importantly, their interest, aid, and enthusiasm, together with the assistance of Colin Greer, helped to bring this venture to fruition.

I consider myself luckier than most in being able to engage in my own personal struggle for equality with three fine and rare men, my husband, Mike, and my sons Jon and Ned. In the course of this and other work, they have been taking steps in the continuing growth process of learning what it means to men when a woman tries to develop "a room of her own." It has disrupted the accustomed pattern of their lives considerably but, hopefully, it has replaced it with something more valuable. My husband has contributed to many discussions of these ideas. But perhaps a sign of greater progress—for ideas are not difficult for him—he merits thanks for doing some of the typing.

J. B. M.

PART I

Pertinent Pioneers

KAREN HORNEY

WHILE STILL a member of the early group around Freud, Dr. Horney presented evidence to support the radical idea that women had their own particular development—not merely a lesser and defective version of the male's. The two selections of her work that follow, written between 1917 and 1933, demonstrated that even within the framework of classical psychoanalytic methodology a new view of women was possible and even necessary. They have been chosen to represent some ideas of the early Freudian psychoanalysts who raised questions about the basic premises concerning the psychoanalytic conception of women. During the twenties and early thirties several other analysts, including Ernest Jones, Josine Muller, and Carl Muller-Braunschweig, also differed with some of Freud's fundamental assumptions about women.

Horney, herself, went on from her studies of women to create a new general psychoanalytic theory in which biological events were no longer crucial determinants of personality development. Thus, she totally revised many of the views presented here. For this reason part of her discussion of the feminine oedipal complex and other issues have been condensed in the first selection. In the second article, part of the detailed plan she proposed for an anthropological study of masochism has also been shortened.

After 1935 Horney did not publish any further papers specifically on women; her later works were addressed to both sexes out of the belief that both men and women needed to develop as full human beings.

Founder and dean of the American Institute for

Psychoanalysis and the American Association for the Advancement of Psychoanalysis, and founding editor of the *American Journal of Psychoanalysis,* Karen Horney was born in Hamburg, Germany, in 1885; she died in New York City in 1952. She is the author of six books, among them *Our Inner Conflicts* and *New Ways in Psychoanalysis.*

The Flight from Womanhood

THE MASCULINITY COMPLEX IN WOMEN AS VIEWED BY MEN AND BY WOMEN

IN SOME OF HIS LATEST WORKS Freud has drawn attention with increasing urgency to a certain one-sidedness in our analytical researches. I refer to the fact that until quite recently the minds of boys and men only were taken as objects of investigation.

The reason for this is obvious. Psychoanalysis is the creation of a male genius, and almost all those who have developed his ideas have been men. It is only right and reasonable that they should evolve more easily a masculine psychology and understand more of the development of men than of women.

The significance of penis envy has been extended quite recently by the hypothesis of the phallic phase. By this we mean that in the infantile genital organization in both sexes only one genital organ, namely the male, plays any part, and that it is just this that distinguishes the infantile organization from the final genital organization of the adult. According to this theory, the clitoris is conceived of as a phallus, and we assume that little girls as well as boys attach to the clitoris in the first instance exactly the same value as to the penis.

The effect of this phase is partly to inhibit and partly to promote the subsequent development. Helene Deutsch has demonstrated principally the inhibiting effects. She is of the opinion that at the beginning of every new sexual function (e.g., at the beginning of puberty, of sexual intercourse, of pregnancy and childbirth), this phase is re-activated and has to be overcome every time before a feminine attitude can be attained. Freud has elaborated her exposition on the positive side, for he believes that it is only penis envy and the overcoming of it which gives rise to the desire for a child and thus forms the love bond to the father.

The question now arises as to whether these hypotheses have helped to make our insight into feminine development (insight that Freud himself has stated to be unsatisfactory and incomplete) more satisfactory and clear.

Science has often found it fruitful to look at long-familiar facts from a fresh point of view. Otherwise there is a danger that we shall involuntarily continue to classify all new observations among the same clearly defined groups of ideas.

The new point of view of which I wish to speak came to me by way of philosophy, in some essays by Georg Simmel.* The point that Simmel makes and that has been in many ways elaborated since, especially from the feminine side, is this: Our whole civilization is a masculine civilization. The State, the laws, morality, religion, and the sciences are the creation of men. Simmel by no means deduces from these facts, as is commonly done by other writers, an inferiority in women, but he first of all gives considerable breadth and depth to this conception of a masculine civilization:

The requirements of art, patriotism, morality in general and social ideas in particular, correctness in practical judgment and objectivity in theoretical knowledge, the energy and the profundity of life—all these are categories which belong as it were in their form and their claims to humanity in general, but in their actual historical configuration they are masculine throughout. Supposing that we describe these things, viewed as absolute ideas, by the single word "objective," we then find that in the history of our race the equation objective = masculine is a valid one.

* See Bibliography, page 408. These essays are not available in an English translation.—ED.

Now Simmel thinks that the reason why it is so difficult to recognize these historical facts is that the very standards by which mankind has estimated the values of male and female nature are

not neutral, arising out of the differences of the sexes, but in themselves essentially masculine. . . . We do not believe in a purely "human" civilization, into which the question of sex does not enter, for the very reason that prevents any such civilization from in fact existing, namely, the (so to speak) naïve identification of the concept "human being" and the concept "man" which in many languages even causes the same word to be used for the two concepts. For the moment I will leave it undetermined whether this masculine character of the fundamentals of our civilization has its origin in the essential nature of the sexes or only in a certain preponderance of force in men, which is not really bound up with the question of civilization. In any case this is the reason why, in the most varying fields, inadequate achievements are contemptuously called "feminine," while distinguished achievements on the part of women are called "masculine" as an expression of praise.

Like all sciences and all valuations, the psychology of women has hitherto been considered only from the point of view of men. It is inevitable that the man's position of advantage should cause objective validity to be attributed to his subjective, affective relations to the woman, and according to Delius the psychology of women hitherto actually represents a deposit of the desires and disappointments of men.

An additional and very important factor in the situation is that women have adapted themselves to the wishes of men and felt as if their adaptation were their true nature. That is, they see or saw themselves in the way that their men's wishes demanded of them; unconsciously they yielded to the suggestion of masculine thought.

If we are clear about the extent to which all our being, thinking, and doing conform to these masculine standards, we can see how difficult it is for the individual man and also for the individual woman really to shake off this mode of thought.

The question then is how far analytical psychology also, when its researches have women for their object, is under the spell of this way of thinking, insofar as it has not yet wholly left behind the stage in which frankly and as a matter of course masculine development only was considered. In other words, how far has the evolution of women, as depicted to us today by analysis, been measured by masculine standards, and how far therefore does this picture fail to present quite accurately the real nature of women?

If we look at the matter from this point of view our first impression is a surprising one. The present analytical picture of feminine development (whether that picture be correct or not) differs in no case by a hair's breadth from the typical ideas that the [little] boy has of the girl.

We are familiar with the ideas that the boy entertains. I will therefore only sketch them in a few succinct phrases, and for the sake of comparison will place in a parallel column our ideas of the development of women.

The Boy's Ideas	Our* Ideas of Feminine Development
Naïve assumption that girls as well as boys possess a penis	*For both sexes it is only the male genital which plays any part*
Realization of the absence of the penis	*Sad discovery of the absence of the penis*
Idea that the girl is a castrated, mutilated boy	*Belief of the girl that she once possessed a penis and lost it by castration*
Belief that the girl has suffered punishment that also threatens him	*Castration is conceived of as the infliction of punishment*

* "Our" refers to psychoanalysts' ideas on this subject.—ED.

8

The Boy's Ideas	Our Ideas of Feminine Development
The girl is regarded as inferior	*The girl regards herself as inferior. Penis envy*
The boy is unable to imagine how the girl can ever get over this loss or envy	*The girl never gets over the sense of deficiency and inferiority and has constantly to master afresh her desire to be a man*
The boy dreads her envy	*The girl desires throughout life to avenge herself on the man for possessing something she lacks*

The existence of this overexact agreement is certainly no criterion of its objective correctness. It is quite possible that the infantile genital organization of the little girl might bear as striking a resemblance to that of the boy as has up until now been assumed.

But it is surely calculated to make us think and take other possibilities into consideration. For instance, we might follow Georg Simmel's train of thought and reflect whether it is likely that female adaptation to the male structure should take place at so early a period and in so high a degree that the specific nature of a little girl is overwhelmed by it. Later I will return for a moment to the point at which it does actually seem to me probable that this infection with a masculine point of view occurs in childhood. But it does not seem to me clear offhand how everything bestowed by nature could be thus absorbed into it and leave no trace. And so we must return to the question I have already raised—whether the remarkable parallelism I have indicated may not perhaps be the expression of a one-sidedness in our observations, due to their being made from the man's point of view.

Now, if we try to free our minds from this masculine mode of thought, nearly all the problems of feminine psychology take on a different appearance.

The first thing that strikes us is that it is always, or

principally, the genital difference between the sexes which has been made the cardinal point in the analytical conception and that we have left out of consideration the other great biological difference, namely, the different parts played by men and by women in the function of reproduction.

At this point I, as a woman, ask in amazement, and what about motherhood? And the blissful consciousness of bearing a new life within oneself? And the ineffable happiness of the increasing expectation of the appearance of this new being? And the joy when it finally makes its appearance and one holds it for the first time in one's arms? And the deep pleasurable feeling of satisfaction in suckling it and the happiness of the whole period when the infant needs her care?

Certainly, regarded from the standpoint of the social struggle, motherhood *may* be a handicap. It is certainly so at the present time, but it is much less certain that it was so in times when human beings were closer to nature.

Moreover, we explain penis envy itself by its biological relations and not by social factors; on the contrary, we are accustomed without more ado to construe the woman's sense of being at a disadvantage socially as the rationalization of her penis envy.

But from the biological point of view woman has in motherhood, or in the capacity for motherhood, a quite indisputable and by no means negligible physiological superiority. This is most clearly reflected in the unconscious of the male psyche in the boy's intense envy of motherhood. We are familiar with this envy as such, but it has hardly received due consideration as a dynamic factor. When one begins, as I did, to analyze men only after a fairly long experience of analyzing women, one receives a most surprising impression of the intensity of this envy of pregnancy, childbirth, and motherhood, as well as of the breasts and of the act of suckling.

In the light of this impression derived from analysis, one must naturally inquire whether an unconscious mas-

THE FLIGHT FROM WOMANHOOD

culine tendency to depreciation is not expressing itself intellectually in the above-mentioned view of motherhood. This depreciation would run as follows: In reality women do simply desire the penis; when all is said and done motherhood is only a burden that makes the struggle for existence harder, and men may be glad that they have not to bear it.

When Helene Deutsch writes that the masculinity complex in women plays a much greater part than the femininity complex in man, she would seem to overlook the fact that the masculine envy is clearly capable of more successful sublimation than the penis envy of the girl, and that it certainly serves as one, if not as the essential, driving force in the setting up of cultural values.

Language itself points to this origin of cultural productivity. In the historic times that are known to us, this productivity has undoubtedly been incomparably greater in men than in women. Is not the tremendous strength in men of the impulse to creative work in every field precisely due to their feeling of playing a relatively small part in the creation of living beings, which constantly impels them to an overcompensation in achievement?

If we are right in making this connection, we are confronted with the problem of why no corresponding impulse to compensate herself for her penis envy is found in woman. There are two possibilities: Either the envy of the woman is absolutely less than that of the man, or it is less successfully worked off in some other way. We could bring forward facts in support of either supposition.

In favor of the greater intensity of the man's envy we might point out that an actual anatomical disadvantage on the side of the woman exists only from the point of view of the pregenital levels of organization. From that of the genital organization of adult women there is no disadvantage, for obviously the capacity of women for coitus is not less but simply other than that of men. On the other hand, the part of the man in reproduction is ultimately less than that of the woman.

Further, we observe that men are evidently under a greater necessity to depreciate women than conversely. The realization that the dogma of the inferiority of women had its origin in an unconscious male tendency could only dawn upon us after a doubt had arisen whether in fact this view were justified in reality. But if there actually are in men tendencies to depreciate women behind this conviction of feminine inferiority, we must infer that this unconscious impulse to depreciation is a very powerful one.

In this discussion I have already touched on a problem that Freud has recently brought into the foreground of interest: the question of the origin and operation of the desire for a child. In the course of the last decade our attitude toward this problem has changed. I may therefore be permitted to describe briefly the beginning and the end of this historical evolution.

The original hypothesis was that penis envy gave a libidinal reinforcement both to the wish for a child and the wish for the man, but that the latter wish arose independently of the former. Subsequently the accent became more and more displaced onto the penis envy, until in his most recent work on this problem, Freud expressed the conjecture that the wish for the child arose only through penis envy and the disappointment over the lack of the penis in general, and that the tender attachment to the father came into existence only by this circuitous route— by way of the desire for the penis and the desire for the child.

This latter hypothesis obviously originated in the need to explain psychologically the biological principle of heterosexual attraction. This corresponds to the problem formulated by [George] Groddeck, who says that it is natural that the boy should retain the mother as a love object, "but how is it that the little girl becomes attached to the opposite sex?"

In order to approach this problem we must first of all realize that our empirical material with regard to the masculinity complex in women is derived from two sources of very different importance. The first is the direct observation of children, in which the subjective factor plays a relatively insignificant part. Every little girl who has not been intimidated displays penis envy frankly and without embarrassment. We see that the presence of this envy is typical and understand quite well why this is so; we understand how the narcissistic mortification of possessing less than the boy is reinforced by a series of disadvantages arising out of the different pregenital cathexes: the manifest privileges of the boy in connection with urethral erotism, the scoptophilic instinct, and onanism.

I should like to suggest that we should apply the term *primary* to the little girl's penis envy, which is obviously based simply on the anatomical difference.

The second source upon which our experience draws is to be found in the analytical material produced by adult women. Naturally it is more difficult to form a judgment on this, and there is therefore more scope for the subjective element. We see here in the first instance that penis envy operates as a factor of enormous dynamic power. We see patients rejecting their female functions, their unconscious motive in so doing being the desire to be male. We meet with fantasies of which the content is: "I once had a penis; I am a man who has been castrated and mutilated," from which proceed feelings of inferiority that have for aftereffect all manner of obstinate hypochondriacal ideas. We see a marked attitude of hostility toward men, sometimes taking the form of depreciation and sometimes a desire to castrate or maim them, and we see how the whole destinies of certain women are determined by this factor.

It was natural to conclude—and especially natural because of the male orientation of our thinking—that we could link these impressions on to the primary penis envy and to reason a posteriori that this envy must possess an enormous intensity, an enormous dynamic power, see-

13

ing that it evidently gave rise to such effects. Here we overlooked the fact, more in our general estimation of the situation than in details, that this desire to be a man, so familiar to us from the analyses of adult women, had only very little to do with that early, infantile, primary penis envy, but that it is a secondary formation embodying all that has miscarried in the development toward womanhood.

From beginning to end, my experience has proved to me with unchanging clearness that the Oedipus complex in women leads (not only in extreme cases where the subject has come to grief, but *regularly*) to a regression to penis envy, naturally in every possible degree and shade. The difference between the outcome of the male and the female Oedipus complexes seems to me in average cases to be as follows. In boys the mother as a sexual object is renounced owing to the fear of castration, but the male role itself is not only affirmed in further development but is actually overemphasized in the reaction to the fear of castration. We see this clearly in the latency and prepubertal period in boys and generally in later life as well. Girls, on the other hand, not only renounce the father as a sexual object but simultaneously recoil from the feminine role altogether.

In order to understand this flight from womanhood we must consider the facts relating to early infantile onanism, which is the physical expression of the excitations due to the Oedipus complex.

Here again the situation is much clearer in boys, or perhaps we simply know more about it. Are these facts so mysterious to us in girls only because we have always looked at them through the eyes of men? It seems rather like it when we do not even concede to little girls a specific form of onanism but without more ado describe their autoerotic activities as male; and when we conceive of the difference, which surely must exist, as being that of a negative to a positive, i.e., in the case of anxiety about onanism, that the difference is that between a castration threatened and castration that has actually taken place! My analytical experience makes it most decidedly possible that little girls have a specific feminine form of onanism (which incidentally differs in technique from that of boys), even if we assume that the little girl practices exclusively clitoral masturbation, an assumption that seems to me by no means certain. And I do not see why, in spite of its past evolution, it should not be conceded that the clitoris legitimately belongs to and forms an integral part of the female genital apparatus.

Whether in the early phase of the girl's genital development she has organic vaginal sensations is a matter remarkably difficult to determine from the analytical material produced by adult women. In a whole series of cases I have been inclined to conclude that this is so, and later I shall quote the material upon which I base this conclusion. That such sensations should occur seems to me theoretically very probable for the following reasons. Undoubtedly the familiar fantasies that an excessively large penis is effecting forcible penetration, producing pain and hemorrhage, and threatening to destroy something, go to show that the little girl bases her Oedipus fantasies most realistically (in accordance with the plastic concrete thinking of childhood) on the disproportion in size between father and child. I think too that both the Oedipus fantasies and also the logically ensuing dread of an internal—i.e., vaginal—injury go to show that the vagina as well as the clitoris must be assumed to play a part in the early infantile genital organization of women.* One might even infer from the later phenomena of frigidity that the vaginal zone has actually a stronger cathexis (arising out of anxiety and attempts at defense) than the clitoris, and this because the incestuous wishes are referred to the vagina with the unerring accuracy of the unconscious.

* Since the possibility of such a connection occurred to me, I have learned to construe in this sense—i.e., as representing the dread of vaginal injury—many phenomena that I was previously content to interpret as castration fantasies in the male sense.

From this point of view frigidity must be regarded as an attempt to ward off the fantasies so full of danger to the ego. And this would also throw a new light on the unconscious pleasurable feelings that, as various authors have maintained, occur at parturition, or alternatively, on the dread of childbirth. For (just because of the disproportion between the vagina and the baby and because of the pain to which this gives rise) parturition would be calculated to a far greater extent than subsequent sexual intercourse to stand to the unconscious for a realization of those early incest fantasies, a realization to which no guilt is attached. The female genital anxiety, like the castration dread of boys, invariably bears the impress of feelings of guilt and it is to them that it owes its lasting influence.

A further factor in the situation, and one that works in the same direction, is a certain consequence of the anatomical difference between the sexes. I mean that the boy can inspect his genital to see whether the dreaded consequences of onanism are taking place; the girl, on the other hand, is literally in the dark on this point and remains in complete uncertainty. Naturally this possibility of a reality test does not weigh with boys in cases where the castration anxiety is acute, but in the slighter cases of fear, which are practically more important because they are more frequent, I think that this difference is very important. At any rate, the analytical material that has come to light in women whom I have analyzed has led me to conclude that this factor plays a considerable part in feminine mental life and that it contributes to the peculiar inner uncertainty so often met with in women.

Under the pressure of this anxiety the girl now takes refuge in a fictitious male role.

What is the economic gain of this flight? Here I would refer to an experience that all analysts have probably had: They find that the desire to be a man is generally admitted comparatively willingly and that when once it is accepted, it is clung to tenaciously, the reason being the desire to avoid the realization of libidinal wishes and fantasies in connection with the father. Thus the wish to be a man subserves the repression of these feminine wishes or the resistance against their being brought to light. This constantly recurring, typical experience compels us, if we are true to analytical principles, to conclude that the fantasies of being a man were at an earlier period devised for the very purpose of securing the subject against libidinal wishes in connection with the father. The fiction of maleness enabled the girl to escape from the female role now burdened with guilt and anxiety. It is true that this attempt to deviate from her own line to that of the male inevitably brings about a sense of inferiority, for the girl begins to measure herself by pretensions and values that are foreign to her specific biological nature and confronted with which she cannot but feel herself inadequate.

Although this sense of inferiority is very tormenting, analytical experience emphatically shows us that the ego can tolerate it more easily than the sense of guilt associated with the feminine attitude, and hence it is undoubtedly a gain for the ego when the girl flees from the Scylla of the sense of guilt to the Charybdis of the sense of inferiority.

When we see how large a part of the strength of primary penis envy is accrued only by retrogression from the Oedipus complex, we must resist the temptation to interpret in the light of penis envy the manifestations of so elementary a principle of nature as that of the mutual attraction of the sexes.

Whereupon, being confronted with the question of how we should conceive psychologically of this primal, biological principle, we would again have to confess ignorance. Indeed, in this respect the conjecture forces itself more and more strongly upon me that perhaps the causal connection may be the exact converse and that it is just the attraction to the opposite sex, operating from a very early period, which draws the libidinal interest of the little girl to the penis. This interest, in accordance with the level of development reached, acts at first in an autoerotic and narcissistic manner, as I have described before. If we view these relations thus, fresh problems would logically present themselves with regard to the origin of the male Oedipus complex, but I wish to postpone these for a later paper. But, if penis envy were the first expression of that mysterious attraction of the sexes, there would be nothing to wonder at when analysis discloses its existence in a yet deeper layer than that in which the desire for a child and the tender attachment to the father occur. The way to this tender attitude toward the father would be prepared not simply by disappointment in regard to the penis but in another way as well. We should then instead have to conceive of the libidinal interest in the penis as a kind of "partial love," to use [Karl] Abraham's term. Such love, he says, always forms a preliminary stage to true object love. We might explain the process too by an analogy from later life: I refer to the fact that admiring envy is specially calculated to lead to an attitude of love.

With regard to the extraordinary ease with which this regression takes place, I must mention the analytical discovery that in the associations of female patients the narcissistic desire to possess the penis and the object libidinal longing for it are often so interwoven that one hesitates as to the sense in which the words "desire for it" are meant.

One word more about the castration fantasies proper, which have given their name to the whole complex because they are the most striking part of it. According to my theory of feminine development, I am obliged to regard these fantasies also as a secondary formation. I picture their origin as follows: When the woman takes refuge in the fictitious male role, her feminine genital anxiety is to some extent translated into male terms—the fear of vaginal injury becomes a fantasy of castration. The girl gains by this conversion, for she exchanges the uncertainty of her expectation of punishment (an uncertainty conditioned by her anatomical formation) for a concrete idea. Moreover, the castration fantasy, too, is under the shadow of the old sense of guilt—and the penis is desired as a proof of guiltlessness.

Now these typical motives for flight into the male role—motives whose origin is the Oedipus complex—are reinforced and supported by the actual disadvantage under which women labor in social life. Of course we must recognize that the desire to be a man, when it springs from this last source, is a peculiarly suitable form of rationalization of those unconscious motives. But we must not forget that this disadvantage is actually a piece of reality and that it is immensely greater than most women are aware of.

Georg Simmel says in this connection that "the greater importance attaching to the male sociologically is probably due to his position of superior strength," and that historically the relation of the sexes may be crudely described as that of master and slave. Here, as always, it is "one of the privileges of the master that he has not constantly to think that he is master, while the position of the slave is such that he can never forget it."

Here we probably have the explanation also of the underestimation of this factor in analytical literature. In actual fact a girl is exposed from birth onward to the suggestion—inevitable, whether conveyed brutally or delicately—of her inferiority, an experience that constantly stimulates her masculinity complex.

There is one further consideration. Owing to the hitherto purely masculine character of our civilization, it has been much harder for women to achieve any sublimation that would really satisfy their nature, for all the ordinary professions have been filled by men. This again must have exercised an influence upon women's feelings of inferiority, for naturally they could not accomplish the same as men in these masculine professions and so it appeared that there was a basis in fact for their inferiority. It seems to me impossible to judge to how great a degree the unconscious motives for the flight from womanhood are reinforced by the actual social subordination of women. One might conceive of the connection as an interaction of psychic and social factors. But I can only indicate these problems here, for they are so grave and so important that they require a separate investigation.

The same factors must have quite a different effect on the man's development. On the one hand they lead to a much stronger repression of his feminine wishes, in that these bear the stigma of inferiority; on the other hand it is far easier for him successfully to sublimate them.

In the foregoing discussion I have put a construction upon certain problems of feminine psychology, which in many points differs from current views. It is possible and even probable that the picture I have drawn is one-sided from the opposite point of view. But my primary intention in this paper was to indicate a possible source of error arising out of the sex of the observer, and by so doing to make a step forward toward the goal that we are all striving to reach: to get beyond the subjectivity of the masculine or the feminine standpoint and to obtain a picture of the mental development of woman that will be more true to the facts of her nature—with its specific qualities and its differences from that of man—than any we have hitherto achieved.

KAREN HORNEY *

The Problem of Feminine Masochism

INTEREST IN THE PROBLEM of feminine masochism extends far beyond the merely medical and psychological spheres, for to students of the Western culture at least, it touches on the very roots for evaluating woman in her cultural definition. The facts appear to be that in our cultural areas, masochistic phenomena are more frequent in women than in men. Two ways of approaching an explanation of this observation have appeared. By one, there is an attempt to discover if masochistic trends are inherent in, or akin to, the very essence of female nature. By the other, one undertakes to evaluate the weight of social conditionings in the genesis of any sex-limited peculiarities in the distribution of masochistic trends.

In psychoanalytic literature—taking the views of [Sandor] Rado and [Helene] Deutsch as representative in this connection—the problem has been tackled only from the viewpoint of regarding feminine masochism as one psychic consequence of anatomical sex differences. Psychoanalysis thus has lent its scientific tools to support the theory of a given kinship between masochism and female biology. The possibility of social conditioning has as yet not been considered from the psychoanalytical side.

The task of this paper is to contribute to the efforts of determining the weight of biological and cultural factors in this problem; to review carefully the validity of the psychoanalytical data given in this direction; and to raise the question of whether psychoanalytical knowledge can

---

* A biographical sketch of the author appears on page 3.

be utilized for an investigation of a possible connection with social conditionings.

One may summarize the psychoanalytic views thus far presented somewhat as follows:

The specific satisfactions sought and found in female sex life and motherhood are of a masochistic nature. The content of the early sexual wishes and fantasies concerning the father is the desire to be mutilated, that is, castrated by him. Menstruation has the hidden connotation of a masochistic experience. What the woman secretly desires in intercourse is rape and violence, or in the mental sphere, humiliation. The process of childbirth gives her an unconscious masochistic satisfaction, as is also the case with the maternal relation to the child. Furthermore, as far as men indulge in masochistic fantasies or performances, these represent an expression of their desire to play the female role.

Deutsch* assumes a genetic factor of a biological nature, which inevitably leads up to a masochistic conception of the female role. Rado† points out a genetic factor that forces the sexual development into a masochistic channel. There is a difference of opinion as to whether or not these specifically female forms of masochism arise from deviations in the female development, or represent the "normal" female attitude.

It is assumed at least implicitly that masochistic character trends of all kinds also are much more frequent in women than in men. This conclusion is inevitable when one holds the basic psychoanalytic theory that general behavior in life is modeled on the sexual behavior pattern, which in women is deemed masochistic. It then follows that if most or all women are masochistic in their attitude

* Helene Deutsch, "The Significance of Masochism in the Mental Life of Women" (Part 1: " 'Feminine' Masochism and Its Relation to Frigidity"), *International Journal of Psycho-Analysis* 11 (1930): 48–61.

† Sandor Rado, "Fear of Castration in Women," *Psychoanalytic Quarterly* 3–4 (1933).

toward sex and reproduction, they would indubitably reveal masochistic trends in their nonsexual attitude toward life more frequently than would men.

This consideration shows that these authors are dealing in fact with a problem of normal female psychology, and not only with one of psychopathology.

There is no need to question the fact that women may seek and find masochistic satisfaction in masturbation, menstruation, intercourse, and childbirth. Beyond doubt this occurs. What remains for discussion is the genesis and frequency of occurrence. Both Deutsch and Rado, in dealing with the problem, completely ignore discussion of frequency, because they maintain that the psychologic genetic factors are so forceful and ubiquitous that a consideration of frequency becomes superfluous.

On the matter of genesis, both authors assume that the decisive turning point in female development is the awareness of the little girl that she has no penis, the assumption being that the shock of this realization exerts a lasting influence. There are two sources of data for this assumption: the findings in the analyses of neurotic women concerning fantasies and wishes to possess, or to have possessed, a penis; and the observation of little girls expressing the wish to have a penis when they discover its existence in others.

The foregoing observations are sufficient to build a working hypothesis to the effect that wishes for masculinity of some origin or other play a role in female sex life, and this hypothesis may be used in seeking explanations for certain neurotic phenomena in women. It must be realized, however, that this is a hypothesis, not a fact; and that it is not even indisputably useful as a hypothesis. When it is claimed, moreover, that the desire for masculinity is not only a dynamic factor of primary order in neurotic females, but in every human female, independent of individual or cultural conditions, one cannot but remark that there are no data to substantiate this claim. Unfortunately little or nothing is known of psychically

healthy women, or of women under different cultural conditions, due to limitations of historical and ethnological
knowledge.

Therefore, as there are no data about frequency, conditioning, and weight of the observed reactions of the
little girl to the discovery of the penis, the assumption
that this is a turning point in female development is
stimulating, but can scarcely be used in a chain of proof.
Why, indeed, should the girl turn masochistic when she
realizes the lack of a penis? Deutsch and Rado account
for this further assumption in very different ways.
Deutsch believes that "the hitherto active-sadistic libido
attached to the clitoris rebounds from the barricade of the
subject's inner realization of her lack of the penis . . .
and most frequently of all is deflected in a regressive direction to masochism." This swinging in the direction of
masochism is "part of the woman's anatomical destiny."

Let us ask again: What are the data? As far as I can see,
only the fact that there may exist in small children early
sadistic fantasies. This is partly elicited by direct psychoanalytic observation of neurotic children (M. Klein),
and partly by reconstruction out of analysis of neurotic
adults. There is no evidence for the ubiquity of these
early sadistic fantasies, and I wonder, for instance,
whether little American Indian girls, or little Trobriand
girls have them. However, even taking for granted that
this occurrence was in fact ubiquitous, there still remain
three further assumptions necessary for completion of the
picture:

1. That these sadistic fantasies are generated by the
active-sadistic libido cathexis of the clitoris.

2. That the girl renounces her clitoris-masturbation
in consequence of the narcissistic injury of having no
penis.

3. That the hitherto active-sadistic libido turns automatically inward and becomes masochistic.

All three assumptions seem highly speculative. It is
known that people can become frightened of their hostile

aggressions and subsequently prefer the suffering role, but how a libido-cathexis of an organ can be sadistic and then turn inward seems mysterious.

Deutsch wanted "to examine the genesis of femininity," by which she means "the feminine, passive-masochistic disposition of the mental life of women." She affirms that masochism is the most elemental power in female mental life. No doubt that is the case in many neurotic women, but the hypothesis offered that it is psycho-biologically necessary in all women is unconvincing.

Rado proceeds in a more careful way. First, he does not start with the endeavor to point out the "genesis of femininity," but wants to account only for certain clinically observable pictures in neurotic women and he gives valuable data about various defenses against masochistic drives in women. Furthermore, he does not take the wish for penis-possession as a given fact, but recognizes that there may be a problem here.

Rado offers the following formula for the masochistic development in women following the discovery of the penis: He agrees with Freud that this discovery is inevitably a narcissistic shock for the girl, but he thinks the effect varies with different emotional conditions. If it occurs in the period of early sex efflorescence, it represents, according to Rado, in addition to the narcissistic blow, a peculiarly painful experience because it arouses in the girl the belief that the male can derive much more pleasure from masturbation than the female. This experience, he thinks, is so painful that it destroys forever the pleasure the girl hitherto found in masturbation. Before we see how Rado deduces the genesis of female masochism from this alleged reaction, it is necessary to discuss the underlying premise that the awareness of the possibility of a major pleasure definitely destroys the enjoyment of an attainable pleasure that is considered inferior to it.

How does this assumption coincide with the data of everyday life? It would imply, for instance, that a man who thought Greta Garbo more attractive than other women, but had no chance of meeting her, would as a result of the "discovery" of her superior charms lose all pleasure in having relations with other women available to him. It would imply that one who is fond of mountains would find his pleasure in them utterly spoiled by imagining that a sea resort might offer a greater pleasure. Of course, reactions of this kind are occasionally observed, but only in persons of a certain type, namely, in persons excessively or pathologically greedy. The principle applied by Rado is certainly not the pleasure principle, but might better be called the greediness principle, and as such, though valuable for the explanation of certain neurotic reactions, can scarcely be assumed to work in "normal" children or adults, and is in fact contradictory to the pleasure principle.

Let us, however, accept for a moment Rado's assumption that the girl hitherto satisfied in her sexual outlets finds her pleasure in masturbation destroyed by the discovery of the penis. What then might one expect this to contribute toward her development of masochistic drives? Rado argues as follows. The extreme mental pain caused by the penis discovery excites the girl sexually and this provides her with a substitute gratification. Having been robbed thus of her natural means of satisfaction, she has thenceforth only the one way of craving satisfaction through suffering. Her sexual strivings become and remain masochistic. She may then later, conceiving the aim of her strivings as dangerous, build up various defenses, but the sex strivings themselves are definitely and permanently shifted into masochistic channels.

One question intrudes itself. Granting that the girl would really suffer severely from the vision of an unattainable major source of pleasure, why should this pain excite her sexually? As this assumed reaction is the cornerstone upon which the author builds a subsequent lifelong masochistic attitude, one would like to hear evidence of its factual occurrence.

Following Rado's train of reasoning, is it not curious

26

indeed that the little boy does not turn masochistic? Nearly every little boy obtains a view of the much larger penis of some adult. He perceives that the adult—the father—can obtain a much greater pleasure than he does. The idea of the greater obtainable pleasure should spoil his own enjoyment in masturbation. He should give up masturbation. He should suffer a severe mental pain, which excites him sexually, and he should adopt this pain as a substitute gratification and from then on be masochistic. This seems to happen very infrequently.

I proceed to a last critical point. Assuming the girl did react to the discovery of the penis with a severe mental pain; assuming the idea of a possibly greater pleasure destroying her attainable pleasure; assuming she did become sexually excited by the mental pain and found a substitute sexual satisfaction in it; assuming all these debatable considerations for the purpose of argument: why then should she *lastingly* be driven to seek satisfaction in suffering? There seems to be a discrepancy between cause and effect here. A stone that has fallen to the ground will remain there unless it is removed by some external power. A living organism, when hit by some traumatic event, adapts itself to the new situation. While Rado assumes subsequent defense reactions built up as a protection against the dangerous masochistic drives, he does not question the enduring character of the strivings themselves, which once established are believed to retain their motivating force unchanged. It is one of the great scientific merits of Freud to have vigorously stressed the tenacity of childhood impressions; yet psychoanalytic experience shows also that an emotional reaction which has once occurred in childhood is maintained throughout life only if it continues to be supported by various dynamically important drives. If Rado does not assume that a single traumatic shock can exert a lasting influence without being supported by any needs within the personality, then he must assume that though the shock is passing, the allegedly painful fact of lacking a penis remains, with

27

the consequence that masturbation is abandoned, and the sexual libido is permanently redirected along masochistic channels. But clinical experience indicates that absence of masturbation is by no means invariable in masochistic children.* This chain of alleged causation therefore also fails.

Although Rado does not assume, as does Deutsch, that this traumatic event is a regular, inevitable occurrence in female development, he states correctly that it is bound to happen with "striking frequency," and in fact a girl could, according to his assumptions, only exceptionally escape the fate of a masochistic deflection. In coming to this implied conclusion that women must be almost universally masochistic, he has made the same error that physicians tend to make if they endeavor to account for pathologic phenomena on a broader basis—namely, unwarranted generalization from limited data. It is in principle the same error that psychiatrists and gynecologists have made before him: Krafft-Ebing, observing that masochistic men often play the role of the suffering female, speaks of masochistic phenomena as representing a sort of rank overgrowth of female qualities; Freud, starting from the same observation, assumes a close connection between masochism and femininity; the Russian gynecologist Nemilow, being impressed by women's suffering in defloration, menstruation, and childbirth, speaks of the "bloody tragedy of woman"; the German gynecologist Liepman, being impressed by the frequency of illnesses, accidents, and pains in the life of women, assumes that vulnerability, irritability, and sensitivity are the fundamental triad of female qualities.

Only one justification could be adduced for such generalizations, namely, Freud's hypothesis that there is no

* In a communication from David M. Levy he cites instances in which girls with fantasies of being beaten also masturbated while indulging in these fantasies. He states that he knows of no direct relationship between masochistic phenomena and the absence of genital manipulation.

fundamental difference between pathologic and "normal" phenomena; that pathologic phenomena merely show more distinctly as through a magnifying glass the processes going on in all human beings. There can be little doubt that this principle has broadened the horizon, but one should be aware of its limitations. These have had to be considered, for instance, in dealing with the Oedipus complex. First, its existence and implications were seen distinctly in neuroses. This knowledge sharpened the observation of psychoanalysts, so that slighter indications of it were frequently observed. The conclusion was then drawn that this was an ubiquitous phenomenon, which in neurotic persons was only more accentuated. This conclusion is disputable, because ethnological studies have shown that the peculiar configuration denoted by the term Oedipus complex is probably nonexistent under widely different cultural conditions. One must, therefore, narrow down the assumption to the statement that this peculiar emotional pattern in the relations between parents and children arises only under certain cultural conditions.

The same principle can in fact be found to apply to the question of feminine masochism. Deutsch and Rado have been impressed by the frequency with which they found a masochistic conception of the female role in neurotic women. I suppose every analyst will have made the same observations, or will be assisted by their findings in making them more accurately. Masochistic phenomena in women can be detected as a result of directed and sharpened observation, where they might otherwise have passed unnoticed, as in social rencontres with women (entirely outside the field of psychoanalytic practice), in feminine character portrayals in literature, or in examination of women of somewhat foreign mores, such as the Russian peasant woman who does not feel she is loved by her husband unless he beats her. In the face of this evidence, the psychoanalyst concludes that he is here confronted with an ubiquitous phenomenon, functioning on a psychobiological basis with the regularity of a law of nature.

The one-sidedness or positive errors in the results obtained by a partial examination of the picture are due to a neglect of cultural or social factors—an exclusion from the picture of women living under civilizations with different customs. The Russian peasant woman of the tsarist and patriarchal regime was invariably cited in discussions aimed at proving how deeply masochism is ingrained in female nature. Yet this peasant woman has emerged into the self-assertive Soviet woman of today who would doubtless be astonished if beatings were administered as a token of affection. The change has occurred in the patterns of culture rather than in the particular women.

More generally speaking, whenever the question of frequency enters into the picture, sociological implications are involved, and the refusal to be concerned with them from the psychoanalytic angle does not shut out their existence. Omission of these considerations may lead to a false valuation of anatomical differences and their personal elaboration as causative factors for phenomena actually partially or wholly the result of social conditioning. Only a synthesis of both series of conditions can lead to a complete understanding.

For sociological and ethnological approaches, data concerning the following questions would be pertinent:

1. What is the frequency of occurrence of masochistic attitudes toward female functions under various social and cultural conditions?

2. What is the frequency of general masochistic attitudes or manifestations in women, as compared with men, under various social and cultural conditions?

If both these inquiries gave color to the view that under all social conditions there is a masochistic conception of the female role, and if equally there is a decided preponderance of general masochistic phenomena among women as compared with men, then, and only then, would one be justified in seeking further psychologic reasons for this phenomenon.

The task of psychoanalysis in regard to data concerning indications for general masochistic attitudes is much more difficult, because understanding of the whole phenomenon is still limited. In fact, it has not advanced much beyond Freud's statement that it has something to do with sexuality and with morality. There are, however, these open questions: Is it a primarily sexual phenomenon that extends also into the moral sphere, or a moral phenomenon extending also into the sexual sphere? Are the moral and the erogenic masochism two separate processes or only two sets of manifestations arising from a common underlying process? Or is masochism perhaps a collective term for very complex phenomena?

One feels justified in using the same term for widely discrepant manifestations because all of them have some trends in common: tendencies to arrange in fantasies, dreams, or in the real world, situations that imply suffering; or to feel suffering in situations that would not have this concomitant for the average person. The suffering may concern the physical or the mental sphere. There is some gratification or relief of tension connected with it, and that is why it is striven for. The gratification or relief of tension may be conscious or unconscious, sexual or nonsexual. The nonsexual functions may be very different: reassurances against fears, atonements for committed sins, permission to commit new ones, strategy in reference to goals otherwise unattainable, indirect forms of hostility.

The realization of this wide range of masochistic phenomena is more bewildering and challenging than encouraging, and these general statements certainly cannot be of much help to the anthropologist. More concrete data are at his disposal, however, if all scientific worries about conditions and functions are swept aside, and only those surface attitudes that have been observable in patients with distinct and widespread masochistic tendencies within the psychoanalytic situation are made the basis of his investigations. For this purpose, therefore, it may suffice to enumerate these attitudes without tracing them back in detail to their individual conditions. Needless to say, they are not all present in every patient belonging to this category; yet the whole syndrome is so typical (as every analyst will recognize), that if some of these trends are apparent at the beginning of a treatment, one can safely predict the entire picture, though of course the details vary. The details concern sequence of appearance, distribution of weight among the single trends, and particularly form and intensity of defenses built up for protection against these tendencies.

Let us consider what observable data there are in patients with widespread masochistic trends. As I see it, the main lines of the surface structure in such personalities are somewhat as follows:

There are several ways in which one can find reassurance against deep fears. Renunciation is one way; inhibition, another; denying the fear and becoming optimistic, a third; and so on. Being loved is the particular means of reassurance used by a masochistic person. As he has a rather free-floating anxiety, he needs constant signs of attention, and as he never believes in these signs except momentarily, he has an excessive need for attention and affection. He is therefore, generally speaking, very emotional in his relations with people; easily attached because he expects them to give him the necessary reassurance; easily disappointed because he never gets, and never can get, what he expects. The expectation or illusion of the "great love" often plays an important role. Sexuality being one of the most common ways of getting affection, he also tends to overvalue it and clings to the illusion that it holds the solution of all life's problems. How far this is conscious, or how easily he has actual sexual relations, depends on his inhibitions on this score. Where he has had sexual relations, or attempts at such, his history shows a frequency of "unhappy loves"; he has been deserted, disappointed, humiliated, badly treated. In nonsexual relations, the same tendency appears in all gradations from being or feeling incompetent, self-sacrificing, and submissive, to playing the martyr role and feeling or actually being humiliated, abused, and exploited. While he otherwise feels it as a given fact that he *is* incompetent or that life *is* brutal, one can see in the psychoanalytic situation that it is not facts, but an obstinate tendency, which makes him insist upon seeing or arranging it this way. This tendency, moreover, is revealed in the psychoanalytic situation as an unconscious arrangement motivating him to provoke attacks, to feel ruined, damaged, ill-treated, humiliated, without any real cause.

Because other people's affection and sympathy are of vital importance to him, he easily becomes extremely dependent, and this hyperdependency also shows clearly in relations with the analyst.

The next observable reason he never believes in any form of affection he may actually receive (instead of clinging to it as representing the coveted reassurance) lies in his greatly diminished self-esteem; he feels inferior, absolutely unlovable and unworthy of love. On the other hand, just this lack of self-confidence makes him feel that appealing to pity by having and displaying inferiority feelings, weakness, and suffering is the only means by which he can win the affection he needs. One sees that the deterioration of his self-esteem lies rooted in his paralysis of what may be termed "adequate aggressiveness." By this I mean the capacities for work, including the following attributes: taking initiative; making efforts; carrying things through to completion; attaining success; insisting upon one's rights; defending oneself when attacked; forming and expressing autonomous views; recognizing one's goals and being able to plan one's life according to them. In masochistic persons one usually finds widespread inhibitions on this score, which in their entirety account for the feeling of insecurity, or even helplessness, in the life struggle, and explain the subsequent dependency on other people, and a predisposition to look to them for support or help.

Psychoanalysis reveals the tendency to recoil from competition of any kind as the next observable reason for their incapacity to be self-assertive. Their inhibitions thus result from efforts to check themselves in order to avoid the risk of competition.

The hostile feelings inevitably generated on the basis of such self-defeating tendencies also cannot be expressed freely because they are conceived as jeopardizing the reassurance attendant on being loved, which is the mainspring of protection against anxieties. Weakness and suffering, therefore, already serving many functions, now also act as a vehicle for the indirect expression of hostility.

The use of this syndrome of observable attitudes for anthropologic investigation is subject to one source of possible major error, namely, masochistic attitudes are not always apparent as such because they are frequently concealed by defenses, often appearing clearly only after the latter have been removed. As an analysis of these defenses clearly is beyond the sphere of such an investigation, the defenses must be taken at face value, with the result that these instances of masochistic attitudes must escape observation.

Reviewing then, the observable masochistic attitudes, regardless of their deeper motivation, I suggest that the anthropologist seek data concerning questions like these: under what social or cultural conditions do we find more frequently in women than in men

1. the manifesting of inhibitions in the direct expression of demands and aggressions;

2. a regarding of oneself as weak, helpless, or inferior and implicitly or explicitly demanding considerations and advantages on this basis;

3. a becoming emotionally dependent on the other sex;

4. a showing of tendencies to be self-sacrificing, to be submissive, to feel used or to be exploited, to put responsibilities on the other sex;

5. a using of weakness and helplessness as a means of wooing and subduing the other sex.

Besides these formulations, which are direct generalizations of the psychoanalytic experience with masochistic women, I may also present certain generalizations as to the causative factors that predispose to the appearance of masochism in women. I should expect these phenomena to appear in any culture-complex that included one or more of the following factors:

1. Blocking of outlets for expansiveness and sexuality.

2. Restriction in the number of children, inasmuch as having and rearing children supplies the woman with various gratifying outlets (tenderness, achievement, self-esteem), and this becomes all the more important when having and rearing children is the measuring rod of social evaluation.

3. Estimation of women as beings who are, on the whole, inferior to men (insofar as it leads to a deterioration of female self-confidence).

4. Economic dependence of women on men or on family, inasmuch as it fosters an emotional adaptation in the way of emotional dependence.

5. Restriction of women to spheres of life built chiefly upon emotional bonds, such as family life, religion, or charity work.

6. Surplus of marriageable women, particularly when marriage offers the principal opportunity for sexual gratification, children, security, and social recognition.* This condition is relevant inasmuch as it favors [as do also 3 and 4] emotional dependence on men, and generally speaking, a development that is not autonomous but fashioned and molded by existing male ideologies. It is

* It must be borne in mind, however, that social regulations, such as marriage arrangement by families, would greatly reduce the effectiveness of this factor. This consideration also throws a light on Freud's assumption that women generally are more jealous than men. The statement probably is correct so far as the present German and Austrian cultures are concerned. To deduce this, however, from more purely individual anatomical-physiological sources (penis envy) is not convincing. While it may be so in individual cases, the generalization—independent of consideration of the social conditions—is subject to the same fundamental objection as previously mentioned.

pertinent also insofar as it creates among women a particularly strong competition from which recoil is an important factor in precipitating masochistic phenomena.

All the factors enumerated overlap; for example, strong sexual competition among women will be more potent if other outlets for competitive strivings (as for professional eminence) are concurrently blocked. It would seem that no one factor is ever solely responsible for the deviating development, but rather a concatenation of factors.

In particular one must consider the fact that when some or all of the suggested elements are present in the culture complex, there may appear certain fixed ideologies concerning the "nature" of woman; such as doctrines that woman is innately weak, emotional, enjoys dependence, is limited in capacities for independent work and autonomous thinking. One is tempted to include in this category the psychoanalytic belief that woman is masochistic by nature. It is fairly obvious that these ideologies function not only to reconcile women to their subordinate role by presenting it as an unalterable one, but also to plant the belief that it represents a fulfillment they crave, or an ideal for which it is commendable and desirable to strive. The influence that these ideologies exert on women is materially strengthened by the fact that women presenting the specified traits are more frequently chosen by men. This implies that women's erotic possibilities depend on their conformity to the image of that which constitutes their "true nature." It therefore seems no exaggeration to say that in such social organizations, masochistic attitudes (or rather, milder expressions of masochism) are favored in women while they are discouraged in men. Qualities like emotional dependence on the other sex (clinging vine), absorption in "love," inhibition of expansive, autonomous development, and so on are regarded as quite desirable in women but are treated with opprobrium and ridicule when found in men.

One sees that these cultural factors exert a powerful influence on women; so much so, in fact, that in our culture it is hard to see how any woman can escape becoming masochistic to some degree, from the effects of culture alone, without any appeal to contributory factors in the anatomical-physiological characteristics of woman, and their psychic effects.

Certain writers, however—among them H. Deutsch—have generalized from psychoanalytical experience with neurotic women, and have held that the culture complexes to which I have referred are themselves the very effect of these anatomical-physiological characteristics. It is useless to argue this overgeneralization until the type of anthropological investigation suggested has been made. Let us look, however, at the factors in the somatic organization of women, which actually contribute to their acceptance of a masochistic role. The anatomical-physiological factors in women that may prepare the soil for the growth of masochistic phenomena, seem to me to be the following:

1. Greater average physical strength in men than in women. According to the ethnologists this is an acquired sex difference. Nevertheless it exists nowadays. Although weakness is not identical with masochism, the realization of an inferior physical strength may fertilize an emotional conception of a masochistic female role.

2. The possibility of rape similarly may give rise in women to the fantasy of being attacked, subdued, and injured.

3. Menstruation, defloration, and childbirth, insofar as they are bloody or even painful processes, may readily serve as outlets for masochistic strivings.

4. The biologic differences in intercourse also serve for masochistic formulation. Sadism and masochism have fundamentally nothing whatsoever to do with intercourse, but the female role in intercourse (being penetrated) *lends* itself more readily to a personal misinterpretation (when needed) of masochistic performance; and the male role, to one of sadistic activity.

These biological functions have in themselves no masochistic reactions; but if masochistic needs of other origin are present, they may easily be involved in masochistic fantasies, which in turn causes them to furnish masochistic gratifications. Beyond admitting the possibility of a certain preparedness in women for a masochistic conception of their role, every additional assertion as to the relation of their constitution to masochism is hypothetical; and such facts as the disappearance of all masochistic tendencies after a successful psychoanalysis, and the observations of nonmasochistic women (which, after all, exist), warn us not to overrate even this element of preparedness.

In summary: The problem of feminine masochism cannot be related to factors inherent in the anatomical-physiological-psychic characteristics of woman alone, but must be considered as importantly conditioned by the culture complex or social organization in which the particular masochistic woman has developed. The precise weight of these two groups of factors cannot be assessed until we have the results of anthropological investigations using valid psychoanalytical criteria in several culture areas significantly different from ours. It is clear, however, that the importance of anatomical-psychological-psychic factors has been greatly overestimated by some writers on this subject.

ALFRED ADLER

ALFRED ADLER was the first psychoanalyst to condemn society's conception of women and to see this conception, in itself, as a root contributing cause of the psychological problems not only of women but also of men and children. In this selection he long predates Kate Millett in his statement that both sexes have fallen into a morass of "prestige politics" which robs them of candor and deprives them of love and happiness.

By the time of this writing Adler had long broken with Freud. A physician, born in Vienna in 1870, Adler initiated his own psychological investigations and then joined the group around Freud during the early years of this century. In 1911 Adler withdrew from the Freudian group and went on to develop his own school of psychoanalytic thought, which he called "individual psychology," the study of the individual as he or she differs from others and yet is affected by the larger social forces. He established several institutes and clinics based on this theory and founded the journal *Individual Psychology.* He died in 1937.

Adler was concerned with bringing new psychological understanding to all people, and strove particularly to influence education and training of the young. The paper that follows is condensed from a chapter of his book, *Understanding Human Nature,* and reflects one of the many efforts he made in that direction.

Sex

From our previous considerations we have learned that two great tendencies dominate all psychic phenomena. These two tendencies, the social feeling and the individual striving for power and domination, influence every human activity and color the attitude of every individual.

All our institutions, our traditional attitudes, our laws, our morals, our customs, give evidence of the fact that they are determined and maintained by privileged males for the glory of male domination. These institutions reach out into the very nurseries and have a great influence upon the child's soul. This occurs even when fathers and mothers with considerable insight are disposed to overlook those privileges that we have inherited from ancient days, in favor of a greater equality. It is very difficult to make it clear to a child that a mother who is engaged in household duties is as valuable as a father.

Think what it means to a young boy who sees the prevailing privilege of manhood before his eyes from his earliest days. He is reinforced in his sentiments by the fact that women in his environment are not at all convinced of their equality with men. That most important question which all women should ask their prospective husbands before marriage: "What is your attitude toward masculine domination, particularly in family life?" is usually never answered.

What we consider "masculine" nowadays is common knowledge. Above all it is something purely egoistic, something which satisfies self-love, gives a feeling of superiority and domination over others, all with the aid of seemingly "active" characteristics such as courage, strength, duty, the winning of all manner of victories, especially those over women, the acquisition of positions, honors, titles, and the desire to harden himself against so-called feminine tendencies, and the like. There is a constant battle for personal superiority because it counts as a "masculine" virtue to be dominant.

In this manner every boy assumes characteristics he sees in adult men, especially his father. We can trace the ramifications of this artificially nourished delusion of grandeur in the most diverse manifestations of our society. At an early age a boy is urged to secure for himself a reserve of power and privileges. This is what is called "manliness."

The advantages of being a man are, under such conditions, very alluring. We must not be astonished, therefore, when we see many girls who maintain a masculine ideal either as an unfulfillable desire, or as a standard for the judgment of their behavior; this ideal may evince itself as a pattern for action and appearance.

It is a frequently overlooked fact that a girl comes into the world with a prejudice sounding in her ears which is designed only to rob her of her belief in her own value, to shatter her self-confidence and destroy her hope of ever doing anything worthwhile. If this prejudice is constantly strengthened, if a girl sees again and again how women are given servile roles to play, it is not hard to understand how she loses courage, fails to face her obligations, and sinks back from the solution of her life's problems.

It is easy enough for a girl to lose her courage and her self-confidence in our civilization, yet, as a matter of fact, certain intelligence tests proved the interesting fact that in a certain group of girls, aged fourteen to eighteen, greater talent and capability were evinced than was shown by all other groups, boys included. Further researches show that these were all girls from families in which the

mother was either the sole breadwinner, or at least contributed largely to the family support. What this means
is that these girls were in a situation at home in which the
prejudice of the lesser capability of woman was either not
present or existed only to a slight extent.

One of the bitter consequences of the prejudice concerning the inferiority of women is the sharp division and
pigeonholing of concepts according to a scheme: thus
"masculine" signifies worthwhile, powerful, victorious,
capable, whereas "feminine" becomes identical with
obedient, servile, subordinate. This type of thinking has
become so deeply anchored in human thought processes
that in our civilization everything laudable has a "masculine" color whereas everything less valuable or actually
derogatory is designed "feminine." We all know men
who could not be more insulted than if we told them that
they were feminine, whereas if we say to a girl that she is
masculine it need signify no insult. The accent always
falls so that everything reminiscent of woman appears
inferior.

The obvious advantages of being a man have caused
severe disturbances in the psychic development of women
as a consequence of which there is an almost universal
dissatisfaction with the feminine role. The psychic life of
woman moves in much the same channels, and under
much the same rules, as that of any human beings who
find themselves the possessors of a strong feeling of inferiority because of their situation in the scheme of
things. The prejudice of her alleged inferiority as a
woman signifies an additional aggravating complication.
If a considerable number of girls find some sort of compensation, they owe it to their character development, to
their intelligence, and sometimes to certain acquired
privileges. This shows simply how one mistake may give
rise to others. Such privileges are the special dispensa-
tions, exemptions from obligations, and the luxuries,
which give a semblance of advantage in that they simulate
what purports to be a high degree of respect for woman.

There may be a certain degree of idealism in this, but finally this idealism is always an ideal which has been fashioned by men to the advantage of men. George Sand once described it very tellingly when she said: "The virtue of woman is a fine invention of man."

In general we can distinguish three types of women in the battle against the feminine role. One type has already been indicated: the girl who develops in an active, "masculine," direction. She becomes extraordinarily energetic and ambitious, and is constantly fighting for the prizes of life.

The whole history of civilization, however, shows us that the pressure exerted upon woman, and the inhibitions to which she must submit today, are not to be borne by any human being; they always give rise to revolt. If this revolt now exhibits itself in the direction which we call masculine, the reason for it is simply that there are only *two* sex roles possible. One must orient oneself according to one of two models, either that of an ideal woman, or according to that of an ideal man. Desertion from the role of woman can therefore appear only as masculine, and vice versa. This does not occur as the result of some mysterious secretion, but because in the given time and place, there is no other possibility. We must never lose sight of the difficulties under which the psychic development of a girl takes place. So long as we cannot guarantee every woman an absolute equality with man, we cannot demand her complete reconciliation with life, with the facts of our civilization, and the forms of our social life.

The woman who goes through life with an attitude of resignation, who exhibits an almost unbearable degree of adjustment, obedience, and humbleness, belongs to the second type. Seemingly she adjusts herself everywhere, takes root wherever placed, but demonstrates such a high degree of clumsiness and helplessness that she accomplishes nothing at all! She may produce nervous symptoms, which serve her in her weakness, to demonstrate to others her need for consideration. Her submission, her humility, her self-repression, are founded on the same re-volt as that of her sister of the first type, a revolt which says clearly enough: "This is no happy life!"

The woman who does not defend herself against the womanly role but carries in herself the torturing con-sciousness that she is condemned to be an inferior being and ordained to play a subordinate role in life, makes up the third type. She is fully convinced of the inferiority of women, just as she is convinced that man alone is called upon to do the worthwhile things in life. As a conse-quence, she approves his privileged position. Thus she swells the chorus of voices that sound the praises of man as the doer and the achiever, and demands a special posi-tion for him. She shows her feeling of weakness as clearly as if she wanted recognition for it, and demanded addi-tional support because of it; but this attitude is the begin-ning of a long-prepared revolt. By way of revenge she will shift her marital responsibilities upon her husband with a lighthearted catchword to the effect that "Only a man could do these things!"

What of those cases in which marriage occurs, in which one could believe that the role of woman had been volun-tarily assumed? We learn that marriage need not neces-sarily be an indication that a girl has reconciled herself with her womanly role. The example of a thirty-six-year-old woman is typical of this. She comes to the physician complaining of various nervous ills. She was the oldest child of a marriage between an aging man and a very domineering woman. The mother ruled the house with clamor, and insisted upon having her will carried out at all costs, and regardless of anyone else's pleasure. The old man was forced into his corner at every opportunity. Her mother's whole activity consisted in maintaining cer-tain "principles of domestic economy" which she felt were desirable to enforce. These were an absolute law to the family.

Our patient grew up a very capable child who was much

pampered by the father. On the other hand, her mother was never satisfied with her and was always her enemy. Later, when a boy, toward whom the mother was far more favorable, was born, the relationship became unbearable. The little girl was conscious that she had a support in her father, who, no matter how modest and retiring he was in other things, could take up the cudgel when his daughter's interests were at stake. Thus she began to hate her mother cordially.

In this stubborn conflict the cleanliness of the mother became the daughter's favorite point of attack. The child made it a point of special pleasure to go about as dirty and ill-clad as possible, and to soil the house whenever the occasion offered.

When this little girl was eight years old the following situation existed. The father was permanently on his daughter's side; her mother went about with a bitter face, making pointed remarks, enforcing her "rules," and reproaching the girl. The girl, embittered and belligerent, availed herself of an extraordinary sarcasm which crippled the activity of her mother. An additional complicating factor was the valvular heart disease of the younger brother, who was his mother's favorite and a very much pampered child, who used his sickness to hold the attentions of his mother to an even more intensive degree. One could observe the constantly thwarted activities of the parents toward their children. Under such circumstances did this little girl grow up.

It then occurred that she fell sick of a nervous ailment no one could explain. Her sickness consisted in the fact that she was tortured by evil thoughts directed against her mother, the consequence of which was that she felt herself hindered in all her activities. Finally she occupied herself very deeply, and suddenly, and without success, in religion. After some time these evil thoughts disappeared. Some medicine or other was given the credit for the disappearance, although it is more probable that her mother was forced into the defensive. A residue which expressed itself in a remarkable fear of thunder and lightning remained.

The little girl believed that the thunder and lightning came only as a result of her bad conscience, and would someday cause death because she had such evil thoughts. One can see how the child was attempting to free herself of its hate for its mother at this time. The development of the child went further, and it seemed that a bright future was beckoning her. The statement of a teacher who said: "This little girl could do anything that she wanted to!" had a great effect on her. These words are unimportant in themselves but for this girl they meant, "I can accomplish something if I wish." This realization was followed by an even greater intensity in the combat against her mother.

Adolescence came, and she grew up into a beautiful young woman, became marriageable, and had many suitors; yet all opportunities of a relationship were broken off because of the peculiar sharpness of her tongue. In the bitter battle she had been carrying on against her mother ever since her childhood, she had become unbearably quarrelsome. War was her victory. The behavior of her mother had constantly irritated this child and caused her to seek for fresh triumphs. A bitter word battle was her greatest happiness; in this she showed her vanity. Her "masculine" attitude expressed itself also in that she desired such word battles only where she could conquer her opponent.

When she was twenty-six years old she made the acquaintance of a very honorable man who did not allow himself to be repulsed by her belligerent character and paid court to her very earnestly. After two years of resistance she finally accepted him in the deep conviction that she had made a slave of him, and that she could do with this man whatever she wished. She had hoped secretly that she would find in him a second edition of her father, who would give in to her whenever she wanted.

She soon learned that she had made a mistake. He

[her husband] demanded cleanliness, tenderness, punctuality, and all manner of unjustified requests which she was not prepared to fulfill. He continued his demands with an inexorableness which caused her to have very unhappy prospects for the future. In an intoxication of self-effacement this righteous, dutiful man had wooed her, but no sooner did he have her in his possession than his intoxication had disappeared.

No change in the lack of harmony that existed between them appeared when she became a mother. She was forced to assume new duties. In the meantime, her relationship to her own mother, who was energetically taking up the cudgels for her son-in-law, became worse and worse. The constant warfare in her house was carried on with such heavy artillery that it is not to be wondered that her husband occasionally acted badly, and without consideration, and that occasionally the woman was right in her complaints. The behavior of her husband was the direct consequence of the fact that she was unapproachable, which, again, was a result of her lack of reconciliation with her womanliness. She had believed originally that she could play her role of empress forever, that she could wander through life surrounded by a slave who would carry out all her wishes. Life would have been possible for her only under these circumstances.

What could she do now? Should she divorce her husband and return to her mother and declare herself beaten? She was incapable of leading an independent life for she had never been prepared for it. A divorce would have been an insult to her pride and vanity. Life was misery for her; on the one hand her husband criticized her, and on the other side stood her mother with her heavy guns, preaching cleanliness and order.

Suddenly, she, too, became cleanly and orderly! She did washing and polishing and cleaning the whole day. The disease that manifests itself in continual washing and cleaning is an extraordinarily frequent occurrence in women who are belligerent against their womanliness and attempt in this fashion to elevate themselves, by their complete virtue in cleanliness, over those who do not wash themselves so frequently. Unconsciously all these efforts are aimed solely at exploding the entire household. Few households were ever more disorderly than the household of this woman. Not cleanliness, but the discomfiture of her entire household, was her goal.

We could tell of very many cases in which a reconciliation with the role of being a woman was only *apparently* true. That our patient had no friends among women, could get along with no one, and knew no consideration for another human being fits very well into the pattern that we might have expected in her life.

It will be necessary for us to evolve better methods of educating girls in the future, so that they shall be better prepared to reconcile themselves with life. We must therefore be on the watch to recognize and counter the whole technique of society's mistaken behavior in this connection. We must take up the battle not because we have some pathologically exaggerated respect for woman, but because the present fallacious attitude negates the logic of our whole social life.

Let us take this occasion to discuss another relationship often used to degrade woman: the so-called dangerous age, that period which occurs about the fiftieth year, accompanied by the accentuation of certain character traits. Physical changes serve to indicate to a woman in the menopause that the bitter time in which she must lose forever that little semblance of significance that she has so laboriously built up during the course of her life has come. Under these circumstances she searches with redoubled efforts for any instrument that will be useful in maintaining her position, now grown more precarious than ever before. This amounts to a virtual degradation and enslavement. Imagine the anxiety of an adolescent girl who thinks of this epoch in her life which lies in her future. Womanliness is not extinguished with the fiftieth year.

The honor and worth of a human being lasts unaltered beyond this age. And it must be guaranteed.

The foundations of all these unhappy manifestations are built upon the mistakes of our civilization. If our civilization is marked by a prejudice, then this prejudice reaches out and touches every aspect of that civilization, and is to be found in its every manifestation. The fallacy of the inferiority of woman, and its corollary, the superiority of man, constantly disturbs the harmony of the sexes. As a result, an unusual tension is introduced into all erotic relationships, thereby threatening, and often entirely annihilating, every chance for happiness between the sexes. Our whole love life is poisoned, distorted, and corroded by this tension. This explains why one so seldom finds a harmonious marriage, this is the reason so many children grow up in the feeling that marriage is something extremely difficult and dangerous.

Prejudices such as we have described prevent children, to a large measure, from understanding life adequately. Think of the numerous young girls who consider marriage only as a sort of emergency exit out of life. This is an aspect of our life which is so widespread and important that every one of us is involved in it. It becomes the more complicated since in our day a child is forced into a behavior pattern that is a depreciation and negation of the other sex.

A calm education certainly could overcome these difficulties, but the hurry of our days, the lack of really proved and tested educational methods, and particularly the competitive nature of our whole life, which reaches even into the nursery, determine only too harshly the tendencies of later life. The fear that causes so many human beings to shrink from assuming any love relationships is caused largely by the useless pressure that forces every man to prove his masculinity under all circumstances, even though he must do it by treachery and malice or force.

That this serves to destroy all candor and trust in the love relationships is self-understood. We have no reason to combat the former purposes of the emancipation-for-women movements. It is our duty to support them in their efforts to gain freedom and equality, because finally the happiness of the whole of humanity depends upon effecting such conditions that a woman will be enabled to be reconciled with her womanly role, just as the possibility of a man's adequate solution of his relationship to woman likewise depends upon it.

It would require the creative power of a poet to give an adequate picture of this whole situation. We must be content to indicate only the main points. An adolescent girl acts very much as though she were inferior. The belief in her inferiority is forced upon a girl by her environment. She is so irrevocably guided into this channel of behavior that even investigators with a great deal of insight have from time to time fallen into the fallacy of believing in her inferiority. The universal result of this fallacy is that both sexes have finally fallen into the hasty pudding of prestige politics, and each tries to play a role for which he is not suited. What happens? Both their lives become complicated, their relationships are robbed of all candor, they become surfeited with fallacies and prejudices, in the face of which all hope of happiness vanishes.

CLARA THOMPSON

Clara Thompson (1893–1958) was originally trained in the classical psychoanalytic tradition but went on to become one of the leaders of the newer school of psychoanalysis based on the theories of Harry Stack Sullivan. Thompson stands as the major figure of the 1940s who pointed to the cultural complications affecting women's development and who reoriented psychological understanding of many major problems of women.

Dr. Thompson was a leading figure at the William Alanson White Institute, serving as executive director, president, and a member of the board of directors; she was the first president of the Washington-Baltimore Psychoanalytic Institute and the first vice-president of the American Association for the Advancement of Psychoanalysis.

In addition to her other writings, her many papers on women are collected in the volumes *Interpersonal Psychoanalysis* and *On Women.*

"Penis Envy" in Women

Penis envy" is a term coined by Freud and used by him to describe a basic attitude found in neurotic women. The term had more than symbolic meaning to him. He was convinced that this envy in women grew out of a feeling of biologic lack beginning with the little girl's discovery in early childhood that she lacked something possessed by the little boy. Because of this, according to Freud, she believed she had been castrated, and she dealt with this shock either by sublimating the wish for a penis in the wish for a child, that is, becoming a normal woman, or by the development of neurosis, or by a character change described as the masculinity complex, a type of character which seeks to deny that any lack exists.

Critical evaluations of Freud's theory on the subject have already been published by Horney and myself. In brief, it has been shown that cultural factors can explain the tendency of women to feel inferior about their sex and their consequent tendency to envy men; that this state of affairs may well lead women to blame all their difficulties on the fact of their sex. Thus they may use the position of cultural underprivilege as the rationalization of all feelings of inferiority.

The position of underprivilege might be symbolically expressed in the term penis envy using the penis as the symbol of the more privileged sex. Similarly, in a matriarchal culture one can imagine that the symbol for power might be the breast. The type of power would be somewhat different, the breast standing for life-giving capacity rather than force and energy. The essential significance in both cases would be the importance in the cultural setting of the possessor of the symbol.

Thus one can say the term penis envy is a symbolic representation of the attitude of women in this culture, a picturesque way of referring to the type of warfare that so often goes on between men and women. The possibility of using the term in two ways, that is, as actually referring to a biologic lack, or as symbolically referring to a feeling of inferiority, has led to some confusion in psychoanalytic writing and thinking. It would make for greater clarity if the term were used only in representing Freud's concept. However, as psychoanalysis has developed, new meanings and different emphases often have become attached to an old term without any attempt at precise restatement. Consequently, the term penis envy is used by many without very exact definition. This may lead one to assume that Freud's concept is meant when the thinking is actually along cultural lines. It, therefore, seems worthwhile to clarify the present-day meaning of the term.

It seems clear that envy of the male exists in most women in this culture, that there is a warfare between the sexes. The question to be considered is whether this warfare is different in kind from other types of struggle that go on between humans and if it is not actually different, why is there such preoccupation with the difference in sex? I believe that the manifest hostility between men and women is not different in kind from any other struggle between combatants, one of whom has definite advantage in prestige and position. Two things have contributed to giving the fact of sexual difference a false importance. Penis envy and castration ideas are common in dreams, symptoms, and other manifestations of unconscious thinking. Body parts and functions are frequent symbols in archaic thought. These ideas then may be only the presentation of other problems in symbolic body terms. There is not necessarily any evidence that the body situation is the cause of the thing it symbolizes. Any threat to the personality may appear in a dream as a castration. Furthermore, there is always a temptation to use some obvious situation as a rationalization of a more obscure one. The penis-envy concept offers women an explanation for their feelings of inadequacy by referring it to an evidently irremediable cause. In the same way, it offers the man a justification for his aggression against her.

Sexual difference is an obvious difference, and obvious differences are especially convenient marks of derogation in any competitive situation in which one group aims to get power over the other.

Discrimination because of color is a case in point. Here, a usually easily distinguishable difference is a sign that is taken as adequate justification for gross discrimination and underprivilege. A Negro should feel himself inferior because he has a black skin. Obviously, the black skin is important to the group in power because it is such an easily recognized characteristic with which to differentiate a large number of people from themselves. Everything is done to make it a symbol for all the inferiority feelings Negroes have. Few indeed of the governing class can be so fatuous as to believe that black skin implies an intrinsic inferiority. It is amazing, however, to discover how near to this superficiality many of their rationalizations actually come.

In the same way, the penis or lack of penis is another easily distinguishable mark of difference and is used in a similar manner. That is, the penis is the sign of the person in power in one particular competitive setup in this culture, that between man and woman. The attitude of the woman in this situation is not qualitatively different from that found in any minority group in a competitive culture. So, the attitude called penis envy is similar to the attitude of any underprivileged group toward those in power.

The clinical picture of penis envy is one in which the woman is hostile. She believes the man wishes to dominate her or destroy her. She wishes to be in a position to do similar things to him. In other words, the penis symbolically is to her a sword for conquering and destruction. She feels cheated that she has not a similar sword for the same purpose. This attitude need not have a specific relationship to the sexual life and genitals as such, but may be found as a part of a more general attitude of envy and may only secondarily affect the sexual life. In fact, it may be accompanied by evidences of envy in other relationships. Other women who in some way have more assets and opportunities may also be objects of envy. One may thus find a woman supposedly suffering from penis envy showing a general tendency to envy anyone who has something she does not have and which she desires.

Envy is a characteristic of a competitive culture. It implies comparison to one's disadvantage. There are three general directions in which character can develop in an effort to cope with this feeling. One outstanding type of character development in Western society is the one in which the person tries to excel over others. One does away with envy by achieving success. If one fails in proving that one is as good or better than the envied one, tendencies to revenge may develop. The person seeks then to pull the superior one down and in some way humiliate him. Or a person may withdraw from competition, apparently have no ambition, and desire to be inconspicuous. In such a situation, although there may be a feeling of helplessness and increased dependency, there may also be a secret feeling of power from being aloof to the struggle.

As has been said, the relationship between men and women has special features not found in the relationship with one's own sex. These special features are of two kinds. They have to do with the attitude of a minority group to a dominant group, and they have to do with the fact that the most intimate type of interpersonal situation, the sexual act, is an important part of and usually exclusively limited to the relationship between the two sexes. Thus any problem of interpersonal intimacy would be accentuated in this relationship.

In a patriarchal culture the restricted opportunities afforded woman, the limitations placed on her development and independence, give a real basis for envy of the male quite apart from any neurotic trends. Moreover, in an industrial culture in which the traditional family is no longer of central importance, the specific biologic female contribution, the bearing of children, loses value coordinate with the various factors which encourage a diminishing birthrate. This, although it is not a biologic inferiority, acts as if it were in that a woman can feel that what she has specifically to contribute is not needed or desired.

Therefore, two situations in the culture are of importance in this discussion: the general tendency to be competitive which stimulates envy; and the tendency to place an inferior evaluation on women. No one altogether misses some indoctrination with these two trends. If the competitive attitude is greatly developed by personal life experiences, the hatred of being a woman is correspondingly increased. The reverse is also true; that is, if there has been emphasis on the disadvantages of being a woman, a competitive attitude toward men tends to develop. Out of either situation may appear character developments that fit into the clinical picture of penis envy, and it is not necessary to postulate that in each case an early childhood traumatic comparison of genital organs took place. Such early experiences do sometimes occur, but it is my impression, as well as that of [Frieda] Fromm-Reichmann, that they are traumatic only in the setting of other serious traumatic factors and that they derive their importance chiefly from offering a kind of rationalization for the feeling of inferiority and defeat.

One scarcely can overemphasize the fact that the sexual relationship is one of the most important interpersonal situations. Any competitiveness in the personality of either participant is bound to have an effect upon the sexual relationship. Any actual social underprivilege of one partner must also have an effect on the sexual relationship. This should not be confused with any idea that a biologic sexual inequality was the cause of the competitive attitude or the condition of underprivilege of one partner. The sexual life is merely one important situation in which the problem appears.

Thus it may be seen that the clinical picture of penis envy has little to do with the sexual life, except secondarily, and that it has to do with all aspects of living. If one rejects the idea that inferiority feelings in women are due to a feeling of biologic lack, one must conclude that the term does not describe a clinical entity deriving from a constant origin, but has become a symbol and rationalization for various feelings of inadequacy in women. The situation of cultural underprivilege gives the impression of validity to the rationalization.

CLARA THOMPSON*

Some Effects of the Derogatory
Attitude toward Female Sexuality

IN AN EARLIER PAPER entitled " 'Penis Envy' in Women" I
stressed the fact that the actual envy of the penis as such
is not as important in the psychology of women as their
envy of the position of the male in our society. This position of privilege and alleged superiority is symbolized by
the possession of a penis. The owner of this badge of
power has special opportunities, while those without have
more limited possibilities. I questioned whether the penis
in its own right as a sexual organ was necessarily an object of envy at all.

That there are innate biological differences between
the sexual life of man and woman is so obvious one must
apologize for mentioning it. Yet those who stress this
aspect most are too often among the first to claim knowledge of the psychic experiences and feelings of the opposite sex. Thus for many centuries male writers have been
busy trying to explain the female. In recent years a few
women have attempted to present the inner life of their
own sex, but they themselves seem to have had difficulty
in freeing their thinking from the male orientation. Psychoanalysts, female as well as male, seem for the most
part still to be dominated by Freud's thinking about
women.

Freud was a very perceptive thinker but he was a

* A biographical sketch of the author appears on page 51.

male, and a male quite ready to subscribe to the theory of male superiority prevalent in the culture. This must have definitely hampered his understanding of experiences in a woman's life, especially those specifically associated with her feminine role.

Of course this thinking can be carried to extreme lengths and one can say that no human being can really know what another human being actually experiences about anything. However, the presence of similar organs justifies us in thinking that we can at least approximate an understanding of another person's experiences in many cases. A headache, a cough, a pain in the heart, intestinal cramps, weeping, laughter, joy, the sense of well-being we assume feels very similar to another person to what we ourselves experience under those titles.

In the case of sexual experiences, however, one sex has no adequate means of identifying with the experience of the other sex. A woman, for instance, cannot possibly be sure that she knows what the subjective experience of an erection and male orgasm is. Nor can a man identify with the tension and sensations of menstruation or female genital excitation or childbirth. Since for many years most of the psychoanalysts were men, this may account for the prevalence of some misconceptions about female sexuality. In 1926 in her paper "Flight from Womanhood" Horney pointed out that Freud's theory that little girls believed they had been castrated and that they envied boys their penises is definitely a male orientation to the subject. In this paper she listed several ideas which little boys have about girls' genitals. These ideas, she shows, are practically identical with the classical psychoanalytic conception of the female. The little boy's ideas are the assumption that girls also have penises, resulting in a shock at the discovery of the absence. The boy, reasoning from his own life experience, assumes this is a mutilation, as a punishment for sexual misdemeanor. This makes more vivid to him any castration threats which have been made to him. He concludes that the girl must feel inferior and envy him because she must have come to the same conclusions about her state. In short, the little boy, incapable of imagining that one could feel complete without a penis, assumes that little girls must feel deprived. It is doubtless true that her lack of a penis can activate any latent anxiety the boy may have about the security of his own organ, but it does not necessarily follow that the girl feels more insecure because of it.

In the "Economic Problem of Masochism" Freud assumes that masochism is a part of female sexuality, but he gives as his evidence the fantasies of passive male homosexuals. What a passive male homosexual imagines about the experience of being a woman is not necessarily similar to female sexual experience. In fact, a healthy woman's sexual life is probably not remotely similar to the fantasies and longings of a highly disturbed passive male personality.

Recently I heard to my amazement that a well-known psychiatrist had told a group of students that in the female sexual life there is no orgasm. I can only explain such a statement by assuming that this man could not conceive of orgasm in the absence of ejaculation. If he had speculated that the female orgasm must be a qualitatively different experience from that of the male because of the absence of ejaculation, one could agree that this may well be the case. I think these examples suffice to show that many current ideas about female psychosexual life may be distorted by being seen through male eyes.

In "Sex and Character" [Erich] Fromm has pointed out that the biological differences in the sexual experience may contribute to greater emphasis on one or the other character trends in the two sexes. Thus he notes that for the male it is necessary to be able to perform, while no achievement is required of the female. This, he believes, can have a definite effect on the general character trends. This gives the man a greater need to demonstrate, to produce, to have power, while the woman's need is more in the direction of being accepted, being desirable. Since her satisfaction is dependent on the man's ability to produce, her fear is in being left, being frustrated, while his is fear of failure. He points out that the woman can make herself available at any time and give satisfaction to the man, but the man's possibility of satisfying her is not entirely within his control. He cannot always produce an erection at will.

The effect of basic sexual difference on the character structure is not pertinent to this paper. Fromm's thesis that the ability to perform is important in male sexual life and that it is especially a matter of concern to him because it is not entirely within his control, while the female may perform at all times if she so wishes, are points of importance in my thesis although I should like to develop somewhat different aspects of the situation.

Fromm shows that the woman can at any time satisfy the male and he mentions the male's concern to perform successfully for the female, but he does not at any point discuss how important obtaining satisfaction for themselves is in the total reaction.

In general, the male gets at least some physiological satisfaction out of his sexual performance. Some experiences are more pleasurable than others, to be sure, and there are cases of orgasm without pleasure. However, just because he cannot force himself to perform, he is less likely to find himself in the midst of a totally uncongenial situation.

The female, however, who is permitting herself to be used when she is not sexually interested or at most only mildly aroused, frequently finds herself in the midst of an unsatisfactory experience. At most she can have only a vicarious satisfaction in the male's pleasure. I might mention parenthetically here that some male analysts, for example Ferenczi, are inclined to think that identification with the male in his orgasm constitutes a woman's true sexual fulfillment. This I would question.

What one frequently finds in women who have for some

reason consented to being used for the male's pleasure is resentment. This is in many cases covered by an attitude of resignation. A frequent answer from women about marital sexual relations is "It is all right. He doesn't bother me much." This attitude may hold even when in other respects the husband and wife like each other. That is, such an attitude may exist even when the woman has not been intimidated by threats or violence. She simply assumes that her interests are not an important consideration.

Obviously the sexual act is satisfactory to the woman only when she actively and from choice participates in her own characteristic way. If she considered herself free to choose she would refuse the male except when she did desire to participate.

This being the case, it might be fruitful to examine the situations in which the woman submits with little or no interest. There are, of course, occasions when she genuinely wishes to do this for the man's sake. This does not create a problem. More frequently the cause is a feeling of insecurity in the relationship. This insecurity may arise from external factors, i.e., the male concerned may insist on his satisfaction or else! The insecurity may also arise from within, from the woman's own feelings of inadequacy. These feelings may be due simply to subscribing to the cultural attitude that her needs are not as insistent as the man's, or there may be in addition personal neurotic difficulties.

The question arises—how has it become socially acceptable for a man to insist on his sexual rights whenever he desires? Is this because rape is a possibility and the woman is physically relatively defenseless? This must have had some influence in the course of society's development. However, it has often been proved that even rape is not easy without some cooperation from the woman. The neurotic condition of vaginismus illustrates that in some conditions even unconscious unwillingness on the part of the woman may effectively block male performance. So, while the superior physical power of the male may be an important factor in the frequency of passive compliance, there must be other factors. Those other factors are not of a biological nature, for apparently the human being is the only species in which the female's participation in the sexual act without sexual excitement occurs.

We must look to cultural attitudes for the answer. We find two general concepts that are significant here, and to which both men and women subscribe in our culture. One is that the female sexual drive is not as pressing or important as the male. Therefore, there is less need to be concerned in satisfying it or considering it. The other is the analytically much-discussed thesis that the female sex organs are considered inferior to those of the male.

In recent years there has been a definite tendency to move away from the first idea as far as actual sexual performance is concerned. With the increasing tendency to be more open in observing facts about sex, women in many groups have become able not only to admit to themselves but also to men that their sexual needs are important. However, this is still not true of all groups. Moreover, at almost the same time another important aspect of women's sexual life has diminished in importance. That is the bearing of children. Woman's specific type of creativeness is no longer highly desired in many situations.

As we know, during the Victorian era a woman's sexual needs were supposed to be practically nonexistent. A woman was expected to be able to control her sexual desires at all times. Thus an extramarital pregnancy was allegedly entirely due to the woman's weakness or depravity. The man's participation was looked upon with more tolerance, and there was little or no social disgrace attached to him. The double standard of sexual morality also implied an assumption that woman's sexual drive was not as insistent as the male's.

The fact that evidence of erotic excitement could be concealed much better by women than by men made the development of such thinking possible. Since she was not supposed to be erotic and since the man must have his satisfaction, a pattern was developed in which the dutiful wife offered herself to her husband without actively participating in the act herself. I am sure many women were sufficiently normal to find nonparticipation difficult and doubtless many men did not subscribe to the feeling that they should be horrified at any evidence of passion in their wives. Nevertheless, as recently as twenty years ago a woman consulted me over her marital difficulties. It seemed that her husband felt disgust whenever she responded sexually to him. She tried to conceal her sexual responses, including orgasm, from him, then would lie awake the rest of the night in misery and rage. Since I saw this woman only twice, I am not in a position to say how much this situation contributed to her suicide about a year later. Undoubtedly there were many other difficulties in her relation to her husband of which the sexual may have been only one expression. Certainly this extreme denial of sexual interest is seldom required of women today, but an attenuated form still remains, especially in marriage. Here it is found not only in frigid women who, realizing their inadequacy as mates, make amends as best they can by a nonparticipating offering of themselves. But also one finds the attitude even in women with adequate sexual responsiveness in many situations. They have accepted the idea that the male's needs are greater than their own; therefore, his wishes and needs are paramount.

So the feeling that woman's sexual life is not as important or insistent as the male's may produce two unfortunate situations. It may inhibit the woman's natural expression of desire for fear of appearing unwomanly, or it may lead her to feel she must be ready to accommodate on all occasions, i.e., she has no rights of her own. Both extremes mean an interference with her natural self-expression and spontaneity with resulting resentment and discontent.

Moreover, since the male has often been indoctrinated with the idea that woman's sexual life is not important, he may not exert himself much to make her interested. He fails to see the importance of the art of love.

When an important aspect of an individual's life becomes undervalued this has a negative effect on the self-esteem. What a woman actually has to offer in sexual responsiveness becomes undervalued and this in turn affects her own evaluation of herself as a person.

The second way in which our culture has minimized woman's sexual assets is in the derogation of her genitals. I feel you will all settle back now and say, "Oh, yes—penis envy." But that is not what I am going to talk about. As I said earlier, the idea of penis envy is a male concept. It is the male who experiences the penis as a valuable organ and he assumes that women also must feel that way about it. But a woman cannot really imagine the sexual pleasure of a penis—she can only appreciate the social advantages its possessor has. What a woman needs rather is a feeling of the importance of her own organs. I believe that much more important than penis envy in the psychology of woman is her reaction to the undervaluation of her own organs. I think we can concede that the acceptance of one's body and all its functions is a basic need in the establishment of self-respect and self-esteem.

The short, plump, brunette girl may feel that she would be more acceptable if she were a tall, thin blond—in other words, if she were somebody else. The solution of her problem lies, not in becoming a blond, but in finding why she is not accepting of what she is. The history will show either that some significant person in her early life preferred a tall blond, or being brunette becomes associated with other unacceptable characteristics. Thus, in one case where this envy of the blond type was present, being brunette meant being sexy and being sexy was frowned upon.

Sex in general has come under the disapproval of two kinds of thinking in our culture. The puritan ideal is de-

65

nial of body pleasure and this makes sexual needs something of which to be ashamed. Traces of this attitude still remain today in the feelings of both sexes.

We also have another attitude that derogates sexuality, especially female sexuality. We are a people with great emphasis on cleanliness. In many people's minds the genital organs are classed with the organs of excretion and thus become associated with the idea of being unclean. With the male, some of the curse is removed because he gets rid of the objectionable product. The female, however, receives it, and when her attitude is strongly influenced by the dirty excretion concept, this increases her feeling of unacceptability. Moreover, the men who feel the sexual product is unclean reinforce the woman's feeling that her genitals are unclean.

The child's unrestrained pleasure in his body and its products begins to be curbed at an early age.

This is such a fundamental part of our basic training that most of us would have difficulty imagining the effect on our psychic and emotional life of a more permissive attitude. What has happened is that this training has created a kind of moral attitude toward our body products. Sphincter morality, as Ferenczi called it, extends to more than the control of urine and feces. To some extent genital products come also under the idea of sphincter morality. Obviously, this especially has an influence on attitudes toward the female genitals where no sphincter control is possible. My attention was first called to this by a paper written in German by Bertram Lewin twenty years ago. In this paper, among other things, he presented clinical data in which the menses were compared to an unwanted loss of feces and urine due to lack of sphincter control. In one case he reported, the woman had become very proficient in contracting the vaginal muscles so that she attained some semblance of control of the quantity of the menstrual flow. Although in my own practice I have never encountered a patient who actually tried to produce a sphincter, I have frequent evidence that the inability not only to control menstruation but all secretions of the female genitals has contributed to a feeling of unaccept-ability and dirtiness. One patient, on being presented by her mother with a perineal napkin on occasion of her first menses, refused to use it. To her it meant a baby's diaper and she felt completely humiliated. Obviously, she pres-ently felt even more humiliated because of the inevitable consequences of her refusal.

Also, due to our overevaluation of cleanliness another attribute of the female genital can be a source of distress, i.e., the fact that it has an odor. Thus one of the chief means by which the female attracts the male among animals has been labeled unpleasant, to many even dis-gusting. For example, a female patient whose profession requires her appearing before audiences has been greatly handicapped for many years by a feeling of being "stink-ing" which is greatly augmented whenever she is in a position to have her body observed. Thus she can talk over the radio but not before an audience. Another pa-tient felt for years that she could never marry because she would not be able to keep her body clean at every moment in the presence of her husband. Whenever she had a date with a man she prepared for it by a very vigorous cleans-ing of the genitals, especially trying to make them dry. When she finally had sexual relations she was surprised and greatly helped in her estimation of her body by dis-covering that this highly prized dryness was just the op-posite of what was pleasing to the man.

In two cases the feeling of genital unacceptability had been a factor in promiscuity. In each case an experience with a man who kissed her genital in an obviously ac-cepting way was the final step in bringing about a com-plete transformation of feeling. In both cases all need to be promiscuous disappeared and they felt loved for the first time.

I am obviously oversimplifying these cases in order to make my point clear. I do not wish to leave the impression that the feeling of dirtiness connected with the genitals was the sole cause of a feeling of unacceptability in these patients. There was in each case a feeling from early childhood of not being acceptable produced by specific attitudes in the parents. The feeling of unacceptability became focused on the genitals eventually for different reasons in each case. For example, in three cases the woman had risen above the lowly social position of her parents and with these the feeling of having dirty genitals became symbolic of their lowly origin of which they were ashamed. Their parents had not placed such an emphasis on baths as they found to be the case in the new social milieu. Therefore, any evidence of body secretion or odor betrayed them and this made sex itself evidence of lower-class origin. On the other hand, two other patients suffered from their own mothers' overemphasis on body cleanliness. In each of these two cases the mother was cold and puritanical as well as overclean, and the patient felt humiliated because she had a more healthy sexual drive which she felt was proclaimed to the world by her body's odors and secretions.

From these observations I hope I have emphasized the fact that the problem of a woman's sexual life is not in becoming reconciled to having no penis but in accepting her own sexuality in its own right. In this she is hampered by certain attitudes in the culture such as that her sexual drive is not important and her genitals are not clean. With these two deprecatory cultural attitudes in the background of women's lives, it is to be expected that both are important points at which difficulties in interpersonal relations may be expressed.

CLARA THOMPSON*

Cultural Pressures in the Psychology of Women

IN MY STUDY of *The Role of Women in This Culture* I presented a survey of the present status of women in the United States. I pointed out the basic situation and the changes that are going on. Although the paper was chiefly concerned with the positive aspects of woman's evolution, I spoke also of the problems still remaining, and the new problems arising in the new situations.

It is this problem aspect of woman's present cultural situation that I shall now discuss. I shall approach this through a consideration of Freud's theories about women, viewing these in the light of cultural factors.

The importance of cultural influences in personality problems has become more and more significant in psychoanalytic work. A given culture tends to produce certain types of character. In *The Neurotic Personality of Our Time* Karen Horney has well described certain trends found in this culture. Most of these neurotic trends are found working similarly in both sexes. Thus, for example, the so-called masochistic character is by no means an exclusively feminine phenomenon. Likewise the neurotic need to be loved is often found dominating the life of men as well as women. The neurotic need of power, and insatiable ambition drives, are not only found in men but also in women.

---

* A biographical sketch of the author appears on page 51.

Nevertheless, in some respects the problems of women are basically different from those of men. These fundamental differences are due to two things. First, woman has a different biological function and because of this her position in society necessarily differs in some respects from that of the man. Second, the cultural attitude toward women differs significantly from that toward men for reasons quite apart from biological necessity. These two differences present women with certain problems that men do not have to face.

[Here, Thompson explains Freud's theory and some of the criticisms she and Horney have made in the previous papers. She adds that Freud's pessimism about successful psychoanalysis of women seems unwarranted since it was based on his view that women ultimately desired a penis. Reviewing clinical evidence on the young girl's awareness of either the vagina or the clitoris, she questions whether there is yet any adequate information on the innate sexual interests of women.—Ed.]

The biological problems of a woman's life cannot be ignored although it would seem that in most cases biology becomes a problem chiefly when it produces a situation that is unsatisfactory in the cultural setup. Menstruation, pregnancy, and the menopause can bring to a woman certain hazards of which there is no comparable difficulty in the male biology. Freud was so impressed with the biological difficulties of woman that, as is well known, he believed all inferiority feelings of woman had their root in her biological inadequacies. To say that a woman has to encounter certain hazards that a man does not, does not seem to be the same thing as saying woman is biologically inferior, as Freud implies.

The women observed by psychoanalysts are distinctly women living in a particular culture, the Western culture, a patriarchal culture in a state of transition. It is impossible to separate from the total picture something one can safely call biological woman. It is assumed that she exists, that she has her reactions to her particular organic makeup, but it is increasingly clear that not all that seems biological is biological. That women behave differently in different types of culture is now beginning to be known, although intensive analyses of women in other cultures have not yet been made. Freud, ignoring these considerations, thought the attitudes, interests, and ambitions of the middle- and upper-class women whom he analyzed to be the characteristic attitudes, interests, and ambitions of women in general.

Today one realizes that much which even woman herself may attribute to the fact of her sex can be explained as the result of cultural pressures. At the same time, the fact that bearing children must influence women's personality development cannot be denied. Also, the type of sexual response characteristic of a woman conceivably has its influence on her character.

For example, it seems probable that the very fact that the male must achieve an erection in order to carry out the sexual act, and that any failure in this attempt cannot be hidden, while the female can much more readily hide her success or nonsuccess in intercourse, may well have an effect in the basic character patterns of both. Even here, however, more complete understanding of the cultural pressures is necessary before it can be stated in what way or to what extent biology plays a part. But one thing seems fairly certain, namely, that to the extent to which a woman is biologically fulfilled—whatever that may mean —to that extent she has no tendency to envy man's biology, or to feel inferior about her biological makeup.

In certain cultures woman can meet with difficulties that would make her biological makeup appear to be a handicap. This would be true when her drives are denied expression or when fulfillment of the role of woman puts her at a disadvantage. Both these situations are true in many respects in the United States today. This is essentially a patriarchal culture and although many values are changing and these changes on the whole are working to the advantage of women, the patriarchal situation still presents limitations to a woman's free development of her interests. Also, the newer situations have their hazards in that they usually throw women into unequal competition with men. By unequal, the reference is not to biological inequality, but an inequality resulting from prejudice and the greater advantages offered the male.

The official attitude of the culture toward women has been and still is to the effect that woman is not the equal of man. This has led to the following things: Until very recently woman was not offered education even approximately equal to that given a man; when she did secure reasonably adequate education, she found more limited opportunities for using the training than did a man; woman was considered helpless, partly because she was not given an opportunity to work and partly because she had no choice but to be economically dependent on some man; and social restrictions were placed on her, especially in connection with her sex life. These restrictions seemed to work to the advantage of the man.

The assumption of woman's inferiority was a part of the prevalent attitude of society and until very recently was accepted by both sexes as a biological fact. Since there is obvious advantage to the male in believing this, he has proved much more resistant to a new point of view on the matter than have women. Women, at the same time, have had difficulty in freeing themselves from an idea that was a part of their life training. Thus it has come about that even when a woman has become consciously convinced of her value she still has to contend with the unconscious effects of training, discrimination against her, and traumatic experiences which keep alive the attitude of inferiority.

The women whom Freud observed were women in this situation, and it was easy for him to generalize the effects of the attitude of the culture as a fact of biology.

It seems justifiable, therefore, not only to consider Freud's theory in the light of his masculine bias but to examine closely the particular cultural pressures which may have produced the picture of woman as he saw her.

He found that the central problem in the neurotic diffi-culties of most women was penis envy. If this is inter-preted symbolically it will be agreed that in this culture where the advantages go to the possessor of the penis women often find themselves in situations which arouse their envy of men, and so, in their relations to men, they show an attitude which can be called "penis envy."

An awareness of the advantage of a penis might be vaguely conscious in a little girl's mind at the age of three —for already at that age evidences that the son is more privileged are apparent in many middle-class families. Before one can settle the question of whether this early experience takes place in terms of actual envy of the penis, or whether the boy is envied in a more general way, it must be noticed that until very recently the average girl at puberty was made decidedly aware of the disadvantages of being female. In the Victorian era the transition from the freedom of childhood to the restrictions of adoles-cence must have been especially conducive of unhappi-ness. An experience of a patient as recently as fifteen years ago shows vividly the still existing cultural situation. Two children, a boy and a girl, the boy a year and a half older than the girl, grew up in a family where freedom of de-velopment was encouraged. They were both very fond of outdoor life, and went on long hikes together, often camp-ing out overnight. At the age of twelve suddenly a great change was introduced into the girl's life. She was told that now since she was about to become a woman she could no longer go away with her brother on overnight trips. This was only one evidence, but one very impor-tant to her, of the beginning limitation of her activities. She was filled with bitterness and envy of her brother and for several reasons centered her whole resentment on the fact of menstruation. This seemed to her to be the sign of her disgrace, the sign that she had no right to be a person. She became withdrawn and depressed. Her one strong feeling was that she hated to be a woman and did not want to grow up. The condition developed decisively because of the restrictions of adolescence, restrictions that actually changed her whole way of life. I do not wish to imply that this pathological reaction to the situation at puberty developed in a hitherto healthy girl. Envy of her brother had existed in childhood because of her mother's marked preference for him, but a long period of equality with him had done much to restore her self-esteem. The situation at puberty reestablished the idea that he was the more favored person.

The changes brought about by cultural restrictions at the girl's puberty are not of a superficial nature. At this time in the Victorian picture a girl passed from a position of relative equality with boys to one of inferiority. This inferiority was shown in several ways. An outstanding point of the picture was the inhibition of natural aggression. A girl might no longer make demands and go about freely. If she was interested in a boy she must not show it directly. She must never expose herself to possible rejection. This would mean she had been unwomanly. She might no longer pursue her own interests with the same freedom as a boy. Obstacles were placed in the way of her education, her play, and her social life. But especially in her sexual life her freedom of development was curbed. The punishment for spontaneous expression of sexual interests was very great. One impulsive act resulting in pregnancy could ruin a girl's whole life. Her training was in the direction of insincerity about her sexual interests. She was taught to be ashamed of menstruation. It was something to be concealed and any accident leading to its discovery was especially humiliating. In short womanhood began with much unpleasantness. It was characterized by feelings of body shame, loss of freedom, loss of equality with boys, and loss of the right to be aggressive. The training in insincerity especially about her sexual being and sexual interests has undoubtedly contributed much to a woman's diminished sense of self. When something so vitally a part of her must be denied, it is not a great step further to deny the whole self. The fact that much of this has noticeably changed in the last fifty years seems sufficient proof that this situation was due to a cultural attitude and had nothing to do with innate femininity. Freud, observing this cultural change in the girl's status at puberty, attributed it to the necessity of accepting her feminine passivity, which as he said she could not do without a struggle. Is it not more accurate to say that at puberty it became necessary for the girl to accept the restrictions placed on women, and that this was usually unwelcome. In a word, the difficulties of adjustment found in the girl at puberty are the results of social pressures and do not arise from the difficulty of giving up the clitoris in favor of the vagina.

The cultural attitude about the sexual life of women has been one of denial. In former years there was denial almost of its very existence. Today there is still some tendency to deny that it is as important or urgent as the sexual life of men. Passivity and masochism are usually considered essential characteristics of a woman's sexual drive. Passivity was clearly forced upon her by the inhibition of the right to aggression. Her masochism also often proves to be a form of adaptation to an unsatisfactory and circumscribed life.

Not only in her sexual life has the woman had reason to envy the man. The circumscribing of her intellectual development and the discouragement of personal initiative have been frustrating. Partly from lack of training and partly because of man's desire for ownership, woman has had to accept a position of economic dependence on man, and this is still the rule.

Out of this situation come several personality traits that are generally considered typically feminine and that have even been described in psychoanalytic literature as the outcome of woman's biological makeup. Women are supposed to be more narcissistic than men, to have a greater need to be loved than men, to be more rigid than men, and to have weaker superegos than men, these in addition to the already mentioned attitudes of passivity and masochism.

A review of the actual position of economic helplessness of women of the recent past and the relative economic helplessness of many women today leads one to question the innateness of these personality traits. The function of childbearing cannot but have some effect on the personality of woman, but when this function is accompanied by the necessity to legalize the process by marriage and economic dependency—with the only alternative social ostracism and added difficulties in the economic sphere, if she does not marry—one cannot help thinking that woman's greater need to be loved and to have one meaningful sexual relation rather than the more casual sexual life of the man comes about chiefly because she lives in a culture which provides no security for her except in a permanent so-called love relationship. It is known that the neurotic need of love is a mechanism for establishing security in a dependency relation. In the same way, to the extent that a woman has a greater need of love than a man it is also to be interpreted as a device for establishing security in a cultural situation producing dependency. Being loved not only is part of woman's natural life in the same way as it is part of man's, but it also becomes of necessity her profession. Making her body sexually attractive and her personality seductive is imperative for purposes of security. In the past centuries she could feel safe after she had married and could then risk neglecting her charms, but today, with the present ease of divorce, the woman who depends on a man for her means of support and social position must continue to devote a great deal of her time to what may be called narcissistic pursuits, that is, body culture and concern about clothes. One sees that woman's alleged narcissism and greater need to be loved may be entirely the result of economic necessity.

The idea that women must have weaker superegos than men, as stated by Freud, derives from the notion that in the little girl the Oedipus complex is usually not repressed. Because she enters the Oedipus phase after accepting the fact of castration she has no fear to drive her to repression and the formation of a superego. Not only Freud but other writers, notably Sachs, have pointed out that women, therefore, often lack strong convictions, strong consciences, but rather tend to take on the convictions and standards of any men on whom they become dependent in the course of their lives. This is said to be especially noticeable in women who have loved several men. Such a woman is supposed to adopt in succession the attitudes of the various men.

Undoubtedly there are many women who answer this description, but the character trait of having no strong beliefs or convictions is not found universally in women and also occurs frequently in men in this culture.

It is an attitude typical of people who have found that their security depends on approval of some powerful person or group. It is relatively easy to become converted to any ideology that will bring one advantage, especially if one has never for neurotic or reality reasons been able to achieve sufficient independence to be able to know one's own mind. This could scarcely but be the case with the Victorian girl who was not permitted to free herself from her father until she was safely entrusted to the protection of another man. For cultural reasons, the girl had to continue to be dependent on her father and emancipation from the childhood tie was not encouraged. Such a situation is not conducive to the development of independent standards. That some women became independent despite this is remarkable.

One other statement of Freud's requires consideration: the idea that women are more rigid than men and lose their capacity for intellectual and emotional growth earlier. He points to the fact that a woman of thirty often seems already incapable of further development while a man of the same age is at the beginning of his best period of achievement. Although he does not explain just how this is the result of a woman's sex, the implication is that it is the outcome of the difficulties of her sexual development. To quote him: "It is as though the whole process had been gone through and remained inaccessible to influence for the future; as though in fact the difficult development which leads to femininity had exhausted all the possibilities of the individual." One might be tempted to believe that because a woman's period of sexual attractiveness is shorter than that of a man, she grows old mentally and emotionally earlier. However, here too the cultural factors so dominate the picture that it is hard to see anything else. As long as a woman's sole opportunity for success in life was in making a successful marriage, her career was made or lost by the age of thirty. A woman of thirty in the Victorian era and even in some situations today has no future. It is well known in psychoanalytic therapy that for successful outcome of treatment an actual opportunity for further development of the person must exist. This consideration would seem to offer an adequate explanation of the greater rigidity of women, if in fact any such greater rigidity can be demonstrated. I believe that there is no dearth of inflexible personalities among men who have reached the height of their development by the age of thirty, whether because of inferior mental equipment, unfortunate early training, or lack of opportunity. Moreover, today there are many examples of women not dependent on their sexual value for security who remain flexible and capable of development. All that may be said with certainty is that woman's lack of opportunity and economic dependence on men can lead to early rigidity and a narrowed outlook on life, as can any situation that curbs spontaneous development in either sex.

What I have said thus far shows that the characteristics of woman which Freud has explained as the result of her biological vicissitudes, beginning with the discovery that she has no penis, can be quite as satisfactorily explained in terms of the cultural pressures to which she is subjected. The latter hypothesis must certainly be entertained—if only for economy's sake—before separating the female of man from the realm of general biological principles and making her something biologically unprecedented.

It is clear that Freud's theories were originally developed about Victorian women. Let me now discuss in contrast the woman of today. The position of women has changed greatly, and if the cultural factors are important she is no longer as sexually inhibited and restricted, her opportunities for self-development are greatly increased, and marriage is no longer the only means of economic security. These facts have undoubtedly influenced the character of women. So much so that a new type of woman is emerging, a woman capable of independence and whose characteristics differ from those described by Freud. However, the present is still a situation of transition. It takes a long time for a cultural change to come about, especially in its psychological i nplications for nondependent persons. Something of the Victorian attitude still persists in the psychology of most women. One finds several remnants of it, for example, the notion that it is more womanly for a woman to marry and let a man support her. The majority of women still accept this idea, to be sure not as early in their lives as their grandmothers did. They often have a few years of independence first. For some the alternative of marriage with economic dependence, or independence with or without marriage, presents a serious conflict. Also, under the influence of tradition and prejudice, many women are convinced that their adequate sexual fulfillment, including children, and an adequate self-development are not to be reconciled. Men have no such tradition and with them the two interests usually reinforce each other. In this, certainly, women still have real grounds for envying men.

In this specific, limited sense Freud's idea that women have envy because they have no penis is symbolically true in this culture. The woman envies the greater freedom of the man, his greater opportunities and his relative lack of conflict about his fundamental drives. The penis as a symbol of aggression stands for the freedom to be, to force one's way, to get what one wants. These are the characteristics a woman envies in a man. When this envy is carried to a more pathological degree the woman thinks of the man as hostile to her, and the penis becomes symbolically a weapon he uses against her. In the pathological picture called penis envy by Freud, the woman wishes to have the destructive qualities she attributes to the man and she wishes to use this destructiveness against him.

There remains to be dealt with the ways in which women have met the problem of feeling inferior to and hating men, or to use the Freudian language, have dealt with their penis envy. Freud outlined three solutions: A woman may accept her feminine role; she may develop neurosis; or her character may develop in the direction of a "masculinity complex." The first of these seemed to him to be the normal solution.

Here again the problem arises as to what is biological woman and what is cultural woman. Certainly biologically woman can only find her fulfillment as a woman and to the extent to which she denies this she must be frustrated. However, there are other implications in the idea of accepting the feminine role—it may include the acceptance of the whole group of attitudes considered feminine by the culture at the time. In such a sense acceptance of the feminine role may not be an affirmative attitude at all but an expression of submission and resignation. It may mean choosing the path of least resistance with the sacrifice of important parts of the self for security.

The solution of envy of the male by way of neurosis may be considered a solution by evasion, and although many interesting facts could be considered here, the influence of the cultural pressures does not differ greatly from that found in the next type of situation.

The solution by way of developing a masculinity complex deserves careful consideration. One significant difference of neurotic character structure from neurosis arises from the fact that the character pattern is in many ways acceptable to the culture. It represents not only a working compromise of the person's conflicting trends, but also takes its pattern directly from the culture. The culture invites masculinity in women. With the passing of the old sheltered life, with the increasing competition with men growing out of the industrial revolution as well as out of women's restlessness, it is not strange that her first steps toward equality would be in the direction of trying to be like men. Having no path of their own to follow, women have tended to copy men. Imitating of a person superior to one is by no means unusual. The workingman seeking to move up the social and economic scale not only tries to copy the middle-class way of life but may try to adopt the middle-class way of thinking. He may try so hard that he becomes a caricature of the thing he wishes to be, with loss of sight of his real goals in the process.

In the same way women, by aping men, may develop a caricature situation and lose sight of their own interests. Thus, one must consider to what extent it is profitable for a woman to adopt the ways of a man. To what extent can she do it without losing sight of her own goals. This leads inevitably to a consideration of what characteristics are biologically male and what have developed secondarily as a result of his way of life. Here, as in the consideration of femininity, the same difficulty in separating biological and cultural factors is found. Not many years ago a woman's decision to follow a profession—medicine, for example— was considered even by some analysts to be evidence of a masculinity complex. This rose from the belief that all work outside the home, especially if it called for the exercise of leadership, was masculine, and anyone attempting it, therefore, was trying to be a man.

It is true, practically speaking, that in the business and professional world it often paid to act like a man. Women were entering a domain that had been in the possession of men, in which the so-called masculine traits of decisiveness, daring, and aggression were usually far more effective than the customarily ascribed feminine traits such as gentleness and submissiveness. In adaptation to this new way of life, women could not but tend to change the personality traits acquired from their former cultural setting. The freedom that economic independence brought to women also had its influence in developing characteristics hitherto found only in men. It seems clear, however, that such changes are not in themselves in any fundamental sense in the direction of masculinity. It is not useful to confuse the picture of the independent woman with that of an essentially pathological character structure, the masculinity complex.

By this I mean that the culture now favors a woman's developing certain characteristics which have been considered typical of men; but that in addition she may be neurotic and may exploit the cultural situation to protect herself from certain anxieties which have arisen in part from her difficulties of self-development because she is a woman and, in part, from other privations and traumata. Obviously, if a woman develops characteristics which indicate that she unconsciously considers herself a man, she is discontent with being a woman. It would be fruitful to inquire what this "being a woman" means to her. I have suggested the possibility of several unpleasant meanings. Being a woman may mean to her being inferior, being restricted, and being in the power of someone. In short, being a woman may mean negation of her feeling of self, a denial of the chance to be an independent person. Refusal to be a woman, therefore, could mean the opposite, an attempt to assert that one is an independent person. The woman with a masculinity complex shows an exaggerated need for "freedom" and a fear of losing her identity in any intimacy.

It has become clear in the treatment of some related situations that the development of this character pattern is not solely the result of conditioning against being a woman. More basic may be a threat to the personality integrity from an early dependency, a domineering selfish mother, for example, or from the undermining of self-esteem by a destructive mother. In short, many of the forces that make for the development of neurotic mechanisms in general can contribute to this one. These women fear dependency because dependency has been a serious threat to them. Such women are often unable to have any intimate relationship with men; and if they marry, show a hostile revengeful attitude toward the husband. The marriage relationship is sometimes, however, quite successful when circumstances leave them free to work and at least partially support themselves after marriage. Pregnancy is apt to be a special difficulty because of its at least temporary threat to this independence. And they are always afraid of getting into someone's clutches and losing control of the situation.

If the masculinity complex is not developed primarily as a defense against a feeling of biological lack, if the feeling of cultural inferiority at being a woman is not the sole cause of its development, but on the other hand any difficulty in any important dependency relation can contribute to its formation, why then does it take the particular form of wishing to be or pretending to be a man with associated hatred of men?

Two things in the situation encourage this type of character defense. First, because of the general cultural trend there is secondary gain in such an attitude. It looks like progress and gives the woman the illusion of going along in the direction of the freedom of her time. Second, it offers a means of avoiding the most important intimacy in life, that with a man. This relationship because of its frequent implication of dependency and subordination of the woman's interests especially reactivates all of the dangers of earlier dependencies. The struggle for some form of superiority to men is then an attempt to keep from being destroyed. Men are punished for all that women have been suffering in all sorts of dependency situations. So it would seem that solution of envy of the male by the development of the masculinity complex does not have a simple origin and that sources not simply relating to sexual comparisons are important in it.

In conclusion, let me say that psychoanalysis thus far has secured extensive acquaintance with the psychology of women in only one type of culture. Facts observed in a particular part of the Western world have been interpreted by Freud as an adequate basis for an understanding of female psychology in general and as evidence for a particular theory about specific biological factors in the nature of woman. I have pointed out that characteristics and inferiority feelings which Freud considered to be specifically female and biologically determined can be explained as developments arising in and growing out of Western woman's historic situation of underprivilege, restriction of development, insincere attitude toward the sexual nature, and social and economic dependency. The basic nature of woman is still unknown.

FRIEDA FROMM-REICHMANN

IN COMMENTING on one of Clara Thompson's papers on women, Frieda Fromm-Reichmann in fact presented a new paper on the subject. Like Horney and Thompson, Fromm-Reichmann is recognized as a giant in the psychoanalytic field. She is especially admired for the great impetus she gave to the treatment of the most severe psychological problems, particularly the so-called psychoses. Because of her understanding and genius for teaching others to understand people who had often been considered unapproachable, she holds a special place in psychiatry and psychoanalysis.

Trained in Europe in the more traditional psychoanalytic school, she came to the United States and joined the group surrounding Harry Stack Sullivan. She developed her work in this country during the 1940s and '50s. Dr. Fromm-Reichmann provided a leading spirit as Director and Supervisor of Psychotherapy at the Chestnut Lodge Sanitarium in Rockville, Maryland, and was chairman of the Council of Fellows of the Washington School of Psychiatry in Washington, D.C. She died in 1957.

The paper that follows, which is addressed to the ideas presented in Thompson's article "Some Effects on the Derogatory Attitude toward Female Sexuality," was presented at a symposium on feminine psychology held in 1950 by the faculty of the comprehensive course in psychoanalysis at New York Medical College. The symposium brought together psychoanalysts of widely differing orientations in the hope of creating an ongoing interchange on the psychology of women.

FRIEDA FROMM-REICHMANN AND
VIRGINIA K. GUNST

On the Denial of Women's
Sexual Pleasure

Discussion of Dr. Thompson's Paper

After reading Dr. Thompson's paper, we wondered about one point which she mentioned a little too much in passing, to our taste. We refer to the low esteem that procreation and natural female productivity has in our culture. Perhaps more than all of the other factors which of course hold true, this one is, in our judgment, the basis of the cultural depreciation of female sexuality.

Yesterday we heard about how great this depreciation is and about the slight value our present culture puts upon female procreation. Could this be due to the lack of need for human manpower in our highly mechanized and intellectualized culture?

Before elaborating on the influence of the reduced significance of procreation in our culture, one or two other aspects of women's conflicting sexual role in this culture may be added to those offered by Dr. Thompson. Margaret Mead in her last book, *Male and Female,* mentions one conflict for women in the cultural acceptance of the fact that girls and boys engage in heavy necking with the understanding that actual sexual gratification has to be excluded until marriage. With this cultural pattern it will be very difficult for women ultimately to use their sexual organs properly, to accept them as important and to draw satisfaction from them. We may recall also the inference made by D. H. Lawrence in *Lady Chatterley's Lover.* In effect, Lawrence says that in a culture where such great significance is given to he-men, we do not find too many such he-men, i.e., potent men, who at the same time give great significance to their sexual role and combine sensuousness with sensitivity. He goes on to say, through his characters, that it is this combination that gives men the appreciation of the female partner and her sexual organs and that this, in turn, makes the female herself appreciate her sexual organs.

We may add one other excerpt from Margaret Mead's book. She states that regardless of how much women and little girls may envy the visible organ or the greater superiority which is granted to men in this culture, regardless of how much symbolical or actual penis envy they may feel, they seem to have deep down inside themselves, at a very early age, an appreciation of the fact that their important organs are on the inside. As an illustration, Margaret Mead offers the following observation: If a naked little boy trips and falls while playing, he puts his hands around his penis to protect it. If a naked little girl trips and falls, she embraces herself, that is, she puts her arms around herself as if to protect that which is inside her.

Why then, we ask again with Dr. Thompson, do women later forget, bar from awareness, and have men bar from awareness, the fact that women's important organs are on the inside and that there is no reason to devaluate them?

We believe, as we said, that the answer to this question lies in the devaluation of the significance of procreation and natural creativity in women. Let us follow a good old psychoanalytic practice and look a little further for the answer in myth and folklore, which offer such a great source of understanding of human psychology. You all remember that the biblical creation of the world is conceived as having been done by a male figure, the Lord. This experience seems to have elicited the fantasy that a male God can create the world by virtue of verbalized thought. ("In the beginning God created the heaven and the earth and God said that there be light: and there was light.") As we know, men can produce impressive visible change (erection, ejaculation) in their organ of procreation by thought and fantasy. And so fantasy and thought, which first influence the functioning of the male procreative organ, are given the significance, the significant job, of creating the world. However, there is a Persian myth of the creation of the world which precedes the biblical one. In that myth a woman creates the world, and she creates it by the act of natural creativity which is hers and which cannot be duplicated by men. She gives birth to a great number of sons. The sons, greatly puzzled by this act which they cannot duplicate, become frightened. They think, "Who can tell us, that if she can *give* life, she cannot also *take life*." And so, because of their fear of this mysterious ability of woman, and of its reversible possibility, they kill her.

We believe that in three ways this myth helps us to understand the devaluation of female sexuality and sexual organs in terms of the present cultural devaluation and the ancient, unconscious psychological devaluation of female sexuality. In the latter, woman, proud of her natural creativity, is able to give life to sons. However, if men are frightened by and devaluate this capacity of women, there is only one way for women to gain appreciation from and be protected by men. They must do this by first concealing from men their genuine pleasure in their natural creativity. Then, unfortunately, they must conceal their pleasure from themselves and lay stress upon the other side of their role: the pain of labor connected with childbirth, the discomfort accompanying pregnancy, and the pain and discomfort of menstruation. Hence they call the latter "the curse" or "the cramps," etc.

Now you will say, why is it that women react this way? We believe we have the answer—or one of the answers—in the fact that in spite of their great ability to enjoy their own creativity, they are dependent upon men. No woman can fulfill herself unless a man creates a bridge, as it were, between her inner organs and outer reality. Therefore, she complies with the cultural values as presented by men. Should she try not to, she might appear ridiculous in this culture. We know, from some Indian tribes, that the fear of being ridiculous is considered to be the greatest fear in human beings. Samson Raphaelson, the playright, recently wrote a book, *The Human Nature of Play Writing,* in which he says that the fear of appearing ridiculous is so poisonous that it may dangerously interfere with spiritual creativity. As we see it, what holds true for spiritual creativity, also holds true for the natural creativity in women. Therefore, women must conceal from men how much their natural creative ability means to them. Because of this, women have to depreciate their procreative organs and abilities also in their own minds, and so they learn to put stress only on the painful aspect, the uncomfortable side of it. Consequently, all that which is connected with it, such as menstruation, glandular secretion, and normal discharge, appears dirty and meaningless.

The truth of the matter is, however, that women, if they do not try to bar the real facts from awareness, have a great source of spiritual gratification in being able to perform the greatest act of natural creativity. Moreover, they have a great sexual gratification in delivery and in the nursing period. My great friend and teacher, George Groddeck, has written about this in *The Book of the It,* to which Freud refers in *The Ego and the Id,* as many of you may remember. We know it to be true, that actually pregnancy, delivery, and the nursing period are very great experiences of spiritual gratification and of sexual satisfaction. We know this from clinical experience with those women who speak frankly, if they are not fearful of appearing ridiculous. Knowing this, we may then have to ask as psychiatrists and clinicians: Is it very regrettable that, in this country, there is a routine practice of anesthetizing women while they are in delivery? Does that mean excluding from awareness the greatest experience of spiritual gratification and of sexual satisfaction which a woman can have? We psychoanalysts know it to be true that the barring of sexual fulfillment, and the barring from awareness of sexual wishes from a person's knowledge, may lead to neurosis. This being so, we believe it to be even more true that to bar from awareness the gratifying and sexually satisfying act of procreation may lead to neurosis. Therefore, we further believe that the present practice of women giving birth without being in awareness while doing so may contribute to the development of neuroses in women and that this should be made a topic of extensive psychoanalytic investigation.

There are three psychoanalytically trained obstetricians in San Francisco, Marsh, Moore, and Vollmer, who have developed a technique of preparing and training women for delivery. They have a mirror in front of the delivery table where women, prepared by their training, can observe their own deliveries. In their recently published material the authors say that the effect this method has upon women in labor is that pain is at a minimum and enjoyment of the great experience is tremendous after women overcome the short, initial period of embarrassment. You all know of Read's book about fearless childbirth, which follows the same idea.

There is another means of evidence, known to all obstetricians and psychiatrists, which indicates that childbirth is a real source of wished-for gratification. There are few, if any, women who, after an abortion, regardless of whether the abortion was strictly medically indicated or not, or after sterilization, regardless of how late in their procreative life span it is done, and regardless of how much it was indicated, will not go into temporary depressions.* This eventuates because abortion or sterilization mean that women are deprived of the spiritual and sexual satisfaction of procreation and childbirth. And so if this holds true for procreation and childbirth, then, of

* In more recent investigations these findings have not proved to be so clear-cut.—Ed.

course, it holds true for all the things connected with it, for instance, menstruation.

If young girls are enlightened about the fact that menstruation is not "a curse," but may be a "friendly visitor" who perhaps brings them a message about the functioning of their inner organs, which potentially makes them able to be mothers, their cramps may stop and menstruation may cease to be "a curse." One of us recently had an experience of this kind with a young patient who analytically had gone through all of the reasons for her self-depreciatory attitude toward her role as a woman. Finally the therapist gave her the facts of life and ended by cupping her hands around her mouth and whispering, "And you know, I'll tell you a big secret. Delivery is not only painful!" The girl went back on the ward at the hospital and spread the good news among other girl patients. Six months later she said to the doctor, "Do you know that Mary and I haven't had any cramps for six months and until then we had them every month."

So much about the great act of secretiveness about and depreciation of the gratifying functions of their procreative organs that the women themselves must accomplish because of cultural pressure. Let us add some remarks about the more or less unconscious psychological reactions to female psychosexuality on the part of men, in addition to those that were brought home to us by the Persian myth of the creation of the world. The myth says that men are afraid of women who, since they can give life, may also be able to cause death. Because men are unable to duplicate the experience of childbirth, they *are* afraid. This, of course, is no news to us. We know of the occurrence sometimes of men's fear of the dark hole into which they cannot see. We know of their fear of women because the female does not have as many visible signs of orgastic satisfaction within her own body as the male has. And we know of that which Freud called castration fear, and which in many cases really amounts to castration fear. Men are not only unconsciously afraid of women as childbearers but many men are also envious of this ability of women. We hear so much about penis envy but it is not fashionable in a patriarchal culture to talk about birth envy, although many of us know it exists. The German psychoanalyst [Felix] Boehm described it as early as 1929. We also know it from our clinical experience. Let us briefly repeat here the experience that one of us had with a patient, about which I was privileged to speak to you in another connection here last year. This patient's wife was pregnant with her third child. The patient said to the analyst, "I have a repeated, extremely pleasurable experience. I fill my chest to capacity, hold the air as long as I can, and then I eliminate some parts of my body." It appeared that he was eliminating his penis and that he was trying to fill his "cavity" so as to appear pregnant to himself. It furthermore appeared that he was extremely envious of his wife's pregnancy.

Suppose, then, that it is true that women gain not only spiritual satisfaction but also sexual gratification from carrying a child, from delivering it and from breast feeding the child. That means that women, unless they dissociate these facts from awareness, are sexually gratified with each impregnation for well over a year's time, if they nurse their children over a period of several months. This extended period of satisfaction available to women in pregnancy, delivery, and lactation may very easily account for some difference between men and women regarding the importance of sexual gratification in the sex act per se and as to its frequency. A further prolonged source of sexual satisfaction is given to childbearing women in addition to that available in sexual intercourse. Its influence on women's sex behavior needs further psychoanalytic investigation.

In olden times women really knew that in spite of their basic biologic dependence upon men for their gratification they possessed in pregnancy, delivery, and lactation a great privilege as compared with men. Think of our fairy tales. In one, "The Wolf and the Seven Little

ON THE DENIAL OF WOMEN'S SEXUAL PLEASURE

Goats," the wolf eats six little goats, the mother discovers it, fills his belly with stones, he goes to a little brook, and he falls into it. In the tale of "Little Red Ridinghood," the wolf eats the grandmother and her little grandchild, and he is not able to carry them. He, too, goes to drink water and falls into a brook. From these ancient tales we see that women actually realized that only they possessed the privilege of carrying human beings inside their bodies. We also see men's envy of women's special ability to do so, in their crude attempts to duplicate it, and women's deriding them for it.

Let us repeat, in summary. We believe that the present cultural attitudes we have mentioned—little value being placed on procreation; the more or less unconscious fear and envy of women's maternal ability by men; the need for women to conceal the great positive significance of their sex organs from themselves and from men—may have more to do with the cultural and sexual psychological complications in women's lives in this world of ours than all of the other important reasons which Dr. Thompson has mentioned.

In this unique paper Gregory Zilboorg added a new dimension to the study of the relationship between the sexes. Drawing on his wide knowledge of anthropology, history, and biology in addition to psychoanalysis, he tackled those still outstanding questions: How did it all begin? And why has the oppression of women been so universal and persistent?

Zilboorg was well equipped for his task. He had a most varied background; an esteemed psychoanalyst, he was also highly regarded as a historian, as a man of great erudition, and as an adviser in legal and public matters. In view of his prominence, it is striking that this major work is so little known.

Unlike the preceding authors, Zilboorg never departed from the basic Freudian frame of thought: that culture can be understood as a product of biology. He had, however, a very rich concept of the interweaving of biology and culture.

The following paper is drawn from the much longer original work, in which the author provided more copious documentation of all his major theses.

Since the time of this writing there have been, of course, many additions to our knowledge of the several fields Zilboorg covers. Some of these areas, for example, biology and embryology, are covered in subsequent papers in this book. Other aspects, such as Zilboorg's anthropological evidence, can, obviously, be evaluated only with reference to his full paper and to later data provided by that field.

At the time of his death in 1958 Dr. Zilboorg was clinical professor of psychiatry at Downstate Medical Center and at New York Medical College.

GREGORY ZILBOORG

Masculine and Feminine

Some Biological and Cultural Aspects

The first world war seemed as if suddenly to challenge traditional views on that which is called femininity. Women appeared in a number of places theretofore occupied exclusively by men; they took over the jobs of many a streetcar conductor, taxi driver, elevator boy. Cigarette smoking, theretofore almost totally the prerogative of man, was begun by women; today tobacco-smoking and cocktail-drinking ladies are a normal feature of society, and it is the woman abstainer who has become a rarity. During the last years of the last war, and approximately for a decade thereafter, even the general appearance of women underwent a considerable change. The boyish bob or bobbed hair became almost universal; the hard-spoken, angular, flat-chested "flapper" became such a usual phenomenon that she no longer appeared conspicuous. The knee-length skirt, the masculinized *tailleur* or street suit, and the apparently total discard of the prewar *corsette* exposed the postwar woman to the gaze of the male in a manner of self-contained provocativeness, self-assured initiative, and almost complacent challenge.

From the psychological point of view, all these changes were perhaps more revolutionary than the acquisition and extension of women's suffrage—also primarily a postwar phenomenon. The mid-Victorian cast of chastity, innocent prudery, coyness, and romantic passivity was dealt a more substantial blow by the before-mentioned, seemingly external changes than the admission of women to the bar and jury duty and politics. After all, history had known, acknowledged, and accepted great women in politics. Those women were exceptions, to be sure; they had to be queens, or saints, or unique powers behind the scenes, or semilegendary, or revolutionary heroines— Victoria, Joan of Arc, Lucrezia Borgia, Portia, Charlotte Corday. But throughout history the woman in the street or in the drawing room had remained what is vaguely called feminine. True psychological equality with man, individual initiative, executive ability, frank assertion of her right to choose a sexual partner instead of always being chosen and "kept" by man—all this was truly revolutionary.

As is always the case with such matters, the purely external aspects of this revolution—the fashion in clothes and finery—soon began to dwindle; dresses gradually returned almost to their "prerevolutionary" respectable length, the hair became longer, the hairdo more ornate. But the fundamental psychosociological change held its newly conquered position and consolidated it, despite the fact that even in 1943 the Commonwealth of Massachusetts was still unwilling to admit women to jury duty, because a woman juror might have to be locked up with men in the jury room and supposedly would not be able to take care of matters with safety to herself and propriety to the public. The nature of this new advance of women in civilized independence and cultural equality with men is still not very clear, but the fact of this change is incontestable.

Psychoanalysis, which almost from its inception dealt with the psychological difference between man and woman, has failed surprisingly to analyze this new shift in culture. As a matter of fact, it has even failed to discuss it directly. A perusal of the psychoanalytic literature between 1914 and the early twenties fails to disclose anything more than an occasional discussion of the biopsychological differences between man and woman which were accounted for, so it was asserted, primarily or exclusively by the anatomical differences between the sexes. Freud called attention to Napoleon's acidulous bon mot, "Anatomy is destiny." Psychoanalysis, which in all other aspects of human psychology was iconoclastic, seems to have resigned itself to this accepted decree of destiny. Not that psychoanalysis continued actually to discriminate against women, as biology, sociology, philosophy, and industrial civilization did; on the contrary, it accepted women as partners in the profession, on the basis of total equality. But it did seem to remain rather complacent about the problem, and it did not agitate many discussions on the subject with any particular originality or true appreciation of its import.

In the middle of the twenties, and for approximately the whole decade between 1925 and 1935, the discussion appeared to come into its own. The question as to the phenomenology and genesis of the psychological differences between the sexes began to be debated with considerable frequency and vigor, and toward the end of the decade even with some bristling intensity if not acrimony. Clinical evidence as to essential masculine activity and feminine passivity and the feminine castration complex were cited in support of what [Ernest] Jones once dubbed the "phallocentric" hypothesis; soon apparently just as good clinical evidence was brought forward which questioned or cast doubt on what has become the official Freudian tradition on the subject.

[Karl] Abraham, Helene Deutsch, Horney, Josine Muller, Ernest Jones, Melanie Klein, van Ophuijsen, and Muller-Braunschweig—to mention only the most prominent participants in this discussion besides Freud himself—showed considerable interest in the subject. Amendments to the basic hypothesis of Freud and divergent hypotheses were offered, at first in vague outline and later with increasing definiteness.

Freud entered this discussion with authority and his usual earnestness. In 1927 he presented "Some Psychological Consequences of the Anatomical Distinction between the Sexes," and in 1932 he once more attempted to summarize his findings and views and clear up the issue with his "Female Sexuality." But except for the introduction of the hypothesis of the preoedipal phase, Freud added little to what he had stated previously on the subject. On the whole the problem continued in the state of a highly complex puzzle.

Helene Deutsch made brilliant contributions to the discussion; her conception of the psychogenesis, evolution, and dynamics of the woman's sexual life remained on the whole in harmony with the views of Freud and Abraham. Horney from the very outset approached the whole problem with great boldness. She showed a consistent and promising trend of thought which bode fair to shed new and true light on the problem.

Ernest Jones appeared in the role of mediator and reconciler of the divergences. From his "Early Development of Female Sexuality"—1927—to "Phallic Phase"—1933—he attempted with a great deal of skill and intellectual elasticity to formulate a hypothesis which stood halfway between a synthesis and an eclectic digest of the various divergent trends. Jones was inclined to consider the phallic stage in women a regressive, neurotic phenomenon rather than a normal developmental phase; he was inclined to view the fear of total destruction of sexuality—for which he suggested the term "aphanisis"—as fundamental and as the deepest psychological content of castration anxiety.

It is worthwhile to record that while this discussion of female sexuality occupied a position of prominence in psychoanalytic literature, the apparently central position of this problem was not due to the fact that psychoanalysis during this period was interested in little else. This was the time when such issues as beyond the pleasure principle, the topography of the psychic apparatus, and inhibition, symptoms, and anxiety came to the fore. New viewpoints were introduced, and a considerable reorientation in clinical and theoretical approaches to psychoanalytic problems was brought about. Under the impact of these issues the libido theory, while far from being abandoned, was yet overshadowed by newer problems. Still, the question of female libidinous development stood out as a paramount issue, even against the background of the welter of new problems. This fact alone testifies to the importance and rather disquieting nature of the problem.

After 1933 the discussion of the subject seems to have receded in prominence, but no really new answers to the old questions had been found, and the old answers failed fully to meet the new and legitimate queries about female sexuality.

The organic inferiority of woman, as Freud put it, and the superiority of man, both implied and asserted in psychoanalytic theory, continued to be treated with postulative conviction. Man's psychological road to fatherhood appeared direct and rather simple and easy; woman's psychological road to motherhood appeared circuitous, labored, complex. Even the theory of bisexuality did not relieve the woman of her difficulties. The discussion unhappily seemed to wilt under its own weight. To what extent it failed to be really productive can be seen from the fact that from 1918, when Freud wrote his "Taboo of Virginity," to 1932, when he wrote his "Female Sexuality," he himself failed to suggest any new methodological approach to the problem, although he did note that there was much still to learn and that the discussion started early in the twenties had not proved very profitable.

That the problem was not solved, Freud would readily admit. That it is a problem fraught with a great many dangers to psychoanalysis and to its scientific solidity, all would agree. How is it, then, that psychoanalysis— which revolutionized psychological insight and opened new vistas in the methodology of social sciences, particularly sociology and anthropology, produced new approaches to history and even economics, influenced general orientation even in some aspects of organic pathology and in many trends in biology, literature, and art—yet seems to have stumbled and even failed thus far to offer a truly satisfactory solution of or a comprehensive hypothesis regarding the problems of feminine sexuality and the so-called battle between the sexes— problems peculiarly its own, specifically psychoanalytic?

The same problem, although in a different form, preoccupied the best sociological and biological minds for over a century. It stood out as a major problem in literature and drama. Turgeniev was deeply preoccupied with the role of woman and womanhood in civilization; so were Ibsen, Tolstoy, Zola, and George Bernard Shaw. The ideals and solutions offered abounded in contrasts and self-contradictions. Tolstoy saw in the woman's absolute passivity the very fulfillment of her biological and cultural mission; he commended Chekhov with great enthusiasm for his short story "Darling," which depicts the chameleonic passivity of the woman as little more than the human species of *vacca domestica*. Ibsen—*Nora*— and Shaw—*Candida*—felt and thought in terms of woman's emancipation, and yet it was not fully clear as to what the essential goal of that emancipation was to be; their ideals seemed more pronounced as far as the negative goal was concerned. They seemed to know more what woman should be free from than what she should be free for; the purpose of this emancipation and the role of the emancipated woman remained undetermined. Essentially, the whole struggle between the two age-long ideals of *la femme mère* and *la femme maîtresse* came to full expression without any positive solution of the riddle in sight. The type of Nana, or *La Dame aux Camélias*, alternated with the type of a modern edition of an Aspasia in the form of Hedda Gabler—embittered, man-hating, and yet aspiring toward man's love and a manhood with all the anguish and dissatisfaction of a motherhood at once attained and rejected.

Psychoanalysis did explain the major dynamics of this feminine tragedy, its psychological structure, and the nature of its conflicts as far as the inner war with man and his world is concerned. But admittedly, psycho-analysis failed to shed much light on man's fundamental hostility toward woman, and failed to give in substance any more satisfactory answer than that this is a man's world, the woman has a hard time in it, and that this is her fate. More than that, psychoanalysis seemed to lend some support to the traditional attitude of modern civilization by pointing to the woman's organic, psychological, and cultural inadequacy.

[Zilboorg carries this line of thought further to explore the theme of woman as a castrated being devoid of super-ego as it recurred through the history of philosophy and literature, and as it was especially exemplified in the *Malleus Maleficarum,* the theoretical rationalization for the witch hunts of the fifteenth century.—ED.]

It may be temporarily considered established that there is more than mere conjecture in the thought that hostility between the sexes is real and very old, that this hostility bears all the earmarks of an unconscious drive of con-siderable potency, and that the existing psychoanalytic hypotheses and theories do not sufficiently explain the nature and quality of this hostility, nor do they offer a comprehensive idea as to its origin and development.

It might then be said: Psychoanalysis is fifty years old. It was born and it grew to apparent maturity within half a century replete with changes, the depth and impor-tance of which well surpass the nature and the effects of the French Revolution and possibly even of the Renais-sance. Let psychoanalysis itself, therefore, be treated as a phenomenon, as a part of the history of scientific thought, and let it be examined by means of the very psychological tools that psychoanalysis has provided. Let it be deter-mined what place it does occupy within the scheme of scientific orientation, what it overthrew as something that had outlived its scientific usefulness, and what it kept, or failed to overthrow or to modify.

Freud can be viewed historico-psychologically, from the point of view of what revolution psychoanalysis represents and what transformations it brought about in the field of psychology as a result of the evolution of thought in the course of the past seventy-five or one hundred years. To carry out this immense task properly, a number of comprehensive studies and restudies will have to be made; it is definitely a task for the future. My objective must of necessity be limited to some one feature or aspect of the dynamic psychosociological place of psychoanalysis in the development of scientific thought.

It is all too well known that just as cultural evolution from time to time produces revolutionary changes for which the personality is found with whose genius this revolution is identified, so it almost always happens that the revolutionist, political or scientific, retains frequently one or more of the elements of the past which he himself overthrew so successfully. He suffers from what might be called a "cultural lag" akin to the cultural lag in social development demonstrated by Ogburn.

By way of anticipation, one wonders whether, as regards female sexuality, psychoanalysis also betrays a definite cultural lag. I am inclined to believe that it is the introduction of the concept of the superiority of man in the psychoanalytic theory of sexual development—a concept of values—that is responsible for the general lack of clarity.

Let me leave psychoanalysis for a moment and consider the social and psychological history of man's self-assertion. The impression will at once be gained that man never consciously questioned his own superiority; he always suspected the reliability and the stability of woman. *Varium et mutabile semper femina,* exclaimed Virgil. The Old Testament definitely rejected woman, although on occasion ancient Israel recognized a prophetess. Greece after the Homeric Age and Rome in its philosophies, organizations of state, and jurisprudence not only favored man but kept woman at a social, intellectual, and economic disadvantage. A woman in ancient

Greece could not take possession of what she inherited; she was called an *epicleros,* an heiress who could not possess her heritage.

The harsh opposition to women as it finally evolved into a system of thought toward the fifteenth century has already been cited here when speaking of the *Malleus Maleficarum.* Toward the seventeenth century the theological rationalizations concocted to prove woman's inferiority became more secular. The budding scientific spirit was quick to adopt or rather incorporate the perennial opposition to women, and the panoply of rationalistic philosophy of the eighteenth century as well as the biological science of the nineteenth was utilized to support the hypothesis, with the new "proofs" at their disposal, that man has always been right in his claim that he was superior.

The French Revolution, like all great social crises, brought woman forward as an equal partner of man in the historic struggle for freedom, and here and there a voice could be heard in defense of woman. Not all of them were Marie Antoinettes; there were the Charlotte Cordays as well as the numerous nameless companions of the sans-culottes and their sisters in arms. [Marie Jean] Condorcet was one of the first to raise his voice against man's self-appropriated superiority, against the androcentric philosophy of mankind. He insisted:

If we try to compare the moral energy of women with that of men, taking into consideration the necessary effect of the inequality with which the two sexes have been treated by laws, institutions, customs, and prejudices, and fix our attention on the numerous examples that they have furnished of contempt for death and suffering, of constancy in their resolutions and their convictions, of courage and intrepidity, and of greatness of mind, we shall see that we are far from having the proof of their alleged inferiority. Only through new observations can a true light be shed upon the question of the natural inequality of the two sexes.*

* Marie Jean Condorcet, quoted in Lester F. Ward, *Pure Sociology; a Treatise on the Origin and Spontaneous Development of Society* (New York: Macmillan, 1914), p. 350.

New observations for some reason were not forth-coming, or perhaps they were not considered with the proper amount of attention and respect; all through the nineteenth century the tradition continued. Man became perhaps less openly demonstrative of his self-assertion; he was perhaps willing to concede a purely formal point or two. But the fundamental trend continued to prevail.

"The androcentric world view will probably be as slow to give way as was the geocentric, or as is still the anthropocentric."*

This is the psychosociological heritage bequeathed to the generation that was called upon to create and to de-velop the psychoanalytic theory.

It does seem that androcentric bias interferes with recognizing some fundamental error. Should one admit that he has been in error, he will be confronted with the necessity of recognizing woman's biopsychological inde-pendence, so to speak—the equality of the sexes in the scheme of things. One wonders then whether this suggestion might not be resisted rather sternly, for fear that the genetic theory of sex which was formulated by psychoanalysis might then have to fall by the wayside, and with it perhaps the whole structure of psychoanaly-sis. That this eventually is totally improbable even if the sexes be granted full psychoanalytic equality is not at first clear; it is quite possible that it is one's cultural lag which makes it extremely difficult to give up the androcentric bias to which one still unwittingly but sternly adheres and which interferes with serene consideration of the problem.

There is a penetrating passage in "The Taboo of Vir-ginity" which for some reason seems forgotten, since that which I consider to be its fundamental idea is ascribed generally to Melanie Klein. Freud says:

On the other hand, however, he [man, or primitive man] has the habit of projecting his own inner feelings of hostility on to

* *Ibid.*, p. 332.

the outside world, that is, of ascribing them to whatever objects he dislikes, or even is unfamiliar with. Now woman is also
looked upon as a source of such dangers and the first sexual
act with a woman stands out as a specially perilous one.

One wonders whether here Freud did not actually touch
upon some fundamental hostility man has against woman,
a hostility which he projects into the woman at his first
sexual approach to her, or in general when he comes to
her with his sexual demand.

The basic thought in this passage seems to have been
lost in the traditional view; let me now make careful note
of this thought, for it will prove highly useful. That man
as a rule approaches woman with primordial hostility,
and therefore that his fear of castration by her might
prove a projection of his own hostility, is definitely implied by this passage. When Freud said that "Sexual
need does not unite men, it separates them," he definitely
suggested that the sexual drive from its very beginning
contains primordially a hostility which is directed against
man as a rival. Considering the statements previously
cited, I believe I am not in error if I at least assume that
Freud considered that this primordial hostility is also
directed against the very woman man approaches
sexually.

Both Josine Muller and Jones stated that the girl feels
guilty not in terms of being castrated but in terms of
never being "able to bear children, i.e., that her internal
organs have been damaged." Horney repeatedly called
attention to the woman's fear of being raped and to the
attitude of revenge against men which is directed "with
particular vehemence against the man who performs the
act of defloration," that the girl is afraid "that the con-
tents of her body will be destroyed, stolen, or sucked out."
All these observations do seem to suggest that woman's
fears are in some way deeply connected with her physical
fear of man and of childbearing.

The seemingly iconoclastic suggestion of Karen

Horney's, that one of the fundamental issues in the development of male and female sexuality is the fact that woman stands in relation to man as slave to master, is found rather clearly stated by Freud. In "The Taboo of Virginity" Freud says that the insistence on virginity before marriage "is after all nothing but a logical consequence of the exclusive right of possession over a woman which is the essence of monogamy—it is but an extension of this monopoly on to the past." That Freud saw this fact in the proper light is incontestable. It is equally clear that his androcentric bias saw nothing unusual or deviatory from the normal human course of things in man's proprietary superiority over woman.

Fragmentary as this list is, and desultory as some of the suggestions made are, they may nevertheless serve as ample background for supporting the assumptions: that neither the problem of the development of female sexuality, nor the true bio- and psychosociological role of woman has thus far been sufficiently understood by psychoanalysis; that Freud was aware of this in most of his studies; that he was guided by the androcentric bias or, in other words, was hampered by the cultural lag caused by the androcentric bias; that he was fully aware that such problems as matrilineal inheritance, feminine deities, man's hostility against woman, the motif of rape, and man's subjugation of woman were worthy of consideration. For some reason he merely hinted at these problems and offered no inkling of a solution. His point of departure was that status of humanity which he, following Darwin, called the primitive horde. He caught glimpses of certain things that perhaps preceded the horde; he observed facts which he related to an earlier period; but he did not happen to venture into pondering upon and visualizing the remote past of man which stood historically many ages before the primitive horde.

Freud cannot be reproached for not having gone further back, but the fact once stated might warrant a tentative explanation. The cultural lag of the androcentric bias is well satisfied by the choice of the primitive horde as a point of departure. The very brilliance of Freud's conception as it was outlined in "Totem and Taboo" was so satisfying and so convincing that the followers of Freud overlooked the fact that this anthropological construction alone, if given the primary and exclusive position which it has occupied until now, throws the problem of feminine sexuality out of perspective. The cultural aspects of the problem were illuminated by many rich ideas, while the biological ones were neglected and observers had to fall back on static anatomy and embryology rather than on a dynamic genetic, biological hypotheis.

As far as I know, only Ferenczi sensed this methodological impasse in psychoanalysis. He wanted to overcome the difficulty by means of certain biological speculations, but he never brought these speculations together with anthropological and consequently psychological conceptions in the psychoanalytic sense of the words—that is to say, in the sense of the synthesis between biology and anthropology and the corresponding dynamic manifestations of all the forces they embrace in the functioning of the psychic apparatus.

Pondering over this complex and unsolved problem, I found myself one day perusing the works of Lester F. Ward, who is known to few psychoanalysts, and with whose writing I had been familiar some years ago but had for some reasons repressed. The reasons for the repression were not far to seek, and this time not difficult to discover. I recalled that it was Lester F. Ward who, toward the end of the past century, made the first effective attempt to review and even to reject the androcentric theories which underlie all systems of "humanities": anthropology, sociology, philosophy. Now, when I had arrived at the point of wondering about the androcentric cultural lag, it was not difficult to recall many details of Ward's conceptions and to restudy them with a more eager curiosity, if not with a little more enlightened mind.

I think that these views, first expressed in 1888, are of

sufficient value to psychoanalysts, and particularly to the solution of the problem of masculine and feminine sexuality, for me now to outline them, and while doing so to combine them with my own views so far as mine are based on a psychoanalytic experience which Ward obviously lacked.

Lester F. Ward's theory first appeared inauspiciously in the form of a summary of an address he delivered before the Six O'clock Club in Washington, in 1888. This summary was published in June of that year in the *Household Companion.* It later reappeared in full in Ward's *Pure Sociology; a Treatise on the Origin and Spontaneous Development of Society,* which was written in the closing years of the century at the time Freud completed his *Interpretation of Dreams.*

Ward's views are supported by such a wealth of facts from entomology, botany, zoology, biology, anthropology, and sociology that no summary would do justice to the scholarly and comprehensive presentation of which Ward was a master. It is a pity that this American name, well known to European sociologists, is so little known to Americans and almost totally unknown to psychoanalysts. Ward was the first in American and I believe also in European thought who simultaneously with and independently of Freud—in many respects before Freud— spoke of the importance of the instinct which he defined in a masterful fashion as "a conversion of means [biological] to an end." He was the first to recognize the true value of emotions in human psychology: he recognized the importance of what psychoanalysts have learned to know under the name of "psychic pain." He was the first to describe—almost in Freudian terms—the tensions arising from damming up of libido, which first is accompanied by pleasure, then by pain, then by pleasurable discharge. He defined this process with utmost succinctness by saying that "desire is pain." He emphasized the role of the sexual factors in human life, and he looked forward to the day when all these factors would be studied with greater frankness and would bring about a true psychosociological synthesis. He was acquainted with some of the writings of Havelock Ellis but did not know any of Freud's; Freud had not yet written his *Defense Neuropsychoses* when Ward formulated his views.

Ward begins by calling attention to the fact that reproduction was, and in many classes of living forms still is, nothing more than nutrition. Haeckel's dictum that the process of reproduction is nothing more than "the growth of the organism beyond the individual" is emphasized. Looking beyond the protozoa onto mankind, Ward aptly states that nutrition and the splitting off of an individual from the overgrown primitive organism represents a loss of a part of one's body in favor of reproducing a new organism.

When sexual differentiation gradually did set in, the male played a very secondary, or if you wish a highly specialized, role, in the kingdom of plants and of animals.

If we regard stamens and pistils as individuals, it becomes obvious that in the higher plants generally, and to a much greater extent than in animals, the male is simply a fertilizer, while the female goes on and develops and matures the fruit. Stamens always wither as soon as the anthers have shed their pollen. They have no other function.*

If anthropomorphic and anthropocentric propensities be held in check and an effort be made to look upon the above phenomena dispassionately, one should not flinch from the assumption that the primordial role of the male was highly specialized as no more than a temporary and ephemeral appendage to life.

The phenomenon of minute parasitic males is not rare among the lower forms, and that their sole office is fertilization may be clearly seen from the following statement of Milne Edwards: "It is to be noted that in some of these parasites

* *Ibid.*, p. 320.

(Ex. *Diplozoon paradoxum*—a nematode) the entire visceral cavity was occupied by the testicles, and that Mr. Darwin could not discover in it any trace of digestive organs." Van Beneden also says that the males are reduced to the rôle of spermatophores: "The male of Syngami (nematodes) is so far effaced that it is no longer anything but a testicle living on the female."*

Without entering into teleological speculations, which are always as inconclusive as they are tempting, the process might be formulated as follows: As a result of natural selection a

process was inaugurated that is called *fertilization,* first through an organ belonging to the organism itself (*hermaphroditism*), and then by the detachment of this organ and its erection into an independent, but miniature organism wholly unlike the primary one. This last was at first parasitic upon the primary organism, then complemental to it and carried about in a sac provided for the purpose.†

Ward—using the criterion of racial efficiency—is inclined to consider the female primary, more essential for the preservation of the race of living things, and therefore superior. This theory definitely clashes with androcentric bias, and Ward gives his theory the name "gynecocentric."

Ward does not limit himself to the above few observations on plants and lower animals. To give body and substance to his theory he proceeds gradually along the scale.

From the biogenetic point of view, Ward thinks that the female originally reigned supreme, as she still does in the animal kingdom, and that the male was but "an afterthought of nature." In the animal kingdom as well as originally in the human species, "the male therefore does not select or exercise any choice."

* *Ibid.,* p. 315.
† *Ibid.,* p. 373.

Ward puts together rather compactly certain of the claims in favor of male superiority:

We have the general fact that in all the principal animals with which everybody is more or less familiar, including the classes of mammals and birds at least, the males are usually larger, stronger, more varied in structure and organs, and more highly ornamented and adorned than the females. One has only to run over in his mind the different domestic animals and fowls, and the better known wild animals, such as the lion, the stag, and the buffalo, and most of the common song birds of the wood and meadow, to be convinced of the truth of this proposition.*

If one is to remain on a sound biological basis, it would seem more logical and more in accordance with the basic principles of biological science to consider the above attributes of the male not the manifestation of his primary biological superiority but rather a result of natural selection which was imposed upon him by the female's original power of choice. It was the female who sensed instinctively which mate was more eligible from the standpoint of health and general biological fitness, and by the process of natural selection the male developed into what he is in order best to suit the exacting demands which the female made upon him from this point of view.

Even aggressiveness and combativeness, which are traditionally considered the very essence of masculinity, appear now in a different light.

The battles of the males, however fierce, rarely result fatally, and they often take the form of quasi mock battles in which some do, indeed, "get hurt," but it rarely happens that any get killed. Still less is it true that the strongest and ablest males use their powers to coerce the female into submission. The female, even when greatly surpassed in size and strength by the male, still asserts her supremacy and exercises her pre-

* *Ibid.*, p. 292.

rogative of discrimination as sternly and pitilessly as when she far surpassed the male in these qualities. This is why I reject the usual expression "male superiority" for those relatively few cases in which the male has acquired superior size and strength along with the various ornaments with which the female has decked him out. And nothing is more false than the oft repeated statement inspired by the androcentric world view, that the so-called superior males devote that new-gained strength to the work of protecting and feeding the female and the young. Those birds and mammals in which the process of male differentiation has gone farthest, such as peacocks, pheasants, turkeys, and barnyard fowls, among birds, and lions, buffaloes, stags, and sheep, among mammals, do practically nothing for their families. It is the mother and she alone that cares for the young, feeds them, defends them, and if necessary fights for them. It is she that has the real courage—courage to attack the enemies of the species. Many wild animals will flee from man, the only exception being the female with her young. She alone is dangerous. Even the male lion is really somewhat of a coward, but the hunter learns to beware of the lioness. . . . How much does the bull or the cock care for its mate or offspring? Approach the brood with hostile intent and it is the old hen that ruffles up her feathers so as to look formidable and dares to attack you.*

There seems to be no reason for thinking that the human species developed in any different manner, as far as early sexual differentiation is concerned. At the present stage of knowledge it is impossible to go back far enough to glean the early development of man at that biological level or phase when sexual differentiation had just set in. This is avowedly a very obscure region unattainable to reason.

Ward's hypothesis about the earlier states of mankind following the sexual differentiation and before any inkling of social organization appeared is enlightening.

When the human race finally appeared through gradual

emergence from the great simian stock, this difference in the sexes existed, and sexual selection was still going on. Primitive woman, though somewhat smaller, physically weaker, and esthetically plainer than man, still possessed the power of selection, and was mistress of the kinship group. Neither sex had any more idea of the connection between fertilization and reproduction than do animals, and therefore the mother alone claimed and cared for the offspring, as is done throughout the animal kingdom below man. So long as this state of things endured the race remained in the stage . . . of female rule. That this was a very long stage is attested by a great number of facts.*

This might be called the earliest stage of man's social development, or the "protosocial," as Ward prefers, or the "stage of social protoplasm," as [Emile] Durkheim prefers. Whatever label is ultimately found preferable, this stage offers an inkling as to the possible earliest psychological reactions of man, reactions preceding the primitive horde which was Freud's point of departure. At a remote and very primitive gynecocentric period, there was only the mother to be tied to, to worship, or to hate. Her choice of the male was free and supreme and final. Perhaps the reverberation of this remote, primitive "matriarchy" is responsible for the many varieties of the superior position of woman among certain savage tribes. The Awemba of East Africa will serve as an example; one could cite many others. Among the Awemba,

to a female member of the two "royal" clans sexual freedom was extended; she could choose any man as her consort, and he could not refuse her. Moreover, if no child was born within a year of their mating, the consort was dismissed. . . . In the kingdoms of Uganda and Dahomey . . . the princesses enjoyed a similar freedom to that afforded to the Wemba princesses.†

* *Ibid.*, pp. 375–76.
† J. D. Unwin, *Sex and Culture* (London: Oxford University Press, 1934), pp. 142–43.

Ward believes that it is the discovery by man of his paternity that made him assert himself and perform the revolution of dethroning the woman from her high biological position of privilege and primitive maternal authority. He does not cite any specific facts to this effect; on the other hand, a number of facts cited by him and other investigators seem definitely to point to man's very early hostility toward his primordial mother. She certainly had to wean him sooner or later and let him detach himself from her. The little females as they grew and matured might and most probably did find maternal consolation similar to the one their mother seemed always to have, but the young male must have been a very sorry sight indeed: he was young, inexperienced in getting food for himself, and not strong enough yet to be the object of choice by the fastidious, self-assured woman, who instinctively demanded the best and the strongest the race could offer. Perhaps it is in this subsoil of early human life that the earliest and deepest veins of man's hostility toward women, which is familiar on the basis of many clinical experiences, will sooner or later be found. Perhaps too in this subsoil will be found the first rootlets of that "woman envy," or of maternal yearnings in man, which are recognized as active psychological factors operative not only in schizophrenia. The phenomenon of couvade may here have had its first root, as well as the matrilineal inheritance which impressed Bachofen and MacLennan, and which Bachofen called "demetric gynecocracy."

A point has now been reached which seems to be both delicate and crucial. As the evolution of man is traced from his earliest level of living, what happened to man, or what seems to have happened to him, before he reached the stage of the primitive horde—the earliest form of family with a ruling father—must also be considered.

At the time when the sequence coitus, fertilization, pregnancy, childbirth was still unknown to man, the woman was already the mistress of her own self and of her brood. Man did not yet belong anywhere, so to speak. By virtue of the natural selection imposed upon him by woman, he was powerful and healthy, felt his sexual urges with great vigor, and quite probably it came to pass that one day he became sufficiently conscious and sure of his strength to overpower the woman, to rape her. I have often felt that the concluding words of *Totem and Taboo*— "In the beginning there was the deed"—were even more fittingly applied to the act of primordial rape than to the murder of the father. The repetitive appearance of the fantasies of rape and their concomitant hostility against man, which so many psychoanalysts have often observed clinically, may well be rooted in this primordial deed. What kind of deed can one visualize this primordial deed to have been? It certainly was not for purposes of impregnating the woman—not at first, at any rate. It must have been an overwhelming impulse to discharge sexual tension; it was a driving need. In other words, the act was not that of love and of anticipated fatherhood, nor of tender solicitude; it was a *crime passionnel,* a momentary, purely personal orgy. It was an assault—I almost said brutal assault, and recalled Ward's sharp remark:

I must protest against the term "brutal" as characterizing the treatment of women by man. Far too many human sins are attributed to the brute that still lurks in man, but it is flagrantly unjust to do this; as has been seen, no male brute maltreats the female, and the abuse of females by males is an exclusively human virtue.*

The power with which the human male for the first time overwhelmed the human female marked the end of woman's biological security and ability to choose, of her right to be her own mistress and the mistress of her brood. Those who stress man's primordial striving toward paternity overlook the fact that paternity in the true sense of the word must be actually a much later cultural de-

* Ward, p. 347.

velopment. At one time man's relationship to woman must have been purely hedonistic, even antipaternal and infanticidal. During the protosocial phase of human development man, when he discovered that he possessed the physical power to deprive woman of her right of choice, was still very far from that which psychoanalysis calls true geniality; his was a primitive narcissism, a striving to gratify his *organ sexuality,* which was not yet synthesized into true genitality.

Therefore it is really idle to speak of man's need to assert his paternity of offspring as the need that drove him to assert himself, or his rights over the mother of his children, and to establish a family under his own dictatorship. It seems to me that this point of view is rather spurious so far as it assumes a sudden revelatory discovery on the part of man that it was he who made the woman pregnant, that it was he who was the father of the children to come, and that his expectant fatherhood suddenly aroused in him the altruistic object-libidinous sense of responsibility for mother, child, and family. The facts and observations available—clinical, ethnological, and sociological—support more the assumption that the primordial deed, the primal rape—which may be considered the original sin in the true sense of the word—was an act devoid of any genital, object-libidinous strivings. It was a phallic, sadistic act.

That the subjection of woman was due entirely to her physical inferiority to man, or rather to that superior size and strength which men had acquired in common with most of the other higher animals through female selection, seems beyond controversy, the tendency to deny and escape it being inspired wholly by shame at admitting it.*

Before proceeding further, let me note particularly that, to the narcissistic sexual motif which inaugurated the subjugation of woman, the economic motif was added very soon. Thus the evolution of man from this moment

* *Ibid.,* p. 349.

could be conceived as a double one—a psychosexual and a cultural one. In actuality, these two main lines of growth cannot be separated, but for purposes of clarity I shall have separately to examine each of them. Neither man's nor woman's sexuality can be properly understood from the psychoanalytic point of view, unless these two main lines are properly evaluated.

Seemingly to interrupt for a moment, one cannot be forewarned too many times or too strongly against andro-centric bias, which is the bias of the physically strongest, of the successful conqueror; even very scholarly minds have been lost in the mesh of this bias. I must therefore repeat the words of Ward to the effect that "so universal is this attitude that a presentation of the real and funda-mental relation of the sexes is something new to those who are able to see it, and something preposterous to those who are not." Psychoanalysis knows from its own experience how preposterous certain things seem to those who are not able to see them, and it is incumbent upon one not to lose for a moment the clear awareness of andro-centric habits.

Let me now return to the time when man discovered that woman could also serve him.

Almost at the origin of human society woman was sub-jugated by her companion; we have seen her become in succes-sion, beast of burden, slave, minor, subject, held aloof from free and active life, often maltreated, oppressed, punished with fury for acts that her male owner would commit with impunity before her eyes.*

Ward possessed a greater psychological intuition than he himself knew, and in working out certain details of his gynecocentric theory he definitely sensed the importance of the narcissistic, sexual, sadistic drives which drove the human male to overcome the female. His phraseology is perhaps a little too general and even unclear, but his

* Jean Charles Letourneau, quoted *ibid.*, p. 350.

major ideas are easily translatable into psychoanalytic concepts, and with rather astonishing fitness.

Having become larger and physically stronger than woman, his egoistic reason, unfettered by any such sentiment as sympathy, and therefore wholly devoid of moral conceptions of any kind, naturally led him to employ his superior strength in exacting from woman whatever satisfaction she could yield him. The first blow that he struck in this direction wrought the whole transformation. The aegis and palladium of the female sex had been from the beginning her power of choice. This rational man early set about wresting from woman, and although this was not accomplished all at once, still it was accomplished very early, and for the mother of mankind all was lost.*

These sadistic impulses of man which suddenly came to full and successful expression made him momentary master of woman. Once having sensed blood, as it were, man was quick to assert his mastery and take measures to secure and perpetuate it forever.

Apparently man's rise continued to follow the narcissistic anal pattern for a long time. It cannot be repeated too often that it was not love for his companions or his children that motivated him, but the need to possess and master. At this point I might suggest that future researches into the psychology and origin of the economic factors of human culture might very well prove that property originated in the sadistic act of overcoming the free mother. Women may be considered chronologically the first piece of property, in the true sense of the word, in that sense which Ward defined with unique simplicity and brilliance: Property is possession beyond one's immediate needs. It was the possession beyond his immediate purely sexual needs that man established over woman.

The enslaved, like any tool invented by primitive man,

* Letourneau, quoted *ibid.*, p. 336.

becomes but an extension and complement to the en-slaver's organs. Through the mastery over the slave, as through the handling of a tool, the master extends the scope of his influence and the extent of his power; his needs increase correspondingly, and the need to gratify these increased needs becomes enhanced. This is the ordinary history of how the "standard of living" by mastery and conquest gradually becomes the false mea-sure of economic culture for the representative few. It does seem that it is in the light of this developmental eco-nomic process that man's utilization of his conquest of woman must be considered; it is in this light that the development of the human family ought to be viewed. There is ample evidence in all quarters of the globe and in all strata of savage culture to the effect that the idea of the family was originally born not out of love but out of the drive for economic exploitation, the possibility of which dazzled the very early primitive man when he unleashed his sexual aggression to conquer the woman.

Even the demands for premarital chastity of women and the consecration of virginity spring from the need to possess and not from the drive to love. In "Taboo and Vir-ginity" Freud speaks in a manner that leaves no doubt that he was fully aware of the instinctual nature of the pri-mordial relationship between the sexes.

Auguste Comte was aware that the word "family" originally meant the servants or slaves. "The philologists have traced it [the word "family"] back to the Oscan word *famel* from which the Latin *famulus,* slave, also proceeds, but whether all these terms have the same root as *fames,* hunger, signifying dependence for subsistence is not certain" although not improbable.

That the earliest forms of family life, even after the taboo of incest had been duly established, continued to favor the male's sexual mastery is well known. Freud says [in "Totem and Taboo"]:

It is of interest to point out that the first restrictions which the introduction of marriage classes brought about affected the sexual freedom of the younger generation, in other words, incest between brothers and sisters and between sons and mothers, while incest between father and daughter was only abrogated by more sweeping measures.

—much later, I might add. Even the principle of matrilineal inheritance was thus utilized for the purpose of extending or at least preserving the father's sexual and therefore economic rights, the remnants of which, as has been previously indicated, persisted as late as the Age of Pericles in the juridical phenomenon of *epicleros*. Matrilineal inheritance made the mother and children belong to one class, while the father belonged to another. Consequently, as has been mentioned, a daughter could not lie with her brother who belonged to the same class, but the father could copulate with his own daughter because he belonged to a different class. This fact in itself demonstrates conclusively that in establishing a family it was not object-libidinous, genital paternity that prompted the man but assurance and extension of the narcissistic gratification of his primitive sexual drives.

It may be concluded therefore that phylogenetically— and there is ample clinical evidence that ontogenetically as well—man arrives at object-libidinous paternity not in that direct way which many have become accustomed to imagine in psychoanalysis, but in a manner at least as complex and circuitous if not more so than the one by which woman arrives at psychological maternity.

Ward was amply justified in saying:

It thus appears that, whatever the family may be today in civilized lands, in its origin it was simply an institution for the more complete subjugation and enslavement of women and children, for the subversion of nature's method in which the mother is queen, dictates who shall be fathers, and guards her offspring by the instinct of maternal affection planted in her for that express purpose. *The primitive family was an unnatural androcratic excrescence upon society.**

* *Ibid.*, p. 353.

No more than an attempt to cast such a glance into that past is possible at the present state of knowledge.

According to the previously outlined conception of man's coming into power, the human male had not reached the level of psychological parenthood at the time he suddenly arrived at the level of male efflorescence. In other words, at the time man subjugated woman, he made the first step toward the creation of an economic order and of a family. The prerequisites for the creation of this economic order he did possess to the fullest extent: He had the physical power to impose his will; he found himself free to limit and to conquer other human beings; and he was fully secure in that his "wife"—that is to say, his female slave—would roast his meat and attend to any other of his needs. He did possess the sexual organ which served him in good stead, and it aroused him as if by magic to great spurts of intense energy and ever-increasing power. No wonder the worship of Priapus is so frequently in evidence in mankind, from its remote past to date. This was man's first and ultimately the most telling and the most conspicuous organ and symbol of self-appraisal.

That there ever had been or ever would be beings who would think and feel otherwise he could not conceive; this was the origin of his androcentric self-elevation, from which he would not "step down an inch" throughout the history of civilization. That so very recently, indeed in his biological yesterday, he had counted for so little in this world he had forgotten overnight, as it were. That ". . . the male sex was at first and for a long period, and still throughout many of the lower orders of being, is devoted exclusively to the function for which it was created, viz., that of fertilization," that "among millions of humble creatures the male is simply and solely a fertilizer," the human male had wiped out of his awareness. He stood in the full glory of physical, narcissistic, domineering superiority under the sign of Priapus. Not only did he have no conception of paternity, no more than a rooster or a dog, but even his biological, sexual strivings, as has already been indicated, at first failed to awaken him to the need of paternity. When the woman was not able to serve him, he was angry; when she was heavy with child, he drove her to do her work, he was relentless in his egoistic demands; when she was tending her baby he looked upon the latter as an intruder and a useless one— because babies do no useful work and keep a useful worker away from her toil, which was her duty, fate, and misfortune as a being and as a mother.

These are the deep phylogenetic roots of that hostility which even the civilized father of today harbors against his own offspring. The unconscious hostility against one's own children is well nigh a universal clinical finding among men. Only after the children grow up and become more articulate human beings does the psychological attitude of the father change into increasing affection. This phylogenetic component is of course certainly not the only factor in the development of paternal hostility toward one's children, but the contribution this determinant makes toward the sadistic impulses of the father is great. Thus far psychoanalysis, hampered by the androcentric bias, has failed duly to assess it. There is no doubt that further and deeper studies of man's psyche will yield a great deal of enlightening data, as soon as one learns to discount the androcentric veil which has heretofore covered a number of important psychological data.

At any rate, the primordial male was not a true genital father, and his evolution to fatherhood was as yet to be achieved in some as yet undetermined way. Then too, a mother preoccupied with her baby was undesirable to man for another reason; the mother was less able to respond to the sexual demands of the male—another determinant of his hostility to his own children. Even in a modern civilization in which the family is the very foundation of the community, the reverberation of that narcissistic striving of man to enjoy the economic and sexual advantages of woman which prompted his early behavior may be found. Man does not want the woman to be a mother, but a convenient sexual servant or instrument. It is this opposition to motherhood, which almost perverted the very substance of man's drive, that led Ward to exclaim: "The whole phenomenon of so-called male superiority bears a certain stamp of spuriousness and sham."

Let me then reduce to their simplest terms the psychological reactions of the human male to the female: the male who first overcame the woman by means of rape was hostile and murderous toward the female; he hated her as a sadistic master hates a slave; he hated her as a lecher hates a mother. Of course, when some of the children did develop despite the almost destructive subjugation of the mother, the father did not fail to grasp at the opportunity to enslave the sons and make the daughters a new instrument for the gratification of his sexual pleasures.

But despite all his economic and sadistic and phallic superiority, man could not fail to discover that the woman who only yesterday was a free agent and a free mother still possessed a unique power over mankind. She could produce children who always clung to her, who loved her without stint. Those children of the woman-slave, whom the man hated and who feared him, never loved him and never clung to him. He the master was unable to arouse their confidence, to say nothing of their affection. Thus man, who hated the woman-mother, must have envied her too; her maternal felicity and serenity and her security in being loved were the only things the superior and all-successful male was unable to acquire by any of the means of physical coercion and sexual assaultiveness which were at his disposal. He must have been hopelessly jealous of the woman-mother. In this respect the woman was his undeniable superior, and here he had no biological or psychological means to establish his own

superiority. If only he could also be a mother! His superiority would then be supreme.

It is in this primordial identification with the woman,
fundamentally a hostile or at any rate a profoundly
ambivalent one, that one ought to see the origin of the
couvade. Some earlier writers, like Letourneau, and not
a few of the later and even contemporary ones are inclined to see in the couvade the earliest attempts at man's
assertion of his rightful paternity. But to assume that man
by some miracle discovered his role in the maternity of
the woman even before the woman discovered and asserted her maternity is foolish, of course. The matrilineal traditions even in fully established patriarchal communities, the existence of maternal deities in advance of
paternal ones, are indicative of the fact that the mother
was fully recognized before man even suspected that he
had anything to do with childbirth. All he knew was that
out of the bowels of the woman a new being would come
from time to time.

Not knowing anything about the mechanism of identification, or of ambivalence, or of the dynamics of the unconscious in general, Ward yet was close to the deepest
psychological truth when he said:

In order that a child be born the mother must pass through
the throes of child-birth, must suffer pangs, must remain for a
greater or less period prostrate and helpless, as if the victim of
disease. This temporary illness having always without exception accompanied the birth of a child through the entire history of any horde or race, became indissolubly associated with
it, so that the two constituted a single compound conception
in the savage mind.

And further:

But so firmly did the ideas of temporary illness and childbirth cohere in the mind of the savage that it was not considered an adequate claim to any proprietary title to the child

until this illness had actually been gone through with. But as a father was not really made ill by the birth of the child it was adjudged essential that he should feign such illness and take to his bed for the prescribed period.*

There is little doubt that this identification with the gravid and parturient woman has a deeper, magic wish-fulfillment value of earlier, more primitive strivings. I am inclined to believe that these strivings are coupled with envy and hostility—hence identification through illness—and that the same dynamic factors are responsible for the myth according to which Zeus took from the burning body of Semele the six-month-old fetus of Dionysus, sewed it up in his own loin, bore it to full term, and gave birth to the young god. Similarly, the birth of Athena from the head of Zeus is but another form of identification on the basis of the same type of envy. It is known that schizophrenics occasionally believe, and neurotics not infrequently have dreams, that a baby comes out of the penis—or the head.

Considering all these facts, the existence of maternal deities and the great envy and hatred man must have felt for his primordial mother can be easily understood. Semele means "mother earth." The great Cretan Mother was never admitted to Olympus. One of the names of Artemis was Mâ, and Cybele also was called by that name. Cybele was the Phrygian goddess, a fecund mother; during the ceremonials of worshiping her, her priests castrated themselves—a striking and convincing example of hostile identification and worship.

To return to Ward, allowances must of course be made for his ignorance of the psychodynamics of the unconscious, and his recently quoted suggestion as to the conscious motivation of the couvade overlooked. It is interesting to observe that Ward, perhaps not fully aware himself of the psychological import of his words, does not speak of paternity but of the "proprietary title"—a motivation much more in conformity with the possessive and

* *Ibid.*, pp. 342–43.

domineering characteristics of the primitive male who has become a conscious master, after a long period of being nothing more than an ever-murderous, unconscious fertilizer.

If one is to adhere for a moment to the traditional idiom and speak in terms of superiority and inferiority, "the idea that the female is naturally and really the superior sex seems incredible, and only the most liberal and emancipated minds, possessed of a large store of biological information, are capable of realizing it." Therefore, if the discussion of the biological superiority of one of the sexes and of the discomfort of conscious and unconscious inferiority of the other is to be continued, I must submit that it was man who perceived himself biologically inferior, and it was this sense of inferiority and concomitant hostility that led to the phenomenon of couvade—a magic, compulsion-neurotic, hostile identification with the mother. *It is out of this identification with the mother that psychological fatherhood was achieved.* There may very well be not a little surprise at the paradoxical conclusion to which this study seems to have led, but it seems almost inevitable: The sense of paternity is essentially a feminine attribute ultimately acquired by the human male in his attempt to keep his mastery of the female more secure and less disquieting in the light of periodic demonstrations of female superiority by way of having children. I am inclined to think that it is not penis envy on the part of woman, but woman envy on the part of man, that is psychogenetically older and therefore more fundamental.

The persistent adherent to the androcentric bias might very well raise most violent objections to this point of view; he might assert that the gynecocentric hypothesis is preposterous in that it even deprives man of one of his most natural, if not most important, primary and inalienable attributes and privileges—paternity. To this one can answer only by saying that the androcentric bias has hardly proved more charitable, in that it recognized paternity as a primary psychobiological phenomenon, deprived the woman of her birthright, and led to the construction in psychoanalysis of a hypothesis according to which the woman achieves her birthright in a circuitous and highly complex series of psychobiological gyrations. Moreover, the biological data, some of which have been cited here, would forcefully suggest that it is man who arrived at paternity by way of a circuitous and complex series of psychobiological gyrations, while woman was a mother to begin with, long before man chose to rape her, hate her, enslave her, and then envy and imitate her. In the same manner it could be concluded that paternal affection and solicitude for the children were achieved again through man's identification with woman—for there is no doubt that in this respect at least woman was the first and most impressive as well as the most convincing. Admittedly it seems highly paradoxical to say that fatherhood is a maternal trait of man, but it does seem as true as it is paradoxical.

I wish to repeat that the first cultural act and the first sexual act which led to the formation of a family were identical—the successful physical, narcissistic, sexual assault on woman. Perhaps it is here that one ought to look for the sources of that controversy, cultural or sexual, which has been raging in and around psychoanalysis and confusing the real issues. The first economic and the first sexual self-assertion of the male were one and the same act; the family and the later cultural institutions were born from the first explosive self-assertion. Man was unable to maintain the advantages he had momentarily gained through this act, unless and until he resolved his rivalry with the primordial mother by way of projecting into her a good part of his own sadism as well as and perhaps particularly by way of his identification with the mother. Without this identification, not only would he have been unable to establish his psychological paternity, but he would have been unable to develop that affection for his offspring, that feeling of tenderness and need to provide and care for his children, which is preeminently a paternal attribute. It was this ability of man to borrow from the primordial mother some of her virtues which made the human family, and for that matter human civilization, at all possible.

The above observations and considerations can hardly overcome all the intricate difficulties with which one is confronted when trying to understand the course and development of female sexuality. Nor can it be presumed that the obscurities of these developments will easily disappear in the light of the gynecocentric theory and the additions to it which psychoanalytic insight permits. But one may very well be justified in expecting that the above observations will aid in sharpening psychological wits and in gaining a little more insight into a number of psychological phenomena which, because of their singular nature, have heretofore aroused more contentiousness and censoriousness than detached curiosity and tolerant objectivity. When it is resolved not to overlook how much feminine there is in the masculine attributes of that which was heretofore marked as most primary and unquestionably most masculine, and when the fundamental envy with which man treats woman and the essential hostility which he has for her is borne in mind, then I am certain that clinical observations will become enriched with new material which heretofore was obscured by androcentric bias and therefore escaped direct observation and scientific analysis.

As I have already said, the whole problem cannot be solved fully at the present stage of psychoanalytic knowledge. Only directional lines for further study can be traced; only the points of concentration of misunderstanding can be taken into account and properly reexamined. The whole question of so-called passivity and activity will have to be restudied, as well as the question of masculine and feminine narcissism. The question of many other attributes which have customarily been considered masculine or feminine without questioning will also have to be restudied. Only then will it be possible, for instance, to establish whether elaborateness of dress and fashions and makeup—unquestionable feminine characteristics— are really purely feminine, or whether they are not masculine characteristics which the woman in her state of psychological and cultural subjugation to man gradually learned to acquire—even as man had them in the remote days when he was still a mere fertilizer, and even as the male in the animal kingdom still has them in plumage, color, and other traits and manners of being conspicuous and attracting the benevolent eye of the female.

It will also be necessary to restudy the cultural changes which eventuate on the current scene and revise many of the traditional views on the psychology of striving for equality among the sexes. Perhaps a part of this striving for equality is actually a reassertion of the woman's original state of freedom, which she possessed long before man had a conception of freedom. Perhaps it will also be discovered why those who find themselves unable to solve some of these problems in the light of psychoanalysis choose to stress only the cultural determinants of psychology and omit entirely the biological, instinctual foundation without which there is no culture, or even no mankind.

It does appear to the one who is not fully aware of the role the androcentric bias has played in psychological formulations, who is indeed not even aware of his own androcentric bias, that it was only a cultural revolution— man's self-assertion over woman, the striving toward power, and the being thwarted in this striving to power— that brought mankind and the individual person to the grief of psychopathological reactions. Perhaps it will be possible to demonstrate that behind this stress of cultural factors lies the true awareness that in the beginning culture and biology were one; that they are still one so far as none of the cultural manifestations is possible without instinctual drives; and that instinctual drives, the most primitive as well as the most complex, have no other medium through which to express themselves than cultural patterns—unless they be the purely physiological ones like digestion, assimilation, and elimination. The moment the term psychology is used one must have in mind the whole complexity of instincts functioning not in vacuo but in life—which is culture.

I have been deliberately emphatic here when demonstrating certain facts which psychoanalysis, I believe, has not yet taken fully into account. I have been equally emphatic in indicating that a great deal is as yet to be learned before final answers are formulated. May I conclude with a quotation from Frazer's preface to *Totemism and Exogamy,* which Freud cites in his "Totem and Taboo," calling it an "excellent statement."

"That my conclusions on these difficult questions are final, I am not so foolish as to pretend. I have changed my views repeatedly, and I am resolved to change them again with every change of the evidence, for like a chameleon the inquirer should shift his colours with the shifting colours of the ground he treads."

I am fully aware that to some psychoanalysts the conceptions here suggested, so far as they are new in the psychoanalytic literature, may appear based on rather humble and even unsavory aspects of man's functioning as man. Even in certain psychoanalytic circles one hears of late, with greater frequency than is scientifically desirable, that analysts pay too little attention to that which people call the dignity of the human personality. To this one can answer only in the words of Mephistopheles which take fully into consideration the ill will and the unsavory drives of man. One ought to be fully cognizant of these and know that man and woman are

Ein Teil von jener Kraft
Die stets das Böse will und stets das
　　Gute schafft.

PART II

The Emergence
of New Evidence

MARY JANE SHERFEY

WHILE RETAINING the original psychoanalytic premise that biology determines psychology, Mary Jane Sherfey presents a totally new and striking formulation of women's biology. Her research gathered and synthesized massive amounts of evidence from sources such as embryological studies, primate research, and the work of Masters and Johnson, to arrive at some surprising conclusions.

This excerpt begins with Sherfey's summary of the data presented. It is followed by a section that indicates only a small part of the extensive practical consequences of her work and only a brief hint of the larger implications of her ideas. Sherfey relates them to the major issues involved in the origin of human civilization and the development of human culture. Dr. Sherfey's formulations are challenging and controversial. As she, herself, states, some portions of them may ultimately lead to interpretations different from those she suggests here. It is from the full work, in her book *The Nature and Evolution of Female Sexuality,* that one can appreciate the originality and scope of her contribution.

Dr. Sherfey was formerly assistant professor of psychiatry at Cornell University. She is currently in private practice in New York City.

On the Nature of Female Sexuality

Recent EMBRYOLOGICAL RESEARCH has demonstrated conclusively that the concept of the initial anatomical bisexuality or equipotentiality of the embryo is erroneous. All mammalian embryos, male and female, are anatomically female during the early stages of fetal life. In humans, the differentiation of the male from the female form by the action of fetal androgen begins about the sixth week of embryonic life and is completed by the end of the third month. Female structures develop autonomously without the necessity of hormonal differentiation. If the fetal gonads are removed from a genetic female before the first six weeks, she will develop into a normal female, even undergoing normal pubertal changes if, in the absence of ovaries, exogenous hormones are supplied. If the fetal gonads are similarly removed from a genetic male, he will develop into a female, also undergoing normal female pubertal changes if exogenous hormones are supplied. The probable relationship of the autonomous female anatomy to the evolution of viviparity is described.

From this surprising discovery of modern embryology and other biological data, the hypothesis is suggested that the female's relative lack of differentiating hormones during embryonic life renders her more sensitive to hormonal conditioning in later life, especially to androgens, since some embryonic and strong maternal estrogenic activity is present during embryonic life. This ready androgen responsivity provides the physiological means whereby androgen-sensitive structures could evolve to enhance the female's sexual capacity. In the primates, the marked development of the clitoral system, certain secondary sexual characteristics including skin erotism, and the extreme degree of perineal sexual edema (achieved in part by progesterone with its strong androgenic properties) are combined in various species to produce an intense aggressive sexual drive and an inordinate, insatiable capacity for copulations during estrus. The breeding advantage would thus go to the females with the most insatiable sexual capacity. The infrahuman female's insatiable sexual capacity could evolve only if it did not interfere with maternal care. Maternal care is ensured by the existence of the extreme sexual drive only during estrus and its absence during the prolonged postpartum anestrus of these animals.

The validity of these considerations and their relevance to the human female are strongly supported by the demonstration of comparable sexual physiology and behavior in women. This has been accomplished by the research of Masters and Johnson, and a summary of their findings of the actual nature of the sexual response cycle in women is presented. Their most important observations are:*

* The following definitions may be helpful in understanding some of the anatomical explanations that follow—ED.: (1) *circumvaginal venous plexi:* network of veins around the vagina. (2) *vestibular bulbs:* structures which lie in the superficial tissues alongside the opening of the vagina, composed of large veinlike chambers which fill with blood upon sexual stimulation. They are directly analogous to the chambers in the penis which cause an erection when filled with blood. (3) *labial-preputial-glandar mechanism:* the glans is the end portion of the clitoris; the labia minora surrounds the vaginal opening; the prepuce surrounds the glans. Together, the labia minora and the prepuce form a mucous membrane stretching around the vaginal opening and the glans. (Sherfey has explained that the thrusting of the penis in the vagina causes a rhythmic pulling on this membrane. This rhythmic traction stimulates the glans. Prior to the orgastic state, during the foregoing sexual arousal, the entire surrounding area, especially the vestibular bulbs and the muscles surrounding the vagina, is enormously swollen and en-

1. There is no such thing as a vaginal orgasm distinct from a clitoral orgasm. The nature of the orgasm is the same regardless of the erotogenic zone stimulated to produce it. The orgasm consists of the rhythmic contractions of the extravaginal musculature against the greatly distended circumvaginal venous plexi and vestibular bulbs surrounding the lower third of the vagina.

2. The nature of the labial-preputial-glandar mechanism which maintains continuous stimulation of the retracted clitoris during intravaginal coition has been described. By this action, clitoris, labia minora, and lower third of the vagina function as a single, smoothly integrated unit when traction is placed on the labia by the male organ during coitus. Stimulation of the clitoris is achieved by the rhythmical pulling on the edematous prepuce. Similar activation of the clitoris is achieved by preputial friction during direct clitoral area stimulation.

3. With full sexual arousal, women are normally capable of many orgasms. As many as six or more can be achieved with intravaginal coition. During clitoral-area stimulation, when a woman can control her sexual tension and maintain prolonged stimulation, she may attain up to fifty or more orgasms in an hour's time.

From these observations and other biological data, especially from primatology, I have advanced four hypotheses:

1. The erotogenic potential of the clitoral glans is probably greater than that of the lower third of the vagina. Additional evidence will be presented in a forthcoming paper showing the importance of the labial-

---

gorged with blood. This labial-preputial-glandar mechanism sets off the contraction of the muscles against the engorged bulbs and circumvaginal veins.) (4) *coition:* intercourse. (5) *edematous:* swollen because of the presence of tissue fluid. (6) *estrus:* "heat" in animals. (7) *vascularization:* growth of more blood vessels. (8) *varicosity:* enlarged vein. (9) *perineal body:* the point behind the vagina which is the joining point of the muscles surrounding the vagina. (10) *vasotension:* distension of blood vessels. (11) *nonparous:* referring to a woman who has not borne a child.

preputial-glandar action in the primates. The evolution of primate sexuality has occurred primarily through selective adaptations of the perineal edema and the clitoral complex, not the vagina.

2. Under optimal arousal conditions, women's orgasmic potential may be similar to that of the primates described. In both, orgasms are best achieved only with the high degree of pelvic vasocongestion and edema associated with estrus in the primates and the luteal phase of the menstrual cycle in women or with prolonged, effective stimulation. Under these conditions, each orgasm tends to increase pelvic vasocongestion; thus the more orgasms achieved, the more can be achieved. Orgasmic experiences may continue until physical exhaustion intervenes.

3. In these primates and in women, an inordinate cyclic sexual capacity has thus evolved leading to the paradoxical state of sexual insatiation in the presence of the utmost sexual satiation. The value of this state for evolution is clear: With the breeding premium going to the primate females with the greatest pelvic edema, the most effective clitoral erotism, and the most aggressive sexual behavior, the satiation-in-insatiation state may have been an important factor in the adaptive radiation of the primates leading to man—and a major barrier to the evolution of modern man.

4. The rise of modern civilization, while resulting from many causes, was contingent on the suppression of the inordinate cyclic sexual drive of women because (a) the hyperhormonalization of the early human females associated with the hypersexual drive and the prolonged pregnancies was an important force in the escape from the strict estrus sexuality and the much more important escape from lactation asexuality. Women's uncurtailed continuous hypersexuality would drastically interfere with maternal responsibilities; and (b) with the rise of the settled agriculture economies, man's territorialism became expressed in property rights and kinship laws.

Large families of known parentage were mandatory and could not evolve until the inordinate sexual demands of women were curbed.

[In the following sections Dr. Sherfey illustrates some of the ways in which she believes that her data will lead to new understanding and treatment of disturbances in sexual functioning. They are followed by a brief discussion of the historical and cultural implications of the statements in hypothesis 4.—ED.]

PHYSICAL FACTORS CAUSING COITAL FRIGIDITY BEGINNING IN ADULTHOOD

From the fundamental framework of the sheer physical aspects of the sexual cycle which has been given, it can be seen that coital frigidity will occur if there exists (1) inadequate erotogenic stimulation; (2) inadequate filling of the venous erectile chambers; (3) inadequate pelvic congestion and edema with their resultant tissue tension; and (4) inadequate response of the responding muscles. Many biological barriers may intervene at any point to produce varying degrees of frigidity. These biological barriers rarely, if ever, operate alone but induce psychological reactions reinforced by cultural pressures in endless vicious circles. Consequently, the differential diagnosis between vaginal insensitivity induced by physical factors or by psychological factors is often difficult to make. The following outline of the biological barriers stresses those problems where this diagnostic difficulty is most apt to arise in psychiatry.

Medical Disorders

Of the many diseases, disorders, and injuries which can affect the sexual structures, the following are most pertinent to psychiatry.

OBSTETRICAL DAMAGE   It has been emphasized that

pregnancies enhance sexual capacity and pleasure by flooding the system with the sexual hormones, producing a sudden and enormous growth and vascularization of the pelvic structures as great as, or greater, I believe, than, the pubertal transformation. So important is the pregnancy effect, I would propose that the varicosities left by pregnancy are both adaptive and nonadaptive: during evolution, their value for the buildup and maintenance of sexual tension is so strong there could be nothing but increasing selective pressure for their presence.

However, evolutionary change often gets hoisted by its own petard, so to speak, and may or may not be able to extricate itself from an adaptational dilemma. These varicosities may be one such dilemma. Another, unfortunately, is the fact that the female sexual and procreative apparatus was evolved for mothers giving birth to small-headed babies. Man is much too recent an evolutionary innovation for the female pelvic adaptations necessary to deliver big-headed babies without trauma to the birth canal. (Of the 75 million years the primates have been working themselves up to us, men with heads big enough to produce consistent maternal damage have been around for only the past 500,000 years at most—and probably much less—perhaps .6 to .3 percent of the total.) Obstetrical damage to the sexual structures is far more frequent than most psychiatrists realize, I believe. Without the best of modern obstetrical care, it occurs to a greater or lesser extent in close to 100 percent of all women bearing their first full-term babies; and even with that care, it occurs to some degree in a very large number of them.

Severe traumas are uncommon in this country; moderate to mild degrees rarely abolish the capacity for orgasmic experience but usually lessen it. Furthermore, all obstetrical damage is most apt to occur during the first delivery. Thus, if a woman is unfortunate enough to suffer such damage before full sexual potency was attained, she may never realize the extent to which the obstetrical damage contributes to her frigidity.

Two most frequent forms of perineal tears are also most pertinent to this study:

Tears of the Bulbar System   Tears of the vestibular bulbs and their muscles are the main reason for episiotomies (which are not always done, done well, or become infected). The importance of the bulbar system to full orgasmic capacity is underscored by the fact that such tears are usually unilateral; yet gynecologists uniformly report that women with one nonfunctioning bulb regularly complain of diminished orgasmic reactions.

Torn or Stretched Perineal Body   The process of tears, scar formation, and stretching of all the muscles that make up the perineal body is one of the most frequent causes of coital frigidity due to childbirth—a gaping vaginal orifice may make intercourse easy from the standpoint of ease of entry but can render the climax impossible to attain.

Masters describes an experiment with one volunteer which is particularly instructive on the nature of this problem as well as the dynamics of normal vaginal action. No history is available, of course, other than that this parous woman suffered coital frigidity as the result of obstetrical damage and had an exceptionally gaping vaginal outlet. The subject was obviously heterosexually oriented; so an experiment was designed to determine if she could possibly reach an orgasm if coitus were prolonged far beyond that which could possibly be achieved in personal life. The subject successfully carried coitus through twenty-seven times to the complete expenditure of nearly as many male partners over a six-and-a-half-hour period. No direct clitoral stimulation was allowed. Throughout this entire period, she remained in the excitement stage of arousal, achieving plateau stages of congestion on five occasions—but no orgasm occurred. At the end of this period, pelvic congestion was severe and painful. The labia majora were three times normal size; the labia minora and lower third of the vagina were greatly swollen and continued so; and it required one and a quarter hours for the breasts to return to normal.

After the last coital effort, the patient was instructed to refrain from any autostimulation in order to determine how long it would require for this degree of pelvic congestion to subside. The pelvic structures were still uncomfortably swollen six hours later when the experiment (lasting twelve and a half hours) was declared terminated. The subject immediately sought relief in clitoral area stimulation and achieved a violent orgasmic release of vasotension within two minutes.

This experiment is important to us on several scores:

1. No matter how great the generalized pelvic congestion and edema, an orgasm will not eventuate unless there is that final surge of localized engorgement of the circumvaginal plexi and bulbs which causes the lower third to tighten around the penile shaft and permits the thrusting friction on the lower third and labia to activate the preputial-glandar action.

2. No matter how swollen the lower third, bulbs, and plexi become, they cannot tighten around the penile shaft if the vaginal outlet is abnormally widened.

3. Most significantly, it is obvious that the lower third was stimulated a great deal during this prolonged coital experience; it was greatly swollen. The weight of the penis on the posterior wall would create friction, if noplace else. Yet this stimulation of the lower third was unable to produce the final high levels of sexual tension necessary for the orgasm. On the other hand, the gaping outlet, the lack of tightening of the lower third, and the elongated, loose, and widened labia minora would completely rule out the possibility of labial traction activating the preputial-glans mechanism. Hence, rhythmic stimulation of the glans could not occur. The rapidity and ease with which the clitorally induced orgasm subsequently occurred again point to the prime importance of this structure in the attainment of the orgasm.

Milder degrees of perineal lacerations are much more frequent than the type presented by this subject. They are, in a sense, more pernicious because they are easier to mistake for psychogenic frigidity. With the more moderate tears, the three all-important ingredients to the production of orgasmic levels of vasotension (gripping of the penile shaft; friction on the tightened lower third [of the vagina] and upper labia; and labial-preputial-glandar action) may take place, but only if all conditions for full erotogenic arousal are optimal. With so little margin for all the innumerable physical and emotional variables that influence sexual performance, the orgasm would be achieved infrequently and, when achieved, would often be weak and disappointing.

CONSTITUTIONAL AND ENDOCRINE DISORDERS Of the many disorders falling in these two categories, only three will be mentioned:

Anatomical Variations A possible cause of coital frigidity, with its origin in genetic and endocrine factors and included here because they usually do not appear until after the pubertal transformation, are the anatomical variations of the labial-preputial anatomy. This subject has received no research interest—but should, in the light of the Masters and Johnson observations.

There seems to be so much variation in this anatomy that it is difficult to assign normal limits. For example, the prepuce may be doubled, tripled, or have accessory [extra] folds. It may be smooth, wrinkled, thick, thin, short, or elongated. Similarly, the labia minora show marked variations in size, may form two loops, or have accessory folds. They may be long, short, wrinkled, folded, or corrugated.

These common variations in the sexual anatomy may render the preputial-glandar action more difficult to attain with intravaginal coition, where only a taut connection between the upper labia around the vaginal orifice and the prepuce can create the necessary traction. Obviously, the adherent prepuce practically precludes the possibility of coital orgasms. The extent to which the other variations may interfere is unknown and requires the necessary research.

Juvenile Pelvic Condition Many adolescents mature quite late and may retain a partially juvenile pelvic condition until after their first pregnancy. They may show scant menses, small breasts, boyish body contour, and coital frigidity. It must be kept in mind that specific levels of specific hormones must be present to permit the development of the congestion and edema which create the strong circumvaginal distension necessary for vaginally induced orgasms. Such hormonal levels are slow in developing in these young women (and may continue at low levels throughout life if they remain childless). The juvenile pelvic condition prevents full vasotension so that the labial-preputial-glandar action is not effective. Most of the time, only a simple bulbar orgasm produced by digital stimulation is possible.

Postmenopausal Frigidity Masters and Johnson now have data on this important subject. Any comments will be withheld until their work appears.

Inadequate Erotogenic Stimulation

Assuming an average good degree of pelvic vascularization in both the parous and nonparous woman with no obstetrical damage or unusual anatomical variation, adequate physical stimulation is still necessary for coital orgasms to occur. Inadequate erotogenic stimulation is unquestionably the most frequent cause of vaginal frigidity. So much has been written on the subject, only some additional points made by Masters and Johnson relating to the central themes of this paper will be elaborated.

CONTINUOUS STIMULATION The fact that every woman's level of sexual tension falls almost instantaneously if stimulation is stopped accounts for many cases of frigidity since most men over thirty (and many under) cannot consistently control their ejaculations long enough to permit the woman to reach full pelvic congestion. The one thing that prevents frigidity from this cause being more frequent is the young man's capacity to have repetitive ejaculations without full loss of the erection. Frequent coital frigidity in women whose husbands cannot have multiple orgasms, have them infrequently, or cannot hold their erections for at least four to five minutes is to be expected.

SLOWER AROUSAL TIME IN WOMEN   A clinical impression is that a woman's inability to reduce the period of foreplay with increasing sexual experience is a frequent source of marital discord, if not of coital frigidity. If a man is quickly aroused and unaccustomed, or afraid, to use delaying techniques, coital frigidity would occur frequently or regularly.

LUTEAL PHASE SEXUALITY   An inability to achieve multiple orgasms, a reduced intensity of orgasmic sensations, and the capacity for only manually induced orgasms at all times other than the luteal phase may be considered normal. However, almost total frigidity (arousal only to an early excitement stage) or the consistent inability to achieve an orgasm with good levels of congestion in the plateau stage is rare enough in the ovulatory phase of the menstrual cycle to be considered evidence of either an abnormal hormonal condition or of psychological inhibitions of clinical significance.

ATTEMPTING CLITORAL STIMULATION DURING COITUS   Masters and Johnson stress that a very prevalent notion exists that the man must somehow keep the clitoral shaft directly stimulated during coitus. The physiodynamics of the sexual act indicate that such action is neither really possible nor helpful. In his effort to "ride high" during coition, a man is often unable to maintain intravaginal positioning unless there is an abnormally wide vaginal outlet; otherwise the main result is often the production of vaginal and rectal discomfort with the tip of the penis directed against the rectum.

SPECIAL PROBLEMS CREATED BY THE PREGNANCY EFFECT AND SEXUAL EXPERIENCE   It has been noted that the orgasmic

146

intensity is normally higher in the young, vigorous male than in the young, nonparous woman. This difference levels off after about the age of thirty in men and after about the second or third child in women, or after considerable sexual experience in nonparous women. With age, experience, and parity, a woman's capacity for intense and multiple orgasms would surpass that of the man. I suggest that the oft-noted observation that modern women so often achieve the capacity for regular and multiple orgasms at about the time their husbands' performance is diminishing is due much more to the pregnancy effect and sexual experience than to any recovery from neurotic fears or inhibitions. The pregnancy effect has become increasingly delayed in many women today because of their more prolonged adolescence, later marriage age, and the use of contraceptives. Fewer women reach their full sexual capabilities until after the age of thirty or so because they do not have their second or third child until that age.

Also, I urge the reexamination of the vague and controversial concepts of nymphomania and promiscuity without frigidity. Until now, it has not been realized that regular multiple orgasms, with either clitoral or vaginal stimulation, to the point of physical exhaustion could be the biological norm for women's sexual performance. Even the nonparous woman without undue inhibitions and with prolonged experience can approximate the high levels of vasocongestion reached by the parous female. It could well be that the "oversexed" woman is actually exhibiting a normal sexuality—although because of it, her integration into her society may leave much to be desired.

SPECIAL PROBLEMS CREATED BY WOMEN'S SATIATION-IN-INSATIATION   No doubt the most far-reaching hypothesis extrapolated from these biological data is the existence of the universal and physically normal condition of women's inability ever to reach complete sexual satiation in the presence of the most intense, repetitive orgasmic experiences, no matter how produced. Theoretically, a woman

147

could go on having orgasms indefinitely if physical exhaustion did not intervene.

It is to be understood that repetitive orgasms leading to the satiation-in-insatiation state will be most apt to occur in parous and experienced women during the luteal phase of the menstrual cycle. It is one of the most important ways in which the sexuality of the primate and human female differs from the primate and human male at the physical level; and this difference exists only because of the female's capacity to produce the fulminating pelvic congestion and edema. This capacity is mediated by specific hormonal combinations with high fluid-imbibing action which are found only in certain primates and, probably, a very few other mammalian species.

I must stress that this condition does not mean a woman is always consciously unsatisfied. There is a great difference between satisfaction and satiation. A woman may be emotionally satisfied to the full in the absence of *any* orgasmic expression (although such a state would rarely persist through years of frequent arousal and coitus without some kind of physical or emotional reaction formation). Satiation-in-insatiation is well illustrated by Masters' statement, "A woman *will usually* be satisfied with 3–5 orgasms. . . ." I believe it would rarely be said, "A man will usually be satisfied with three to five ejaculations." The man *is* satisfied. The woman *usually wills* herself to be satisfied because she is simply unaware of the extent of her orgasmic capacity. However, I predict that this hypothesis will come as no great shock to many women who consciously realize, or intuitively sense, their lack of satiation.

On the basis of these observations, it seems that the vast majority of cases of coital frigidity are due simply to the absence of frequent, prolonged coitus. This statement is supported by unpublished data which Masters and Johnson are now accumulating. Following this logical conclusion of their previous research, they began treating a series of couples with severe, chronic frigidity or impotence. All had received prior medical and, often, psychiatric treatment to no avail. For the women, none of whom had ever experienced orgasms after five or more years of marriage, treatment consisted of careful training of the husband to use the proper techniques essential to all women and the specific ones required by his wife. In many cases this in itself was sufficient. In the others, daily sessions were instigated of marital coitus followed by prolonged use of the artificial phallus (three to four hours or more). Thus far, with about fifty women treated, every woman but one responded within three weeks at most and usually within a few days. They began at once to experience intense, multiple orgasms; and once this capacity was achieved after the exposure to daily prolonged coitus, they were able to respond with increasing ease and rapidity so that the protracted stimulation was no longer necessary. It is too early for thorough follow-ups, but initial impressions are most favorable.

Should these preliminary findings hold, an almost total biological etiology of coital frigidity will be proved. The inordinate sexual, orgasmic capacity of the human female will fall in line with that of the other higher primates—and the magnitude of the psychological and social problems facing modern mankind is difficult to contemplate.

HISTORICAL PERSPECTIVE AND CULTURAL DILEMMA

The nature of female sexuality as here presented makes it clear that, just as the vagina did not evolve for the delivery of big-headed babies, so women's inordinate orgasmic capacity did not evolve for monogamous, sedentary cultures. It is unreasonable to expect that this inordinate sexual capacity could be, even in part, given expression within the confines of our culture; and it is particularly unreasonable to expect the delayed blooming of the sexuality of many women after the age of thirty or so to find adequate avenues of satisfaction. Less than one hundred years ago, and in many places today, women regularly had their third or fourth child by the time they were eighteen or nineteen, and the life span was no more than thirty-five to forty years. It could well be that the natural synchronization of the peak periods for sexual expression in men and women has been destroyed only in recent years.

These findings give ample proof of the conclusion that neither men nor women, but especially not women, are biologically built for the single-spouse, monogamous marital structure or for the prolonged adolescence which our society can now bestow upon both of them. Generally, men have never accepted strict monogamy except in principle. Women have been forced to accept it; but not, I submit, for the reasons usually given.

The human mating system with its permanent family and kinship ties was absolutely essential to man's becoming—and remaining—man. In every culture studied, the crucial transition from the nomadic, hunting, and food-gathering economy to a settled, agricultural existence was the beginning of family life, modern civilization, and civilized man. In the preagricultural societies, life was precarious, population growth slow, and infanticide often essential to group survival. With the domestication of animals and the agriculture revolution, for the first time in all time, the survival of a species lay in the extended family with its private property, kinship lineages, inheritance laws, social ordinances, and, most significantly, many surviving children. Only in that carefully delineated and rigidly maintained large-family complex could the individual find sufficient security to allow his uniquely human potentialities to be developed through the long years of increasingly helpless childhood—and could populations explode into the first little villages and towns.

Many factors have been advanced to explain the rise of the patriarchal, usually polygamous, system and its concomitant ruthless subjugation of female sexuality (which necessarily subjugated her entire emotional and intellectual life). However, if the conclusions reached here are true, it is conceivable that the *forceful* suppression of women's inordinate sexual demands was a prerequisite to the dawn of every modern civilization and almost every living culture. Primitive woman's sexual drive was too strong, too susceptible to the fluctuating extremes of an impelling, aggressive erotism to withstand the disciplined requirements of a settled family life—where many living children were necessary to a family's well-being and where paternity had become as important as maternity in maintaining family and property cohesion. For about half the time, women's erotic needs would be insatiably pursued; paternity could never be certain; and with lactation erotism, constant infant care would be out of the question.

There are many indications from the prehistory studies in the Near East that it took perhaps five thousand years or longer for the subjugation of women to take place. All relevant data from the 12,000 to 8000 B.C. period indicate that precivilized woman enjoyed full sexual freedom and was often totally incapable of controlling her sexual drive.* Therefore, I propose that one of the reasons for the long delay between the earliest development of agriculture (c. 12,000 B.C.) and the rise of urban life and the beginning of recorded knowledge (c. 8000–5000 B.C.) was the ungovernable cyclic sexual drive of women. Not until these drives were gradually brought under control by rigidly enforced social codes could family life become the stabilizing and creative crucible from which modern civilized man could emerge.

Although then (and now) couched in superstitious, religious, and rationalized terms, behind the subjugation of women's sexuality lay the inexorable economics of

* However, I must make it clear that the biological data presented support only the thesis on the intense, insatiable erotism in women. Such erotism could be contained within one or possibly several types of social structures which would have prevailed through most of the Pleistocene period. I hope to elaborate on this complicated subject in a later paper.

cultural evolution which finally forced men to impose it and women to endure it. If that suppression has been, at times, unduly oppressive or cruel, I suggest the reason has been neither man's sadistic, selfish infliction of servitude upon helpless women nor women's weakness or inborn masochism. The strength of the drive determines the force required to suppress it.

The hypothesis that women possess *a biologically determined,* inordinately high cyclic sexual drive is too significant to be accepted without confirmation from every field of science touching the subject. Assuming this analysis of the nature of women's sexuality is valid, we must ask ourselves if the basic intensity of women's sexual drive has abated appreciably as the result of the past seven thousand years of suppression (which has been, of course, only a partial suppression for most of that time). Just within the very recent past, a decided lifting of the ancient social injunctions against the free expression of female sexuality has occurred. This unprecedented development is born of the scientific revolution, the product of both efficient contraceptives and the new social equality and emotional honesty sweeping across the world (an equality and honesty which owe more to the genius of Sigmund Freud than to any other single individual). It is hard to predict what will happen should this trend continue—except one thing is certain: if women's sexual drive has not abated, and they prove incapable of controlling it, thereby jeopardizing family life and child care, a return to the rigid, enforced suppression will be inevitable and mandatory. Otherwise the biological family will disappear and what other patterns of infant care and adult relationships could adequately substitute cannot now be imagined.

Should the hypothesis be true that one of the requisite cornerstones upon which all modern civilizations were founded was *coercive* suppression of women's inordinate sexuality, one looks back over the long history of women and their relationships to men, children, and society since the Neolithic revolution with a deeper, almost awesome, sense of the ironic tragedy in the triumph of the human condition.

Finally, the data on the embryonic female primacy and the Masters and Johnson research on the sexual cycle in women will require amendations of psychoanalytic theory. These will be less than one might think at first sight. Other than concepts based on innate bisexuality, the rigid dichotomy between masculine and feminine sexual behavior, and derivative concepts of the clitoral-vaginal transfer theory, psychoanalytic theory will remain. Much of the theory concerning the "masculine" components of female sexuality will also remain but will be based on a different biological conception. Certainly, much of present and past sexual symbolism will take on richer meanings.

It is my strong conviction that these fundamental biological findings will, in fact, strengthen psychoanalytic theory and practice in the area of female sexuality. Without the erroneous biological premises, the basic sexual constitution and its many manifestations will be seen as highly moldable by hormonal influences, which in turn are so very susceptible to all those uniquely human emotional, intellectual, imaginative, and cultural forces upon which psychoanalysis has cast so much light. The power of the psychic processes will stand the stronger. Therefore it may be safely predicted that these new biological findings will not "blow away" Freud's "artificial structure of hypotheses" but will transpose it to a less artificial and more effective level.

In any event, and regardless of the validity of my own conclusions, it is my hope that this presentation of recent major contributions from biology and gynecology bearing on female sexual differentiation and adult functioning will aid in the integration of psychological and biological knowledge and will provide a firm biological foundation upon which all future theories of female psychosexuality must rest.

MABEL BLAKE COHEN

MABEL BLAKE COHEN was one of the long-time leaders of the school of interpersonal psychoanalysis originated by Harry Stack Sullivan. Her paper is the first among those collected here in which a psychoanalyst integrates evidence from both psychological and psychoanalytic studies in order to examine a central issue. In so doing, Cohen arrived at new and convincing formulations. While this article pertains to both sexes, it is of special importance to the development of a newer psychological understanding of women.

Since the publication of this paper there has been an expansion of the types of studies Cohen surveyed here. In addition, some psychologists have recently begun to examine such data for the specific effects of sexual stereotyping, thus augmenting this pioneering work by Dr. Cohen.

Cohen was a coworker with Frieda Fromm-Reichmann and others of the Sullivan group in Washington, D.C.; she was a former president of the Washington Psychoanalytic Society and editor of the journal *Psychiatry*. Dr. Cohen was a training and supervising analyst at the Washington Psychoanalytic Institute at the time of her death in 1972.

Personal Identity and Sexual Identity

IT SOMETIMES SEEMS to me that the roles of both male and female, as popularly defined in our culture, are impossible to play. There are a number of catchwords applied—for instance, "courage," "strength," "activity," "leadership," to the male; or "receptivity," "passivity," "nurturance," "giving," to the female. When one strives to contemplate the task of being always, or almost always, brave, one becomes rebellious and weary with its naïveté. Yet a boy of fourteen, if asked to confess his fear of anything or anybody, would equate it in his mind and feelings with that terrible thing—being a sissy. Similarly, a woman of complete receptivity or passivity would be not only a startling phenomenon, but also an unpleasing one to contemplate. It may amuse you to have me take these crude stereotypes seriously, yet I hope to show how important they are as influences on the development of our children, and how they linger in the background of the adult's mind, influencing the members of the next generation as they in turn become parents.

Alongside the widely held notion of some essence of masculinity and femininity exists the startling belief among many of us that most of the neurotic illness in our population is mother generated. Such a potency attributed to the mother can only amaze one when put alongside the theory of the female as the weaker vessel. It arouses questions as to the whereabouts of the other parent, and about the depths of dependency on a mother image generated by our philosophy of child rearing. The psychoanalytic theories of infant and early childhood development have certainly played an influential part in

introducing a sense of guilty responsibility into the transactions between mother and child, which goes far toward
undermining the spontaneity of their relationship. The
more recent efforts to look at the family as an organic unit
should in the long run help us to a better balance in our
scientific approach. But how long will it take for such
efforts to affect the folklore of masculinity and femininity,
their powers and their duties, their deeds and their mis-
deeds?

My use of the term "identity" in this paper needs some
clarification. The term was popularized in psychoanalytic
circles by [Erik] Erikson, who found it useful in describing
the social development of the person from child to adult.
He saw the developing child as moving through a series of
self-concepts and developmental crises. At each level the
self-concept differs from the previous one, and the critical
issues which must be solved also change with time. In this
sense, the person could be seen as passing through a
series of identities, as in libidinal terms he is seen as passing through a series of libidinal stages. Erikson emphasized a point which [Harry Stack] Sullivan had made
decades earlier—namely, that the essentials of development are not completed, as previously supposed, by the
end of the childhood oedipal period. Sullivan had stressed
the importance of preadolescent and adolescent experiences. Erikson focused a good deal of attention on the
adolescent era, with its particular threats to identity as
the personality struggles for independence from old authorities. Maturity, with the establishment of adult sexuality, a career, a home, a family, represents the next crisis in
development, and is the one on which I shall focus.

What, exactly, is meant by the term identity? This is a
rather difficult question to answer, partly because it is a
loose term and partly because it has come to be used, like
aspirin, for everything. It is an outgrowth in psychoanalysis of the interest in ego psychology which was
initiated by [Heinz] Hartmann's essay, *Ego Psychology and*

the Problem of Adaptation, published in 1939. Hartmann said that

. . . a concept of health which is conceived solely as the nega-tive of neurosis and disregards the state of conflict-free sphere (of the ego) is too narrow, if only because without taking this sphere into account, the concepts of ego-strength, rank order, and equilibrium cannot be satisfactorily delineated. Another reason why some theoretical concepts of health are too narrow is that they usually underestimate the great variety of per-sonality types which must, practically speaking, be considered healthy and the many personality types which are socially necessary.*

In other words, Hartmann viewed the ego as an active element in the personality, with positive, adaptive functions as well as the more negative, defensive ones pre-viously described. From the structural point of view, the task of maturation can be thought of as the building of psychic structures which represent a composite of in-stinctual drive, defense, reappearance of drive in an al-tered, hopefully more mature form, and so on.

Identity, then, could be thought of as an ego-id-superego complex or continuum, or as the personality-as-a-whole. However, Erikson's more useful contribution, it seems to me, comes from looking at it in social or be-havioral terms, and that is the way I shall use it. It could be thought of as the self as it is experienced and as it functions in life situations. It would, then, include con-scious motivations and also the less conscious identifica-tions, drives, and defenses which give it some of its individual coloring. It would be formed by the interaction of heredity, constitution, and experience, over time. This view gives a great deal of weight to learning experiences throughout the life cycle in influencing behavior and improving adaptation.

It seems to me no coincidence that this concept has

* Heinz Hartmann, *Ego Psychology and the Problem of Adaptation* (New York: International University Press, 1958), p. 81.

come into popularity at the same time that psychoanalysis has been moving out of the consulting room and into the community by way of both the vast increase in the number of those exposed to psychoanalytic concepts and also the greater activity of analysts themselves in tackling the problems of society. One of the tasks of community psychiatry, as it works toward goals of social change, is to develop knowledge about what constitutes learning experiences for either groups or individuals, for it is clearly true that experiences themselves are not necessarily contributory to learning, no matter how good they are. Here, too, questions regarding identity come to have a significant bearing upon whether an experience is going to have a learning effect or not.

My thesis in this paper is that there is a considerable incompatibility between many people's sense of identity as persons and as sexual beings, or, to put it another way, between society's traditional definition of the person's sexual role and the optimal development of his assets as a person.

There is at present, and has been for the past generation or so, a great deal of confusion about principles of child rearing. Philosophies and approaches have ranged from extremes of permissiveness to various kinds of limit setting, as far as discipline is concerned. Attitudes toward the sexual aspects of the child's development have also varied, especially in regard to girls, where there has been a range from completely egalitarian treatment to attempts to redefine femininity in terms of the requirements of modern life. As children grow up, they almost seem to have two identities, the sexual one and the personal one. Since the indoctrination as to sexual role comes earliest, beginning in the very first days of life, it tends to color, and at times to overwhelm, the later development of social skills and intellectual capacities. I shall hope to show, by quoting from longitudinal studies of child development, how some of the various influences on development manifest themselves. Then I shall turn to a current study of pregnancy for material on some of the results of these various developmental influences on adults who are now mothers and fathers.

First, I should like to consider the contrasts between the traditional definitions of masculinity and femininity, on the one hand, and actual adult male or female functioning, on the other. [James] Kagan and [H. A.] Moss, in their recent report of a longitudinal study of children's development, define the traditional masculine model as active sexually, athletic, independent, dominant, courageous, and competitive. His choice of career is not highly intellectual, but is more likely to be that of salesman, businessman, athletic coach, or the like. The feminine model is passive and dependent, showing both sexual timidity and social anxiety, fearing and avoiding problem situations, and pursuing homemaking activities rather than career ones. The actuality of these concepts as models for development of many children in our culture is supported by a number of studies of children's attitudes toward the sexes. For instance, Bandura, Ross, and Ross noted in testing children's tendency to imitate adults that the boys normally regarded the male figure as the source of power and the female figure more as the distributor, regardless of the actual power structure of the experimental situation. And Ruth Hartley's studies of children's concepts of male and female roles showed that the shifts in feminine behavior in our society in recent years have not yet affected these concepts.

The traditional concepts of masculinity and femininity undergo many vicissitudes, of course. From the beginning there is constant pressure on the boy to be active, athletic, and competitive; however, in school, and especially in the high school years, the pressures to develop intellectually, to go to college, and to prepare for a career become more insistent and tend to replace the high valuation of physical activity. But adolescence is also the courtship period, and in this area the older traditions continue to take first place. With the girl, there is considerable indulgence of tomboy behavior up until puberty. After that time, the pressures for traditional femininity, prettiness, ladylike behavior, and apparent passivity in courtship become very strong. Attitudes toward intellectual development in the girl are more ambivalent; in some families intellectual achievements are highly regarded, while in others they are either disapproved or regarded with neutrality. Probably the stereotypes reach their peak in intensity of impact during adolescence and from then on become ameliorated by the necessities of education, careers, and marriage.

It is not until after marriage and the establishment of a family that the carrying out of male and female functions has a weighty impact on behavior. Until the children come, the man and wife can be very much alike, both working, both playing at homemaking, both saving toward the purchase of a home and furniture, and so on. It is only with the conception, gestation, and birth of the baby that a decisive division of labor must occur. Now the man becomes in reality the support of the family, and concomitant with this comes an increased feeling of responsibility. The woman, under the ordinary circumstances of raising her children herself, now must withdraw from her career activities, or at least relegate them to second place. She and her child have to become the supported, and hence she must assume a relatively passive and receptive position in relation to her husband in such important areas as money matters, career interests, and coming and going. She also needs to accept the giving or service role in the family, in such matters as baby tending, meal supplying, and so forth. Now the stereotypes of childhood and adolescence must give way before the realities of everyday adult life, in which neither the masculine nor the feminine one has a chance of success. This brave, strong, dominant male is expected to get up at night with a colicky infant, and this passive, helpless, and dependent woman is expected to deal courageously and with common sense with all the accidents and upsets of life with a small baby. Neither compliance with the cultural stereotypes nor rebellion against them and insistence on differences will solve the problems of the adult marriage partners.

A good deal of new information on childhood development has recently become available from two sources: (1) carefully controlled observations of the earliest days of infancy, and (2) longitudinal studies such as those from Berkeley and from the Fels Institute. Most of this work has been done by psychologists and is in the form of statistical statements of probabilities rather than individual case material. The psychologists are notably reluctant to embody their findings in anybody's theory of personality, even Freud's, but prefer to let the facts stand for themselves. For instance, Kagan and Moss are still uncertain as to the propriety of admitting the concept of repression into their system. The psychologists' reluctance to theorize is, one might say, the psychoanalyst's opportunity, and with an apologetic glance in their direction, I shall feel free to take their observations as starting points for my speculations.

The observations of early infancy point to some patterns of response present from birth which are related to subsequent development. One of the most interesting of these, described by [R. Q.] Bell, is the arousal level of the infant. There appears to be a wide range, with two extreme types. One type of infant is characterized as a newborn by quiescent sleep and lean body build, and at a month's age by low waking arousal, lack of assertion of needs in the face of brief deprivation, and a strong positive response to maternal contact. At two and a half years, this type showed cautious, restless, shifting play and positive orientation toward contact with supportive adults. The other type manifested chubby body build, strong appetite, a high level of arousal during sleep in the newborn period, and a high level of responsiveness and arousal coupled with aversive response to maternal contact at the end of the first month. At two and a half years this type showed intense, fearless play with inanimate objects and low orientation toward adult supportive figures and peers.

Such innate patterns may be argued as being the precursors of passive vs. active orientations later in life. It is of interest that the two extreme types show differences in positive response to maternal cuddling which may have much to do with constitutional makeup. It would seem highly probable that the difference in the baby's response would in turn have considerable influence on what the mother offers. Both types of arousal pattern occur in each sex, although there is a greater proportion of the first, or cuddly, type among girls.

There are other innate differences in the two sexes: the obvious anatomical ones, larger size and greater strength in the male, greater mortality rate of male infants, more rapid rate of maturation for females. Differences in general intelligence cannot be shown early in life and during the preschool years. As the school years progress, the differences in type of ability, level of activity, motivation, interests, and so on became more and more apparent. One difference between the sexes that shows up quite early is the amount of aggressive behavior, which even in nursery school is higher for boys than for girls. However, the influence of social teaching in this type of behavior—manhood being equated with fighting—is hard to rule out.

Differential handling of boys and girls is apparent from birth on. Moss has observed that mothers tend to be more responsive to male infants, holding them proportionately more time and generally attending to them more than do mothers of female infants. Somewhat later, at seven months, both parents use more sugary and baby-talk to girl babies and work harder to get them to smile and vocalize. These differential ways of handling the two sexes were independent of the activity level of the infant. Longitudinal studies so far provide only partial information about influences on child development, since they have in the past only used observations and ratings of the behavior of the mother and the child and have overlooked the father, yet they have found some exciting correlations between experiences early in life and later behavior. The child's behavior up to the age of three does not tend to carry on in similar form to later ages, with some exceptions. Of the exceptions, the passivity-activity level of the child seems to be the most enduring. Following the three-year-old level, more behavior tends to show itself in enduring patterns, but the first three or four grades of school are still periods of rapid change. After that, relative stability of many behavior patterns emerges.

The Berkeley study rated maternal behavior in two aspects—the degree of affection and the degree of control exercised by the mother. The investigators found the predictable better development in infancy and early childhood when the mother was affectionate and not too controlling, but surprisingly also found that with girls the positive correlation between good development and loving maternal behavior dropped out after the age of four. This suggests that the mother-daughter relationship undergoes some troubling changes from about the age of four onward which affect the development of the girl. This is confirmed by some of the findings of Kagan and Moss in the Fels longitudinal study. They observed that strong intellectual strivings in boys were correlated positively with maternal protection in the first six years, while strong intellectual strivings in girls were correlated positively with critical maternal attitudes in the same years. One gets the picture, for the girls, of a mother who is in opposition to the traditional feminine stereotype, and who urges and drives her daughter in the direction of intellectual development.

The boys who showed strong intellectual strivings continued, as adults, to show the same tendencies, but these were also associated with high sexual and social anxiety and a general lack of traditional masculine-type behavior.

When the striving girls reached adulthood, they exhibited intellectual competitiveness and masculine-type interests.

Two other groupings showed opposite trends. Those boys who were most active in childhood became as adults strongly masculine, actively sexual, but weaker in intellectual strivings. The girls who were passive and maternally protected in childhood tended to become passive women, dependent on their families, withdrawing from problem situations, showing high social anxiety, and involved in traditional feminine pursuits.

It might be well to be somewhat critical of the traditional masculine and feminine role definitions used in this and other studies. Admittedly they represent extremes and are far from average or typical behavior. It seems to me that they may well represent pathological overexaggerations rather than pictures of some ideal, as far as their mental-health aspects are concerned. However, one cannot get around the fact that they come up over and over again in studies, for example, of how the child looks at male and female differences.

To continue with some of the other findings, Kagan and Moss compared the vocational choices of the ten boys who were given the highest ratings on masculine activities at three to six years of age with the choices of the seven boys who were rated lowest. They showed no overlap. The ten rated most masculine had become three businessmen, two farmers, two athletic coaches, a carpenter, a machinist, and an engineer. The seven who were rated lowest became three teachers, a chemist, a biologist, a physicist, and a psychiatrist! Their recreational choices showed the same dichotomy; the men in the first group built amplifiers, worked with machines, and engaged in sports, while the men in the other group preferred art, music, and reading. It is important to add that these differences were not correlated with intelligence level. The developmental course for the girls was less consistent, for many of the active and competitive ones dropped these behaviors during adolescence and assumed more feminine interests. The girls also showed a rapid increase during early school years of withdrawal from challenging problem situations, and the IQ levels of the achieving girls did not increase through the early years of school as did those of the boys.

The overall pattern that emerges from this study is that of cultural disparagement of passivity and dependency in the boys and a gradual diminution in the frequency and intensity of these characteristics. However, a substitution occurs of behavior which is less obvious but related in kind, such as a low level of sexual activity, social anxiety, and the choice of a more sedentary and intellectual career rather than an active and manipulative one. With the girls, aggression and activity were discouraged while dependency and passivity were rewarded, with a resulting alteration in these behaviors which was most conspicuous in preadolescence and adolescence when heterosexual interests begin to flower. However, even prior to that the girls began to show timidity and withdrawal from challenging tasks and also a tendency toward stability or stagnation of intellectual development.

If the greatest value is placed on successful development of so-called typical masculine and feminine types of behavior, then creativity and maximum intellectual development seem to suffer in both sexes. With girls, there seems to be greater sexual and social anxiety. If the greatest value is placed on high achievement, then sex-typical behavior is less developed, and, with boys, there is greater evidence of sexual and social anxiety.

To illustrate some of the results of these childhood developmental processes, I would like to turn now to some material from an exploratory and descriptive study of pregnant women and their husbands in which a group of colleagues and I have been engaged for the last several years. When we started, our thought was that the later phases of maturing—marriage, the establishment of adult occupations, and the setting up of new family units—had

had little attention. Pregnancy and the early postpartum period highlight the maturational challenges for both wife and husband, since with the establishment of the family comes the necessity to assume a caretaking responsibility and to devise a division of labor which may or may not have been accomplished before. For this reason, conflicts about both feminine and masculine roles tend to be more sharp and hence more available to study.

We have quite full material on more than fifty subjects, which includes weekly interviews with the wives, beginning in the third or fourth month of pregnancy and continuing through the first three months of the postpartum period. This interview material, which we discussed in weekly seminars, was supplemented by psychological examinations, one in the sixth month of pregnancy and a second one at the end of the subject's participation. In addition, we had two interviews with each husband, one before and one after the child was born. Our subjects came to us by referral from obstetricians in private practice and from local mental hygiene clinics. Women with problems were therefore in the majority, although there were also some well-adjusted ones who volunteered because they were interested in learning about themselves and their children.

On scrutinizing our cases, we were surprised to note that more of the multipara in the study were having pregnancy-connected problems than primipara, by roughly 50 percent. It looked as though these mothers had learned from experience that pregnancy and child raising were sources of conflict and dissatisfaction. Eleanor Pavenstadt, who studied a lower-income group in Boston, made a similar observation—namely, that an evaluation of these women after they had had two or three children showed them to be at a lower level of maturity and adjustment than had the initial testing early in their first pregnancies. Because of their social and economic situation, Pavenstadt's subjects were, she felt, without much hope for the future, looking forward to a life of drudgery and involuntary childbearing. This might account for their apparent downhill course. Our subjects, on the other hand, were mainly middle-class Protestants with reasonable financial security and considerable freedom of choice about their family size. If, despite this, there was an increase in emotional disability with the birth of additional children, we would need to look to other conditions of their lives for an explanation.

When we began our study, we made the obvious assumption that the more emotionally unstable women would have the most trouble during their pregnancies. This turned out to be true in the majority of cases, but to our surprise there was a substantial proportion of quite neurotic women who were no worse or, in some cases, even felt and functioned better during their pregnancies than before or after. We finally distinguished five principal groups: first, those who seemed mentally healthy and had no problems during pregnancy; a second small group who were emotionally well adjusted but had other problems, such as physical illness; a third group who had obvious neurotic difficulties but were not worse during pregnancy; a fourth group of neurotic women who improved during pregnancy; and the fifth and largest group of those who showed signs of neurotic illness and felt and functioned worse during pregnancy.

I must make it clear that I am not referring, when I use the word neurotic, to clinical illness, but rather to psychological problems of adjustment sufficiently severe to be handicapping. Some of our subjects had been in psychiatric treatment earlier; some had not. Some of them went on to psychotherapy after their time with us; most did not.

In general, the more maladjusted subjects had had a history of greater tension and conflict in the childhood home and had more difficulties in their marriages. Most of our first group of problem-free women had come from harmonious childhood homes and were happily adjusted in their marriages, with feelings of affection and security on the part of both husband and wife. It was particularly notable that these subjects all had had good relationships with their mothers, although in some cases the relationships with their fathers had been more conflicted. Also notable was the fact that these women were mature, competent, and quite free of conflicts about femininity. Whether they pursued careers or not, they and their husbands had established a relationship which was satisfying to both, not only sexually but also in their workaday living. In contrast, a high proportion of our fifth group, the most troubled ones, had come from unhappy, frustrated, conflictful childhood homes, and inevitably there were marital problems.

Group three, those who were not worse during pregnancy, is particularly interesting to contrast with group five. Despite serious childhood trauma, almost all of them had made successful marriages. In some, it seemed that the happy fortune of marrying a stable and supportive husband had had a curative effect in a woman who otherwise might have gone on toward increasing maladjustment.

Group four, those whose adjustment improved during pregnancy, also had a particular coloring. For these women the states of being pregnant and of being a mother were so intensely satisfying that other relationships and conflicts faded into the background. One of them had been rejected by her husband and was living alone, but was very content, wrapped up in the phenomena of gestation and in daydreams about her wonderful baby. She was quite efficient in coping with the realistic problems involved in living alone and being pregnant, as though she and the fetus formed an entirely complete unit. Another, who was lonely and bored with her marriage to an overly busy professional man, found in her pregnancy her chief source of satisfaction. A third regarded the pregnancy as proof of her adequacy as a woman, something her marriage had not provided her with. We wondered whether in some of these cases the satisfaction with pregnancy and motherhood would evolve into a damaging symbiotic relationship with the child as time went on.

We found the sharpest identity conflicts in the most problem-ridden group. I shall be speaking of our subjects primarily within the frame of reference of socially conditioned impairments of ego development, rather than in terms of their unconscious conflicts. Looking at them in this way, it soon became apparent that issues around comfortable acceptance of the feminine role, adequacy of personal development, and satisfaction of dependent needs were intimately interwoven and were of prime importance in success or failure during pregnancy. Without due foresight, we had initially focused our attention almost exclusively on the woman, imagining that pregnancy had to do primarily with what went on inside her. But the husband's part was forcibly brought to our attention with our first cases, and we became more and more aware of his crucial effect on his wife's well-being. The issues which determined the adequacy of his collaboration were similar to those in his wife—namely, his feeling about himself as a man, his adequacy as a person, and his handling of his dependent needs vis-à-vis his wife.

We found the problem of dependency to be intimately related to questions of masculine and feminine identity. Dependency is a somewhat confused concept; as most often used, it describes a pathological state of childish demandingness.

There is a tendency to overlook interdependency as a part of healthy human relations, both those of husband and wife and also those of people in general. Sometimes we talk of material dependency for goods and services, and sometimes of emotional dependency, without clearly distinguishing them. On the whole, we are more comfortable with the objective, material types of dependency, as when we depend on the fire department to put out our fires. The emotional type of dependency is more problematic. It involves needs for reassurance, support, proof of love or concern, approval, confirmation of our worth, and so on. This kind of experience is a daily necessity for us, and yet we do not clearly know what is an adequate and "normal" dose and what goes beyond that point.

An added difficulty is the high value we place on self-sufficiency or independence, considering it to be one of the qualities of healthy maturity. Could it be more correctly stated that self-sufficiency consists in knowing how to get one's dependency needs met without blood, sweat, and tears? One criterion of suitable degrees of dependency is that of the willingness of the other to be involved. One reacts against a patient's or friend's dependency needs if he seems to ask more than one is willing to give. Perhaps a bargain is inherent in the relationship between two adequate, self-sufficient, successfully dependent adults—namely, that the giving goes both ways. It would be best, then, to look for a dependency balance or equilibrium between two people, or to look for the unbalancing factors in cases of conflict.

Part of the mythology of the sexes is that the man is independent and the woman dependent, but this is only a myth. The man's dependency needs are largely cloaked beneath the masculinity image, while those of the woman are more in the open, and indeed are exaggerated by the popular stereotype of femininity. The need to feel cared for is present in both and undoubtedly goes back to early experience with the mother. A central condition for satisfaction is that the caring-for, whatever it may be, must be freely given by the other, rather than extracted from him. For the more maladjusted, in whom there is a grave lack of trust in the self and the other, gratification of dependency needs is difficult if not impossible of attainment. On the one hand, the freedom of the giving is doubted, and on the other the needs are frequently not expressed. The person tends to believe that if he asks for something, this invalidates the worth of the gift. He tends to rely, then, on the hope that the other will guess his needs and supply them in such a way as to resolve his doubts, a hope which is forever being frustrated. In those whose self-esteem is sturdier, the need for proof is less intense, requests can be verbalized, and a gift offered by the other is accepted at face value.

Another type of conflict regarding dependency occurs when such needs have to be denied, a situation frequent in those whose serious doubts of their own worth are covered up by compensatory strivings for strength and self-sufficiency. Such a defensive structure is seen most often in men, but it certainly occurs frequently in women too. We then see the person playing the role of bountiful provider, manager, or dictator to the other, but underneath the pseudo self-sufficiency is the expectation of the reward of love on the basis of good deeds or heroic character.

In any marriage, there are initially a good many illusions, both as to the perfection of the other and also as to the promise of fulfillment of all needs. Conflicts and disappointments are inevitable, but in fortunate instances a compromise eventually emerges in which there is sufficient satisfaction for each to make the relationship stable. The particular compromise varies with the characters of the two involved. In the so-called ideal, typical marriage the man carries more of the responsibility; he is the more active one, the initiator or, as current terminology puts it, the instrumental one. The woman tends to be more passive and is responsive rather than initiating. Her role has recently been relabeled by the social psychologists as that of being the expressive one. However, this balance may not suit the particular personalities involved, and it is easy to see instances of a more equal balance, a sort of comradeship arrangement, and, on the other side of the scale, examples of relationships in which the woman exhibits the greater degree of initiative, energy, and decision making, while the man is relatively passive. The active-passive balance between the two is not congruent with the dependency-need balance, since an active person's dependency needs are met when he receives confirmation and appreciation for his actions. In terms of dependency needs, the equilibrium must be flexible enough to allow for shifts in situations of stress, and there must be ways of communicating requests between the two.

Especially during pregnancy and the early postpartum period, there is an increase in the woman's dependency needs. In the early stages of the pregnancy, of course, the stresses are largely symbolic, stemming from fears of the pregnancy, of the ordeal of the delivery, and of the increased responsibility after the baby is born. Fear of loss of attractiveness, physical damage, pain, and death, as well as concern about the welfare of the fetus, all make the woman turn toward her husband with increased demands. Later on, in the third trimester and the postpartum period, there are realistic needs for more care and attention from the husband. Our subjects quite frequently asked for a kind of mothering care from their husbands, wanting sympathy, small favors, interest in the developing child, reassurance about their attractiveness, help with planning, and so forth. [Grete] Bibring and her group have documented the lack in modern, small-family life of easy ways of meeting the increased emotional and realistic needs of the pregnant woman—something which was provided by the larger kinship group of other societies and our earlier generations. In the present day in our culture these pressures fall primarily on the husband's shoulders, and the wife's success in getting her needs met and her consequent feelings of well-being depend very much on her way of asking—whether open and appropriate or devious and inappropriate—and his way of responding.

The women in our study showed a readiness to accept help from us and to change habitual patterns of behavior which was perhaps related to their increased vulnerability during pregnancy. This state of loosening or increased permeability often affected the husband too. Where the husbands were able to offer a more sensitive response to their wives, and where the wives could become more open and realistic in their demands, the relationships improved in ways that promised well for the future. We found that counseling in this area paid big dividends in assuring less traumatic pregnancies and a more comfortable start for the babies.

In our most troubled group, we found patterns of interaction between husband and wife which often represented extreme exaggerations of those in the more normal marriages. Like Jack Spratt and his wife, the two have formed a combination which has all-or-nothing qualities about it, and when the pregnancy demands flexibility and shifts in the various aspects of the relationship, the adjustment breaks down. There are three rather typical groups of maladjustment—those in which sexual identity problems are foremost, those in which personal identity issues predominate, and those in which immaturity in both respects is so abysmal that constructive mutuality is impossible. Of course, not all troubled couples fit into one or the other of these clusters. There are, for instance, cases in which one or the other is borderline neurotic, or otherwise seriously ill, and the partner has to develop unusual qualities of giving or caretaking in order that the marriage may endure at all. However, in spite of these and other exceptions, there is a rather remarkable sameness about the interactions of members of the more typical clusters when viewed in terms of their identity and dependency struggles. I would like to illustrate them with some brief examples.

The first type of couple provides a sort of caricature of ideal, typical masculinity and femininity. The women are usually attractive, feminine in manner, and impeccably groomed. The men are active, energetic, ambitious, and closely follow the masculine model. The women are usually rather idle, with little to do except to run a small apartment and occasionally sew for themselves. The men are usually ambitious and overworked, often going to school at night as well as working hard at their jobs and their hobbies. The women show an increasing trend toward inadequacy, in the sense of leaving more and more up to their husbands; they are often demanding and irritable. The men are increasingly occupied with outside interests and activities and consequently are less and less committed to satisfaction in family life. Both partners accept the idea of the woman as dependent child and the man as active protector. Subjects in this group illustrate one of the imbalances between sexual development and personal development. Although the women are successfully feminine, as the culture defines it, they are limited if not infantile in their growth in the intellectual, social, and mastery aspects of living. The men are successful masculine types but are limited as human beings by rigidity, fear of and avoidance of emotion, and inability to participate in a comfortable intimate relationship.

For example, Mrs. A., who was in her second pregnancy, came to us because she was collapsing in weeping spells with increasing frequency. One obstacle to her participation in this study appeared in the beginning—namely, how was Mrs. A. to get to my office since her husband was afraid to let her drive while she was pregnant? The problem was solved when he was able to figure out a way of adjusting his schedule so that he could accompany her to all appointments, wait for her, and drive her home again. Mrs. A. brought out this concern of her husband's with some pride as an illustration of how careful he was of her. She was an exceptionally pretty, typically feminine woman who described herself as very contented, loving to keep house and have children, tremendously admiring of her strong and handsome husband, yet afflicted with these strange spells of tearfulness and depression which came on her, it seemed, without warning.

Her husband was exceedingly busy, working in a demanding job and also going to night school. He was very ambitious and was pursuing a five-year plan for the family's advancement. In addition, he was an enthusiastic golfer and spent at least one of the weekend days on the golf course. He had to have the car for his work and his school, which meant that Mrs. A., who lived in an apartment well away from the shopping center, was stuck at home with her small child all day and most evenings. Even grocery shopping could only be done

Saturday afternoons after her husband returned from the golf course.

The young couple accepted as a matter of course the concept that the man did almost everything, only excepting the cooking and child rearing. He did the housecleaning, hired the domestic help, and made all the plans. Yet he was very impatient with his wife's childishness. He felt that she was demanding, wanting to tie him down to domesticity, and always expecting him or her family to bail her out of her difficulties. She was growing increasingly helpless and felt unable to do things for herself. It developed that her spells of depression would come on when she was unable to get some desired behavior out of her husband or her child.

The wife's story was that of a pretty, popular teen-ager who had been a cheerleader, a camp counselor, and prominent in her class, but whose developmental course had been downhill since her great success in high school. There was no trouble with pregnancy and childbirth on a physiological level, but in the business of living, in the meeting of even minor crises, there was the unquestioning assumption that her proper role was helplessness.

In some pairs who follow this pattern, the division between the two is even greater, for the husband is oblivious of his wife's emotional needs, acting as though achieving success in the material world and taking total responsibility for the mechanics of living were his only functions. Child rearing is then left up to an exceedingly infantile wife, with disastrous results. Quite commonly such pairs come to child-guidance clinics with problem children, and then it is the experience of the therapists that the husband resists getting involved in the treatment situation and cannot be convinced that he has anything to do with the problem.

The balance of dependency is seen in reverse in another group of subjects in which the wife is the active, efficient one and the husband is quiescent, passive, often openly dependent. Here the woman has often developed herself as an educated, able person and has strong strivings for independency and mastery, while she is more uncertain of herself as an attractive woman and often regards the female as inferior to the male, or has to deny that the female is inferior. The man seems uncertain of himself as a male and tends to demand a good deal of mothering care from his wife. He may be intellectually developed and successful professionally, but on the defensive at home, or he may be relatively unsuccessful and leaning on his wife for practical or emotional support. In these marriages there is more open strife between the two, because the wife, while acting quite independently, at the same time resents the husband's passivity. It seems to outrage her sense of what is due her as a woman. It is as though she still retains an ideal of feminine passivity, while her own needs or the requirements of the marriage push her simultaneously in the direction of activity. The husband, too, while lethargic and inactive, shows signs of ambivalence. He resents his wife's managerial efforts and tends to blame or condemn her for them. He also resists her dependency demands, withholding himself from her. Quite frequently in this combination the husband's potency is impaired, adding yet another reason for resentment and frustration in the wife.

One of our subjects, Mrs. B., was a successful private secretary who had always earned more than her salesman husband until she stopped work at the time of the birth of her first child. She had, by then, grown contemptuous of her husband's inadequacy and had considered leaving him before she learned that she was pregnant. Because of the child, she attempted to accept the marriage, but her sense of grievance and abandonment by him brought about a postpartum depression after her first delivery. Now in a second, unwanted pregnancy, she was fearful of a recurrence of the psychosis and filled to overflowing with resentment. She was preoccupied with a vast array of grievances against her husband, including his lack of sexual prowess, his silent and uncommunicative behavior, his failure to make minor household repairs, and his not noticing her and her needs. She would do household tasks that were too heavy or risky for her, rather than ask his help. Then there would be an accumulation of resentment which would come out in a wild torrent as the result of some minor irritation. He was repelled by her aggressiveness and bounciness and imagined that he wanted a docile, agreeable wife. He opposed her working because it did not agree with his fantasies of a proper family life. She, on her side, was hurt by his lack of interest in her and longed to feel more comfortable as a woman.

Marriages such as this in which the problem is some sort of reversal of the usual sexual roles occur frequently in the patients who find their way to a psychiatrist's office, actually more so than the first type of difficulty which I described. There seems to be a constant dissatisfaction which presses both partners to struggle for a better solution. In part, I would presume that the pressure of discontent comes from the violation of cultural norms. Not many men settle down contentedly to let their wives assume leadership, nor do many women accept with equanimity a passive husband. Hence in these marriages there is more open combat, more neurotic symptomatology, and more rebellion against their lot in life. The woman may be primarily aggressive, demanding, complaining, or reproaching, or she may develop various phobias or depression. The man may show passive resistance, rigidity, moral condemnation, or withdrawal; he may sometimes be impotent and sometimes alcoholic. In the more customary vocabulary of psychiatry, this type of marital pair is frequently referred to as "the castrating wife and castrated husband." The surface appearance does indeed support this description, but the epithets obscure the dynamic interplay of needs and frustrations which leads to this result.

A third style of marital disharmony might be called the sibling-rivalry relationship. Here it seems that both people are intent on having their own needs met without regard to the other. Wife and husband are both immature, not only in their adolescent view of sexuality but also in their inability to assume responsibility, control their impulses, and plan for the future. Sometimes they are in competition as to who will be the dependent one, receiving support, reassurance, and care from the other. There is more concern with competition than cooperation, more interest in outward appearances than inner experiences, and each is preoccupied with getting his own way and with his own grievances.

Mrs. C., for example, had always been relatively irresponsible, putting good times and lots of dates above school achievement. After a year of college she married a man who was as immature as herself. He was a college dropout, working in a low-paid job and anxious to marry in order to feel like a man. Marital trouble beset them from the start. She was insistent on having her own way, he equally determined to have his, and there were frequent noisy quarrels and physical battles. In a moment of relative peace they discontinued contraception and she became pregnant. She was delighted at the prospect of having a little baby to play with. He reacted by quitting his job, intending after a few weeks' rest to get a new and better one. The whole pregnancy was a game to her and an event which Mr. C. ignored. Postpartum she was cared for by her overindulgent mother. Nursing was attempted but promptly discontinued because it tied her down too much. When the baby was about two months old, the husband and wife resumed their rivalrous bickering, and Mrs. C. left him, returning to her parental home with the baby.

One combination which is interesting by its absence in our study is that of the domineering husband and submissive wife, a pattern which is of fairly common recurrence in some European cultures. Its infrequency in this country may to some extent account for the oft-repeated complaint that American culture is woman dominated.

Summarizing our study of pregnancy, I believe that we have shown the importance for the welfare of the family unit of, first, a sense of security on the part of both man and woman as to their worth as sexual beings and as to their development as persons, and, second, a balance of equilibrium between the two people as to their dependency needs, a balance which can take account of the varying intensity of such needs in various kinds of personalities, and which also can shift with the vicissitudes of living. If these two conditions are not present, the pregnancy may be fulfilling to the woman and confirming of her femininity, but a threat to the man, who may be too doubtful of himself to be able to meet his wife's increased needs, assume the responsibilities of fatherhood, and accept without anxiety her absorption in the child and consequent withdrawal from himself. Equally, the woman whose doubts of her worth go deep may find more threat than confirmation in the low-prestige mothering role, so that the pregnancy is fraught with anxiety, and her dependency on her husband rises so high as to render futile any reasonable efforts to support her. For the man, defensive needs to prove his masculinity, or lack of confidence in it, can lead either to overprotection and overcontrol of his wife or to abdication of his supportive and integrating functions in the family.

I believe the evidence presented here shows the invalidity of either activity-passivity or independence-dependence as indices of masculine-feminine development. Unfortunately, these are embedded in the culture. They are passed on to children by mothers and fathers uncertain of their own feminine or masculine worth, reinforced by schooling, by storybooks, by TV programs, and by peer-group attitudes. Regrettably, they are also held by many professional workers in the behavioral sciences. Sometimes the assumption is made that such qualities are inborn, as sexually determined characteristics. The material from observations of children contradicts this. Others assume that these qualities are either taught or reinforced as part of the acculturation process. Again, the evidence from longitudinal studies indicates that such acculturation is far from successful. The constitutional tendencies toward activity and passivity do not reverse themselves under the pressures of socialization. Rather they linger on in one guise or another, and the anxieties that are aroused by social disapproval of passivity in boys or activity in girls can be seen in the multitudinous fears experienced by both sexes about not being thought appropriately masculine or feminine. Much of the castration anxiety in men and its counterpart, penis envy, in women seems to spring from fear of condemnation if one does not conform to the model. The overemphasis on so-called masculine traits throws the boy into conflict regarding the feeling aspects of experience and labels as suspect the development of intellectual and artistic interests. Similarly, the girl is made to feel uneasy in striving toward competence, intellectual development, and independence.

As they reach adulthood and marry, conflicts regarding the division of functions, the dependency balance, and the sharing of responsibility arise. For the woman, emphasis on dependency, passivity, and even inadequacy interferes with her functioning as homemaker, wife, and mother just as severely as with her functioning in a career. Despite the low prestige attached to the career of housewife, doing the job well requires competence, good judgment, and ability to take responsibility. Indeed, constructive use of the long hours alone, which are part of the experience of the housewife, requires a considerable degree of inner richness if retrogression and inertia are not to set in. For the man, the overemphasis on strength, courage, initiative, and leadership does violence to his appropriate needs for rest, receiving emotional support, and getting rid of the tensions of the market place.

I would not be thought to be an advocate of abolishing maleness and femaleness in favor of one uniform sex, as Simone de Beauvoir seems to do. Rather, my aim would be to encourage a more critical scrutiny of our assumptions about sex-typical behavior. Freud's description of feminine masochism, it must be remembered, was based on a Victorian type of female who, when viewed from the twentieth century, looks like a rather hysterical specimen.

But even nowadays, Ralph Greenson is reported in the press as describing the feminization of the United States. He sees women becoming increasingly secure, sexually and socially, and men becoming economically and psychologically more insecure. Although he is careful to state that he is only observing and not condemning, the application of the adjectives "feminized" and "emasculated" to the male are not entirely devoid of value judgment. Also, the idea that, as women become more secure, men become more insecure, and vice versa, makes one wonder. Is it really true that we are on a teeter-totter and that only one sex can be secure at a time? The evidence from our study contradicts this assumption, as does common sense. Forty years ago, in a letter to Romain Rolland, Freud wrote, "Given our drive dispositions and our environment, the love for fellow man must be considered just as indispensable for the survival of mankind as is technology." He was referring, of course, to the powerful influence the social value system, "love for fellow man," has over our instinctual life, serving to moderate our aggression. In a parallel fashion to man's other ills, our narrow conceptions of what is manly and hence not womanly, of what is womanly and hence not manly (conceptions which exclude large areas of thought and feeling which might appropriately be considered as human rather than narrowly sex-bound) can be seen to give rise to difficulties in our development and our relations with each other and with our children. They need to be modified by cultural expectations more flexibly in accord with individual needs as they are actually found in males and females.

PAUL CHODOFF

PAUL CHODOFF is a well-known contemporary psycho-analyst who teaches (clinical professor of psychiatry, George Washington University) and practices in Washington, D.C. Stating that the Freudian view of women stands or falls on Freud's more basic theory of infantile sexuality, he examines this theory in the light of modern scientific perspectives and data.

Additional evidence has since been gathered on many of the points Dr. Chodoff raises. This comment can be applied as well to most of the papers written between 1966 and 1969 that appear in this section. Some of this new material is covered in the later articles, demonstrating that even such relatively recent works lead to increasingly refined formulations.

Feminine Psychology and Infantile Sexuality

IN THE FIFTH chapter of *New Introductory Lectures in Psychoanalysis*—"The Psychology of Women"—Freud paints a dolorous picture of Woman, like a doomed Niobe, forever keening her irremediable genital wound as she lingers disconsolate in the oedipal doldrums. Principally from her festering penis envy stems her narcissism, her passive aims, the blunting of her moral sensibility, her envy and jealousy, her self-depreciation. Such a creature seems fit only to satisfy the sexual needs of her master, Man, but even here her frigidity renders her disappointing. Helene Deutsch added masochism to this catalogue of female characteristics, but otherwise there has been relatively little change in the classical psychoanalytic view of female personality or of its origins in the sexual life of the female infant and child, partly because, as recently stated by Sherfey, "There have been no new psychoanalytic contributions to the understanding of female psychosexual development since Freud and the early analysts."* The unflattering portrait of woman summarized above has, of course, been subjected to the buffeting of certain outraged women analysts who have emphasized the greater weight of cultural factors, and to revisions demanded by the newer knowledge of relevant biological data. However, it is still a fair statement that

---

* Mary Jane Sherfey, *The Nature and Evolution of Female Sexuality* (New York: Random House, 1972). See pp. 136–53 in this volume for excerpts from this work.—ED.

Freudian psychoanalysis regards the vicissitudes of the infantile psychosexual development interacting with woman's fateful anatomy as the dominant influence in shaping feminine personality. Such a point of view is entirely consistent with the Freudian stance which stresses the primary genetic importance of the infantile sexual life in forming human character generally, both healthy and pathological. Thus, the Freudian view of women, which has reverberated so resoundingly within our culture and our clinics, to a certain extent stands or falls with the degree of acceptance of Freud's theories of infantile psychosexuality. It is my intention to examine the evidence on the basis of which these theories have won such widespread assent.

That children sometimes exhibit behavior which is clearly sexual in the genital sense of the word is now accepted with little question by most educated people. This acceptance is a tribute to the genius of Freud and to his success in removing the blinders from the eyes of a world which had preferred not to notice certain goings-on during the then prevalent age of "the innocent child." Thus it is probably more accurate to give credit to Freud's achievement in this respect not as a discovery but, rather, as the disclosure of a phenomenon which had always been there but had been ignored. On the other hand, what Freud claimed to have discovered, and which has remained controversial in the eyes of his critics, was the far more inclusive concept of infantile psychosexuality which comprises not only infantile genital behavior but also the nongenital elements of childhood sexual activity along with the fantasies and other hidden mental activity which accompany it.

Although infantile psychosexuality does not lend itself readily to simple definition, certainly an essential feature is the way the term "sexuality" is broadened to embrace the function of obtaining pleasure from the zones of the body rather than being limited to genital behavior. The motor for sexuality is an hypothecated energic force, libido, which progressively illuminates and activates the zonal areas, and which is responsible for the child's sexual activities as he interacts with objects* in his environment. Under the influence of this unfolding drive, the child engages not only in activities which can be observed but also in other forms of behavior which are much more difficult to observe or which cannot be observed at all. These hidden mental activities include the fantasies, wishes, fears, fixations, identifications of the first five years, which, although they are subject to repression almost as they are coming into being, yet exert a profound influence on later development and, more specifically for the purposes of this discussion, on those characteristics of the adult woman which can be said to constitute her personality signature.

At this point, a brief historical review of certain aspects of Freud's life and contributions during the 1890s and the early 1900s will, I believe, provide a perspective against which a consideration of the evidence for the theories of infantile psychosexuality will be more meaningful. During this period, Freud was working eagerly and with great energy and productivity in attempting to understand the etiology of hysteria and was in hopes that he had discovered the *caput nili* of that condition. In cases of the actual neuroses and neurasthenia, which he was also treating during the same period, it seemed obvious to him that unfulfilled sexual drives were responsible for the symptoms these patients were manifesting. Inevitably, "knowledge acquired in one field will throw light on the other," and for this and other reasons, he became increasingly convinced of the sexual etiology of hysteria. Thus the formidable force of Freud's drive and enthusiasm was concentrated on certain patients from whom he expected a particular kind of material; the possibility must be taken into account that there was an element of

* The word "objects" in this sentence refers to people. It is used in the sense of Freud's original meaning, as the object of the instinctual drive.—ED.

FEMININE PSYCHOLOGY AND INFANTILE SEXUALITY

unconscious imposition of his beliefs on these patients, especially on the more suggestible among them. Supporting this possibility in "The Etiology of Hysteria" in 1895, Freud graphically describes how difficult a task it is to wrest the memories of seductions from his patients, how they protest and deny, and how they insist that they have no feeling of recollecting the traumatic scenes. Again, in "Sexuality and Etiology of the Neuroses" in 1898, he says: "Having accurately diagnosed a case of neurasthenic neurosis, one may proceed to transpose into etiology the symptomatical knowledge so gained, and may fearlessly require the patient's confirmations of one's surmises. Denial at the beginning should not mislead the physician; every resistance is finally overcome by firmly insisting on what has been inferred, and by emphasizing the unshakable nature of one's convictions." Is this a picture of the therapist gently and patiently providing a receptive ear for anxiety laden material, or is it, rather, that of a demanding insistence that the patient confirm "one's surmises"? It seems legitimate to suspect that the uniformity of the memories produced under such conditions, which Freud adduced as a proof of their universality in hysteria, may have been a product, rather, of the uniformity of Freud's expectations. Also, though Freud has been praised for his pertinacity and resilience in revising his theories of the sexual etiology of hysteria in the face of the collapse of the seduction hypothesis, one may wonder whether the need to salvage something from the wreckage may not have had a distorting influence on the accuracy of his observations.* At any rate, and whatever the reasons, Freud's formulations of his theories of infantile psychosexuality over the next ten years, culminating in "Three Contributions to the Theory of Sex" in

---

* With reference to the history of Freud's theories, this hypothesis reflects Freud's early belief that women suffering from hysteria had been seduced in childhood. He later concluded that such seductions had never occurred; they were fantasies created as a result of instinctual drives.—ED.

1905, met with a reaction so uncritically rejecting on the part of the medical profession and so unreservedly accepting on the part of his followers that the atmosphere was not at all favorable for the kind of careful, painstaking, and objective examination that so revolutionary a theory deserved.

Freud and Freudian theorists have relied on three main lines of evidence for infantile psychosexuality: (1) the adult sexual perversions and certain nongenital aspects of normal adult sexual life; (2) recovery or reconstruction of the infantile sexual life through psychoanalysis; (3) direct observation of infants and children.

The fact that adults engage in behavior that is clearly sexual involving oral and anal areas plays an important part in Freudian efforts to establish a relationship between sexuality and preoedipal oral and anal activities of infants. However, such a connection cannot simply be assumed since it seems something of a logical discontinuity to assume that a man or woman who feels sexual pleasure in fellatio or intercourse per anum is regressing to a stage in which his pleasurable sensations are analogous to an infant sucking on his mother's breast or expelling a stool. As [J. H.] Gagnon points out, because the oral and anal mucous membranes are capable of being stimulated pleasurably by a number of different stimuli and in many different settings, it does not follow "that all contacts with, or stimulation of, the end organs of the infant have either a protosexual or completely sexual meaning." The same phenomena may be explained, as [Sandor] Rado does, by postulating a superordinate pleasure organization with contributions from genital, alimentary, and tactile systems, rather than by considering all pleasure functions as sexual.

Certainly there at least appears to be a distinction between the preoedipal oral and anal sexuality and the sexuality of the oedipal phallic stage. Although these are all considered to be successive stages of libido concentration in the course of psychosexual development, yet the postulated mental activity of the phallic era, such as, for instance, penis envy and other fantasies, all have a more direct connection with sexuality in the ordinary accepted sense of the term than the oral and anal activities of the preceding stages. That psychoanalysts find it necessary repeatedly to explain that by "sexuality" they mean the function of obtaining pleasure from the zones of the body rather than genital stimulation leading toward orgasm, is testimony to the popular difficulty in understanding this concept. The reason for this confusion is that sex in the phallic oedipal stage is sex in anybody's lexicon; this cannot be said of the oral and anal behavior of infants and babies, and psychoanalysis has always had to assume the burden of proof in establishing a real rather than simply a semantic connection between sexuality in the special sense in which it is applied to these activities and sexuality in the genital reproductive sense in which it is generally understood. While the situation is one which calls for experimental verification, attempts to establish this connection experimentally have had equivocal results, although it is worth mentioning that Freud's linking of thumbsucking and masturbation has been called into question by Peter Wolff who, as a result of direct observation of infants, challenges the interpretation that any stereotyped rhythmic activity in infancy represents autoerotic behavior.

The more direct evidence for Freudian theories of psychosexuality is derived both from sources peripheral to the main body of psychoanalytic treatment experiences and directly from such experiences.

To begin with the former, the nonanalytic evidence, the chief area of proof outside the realms of psychoanalytic therapy proper are those data obtained from direct observation of children which Freud and later analysts have cited as providing confirmation of the theories of infantile sexuality derived originally from the analyses of adults.

But what do such statements, confidently asserting a proved relationship between direct observation of infants

and children and psychoanalytic theories of infantile psychosexuality, really mean, and how reliable are they? Certainly, although the behavior of infants with regard to
oral and anal functions is capable of being observed
(though their interpretation is open to question) the conditions of such observations become more difficult as the
child gets older and enters the phallic oedipal stage. To
introduce controlled conditions into the observation of
phallic masturbation which Freud called "the executive
agent of infantile sexuality" is extremely difficult for
many reasons, not the least of which is the influence of
the observer on the phenomenon observed, while the
anecdotal accounts of mothers cannot be relied upon for
scientific purposes. The difficulty of the task is not lessened by the fact that the observer is dealing with infants
and children who can tell him either nothing or very little
about what they are feeling or doing, and whose categories of conceptualization of events are different from
those of adults. The almost immediate repression to
which many of the fears and fantasies of the phallic
oedipal stage are subject makes it even theoretically unlikely that these would be consciously available to the
child.

An additional reason why statements that direct observation of children have confirmed psychoanalytic theories are questionable can be inferred from the clear
evidence that psychoanalysis entered the field of child
development at a relatively late stage, a fact which seems
to me to have two possible consequences: (1) that early
statements about the confirmation of psychoanalytic theory by direct observation must be viewed with some
reservations; and (2) at the time psychoanalytically
trained observers began to observe children systematically, Freud's concepts of infantile psychosexuality had
already become so widely and formally accepted in the
psychoanalytic world as to seem essentially uncontestable
—possibly to be modified and extended to some degree,
but not to be basically questioned or critically reex-

amined. I venture to suggest that such preconceptions may have a limiting effect even on the careful and thorough work of Escalona and Heider, Sylvia Brody, and the participants in the Kris-Senn Yale Project and that they mar seriously such earlier works as that of Susan Isaacs in 1933 in which the leap from isolated observations of infants and children to conclusions within the traditional psychoanalytic framework often seems quite startlingly abrupt.

An example of a more critical approach by a psychoanalytically trained observer of childhood behavior, already alluded to, is that of Peter Wolff, who concludes his critique of present-day psychoanalytic propositions and research methods concerning infancy by stating: "That direct observations of infants does not at present corroborate psychoanalytic propositions about early infancy and that the propositions as they stand are descriptive and speculative and are not confirmed explanations."*

In addition to direct observation of infants and children, the nonanalytic evidence for psychoanalytic theories of psychosexuality also includes data derived from experiments by workers who are for the most part not analytically trained. On the whole, the attempts at validation described in such works are disappointing. The methods used include a certain amount of observation of infants, often for relatively short periods without adequate controls, and a series of more or less sophisticated tests, questionnaires, and interviews with parents about their children or with adults about their own childhood experiences. Many of the studies do not take into account, even formally, the existence or influence of that linchpin of psychoanalytic theorizing, the dynamic unconscious, with all its distorting effects on observable behavior. They often are equivocal in their conclusions,

* Peter Wolff, "Panel Report: Contributions of Longitudinal Studies to Psychoanalytic Theory," *Journal of American Psychoanalysis* 13 (1965): 605.

which may support or oppose a particular hypothesis, but are almost never so strong as to rule out alternative explanations, and they tend to be tests of the data on the basis of which theoretical propositions have been advanced rather than of the theoretical positions themselves. However, although there is no doubt about the difficulties of experimental validation or disproof of psychoanalytic theories of infantile psychosexuality, there is reason to hope, on the basis of some experimental and observational findings more recent than those mentioned above, that these theories are not entirely insulated from the processes of scientific inquiry, and that other disciplines are in a position to make relevant comments about them.

Time does not permit a discussion of contributions from such disciplines as neurophysiology, ethology, and cultural anthropology, but I would like to discuss briefly some data stemming primarily from endocrinology which are of particular interest in regard to the process of female identity and personality development. In the classical description of infantile psychosexual maturation, both girls and boys are pictured as passing through the pregenital stage in an essentially similar manner. With the awareness of anatomical sex differences, which comes at the phallic stage, the little girl first wants to be a boy, and then only gradually and torturously achieves a feminine identity, a process that continues well into puberty and adolescence. This transition is so laden with difficulty for the girl because, Freud believed, fetal development passes through a constitutionally bisexual stage which has its reverberations in the mental life. As a result of this constitutional bisexuality, "the girl has a masculine homologue that is a primary source of sexual stimulation during childhood so that she will necessarily have more difficulties with her innate bisexuality than the boy who has no comparable functioning feminine homologue." This concept of a constitutional bisexuality has not been supported by biological and endocrinological research on the process of sexual differentiation. On the contrary, there is

192

much evidence that the early embryo, rather than being bisexual or even undifferentiated, is actually female, and only under the influence of a male genetic code are these female structures transformed into male sexual organs by the action of fetal androgens. These findings call into serious question the psychoanalytic theory that normal female sexuality is derived from innate masculine sexuality, and they also suggest that the notion of a feminine personality colored by penis envy and struggling to relinquish this masculine component lacks, at least, any biologic underpinning.

As for the development of a gender identity, by which is meant the psychological aspects of behavior related to masculinity or femininity, the important work of John Money and of the Hampsons with individuals exhibiting various varieties of hermaphroditism has demonstrated that this gender identity in the human species is determined to an overwhelming degree by experiential rather than by inborn, instinctual factors. Furthermore, the consciousness of being male or female, in most cases, is very firmly fixed by the age of three years, so that developments during the phallic and postphallic psychosexual stages cannot play the decisive role in the formation of psychological femaleness attributed to them by psychoanalytic theory—such as the statement in a recent psychoanalytic contribution, that at the phallic level "a truly feminine identification is still biologically impossible since the clitoris is here the main executive of her sexual needs."

Freud himself did not think very highly of experimental methods of testing his theories. For him these theories, including the theories of infantile psychosexuality, must depend primarily on the information derived from the psychoanalytic treatment of patients, and we now turn to a consideration of these data. Here one is confronted with a voluminous mass of more or less detailed case reports or theoretical articles with case illustrations, and it is primarily on the basis of this corpus of clinical material that psychoanalysts make their confident assertion about the secure position of the theories of infantile psychosexuality. It is difficult not to be impressed by the sheer bulk of this evidence, and by the consistency of its conclusions, all confirmatory with minor changes and extensions of the formulations Freud made many years ago; but in spite of the undoubted brilliance of some of these case reports and papers and the intuitive flashes which hit one with a shock of recognition, certain doubts and reservations are not entirely dispelled.

One cause for such reservations is the unsatisfactory outcome of the various efforts previously described to provide a firmly established, extrapsychoanalytic basis on which to build, and against which to measure, the validity and consistency of these theories. Without such a basis, what Rapaport calls a "canon of interpretation," psychoanalysis operates within a closed system, and must face the possibility (which is in fact supported by certain evidence) that the analyst's preconceptions are influencing what his patient produces, and are thus providing a "proof" of psychoanalytic theory which is essentially a form of petitio principii. As has been somewhat sardonically noted recently by [H. J.] Home, in the event of disagreement in the discussion of psychoanalytic propositions, the appeal is almost invariably to the "literature" and not to the fact.

Case reports from the psychoanalytic literature which utilize genetic reconstructions in the field of infantile sexuality vary a great deal in their ability to impose conviction on the reader even though it is granted that no case report can be written without some selection of the material to be presented. Some of these reports are serious attempts to supply adequate samplings of what the patient said, the interpretive conclusions are reasonable, and their relationship to what the patient said is at least a logical one. Other case studies, however, simply reiterate largely preformed conclusions on the basis of insufficient or inapposite observational data conveying a strong impression that the analyst already "knows," possibly by faith, the meanings of his patient's productions and has them safely tucked away into a convenient theoretical pigeonhole even before the patient has produced them.

Although the psychoanalytic literature maintains that the theories of infantile psychosexuality have been confirmed by direct observation of children and infants, such confirmation is taken only as a triumphant proof of what had been already understood from the analyses of adult neurotics. One objection to this claim is that the patients, whose analyses provided the bases for the theories, were, after all, neurotics with sufficient psychopathology to bring them to the analyst's couch, and may not have provided a sufficiently representative sample to apply universally to all individuals sick or healthy. In fact, Frieda Fromm-Reichmann has suggested that the entire Freudian psychosexual sequence is not a normal development, but is, rather, an exceptional psychopathologic formation. However, assuming that this objection has been overcome by the very widespread variety of reasons for which people have subjected themselves to analysis in recent years, there is no doubt that this considerable feat of excavation of the infantile life from the unconscious of adults has been accomplished by the power of the analysis to loose the veils of repression barring adult individuals from conscious access to the feelings and fantasies of their infancies and childhoods; in other words, by the overcoming of the infantile amnesia. There was no question in Freud's mind at first that the principal object of a well-conducted analysis was to enable the individual being analyzed to recover the lost memories of the early and crucial stage of his life, and that successful therapeutic effect depended on such recovery. However, as the method grew in popularity and as more and more people undertook analysis, the belief that adequate analysis meant the recovery of childhood memories, and that therapeutic efficacy depended on such recovery was the victim of the hard-won experience of psychoanalysts including Freud. One can follow in his writings how Freud's changing attitude re-

flects an increasing caution about the possibility of re-
covering infantile memories, so that, in 1938, in modest
contrast to his previous confident assertions, Freud says:
"Quite often we do not succeed in bringing the patient
to recollect what has been repressed. Instead of that,
if the analysis is carried out correctly, we produce in him
an assured conviction that the truth of the reconstruction
achieves the same therapeutic result as a recaptured memory." By 1938, an era in psychoanalysis has ended in
which the recovery of infantile memories was the therapeutic goal, an era which now survives only in certain
movies and in the disappointed expectations of patients
entering analysis even today. However, the method of
reconstruction, the "this is what must have happened to
you" approach, which followed the period of memory
recovery, itself appears to have undergone rather significant modification and retrenchment since Freud made
the statements quoted above. This gradual retreat from
confidence in the analyst's ability to find out "what really
happened" in his patient's infancy and childhood should
raise questions about the reliability of theories of infantile
sexuality resulting from the analysis of adult neurotics
through the use of methods which have now been seriously questioned; if we can no longer regularly recover
memories of their infancy and childhood from patients in
analysis, and we can no longer be so certain about our
ability to reconstruct the past of these patients, why
should these tasks have been easier or more effectively
carried out in the beginning and unsophisticated days of
psychoanalysis? One explanation of this overconfidence
is that in the early period when the secrets of the infantile
sexual life were apparently being unearthed, Freud and
his first disciples were still insufficiently aware of the
great power of the transference on the tendency of
patients in the rather authoritarian setting of early
analyses to please their analysts by providing them with
the kind of material which the latter seemed eager to
hear.

The belief that the infantile amnesia is a regular concomitant of normal and abnormal development depends entirely upon the evidence available from psychoanalytic treatment, and thus is subject to the same strictures discussed previously in connection with other items of theory which depend for their proof on such methods. There is no question that the vast majority of adults remember very little from the early period of life covered by the presumed infantile amnesia. The scantiness of memories from this period, however, does not necessarily prove that they have all been subjected to repression according to the psychoanalytic explanation. Other explanations are possible, as that childhood memory is simply an as yet immature function in the exercise of which the growing child gradually develops increasing skill as he does with many other functions dependent on the level of central nervous system maturation. If this is true, studies of the remembering abilities of children ought to show a gradual and smooth increase with advancing age, which they do. Information theory emphasizes the intimate relationship between memory and both the ability to reason and the previous store of information. Thus the child whose reasoning powers are not yet developed, and who has little background of information to form a mosaic against which to pin and fix new items, should not be able to remember as well as the adult who is able better to reason and who has far more information to use as an available background. Aristotle said that "Only those animals which perceive time remember," and this statement reminds us that the "blooming, buzzing confusion" of the world of infancy and childhood is not timebound and time structured as is that of the adult, and it is not only in regard to time that children structure their world differently than do grown-ups. This has been pointed out by both [Kurt] Goldstein and [Ernst] Schachtel who have criticized the psychoanalytic concept of a specific infantile amnesia due to repression on the grounds that the adult is unable to remember how he felt the world appeared to him as a child because his categories of experiencing and conceptualizing are so different from a child's. The adult ties down and delimits experience to an extraordinary degree by the use of verbal methods which are either absent or very incompletely developed in the preverbal and early verbal child.

Since young children are actually within or very much closer chronologically to the period when infantile sexual behavior is said to occur, their activities and fantasy lives should be more readily available for analytic uncovering and the task of theory validation ought to be easier. Also parents or parental figures and siblings whose interactions with the patient form so much of the material of analysis are present and accessible for the checking of data acquired from the child. While these advantages would be maintained by the presumption that counter cathectic barriers should be less firmly entrenched at this early stage of their development, and thus more easily breached, this factor may be counterbalanced by the rigidity and uncompromising nature of the archaic superego of the child. Other practical and theoretical difficulties may interfere with the value of child psychoanalysis as a source of evidence and for confirmation of theories. Certainly it is more difficult to communicate with young children and to establish a reasonable consensus with them than it is with most adults: (1) because the child's incomplete mastery of language and individual use of it require that verbal communication be supplemented to a considerable degree by play therapy which must be translated back into verbal terms before it can be utilized for interpretation by the therapist; and (2) because, as has already been pointed out, the child's categories of experience are quite different from those of adults.

Whether and to what extent the adult therapist unconsciously influences the responses of his child patient is not a simple matter to judge. The difficulty here is not so much a matter of the child's falling easy prey to the adult's conscious or unconscious suggestions; many children, especially among those in therapy, are relatively insusceptible to direct adult influence. Rather, the communicative difficulties between child and adult may make it more difficult even than with adult patients for the therapist to know whether the child is in fact really accepting his interpretations in a meaningful way. As a result, there may be little or no check on theorizing about the experience of the child which may rapidly descend to the level of speculation. A perusal of some analytic case histories of children leaves the impression that the behavior of the child, verbal and otherwise, provides a very thin and precarious underpinning for the heavy weight of complicated theoretical inference it often must support, while it also appears that there may be simpler and less ornate interpretations than those advanced by certain authors to explain the child's behavior and relationships to his parents and analyst. As an example, one might wonder whether the inhibiting effects of having a child in analysis on the limit-setting roles of the parents might provide an alternative explanation for the fantasies of omnipotence in the child described by Berta Bornstein in "The Analysis of a Phobic Child," which this author interpreted as a reaction formation against intense passive sexual desire.

To return to feminine psychology, I submit that the role attributed to infantile sexuality in general and to penis envy in particular as genotypic influences influencing what are regarded as the modal personality characteristics of adult women cannot be proved on biologic and other empirical grounds, no matter how widely and repetitiously they are given the status of unassailable truths in large segments of educated opinion in the United States. Although Freud said of his picture of femininity limned at the beginning of his paper that "We have only described women insofar as their natures are determined by their sexual functions," certainly these sexual functions and infantile roots cast a long shadow over the adult female personality as seen through the Freudian spectacles which are so widely worn today. As Sherfey states: "For Freud the woman's entire personality is colored and complicated by the dual nature of her sexuality with its fundamental struggle in childhood and early adolescence to relinquish the aggressive function of masculine sexual pleasures emanating from infantile clitoral activity which in turn is a result of the innately bisexual nature of the embryo." If the evidence for infantile psychosexuality can be shown to be faulty, the reappraisal of the concept which will become necessary must not neglect its putative consequences including those for feminine psychology. This will mean that even in the case of women for whom Freud's portrait is a speaking likeness, reasons other than their early sexual life may be found responsible, while there will be fewer obstacles to the view which has been an article of faith with many of us that most women are really much nicer than Freud's writings suggest.

LEON SALZMAN

LEON SALZMAN has long advocated a reorientation in the psychoanalytic outlook on women. In 1967 he compiled a summary of the data currently available to form a basis for such a new outlook.

Salzman is widely known for his work on obsessions, depression, and a number of other psychoanalytic topics. He has also been a national leader in psychoanalytic and psychiatric affairs.

Formerly professor of psychiatry and director of psychoanalytic medicine at Tulane University and Georgetown University, Dr. Salzman is presently clinical professor of psychiatry at the Albert Einstein College of Medicine in New York City.

Psychology of the Female

A New Look

A MORE ADEQUATE understanding of the psychology of the female must include a thorough examination of the totality of her living as an adapting organism with its own assortment of biological capacities and limitations, as well as a being who must function in a world in which political and socioeconomic factors make demands upon her and influence her psychology. Old-fashioned controversies which range around nurture vs. nature, or instinct vs. culture, can no longer occupy the forefront of such investigations. It is clear that it is not a question of either-or, but of both.

Yet myths and outworn theories die slowly and reluctantly. The notion that an individual's character structure is bound to biology and that the psychology of the female is largely dependent upon the presence of a female reproductive system belongs to this class of one-sided theories which still dominate a great many notions of female psychology.

Such notions persist in spite of the evidence from historical sources that sociological and religious factors have always had a hand in gender status and privilege. The dignity and overpowering influence of Freud have given a scientific coating to some of these notions, which have made them even more impregnable.

THE WOMAN'S ROLE

From the dawn of history the status of the female was dictated not only by her biological role, but also by the

PSYCHOLOGY OF THE FEMALE

prevailing technological limitations and religious doctrines. Her role was presumed to be innate and determined exclusively by divine forces. When scientific observations were called upon to support these notions, her behavior reinforced the prevailing conceptions of character structure. Her behavior, however, was also the result of the prescribed role and status which the culture assigned to her. Major upheavals and historical crises may have altered these stereotypes temporarily, but it has only been in recent years that these supposedly immutable and innate qualities have given way to some scientific clarification.

The first inroads were made by Freud when he acknowledged that the female played a significant role in personality development, and thereby deserved special attention and concern. While previous formulations regarding the significant influences which bear on human development tacitly recognized the importance of mother, they focused mainly on father's role. The female not only became important because of her part in sexual activity, but also because of Freud's emphasis on mother's effect on the infant's early experiences. Yet Freud's theories buttressed all the prevailing prejudices and promoted the notion that the female was a deficient male and a second-class citizen, lacking in muscular prowess, emotionally unstable, and devoid of creative potentialities except in limited areas. Her role was directed almost exclusively to childbearing and child rearing and providing the atmosphere in which the man and the children could be served. It is sad to state that this view is not only widespread among many contemporary cultures, but also among many social scientists of great wisdom and repute, as well as among psychologists and psychoanalysts.

The psychology of the female as elaborated by Freud was strongly influenced by the theological and cultural attitudes which prevailed throughout his lifetime as a student as well as a researcher. He grew up in a patriarchal world in which the [Judeo-] Christian myth of crea tion was the dominant notion of the female's status. Sociological theories and the Darwinian views of evolution tended to support these notions. Freud's libido theory was male centered, and the psychology of the female was forced to fit the male model by introducing a number of additional hypotheses to cover the discrepancies. Many a priori opinions based on cultural and historical prejudices were given scientific status in Freud's theory. He linked biology to psychology, and psychosexual development to character structure. This overemphasis on biology neglected many relevant factors that derived from the culture.

In recent years there has been considerable disagreement with Freud's formulations. While indissolubly linked to that of the male both biologically and therefore sociologically, the psychology of the female must be viewed by studying her as a person in her own right, whose role and function is partly determined by her gender and partly by the assigned limits which the culture imposes upon her and which she accepts for a variety of reasons. The female has adaptive needs and security requirements identical to those of the male; the differences between them lie in the idiosyncratic ways these needs are expressed by biological roles and cultural definitions.

Failure to view the female in this broader perspective does a disservice to her skills and potentialities while perpetuating an invalid myth regarding her limitations. Some of the current psychological concepts such as penis envy, masculine protest, and feminine masochism, while largely unsupported by any convincing clinical or theoretical evidence, still have profound influence on social and economic possibilities for the female.

PSYCHOPHYSIOLOGICAL REAPPRAISAL

In an excellent anatomical, biochemical, and physiological review of the nature of female sexuality, [Mary Jane] Sherfey has asserted that it is the female sex which is primal, and not the male. This has been established by biologists for many years. One can no longer speak of a bisexual phase of embryonic development. While genetic sex is established at fertilization, the early embryo is female; the effect of the sex genes is not felt until the fifth or sixth week of fetal life. During this period all embryos are morphologically female. However, if the genetic sex is male, primordial germ cells stimulate the production of a testicular inductor substance which stimulates fetal androgens, *suppressing* the growth of the ovaries. In this way androgens induce male growth pattern. If the genetic sex is female, germ cells stimulate the production of follicles and estrogen. However, if estrogens are not produced (by artificial removal of gonads before the seventh week), a normal female anatomy will develop. Therefore, no ovarian inductor is required, and female differentiation is the result of the innate, genetically determined morphology of all mammalian embryos. Thus, only the male embryo undergoes differentiation necessary for masculinization, while female development is autonomous. After twelve weeks sex reversals are impossible, since the masculine nature of the reproductive tract is fully established. Thus, it is more correct to say that the penis is an exaggerated clitoris and that the scrotum is derived from the labia. The original libido, if one wishes to assume such a concept, is clearly feminine, not masculine.

In addition, the extensive research of Masters and Johnson has illuminated many hitherto clouded and confused areas of female anatomy. The sequence and significance of the female orgasm has been clarified. Both the Kinsey Report and the investigations of Masters and Johnson definitely affirm that, from a biological point of view, clitoral and vaginal orgasms are not separate entities. It is firmly established that the clitoral glans and the lower third of the vagina are the active participants in the female orgasm and are not separate sexual entities. The tendency to reduce clitoral eroticism to a level of psychopathology or immaturity because of its supposed

masculine origin is a travesty of the facts and a mislead-
ing psychological deduction. While the lower third of
the vagina is an erotogenic zone with some sensitivity, it
does not produce orgasmic contractions and, therefore,
there is no such thing as an orgasm of the vagina.

The stimulation of the clitoral glans is what initiates
the orgasm, which then spreads to the outer third of the
vagina. It is a total body response with marked variations
in intensity and timing. Physiologically, it is a physical
release from vasocongestive and myotonic increments
developed in response to sexual stimuli.

Regardless of the anatomical position of the clitoris,
the penis rarely comes into direct contact with the clitoral
glans. However, it is continuously stimulated throughout
coition, even though it retracts during the plateau stage
of sexual excitement. The erection and engorgement of
the clitoris causes it to retract into the swollen clitoral
head, but the active thrusting of the penis and the traction on the labia minora provides stimulation and energetic friction on the glans of the clitoris. After some time,
the orgasmic contractions begin. The clitoral reaction is
the same, regardless of what is used to stimulate the
clitoris and whether it is direct or indirect. The various
positions described or advocated to increase penile contact with the clitoris are either superfluous or impossible.
However, a female superior or lateral coital position does
allow more direct contact. It is notable in this connection
that such positioning has been discredited and avoided
because of the notion that the female passive role requires
the male to always "be on top."

Orgasms in the male and the female are identical biologically, and in the man consist essentially of the contractions of the responding muscles against the erectile
chambers containing sperm and related products. In the
female the contractions produce expulsion of blood from
the erectile chambers. The lower third of the vagina is
different morphologically from the remaining two thirds,
and is capable of accommodating any size penis. It is a

fallacy to assume that the larger penis will be better able to stimulate the clitoris or to be more effective in coitus. Since the female has a slower arousal time and requires continuous stimulation for orgasm to occur, there is often the anxiety that male orgasm will come too soon to permit female orgasm. This idea has a valid biological base, and is often the cause of premature ejaculation when the anxiety of the male produces tension which results in early rather than delayed ejaculation.

The female is capable of multiple orgasm, while the male requires a refractory period before further orgasm is possible. However, there is a need for continuous stimulation until orgasm, since the sexual tension in the female can fall instantaneously if such stimulation is discontinued. This capacity for multiple orgasm and readiness to respond to sexual stimulation requires regular and consistent sexual activity in the female for her to respond most adequately. It is likely that the most common cause of frigidity and difficulty in achieving orgasm in the female is due to infrequent or insufficiently employed sexual intercourse.

In this area psychology lags behind reality since, in spite of psychological bias, the female rarely behaves in the manner these theories require of her. She is not necessarily passive or dependent, and has invaded the labor market and the political arena and challenged man in his self-appointed domains of science, the arts, and technology. This can be amply documented by statistics from the Department of Labor in the United States, as well as sources throughout the world. The traditional female jobs, such as teaching, have been heavily invaded by men, while the traditional male professions and technological tasks have been infiltrated by women. This is particularly notable in the Soviet Union, for example, where over 75 percent of the physicians are women. A far-reaching reappraisal of the entire body of existing theory regarding the female is in order. In this article I am suggesting areas of inquiry.

There is no doubt at all that some aspects of the biological role of the female inevitably and invariably influence her psychology. First, the role of childbearing, which falls exclusively upon the female, must be distinguished from child rearing, which may or may not be her lot, depending upon the culture. Second, the distribution of muscle and fat and the capacity for physical exertion must be borne in mind in appraising her character development. In addition, the availability of the male genital for visual and tactile perception, in contrast to the largely hidden female genital, must also play a role in her sexual attitudes. The conventional gender attitude, which appears very early and influences dress, appearance, play habits, and playmates, however, appears to be largely a cultural phenomenon which differs from time to time and place to place. The notion of the primacy of the male and the desirability of the penis has had little scientific support. Sherfey has presented considerable data, which led her to say, "Therefore the primacy of the embryonic female morphology forces us to reverse long held concepts on the nature of sexual differentiation." The notion that the male is embryonically the original sex is also challenged by Sherfey. She says: "It is correct to say that the penis is an exaggerated clitoris, the scrotum is derived from the labia major, the original libido is feminine,"* etc. Since gender determination occurs very early in human development and is probably fixed beyond alteration by drugs or psychology after age three, an examination of the prevailing notions of infantile sexuality and its relevance to the psychology of adult sexual behavior is necessary.

DEVELOPMENT OF INDIVIDUAL SEXUALITY

In a recent article on infantile sexuality, Chodoff has reviewed this body of theory in some detail. However, the

* Mary Jane Sherfey, *The Nature and Evolution of Female Sexuality* (New York: Random House, 1972).

presumption that infantile sexuality exists is a persist-ently held doctrine. Without becoming involved in a serious semantic examination of the current confusion between the terms sex, libido, genitality, and other non-specific terms, a clarification of the distinction between genital and sexual might be useful, particularly as it refers to the earliest years of life. I think a provocative but useful question could be asked regarding the existing notions of infantile sexuality: does it exist either in a primitive or libidinal form prior to gonadal maturity? This is a matter that need not be taken for granted and should be re-garded as an open question. Should we not distinguish between gender and sex, as well as between genitality and sexuality?* Gender differentiation in the fetus and dur-ing early infancy merely indicates male or female, without any necessary implications of sexual capacity until a later time, for it is only later that the male or female will have some knowledge and skill with regard to the genitals and their ultimate role in the sex act. This is particularly relevant in the male, since throughout life the male genital shares the dual function of a sexual procreative organ as well as an excretory organ.

While it is clearly established in most instances at birth what the gender of the infant is, we must not assume,

---

* F. A. Beach, ed., *Sex and Behavior* (New York: John Wiley, 1965). Beach, in his summary of the conference on sex and behavior held in Berkeley, Calif., commented on this issue with regard to animal behavior. He said: "Many of the elements involved in the coitus of adult mammals can occur independently long before puberty. As just noted mounting behavior is not uncommonly shown by very young males and penile erection is often possible at birth, but to identify these as 'sexual responses' is most strongly in-advisable. Throughout the individual's life, these reactions may occur in several different contexts with different outcomes. To as-sign them arbitrarily and exclusively to a single functional pattern can lead only to confusion. Defining erection in a week-old puppy as 'sexual behavior' simply because the adult male has an erection while copulating is no more logical than affirming that voiding of urine by the infant male is 'territorial behavior' because the adult urinates upon rocks and trees in connection with the establishment of territorial boundaries." He suggests that this applies equally to human sexual behavior.

therefore, that his early activities can be attributed specifically to his gender. Because a male infant is very active or very passive, we should not assume this to be a sexual factor. Only when the genital as a sexual organ is involved in an activity or influences behavior should it be considered to be part of a gender involvement. The play of infants or children cannot be considered sexual simply because the genitals are involved; otherwise, we presume a knowledge of sex which may be completely lacking, or we make the error of confusing genital with sexual, just as we sometimes fail to make a distinction between a tool and a particular activity carried on with it. The choice of playmates by children could be influenced by availability, similarity of play interest, concordance of energy output, and muscular prowess, and not necessarily by gender determination.

Many other factors come into operation, as the recent research of [John] Money, [J. G. and J. L.] Hampson, and others have suggested. One's behavior as a male or female is strongly influenced by the cultural factors of maleness and femaleness, rather than by an appreciation of the sexual significance of one's gender. This can only occur later, when we are capable of understanding the complicated requirements of sexual rather than gender behavior. Being dressed as a boy or a girl means being identified with privileges or denials regarding gender rather than sexual identity. The abundance of questions, confusion, ignorance, and curiosity about sex roles in both genders need not be the result of repression, but of ignorance. While gender interest and genital manipulation is present in both sexes, it is largely an a priori assumption that sexual knowledge exists and that such interest and play has sexual origins and derivatives. A revision of some of the early notions of female deficits in terms of penis envy and a host of other presumed sexual privileges of the male child will have great influence in clarifying our views on the psychology of the female.

The efforts to study behavior in the framework of instinct, learning, concepts of maturation, or experience have not been illuminating, since they tend to become either-or dichotomies rather than a recognition of the essential role of all elements. Research in primates as well as in man clearly indicates that the physiological mechanisms involved in coitus are functional before the individual is capable of reproduction. In addition, social experience clearly influences the capacity to perform the sex act.

The complex problem of gender role in contrast to morphology or sexual object in sex behavior has been illuminated by a large number of physiological, biochemical, and chromosomal studies in recent years. There are a large number of variables that enter into the total sexual pattern. They are: (1) sex chromatin pattern; (2) gonadal sex as indicated by morphology; (3) hormonal sex, which is correlated to secondary sex characteristics; (4) external genital morphology; (5) internal accessory reproductive structure; (6) psychological sex and rearing; and (7) psychological sex or gender role.

Psychological maleness or femaleness is not attributable to any single one of these variables, and does not appear to have an innate preformed instinctive basis. At the Gender Identity Clinic in Baltimore, it has been discovered that sex assignment and rearing often play the major factor in gender role. Thus, gender role and orientation in man appears to depend on learned experience as well as somatic variables. Hampson concludes: "Psychologic sex or gender role appears to be learned, that is to say it is differentiated through learning during the course of many experiences of growing up. In place of a theory of innate constitutional psychologic bisexuality we can substitute a concept of psycho-sexual neutrality in humans at birth."

Freud's views on the female centered around her desire to obtain the favored male organ. The hopeless striving to obtain a penis was finally abandoned at childbirth, when the woman could accept her child as a substitute for the

211

penis. Freud believed that this struggle left the female with permanent psychological scars, such as insatiable envy and feelings of inferiority, vanity, passivity, and other so-called feminine traits. In addition, he assumed that certain character traits were linked with gender: passivity with femininity, and activity with masculinity. After an elaborate anatomical, biochemical, and physiological appraisal, Sherfey states that: "It is also evidence for the concept that direct sexual aggressiveness or passivity in humans is largely culturally determined."

Freud's view was almost entirely the result of speculation and superficial observation, and the evidence used to support this hypothesis was derived from interpretations which grew from the original assumption. For example, the girl who was curious or admiring of the boy's penis, for whatever reasons and perhaps because of its urinary versatility, was presumed to be envying the genital for its symbolic and procreative capacities. With the assumption of the primacy of the genital, such curiosity would be interpreted as envy of the male because of the superior qualities of the male sexual organ. The reminiscences, fantasies, and overt manifestations of many girls who envied the boys were interpreted as envy or desire to be boys because of an a priori assumption of male genital primacy, rather than other factors such as the possibility of special privilege and status related to the cultural mores and prejudices regarding the male.

Freud's attempts to document this portion of his psychological theory were very unconvincing. The major part of the evidence regarding his views on female psychology were derived from observations of the behavior of young girls in their awareness of sex differences and data from the analyses of neurotic adults. In both instances interpretations of the data are heavily prejudiced by the libido theory, which forms the framework for such interpretations. The psychoanalytic literature on this subject is abundant and reaffirms Freud's views, since it begins with the same premise. In more recent years this notion has not only been shaken by biological studies, but by psychoanalytic data as well. The female is hardly a poorly equipped specimen of manhood, biologically inferior to the male, permanently envious, and perpetually dissatisfied with having been given the less desirable biological role. In many ways the female is better equipped biologically to fulfill her role than the male is. She has a more labile nervous system and a more responsive autonomic system. These physiological findings are undoubtedly related to the need to handle the regularly recurring crises of menstruation, childbirth, and the physiological trials of childbearing. In addition, the notion of a sex-linked character structure has been rudely shaken by recent investigations of the role of the female sexual apparatus. These studies indicate that the woman, far from being passive in the sex act, is an extremely active participant to the extent that vaginal contractions are more responsible than the sperm's own motile powers for sperm reaching the ovum. In almost every phase of Freud's views on the psychology of the female there has been a multitude of objections, revisions, and clarifications.

The attempt to link character and gender overlooked the multicausal bases for character and the crucial significance of the role of the individual in a particular time and place. Character structure is the result of a multiple set of interactions, of which biology is only one factor, along with the cultural determinants of a social, political, economic, and philosophical nature. This is the view of the post-Freudian ego psychologists and cultural psychoanalysts who see character structure as the result of the cultural pressures on the libidinal development. This altered view of character development is particularly significant in elucidating the psychology of the female. The attitudes, characterological traits, and behavioral characteristics of the female may not be due exclusively to her given genital apparatus, but rather to a multitude of demands, restraints, expectations, and controls which the particular culture places on her. The biological and physiological differences, nevertheless, are significant. The marked difference in the size and bulk of the voluntary muscles would obviously produce some divergent attitudes regarding the male and female when the culture requires strength and endurance. While this was the paramount need in primitive cultures, the advent of mechanical contraptions and a technology capable of replacing muscular power in recent years has obviated this advantage. The major differences that revolve about the roles of the male and female in the procreative and child-rearing processes may produce distinctive characterological elements in each sex.

In earlier years the female was entirely divorced from political, economic, and sociological problems. The prevailing cultures limited her significance to the kitchen and bedchamber. Her role was determined by the combination of being a mother completely dependent on the male, both economically and physically. Freud held that the dependency was biologically ordained due to the absence of the penis, and thus maintained that the submissiveness and masochistic attitudes of the female were outgrowths of her gender. However, as greater opportunities opened up for women and as they became less economically dependent on men, it was possible to see that the characteristics Freud assumed to be ubiquitous could be culturally determined. The masochistic tendencies which are frequently evident in the behavior of the female can be completely and sufficiently understood on cultural grounds. Being limited in her social and political influence, she had no other recourse but to swallow her needs, desires, and disappointments. However, the gender enlightenment has produced growing evidence of woman as an outspoken and capable defender of her rights. It is no longer the picture of the masochist—the silent, long-suffering person—but of the participant who expects an equal share of the returns and makes it abundantly clear.

In spite of the changes in her cultural status, childbearing and child-rearing functions still influence a significant portion of the female personality structure. As child-rearing practices change either through the use of crèches, early boarding schools, or day-care centers, major changes in this aspect of her role as mother may change too. Since there is no possibility in the foreseeable future that the childbearing role of the woman will be supplanted by artificial conception and fetal development apparatus, it can be concluded that this will remain a permanent feature in the psychology of the female.

It is now necessary to recognize that what was considered to be the biological consequence of the absence of the male genital system may be more closely related to the cultural attitudes toward the female. The notion of the weak, helpless, and submissive female, which is not supported by any biological or psychological evidence, may also need to be abandoned, even though the woman as well as the man has come to accept this notion and actively to oppose its abolition. This observation requires a chapter in itself, and has great relevance to the notion of identifying with the aggressor. It is analogous to the prisoner, slave, or member of a minority group who comes to accept the derogatory view of his own status in order to achieve maximum security and advantage. As his status slowly changes, he reluctantly examines the realities of the situation. Thus, there is always a time lag in the recognition of one's power and privilege after a long period of subjugation.

The tendency to attribute passivity to the female because the male genital had to penetrate the vaginal canal through an act of positive insertion (activity) describes only one element in a much more elaborate sexual performance. It could hardly be the prime determinant of the man's character structure, as Freud has suggested. The remaining elements of the biology of procreation, such as conception, fetal management, delivery, and child rearing would also play a significant role; in these areas the female could hardly be described as passive.

Since she is the carrier of the young, some provision must be made for the prolonged nurture of the fetus in a warm, protected environment. This is achieved by an internal uterus which can only be reached by a long projective organ which can penetrate deep to deposit the necessary sperm. This is an adaptive device, not a characterological description, since in many animal species, e.g., the cat family, the female is the active aggressive partner, even though she must still be penetrated by an erectile penis. The female genital apparatus is extremely active in the sex act and is not merely a passive receptor of sperm.

Childbearing and the endocrine cycle between pregnancies demand great physiological flexibility and adaptability. The physiological changes that accompany menstruation and conception necessitate, at times, a more sedentary, less generally active existence, although the woman has traditionally carried out practically every function of which a man is capable. Yet, at certain times her procreative role necessitates some restriction of her motion in order to deliver her offspring. The care of the young further limits her mobility. To this extent she is different from the male. Childbearing and motherhood are the biological roles restricted to the female, and it is the special demands of these roles that determines the differences in the sexes, not the presence or absence of particular genital organs or conventional ideas of sexual activity.

A further complication in the comprehension of the psychology of the female was produced by the assumption, wholly unsupported by biological or physiological data, that the female was capable of two types of orgasm—clitoral and vaginal. This assumption was the outgrowth of Freud's attempt to fit the female sexual development into the male model. The distinction between vaginal and clitoral orgasm and the assumption that the vaginal orgasm represented more mature sexual development inevitably made it a more desirable goal and belittled the clitoral orgasm. There has been no valid evidence presented thus far to indicate that such a distinction exists. There are quantitative and qualitative differences in the female's response to the sex act, but there is no reason to assume that this is due to a clitoral rather than a vaginal orgasm. All the available anatomical data indicate that the vagina is devoid of nerve endings and incapable of producing the effect that is described as an orgasm. The clitoris, on the other hand, is generously endowed with a multitude of nerve endings and is capable of tumescence, detumescence, and spasmodic contractions analogous to those of the male genital. There is every reason to believe that the female orgasm is an outcome of clitoral stimulation, and that it consists of a series of spasmodic contractions in the tumescent perineal area. This is also analogous to orgasm in the male, except that in the male there is an ejaculation of seminal fluid.

One of the unfortunate consequences of the clitoral-vaginal orgasm notion is that it tends to encourage discontent in the female, who experiences orgasm when there is clitoral stimulation either by the finger or the penis before or during sexual intercourse. She assumes that her orgasm is inferior and that she is sexually immature, even though it may have been pleasurable. She has rightly insisted on having a vaginal orgasm, and either blames herself or her husband for her failure to experience it. Since there appears to be no validation for this whole notion, there is no reason to assume that an orgasm which is achieved by means of clitoral stimulation with either finger or penis is inferior or imperfect, or that it can be improved by psychoanalytic therapy.

Recent studies of female sexual behavior also fail to support this notion of a clitoral and vaginal orgasm. Sherfey also comments on this matter after an extensive examination of the factors. She says: "It is a physical impossibility to separate the clitoral from the vaginal orgasm as demanded by psychoanalytic theory." Masters and Johnson agree completely with this formulation.

Orgasm, both in the male and the female, appears to be the result of the stimulation of the highly sensitized clitoris in the female and the glans penis in the male. While some means of stimulating these organs may be preferable, nevertheless orgasm results from such stimulation. The presence of the penis in the vagina is a convenient arrangement for the mutual stimulation of both clitoris and penis. Since there is a growing conviction that sex activity is a process to be enjoyed and practiced in whatever manner is conducive to the greatest mutual enjoyment provided no physiological or psychological damage results to either partner, the manner of stimulating both the glans penis and clitoris, whether by means of the mouth, finger, or vaginal insertion, should not be viewed in terms of either normality or maturity. While there is a preferred posture to ensure procreation and mutual orgasm, a more enlightened attitude toward sex should avoid assigning priorities to particular methods of achieving sexual satisfaction. While the laws regarding sex behavior in many parts of the world still cling to the categories "normal" or "deviant," [enlightened] psychological theory has avoided labeling the variations of sex behavior between male and female as deviant so long as they are not physiologically or psychologically injurious to either partner. This is particularly applicable to the variations as they involve the female in terms of activity or passivity in the sex act. There is not an aggressive partner, the male, or a passive partner, the female, in sexual intercourse. Each partner must be passive *and* aggressive, and must participate mutually and cooperatively in a venture that calls for both activity and passivity. The unfortunate persistence of labels attributable to one sex as opposed to the other has led to untold misery in the form of feeling guilty, inferior, inadequate, or even homosexual when one's inclinations are somewhat different from the prevailing notions or prejudices of the role of one sex as opposed to the other. The female has been the major victim in this hangover from Victorian morality and scientific infantilism. Since the mantle of being passive or submissive falls upon her, under this notion she is required to wait upon the desires and demands of the male and be subject to his particular program for sexual activity. To encourage or direct this activity is to step outside the female role. To suggest or recommend some measures that might enhance her enjoyment would be aggressive or too masculine. Consequently, she must must be patient and long-suffering, depending upon the male's good will and competence for her enjoyment. When she has refused to function in these prescribed ways, there still remain some misguided psychologists and psychoanalytic theorists who insist upon calling it penis envy, masculine protest, latent homosexuality, or a refusal to accept her proper biological role. Such labels are remnants of outmoded conceptions of female psychology, and no longer serve to illuminate the conflicts and difficulties in her personal relationships.

The understanding of the psychology of the female has only just begun. We have yet to see the psychological effect of the marked technological changes which have reduced the need for the gross musculature of the male and favor the smaller, more discriminating musculature that characterizes the female. These machines will certainly alter the role and status of the female. As the demand for the equality of opportunity, as well as education and employment, is met, the role of the female may radically enhance her status and view of herself beyond the boundaries of motherhood. Profound changes can be expected in her psychology as she moves out of the confines of a minority into an equal status with the male, economically as well as sociologically.

<h3 style="text-align:center">CONCLUSION</h3>

While the machine that can conceive and incubate a child is a playful science-fiction fantasy, it is most likely that childbearing will remain part of the female role even while child-rearing practices change. In addition, widespread utilization of contraceptive measures for the limitation of family size will also fundamentally alter the woman's role. A psychology that relates character to social and cultural forces will have an easier time understanding the effect of these changes on the female. Only when it is recognized that the psychology of the female, like that of the male, is determined by her inherent biological potentiality in a changing cultural matrix, will it be possible to comprehend fully the changes that will occur in the female personality structure over the succeeding centuries. It is obvious that the psychology of the female is closely linked to that of the male; however, the relationship is not determined by the presence or absence of a penis, but by the fact that male and female paths must collide, integrate, and even overlap in the fulfillment of their separate biological roles. One sex is neither superior nor inferior to another: they are each different to the extent that they serve different biological roles. Otherwise they are alike; both want and need security, status, prestige, and acceptance; and both are capable of envy, greed, hostility, and masochism to the extent that their needs are frustrated. However, one will forever bear children while the other will supply the seed to fulfill his part in the procreative process. In this they will differ until parthenogenesis overtakes the human organism.

JUDD MARMOR

Juᴅᴅ Mᴀʀᴍᴏʀ is a prominent contributor to many areas
of psychiatry and psychoanalysis. He is currently vice-
president of the national American Psychiatric Association, Franz Alexander Professor of Psychiatry at the
University of Southern California School of Medicine,
and a training analyst at the Southern California Psychoanalytic Institute.

Dr. Marmor has generated ideas on many topics ranging from a new conception of "free association" to an
evaluation of the relationship between the individual and
contemporary society. Marmor is additionally a recognized authority on sexuality and homosexuality.

Changing Patterns of Femininity

PSYCHOANALYTIC IMPLICATIONS

THERE IS PROBABLY no area in Freud's writings more fraught with theoretical and clinical contradictions than his pronouncements concerning feminine psychophysiology. In what follows, I shall examine these pronouncements in the light of certain developments and changes in the behavioral patterns of twentieth-century women, with some consideration to the impact of these changes on the institution of Western marriage.

The exact nature of the relationship of primitive man and woman is shrouded in conjecture (the popular fantasy pictures a masterful caveman dragging his willing and passively inert mate along the ground by her hair). We know, however, that since recorded history there has been no fixed pattern to this relationship. There is evidence to suggest that in most primitive nomadic communal societies, family descent was reckoned through the mothers (probably for the obvious reason that maternity, in contrast to paternity, could not be doubted), and clans were consequently organized along matrilineal lines. With the evolution of agriculture, and the gradual development of private property, the transfer of property from father to son became a paramount socioeconomic factor, and families began to be organized along patrilineal lines. The risk of false paternity was protected against by the development of the institution of wifely chastity, and gradually woman began to occupy a more and more subordinate role as a sexual chattel of man.

However, there has not been a straight line of social evolutionary development in the relationship between the sexes. The social status of woman has changed at various times both within the same society and in different societies. Thus, in ancient Greece up to the reign of Cecrops, families were matrilineal; women enjoyed considerable status and voted with men in the popular assembly. Yet subsequently, in the Platonic era, the position of the woman in the family became a degraded and depreciated one, and she was strictly confined to the home, without political or economic rights. There were important social and economic factors involved in these shifting vicissitudes, but they are beyond the purview of this chapter.

THE EMANCIPATION OF MODERN WOMAN

What concerns us more directly here is that in American and European history, up to the end of the eighteenth century, woman's position, for the most part, was distinctly subordinate to that of man. She was totally dependent upon him economically, had no vote and relatively few legal rights, and was denied access to formal education. Early in the nineteenth century, however, in the wake of the egalitarian spirit set into motion by the American and French revolutions and of the sociological changes engendered by the industrial revolution, women in England and America began, for the first time in modern history, to assert their prerogatives in relationship to men. Nevertheless, it was almost a hundred years before they obtained the right to vote and began to move toward fuller equality before the law. Even now, in the second half of the twentieth century, there are many states of the union in which such equivalence does not exist; and the constitutional amendment on equal rights for men and women has repeatedly failed to pass Congress. Despite this, the decades since 1920 have seen remarkable changes in the status of women throughout the world. They are able to vote in most countries where voting franchises exist, to enter many professions previously reserved for men, and to move out of the confines of the home into the broader arena of social, cultural, and political life.

However, even within our lifetime there has been a discernible ebb and flow to this pattern. The "feminine revolt" that was so manifest in the twenties through the forties seems to have given way to the "feminine mystique" of the fifties. Where after World War I women were struggling to get out of the home, the current trend seems to be back to the home. A smaller percentage of college graduates today are women than were thirty years ago, and American women constitute a smaller proportion of the professional world today than they did then. (By contrast, women in some Eastern European countries have more than doubled their representation in professional occupations.)

The reasons for this apparent recession in the revolutionary upsurge of women in America are complex. Some classical Freudians would argue that the entire feminine revolution was essentially a neurotic outbreak of penis envy and that what we are now witnessing is a healthy return to "normal" patterns of femininity. Such a statement, however, merely attaches value-laden labels to the phenomenon without really explaining it. Indeed, there are those who claim that the post-World War II popularity of Freudian theory in America has been in itself a potent factor in "pushing" American women back toward a more subordinate and passive role. While this view may have some validity, it seems more likely that certain broad socioeconomic factors have been involved, notably the gradual increase of automation and the pressure from men to push women out of the shrinking labor market except in those areas traditionally reserved for them (domestic work, secretarial and teaching positions, retail selling, and so forth). [Betty] Friedan suggests that an additional factor may have been the increased awareness of American business and merchandising executives that "women will buy more things if they are kept in the under-used, nameless-yearning, energy-to-get-rid-of state of being housewives."

Nonetheless, the increased emancipation of women that began in the twenties has left an important imprint on the relationship between the sexes that deserves our further consideration.

CHANGING MALE-FEMALE RELATIONSHIPS

What are some of the changes that have taken place?* By and large there has been a considerable relaxation of the social and sexual restrictions placed upon female children born after World War I. Little girls are now allowed to play more vigorously and competitively, with resultant greater muscular strength and athletic capability. During the preadolescent and adolescent years, contacts between the sexes have become freer, and adolescent as well as preadolescent petting occurs with much greater frequency than in previous decades. This increased freedom, both socially and sexually, has led to a higher degree of sophistication and self-confidence in young girls. This, combined with the earlier physiological maturation curves of most girls, tends to give them a considerable degree of relative dominance and mastery over boys of similar age levels, particularly during the adolescent years. Post-World War I mores have also accorded women greater freedom in taking the initiative in reaching out to men both socially and sexually, and as a result much feminine assertiveness that would have been dampened or totally inhibited by the convention of earlier eras has been enabled to flourish. Many other time-hallowed conventions have also changed. For example,

---

* The comments that follow refer to broad trends and are not intended as universal generalizations; obviously there are many individuals who do not fit into these patterns. The existence of these trends, however, regardless of their extent, is sufficient to document the points I shall be making.

it is no longer considered "unfeminine" for women to wear slacks, wear short hair, or smoke cigarettes. Indeed, we are beginning to see evidences that before too long women will also be smoking cigars and pipes without loss of feminine status.

These changing conventions have been reflected in current patterns of marital relationships also. Women have tended to become more dominant in the home, in an interpersonal sense. Discipline, once the exclusive domain of the father, has been increasingly delegated to the mother. Indeed, in many homes it is now father rather than mother to whom the children turn for redress from discipline or as the "soft touch." Similarly, women are playing a more important role in family decision making. The popular joke that wives make all the minor decisions (those concerning the family), while husbands make all the major ones (those concerning international relations), is a reflection of this shift in family dominance.

Another important indication of this shift in marital equilibrium has been the increasing emphasis upon female orgasm. In the Victorian era, "it was considered unfeminine for a woman to acknowledge or display sexual feelings of any kind, even in the conjugal relationship." Now a significant proportion of women express their sexual desires quite openly and engage in the sexual act not as passive recipients but as active participants, indeed often taking the initiative in arousing the man. Sexual intercourse now is expected to culminate in orgasm for the woman no less than for the man, and failure to achieve orgasm is generally as disappointing to the woman as it would be to the man.

The changing status of women has had noteworthy reverberations outside the home also. The percentage of women in the American labor force (excluding the actual war years) has slowly but steadily increased in the past forty years. According to Bureau of Labor statistics for 1962, 24 million, or just over one-third of all working people for that year, were women.

Thirty-six percent of all women were working women. Of these 24 million working women, moreover, less than 25 percent were single, and slightly over 20 percent were widowed, divorced, or separated. The remaining 56 percent, or 13.5 million working women, were married and living with their husbands. These figures indicate that American women are assuming an increasingly important economic role in the family, not merely as the primary spenders of the family income, but also as wage earners. An additional factor in this growing economic importance is the fact that many women outlive their husbands and end up controlling their estates.

Because it is generally easier for Negro women to obtain work than it is for their husbands, the Negro woman in America is often the *only* wage earner in the family, and the Negro family therefore tends to be matriarchal, with the father occupying a depreciated status position. Although these effects are easily recognized in the Negro family, the corresponding, more subtle consequences in the white American family as a result of the economic factors described above are less easily recognizable but no less real.

Women who are not in the labor force also occupy a different psychological position than do men. The man who does not work in our society is apt to be left with a loss of identity and severe impairment of his morale; he generally becomes either depressed or apathetic, or aggressively antisocial.* The nonworking wife, however, still retains a meaningful identity as a wife and mother. She is thus able to use her leisure time more constructively. Increasing numbers of middle-class wives attend adult-education classes, read books, and participate in various artistic and creative activities. The result is that

* This fact may change in coming decades as increasing automation creates larger numbers of unemployed men. The traditional puritan ethos associating personal identity with work identity may in time have to give way to a new ethos in which identities are based on other factors, such as specific cultural interests, or skills, and so forth.

while many working husbands become progressively nar-
rower in their areas of interest and knowledge, their
wives become the chief purveyors of cultural and aesthetic
interests in and outside the home. These factors tend
also to increase the relative importance of the mother in
the family vis-à-vis the father, and their effects upon the
identifications formed by children in the family can be of
great significance. It is possible, for example, that they
play a part in the increasing incidence of homosexuality
in modern society; a common thread in the histories of
many homosexuals is the identification with the "more
cultured and aesthetically oriented mother."

The progressive technological development of society
in the coming decades can be expected to have continuing important effects on the relations between the sexes.
Not only does the increase in automation mean that
women will become more and more able to do "men's
jobs," but also the sharp decline in total jobs available
is bound to mean an enormous increment in leisure time
for both sexes, with profound changes in family relationships.

PSYCHOANALYTIC IMPLICATIONS

The classical psychoanalytic position on women as
outlined by Freud is too well known to require detailing
here.

Let us now consider these formulations in the light of
contemporary knowledge.

Anatomy Is Fate

That the anatomical differences between the sexes must
inevitably be reflected in some personality differences, regardless of variations in cultural patterns, would seem to
be almost axiomatic. Differences in body image, in the experience of menstruation at puberty, in the subsequent
monthly cyclical variations of endocrine function, and in
the experiences of sexual intercourse, pregnancy, child-

birth, and menopause are all aspects of bodily sensation and function that are uniquely different for the woman as compared to the man; and in the biological-environmental interaction that leads to personality formation, these *must* result in significant personality variances between the sexes. To deny this, and to argue, as some strongly oriented feminists have done, that personality differences between the sexes have *nothing* to do with biological differences but are *totally* a reflection of cultural factors is to miss the mark no less than do those who have overemphasized the importance of the biological factor.* The fact is that only by taking into consideration *both* the biological differences between the sexes *and* the variations in cultural reactions to these differences—that is, the *field situation*—can the personality similarities and dissimilarities between men and women, at any given time and place, be fully understood.

Even as sophisticated an observer as Erik Erikson tends to fall into the error of trying to derive some of woman's psychological characteristics *solely* from her anatomical structure. In his recent, beautifully written "Inner and Outer Space: Reflections on Womanhood," he advances the thesis that women are prone to be more concerned with "inner-space" as compared to men's greater preoccupation with "outer-space," and that this is somehow due to "the existence of a *productive inner-bodily space* safely set in the center of female form and carriage." He presents as evidence for this conclusion the fact that in a study of 150 boys and 150 girls, aged ten to twelve, in which they were asked to construct a "scene" with toys on a table, two-thirds of the girls constructed *peaceful interior* scenes, while two-thirds of the boys constructed *aggressive exterior* scenes, or else structures with protruding walls. One need not question the accuracy of Erikson's observations to raise serious doubts concerning

* The reaction of feminists to the latter point of view, however, is understandable since the emphasis on innate differences has almost always been used to prove man's "inherent superiority."

his conclusions that these differences derive somehow only from the anatomical differences between the sexes. What about the enormous multitude of acculturation factors—the toys, the games, the adult expectations, and so forth—that have played a part in shaping the fantasies, the perceptions, and the activities of these ten- to twelve-year-old children? Erikson himself notes that in almost one-third of the subjects the girls constructed "male" configurations and the boys constructed "female" configurations. Obviously these were the results of experiential, not anatomical, variations. The point, simply, is that to attempt to derive such differences solely from anatomical or physiological considerations inevitably results in oversimplifications. One must always take into consideration the interaction between these factors and the experiences they encounter in the environment—in time, place, family, and culture.

Penis Envy

It is, for example, a massive oversimplification to assume, as Freud did, that the lack of a penis must inevitably be considered as a defect by the female child, in all times and cultures. Clara Thompson and others have quite correctly pointed out that the phenomenon of penis envy that Freud observed and described in his women patients was not a universal feminine occurrence but was related to the "culturally under-privileged" position that these women occupied. That this is so is confirmed by what has been happening to this phenomenon as the position of Western women has changed in the past four decades. Not only is it manifesting itself with much lesser intensity than it used to, but more and more psychoanalysts report that they do not even always find evidences of it. Meanwhile, another manifestation has begun to make its appearance with increasing frequency, a phenomenon in men which has been variously described as breast envy, womb envy, and woman envy, and which is derived from men's supposed jealousy of women's ability to bear and suckle children. In the past, when such a reaction was encountered in men, it was assumed to be deeply neurotic,* but now it is beginning to be described as a more "universal" phenomenon. But how is it possible that a clinical genius like Freud would have failed to recognize such a common aspect of male psychology? The answer, of course, is that it was *not* a frequent occurrence in his time, and has become so only as a consequence of the shifting equilibrium between the sexes. The fact is that womb envy, like penis envy, can only be understood by taking into consideration the total field situation in which it appears. The presence or absence of a penis may be regarded by the developing child as an asset *or* a deficit depending on the nature of the cues that he or she is getting from the environment. When a society places greater value on the birth of a son than on that of a daughter, children in the family become aware of this in a myriad subtle ways; the same is true when little boys are accorded greater freedom of movement and play, and when fathers are accorded greater respect and deference than mothers. In such a society little girls, and later women, will inevitably manifest many indications of penis envy, while indications of woman envy in men will be relatively rare. On the other hand, when these conditions no longer hold true, or become reversed (as has begun to happen in Western society in recent decades), *then we can expect to find that unconscious manifestations of penis envy will begin to diminish, and those of woman envy will begin to increase.*

A male patient of mine—not a homosexual—grew up as the only boy and youngest child in a family of three children. The father was a relatively weak and incompetent person in contrast to the mother, who was a warm, competent, and dominant individual. The two older sisters were also extremely effective and assertive children. Little wonder that my patient recalled as a child strongly

* As might have been expected in an androcentric culture, however, women's envy of men was always assumed to be normal and "natural"!

wishing he were a girl, and fantasying that the front of his body was smooth and penisless just like his sisters'! *For his milieu,* his envy reaction was no less "normal" than the penis envy of the little girl who grows up in a male-centered environment.

In this connection, Helene Deutsch's dismissal of the clitoris as "an inferior organ" in terms of its capability to provide libidinal gratification is a remarkable example of culturally influenced amblyopia, coming as it does from a woman. The actual fact, as Dickinson has pointed out, is that although "the female organ is minute compared with the male organ . . . the size of its nerves . . . and nerve endings . . . compare strikingly with the same provision for the male. Indeed . . . the glans of the clitoris is demonstrably richer in nerves than the male glans, for the two stems of the dorsalis clitoridis are relatively three to four times as large as the equivalent nerves of the penis. . . ."* Little wonder that this "inferior organ" enables the orgastically potent female often to have multiple orgasms to every single orgasm of the male!

More recently, in the most definitive article to date on female sexuality in the psychoanalytic literature, Sherfey, leaning heavily on the unprecedented and significant research findings of Masters and Johnson, puts the finishing touch to the myth of clitoral inferiority.† Not only is clitoral stimulation capable of producing multiple orgasms to an extent unknown in men (as many as twenty to fifty consecutive orgasms have been recorded within the span of an hour!), but also the average orgastic re-

---

* R. L. Dickinson, *Human Sexual Anatomy* (2nd ed.; Baltimore: Williams & Wilkins, 1949).

† See the excerpt from *The Nature and Evolution of Female Sexuality* by Mary Jane Sherfey on pp. 136–53 of this volume. The researches of Masters and Johnson explode with finality the fiction of the existence of a vaginal orgasm distinct from clitoral orgasm. Their studies reveal beyond a doubt that the nature of orgasm in the female is the same regardless of the stimulus that produces it, and consists of rhythmic contractions of extravaginal musculature against the greatly distended circumvaginal venous plexi and vestibular bulbs surrounding the lower third of the vagina.

sponse in women is generally more prolonged than that of men and just as intense in terms of their muscular capacities.

Masochism and Passivity

The assumption that normal men are naturally dominant and aggressive, while normal women are naturally submissive and masochistic, is another myth that the changing patterns of relationship between the sexes has begun to dispel. Even the biological evidence has never justified these conclusions. It is well known that among lower animals the female of the species can be fully as vicious and aggressive as the male, while dominance per se, as biologists have long recognized, is not a simple sex-linked trait but depends on a number of variables, including relative size and strength, motivation, previous experiences, social setting, and so forth.*

A variant of this, the effort to justify this myth on the basis of the differences in roles in sexual intercourse, similarly fails to stand up under careful analysis. The common argument advanced here is that in the sexual act it is the male who must be the penetrator, while the woman is merely the recipient, and that the aggressivity of the male and the passivity of the female naturally follow from this. The error here lies in confusing a *behavioral* phenomenon with a *motivational* one. A male can be a passive and submissive penetrator, while a female can be an aggressive and dominant recipient, in the sexual act. Indeed, recent researches indicate that the female genital apparatus during orgasm is extremely active. Receptivity and passivity are not synonymous. It is a striking commentary on the power of a cultural prejudice that both male and female classical Freudians have always assumed

* According to Harlow (personal communication, 1965), in primates, *all other things being equal,* males tend to be dominant to females. If the female is larger and heavier, however, she may be dominant. In human beings, the significant variables in dominance behavior are much more complex and include social and psychological parameters as well as physical ones.

233

that the vagina, as a hollow organ, *had* to be a passive receptacle, although they came to no such conclusions about either the mouth or the anus. "Oral" and "anal" aggression were readily recognized, but the same theoreticians, caught in the meshes of an unconscious common prejudice, were unable to see that, under certain conditions, the vagina too could be an aggressively seeking, grasping, holding, or expulsive organ. The analogy between the mouth and the vagina has, of course, been recognized unconsciously by many males in the symbolism of the "dentate vagina," but most psychoanalysts have tended merely to dismiss this as a neurotic construction, without recognizing the important kernel of truth that it contains.

An additional refutation of the myth of "normal feminine masochism" is that women who are passive and submissive in relation to men are *less* apt to be orgastically potent than those who are more assertive, self-confident, and dominant.

It may be argued by some that one cannot ignore the impact of fantasy on character formation and that the sexual fantasies of men and women are inevitably different: the male adolescent's fantasies deal with penetration; the female's with presumably anxious fears of being penetrated, and deflorated. The experience of periodic menstruation with its bleeding also is supposed to contribute in some way to an inevitable masochistic inclination in women as compared to men. Perhaps. But here too I must caution that the psychological impact of what appear to be simple biological events in men cannot ever be divorced from their sociocultural context. Fantasies of being penetrated *may or may not* be associated with anxiety or masochistic implications. The little girl, relatively early in her life, under conflict-free circumstances, experiences the insertion of objects (or her finger) into her vagina as a pleasurable, not a painful experience. It is man, not woman, who assumes that to experience such penetration is painful and therefore masochistic. The fact that so many women in our culture are indeed apprehensive about their first sexual experience is not a biological inevitability but the result of a puritanical culture which in its effort to maintain a completely artificial sexual morality fills little children, and particularly little girls, with fears of sex as something dirty, sinful, and even dangerous. Even the bleeding of menstruation need not necessarily be anxiety provoking. I have known a number of adolescent girls—and I am sure there are many—who welcomed their first menstrual period with tremendous elation and excitement and could not wait to tell their parents and friends that at last they had achieved the visible evidence of maturity. The fantasies and self-images of men and women are indeed different—and inevitably so, for both biological and cultural reasons—but these differences do not necessarily lead to sex-linked patterns of masochism or sadism.

Faulty Superego Development

Nowhere does the cultural bias inherent in Freud's views about the nature of women become more apparent than in his bland assumption that women have less adequate superegos than men. (One is reminded of Professor Higgins's plaintive cry in *My Fair Lady*: "Why can't women be like men?") Certainly no objective mid-twentieth-century American behavioral scientist would seriously argue any longer that women inherently have a lesser sense of justice, a greater disposition to envy, weaker social interests, or a lesser capacity for sublimation than men. The record of women in England and America in the past four decades on behalf of social justice and human brotherhood compares more than favorably with that of men.

It is important to note, however, that Freud's views on women were not merely an outgrowth of his position as a nineteenth-century Middle European male; they flowed quite logically from his theory about superego development. If they were in error, as they obviously were, his theory of superego development must also be fallacious. It simply cannot be that the development of the superego results only from the resolution of the Oedipus complex, as classical psychoanalytic theory has long held. This is not the place to enter into a detailed dissertation on how the personality phenomenon that Freud designated as superego comes into being, but suffice it to say that it is obviously an acculturation phenomenon that develops from the child's gradual incorporation of the dos and don'ts from its environment—beginning from the time the child is first able to comprehend the significance of such interdictions. The impact of this acculturation process is felt by girls as fully and as early as it is by boys. Indeed, the evidence is that since, culturally, little girls are expected to be better behaved than little boys, the pressure of this process is *greater* upon girls than upon boys. As a result, as might be anticipated, females in our culture, at least in their early years, are apt to show evidence of *better* superego development than do males—the very reverse of Freud's theoretical assumption.

THE PROBLEM OF GENDER ROLE

Actually, much of what we have been talking about in this essay revolves around the problem of what modern social psychologists would call "gender role"—that is, what is considered "masculine" or "feminine" behavior. The fact is that gender-role patterns have varied widely in different times and in different cultures. As Opler has put it:

A Navajo Indian may be a he-man, a gambler, and a philanderer while dressing in bright blouses adorned with jeweled belts, necklaces, and bracelets. French courtiers in the retinues of effete monarchs were equally philanderers, though rouged, powdered, and bedecked with fine lace. The Andaman Islanders like to have the man sit on his wife's lap in fond greetings, and friends and relatives, of the same or opposite sex, greet one another in the same manner after absences, crying in the affected manner of the mid-Victorian woman. Like the

Ute, they value premarital sexual experimentation and sexual prowess and technique in any later life period. Obviously, the style of social and sexual behavior is something of an amalgam and is culturally influenced.*

Gender role and gender identity, although generally related to the biological sex of a child, actually are not shaped by biological factors but by cultural ones. Once the child's biological ascription is settled, a myriad of culturally defined cues begin to be presented to the developing infant which are designed to shape its gender identity to its assigned sex. Little girls are handled more gently than little boys, are given different toys to play with,† are expected to be quieter and cleaner, are spoken to in different tones, and are addressed in different terms. The little girl who wheedles is spoken of fondly as a "charmer" and a "coquette"; the little boy is told to stop being a baby and to act like a man. The little girl's clothes and hairdos are noticed, complimented, and fussed over. Not so the little boy's; he is more apt to be praised for his agility and courage. The girl is expected to help with "inside" chores (cleaning up, doing dishes); the boy, with "outside" ones (shoveling snow, mowing the lawn). So powerful are these acculturation processes that, as the Hampsons have demonstrated, in certain cases of pseudo hermaphroditism in which the child's biological sex is mistaken for that of the opposite sex the incorrect gender identity becomes so powerfully established by the age of two or three that it becomes psychologically destructive to the child to try to change it.

What is important to our present thesis, however, is not that this acculturation occurs, but that, as we have seen, its *content* can and does change. What we have been observing in recent decades is a gradual change in certain

* M. Opler, "Anthropological and Cross-cultural Aspects of Homosexuality," in *Sexual Inversion*, edited by Judd Marmor (New York: Basic Books, 1968), p. 116.
† The assumption that all girls "naturally" prefer dolls to boys' toys is not borne out by objective studies. See Mirra Komarovsky, *Women in the Modern World* (Boston: Little, Brown, 1953).

female gender-role patterns that have previously been traditional in Western culture.

The implications of these changing patterns extend beyond psychoanalytic theory to psychoanalytic therapy. Erich Fromm once observed that a psychoanalyst's value system would profoundly affect how he would treat a female patient who presented the problem of Nora in Ibsen's *Doll House*. If he held to classical psychoanalytical views concerning femininity, he would focus his interpretations upon her penis envy and her rejection of the "normal" feminine goals of wifehood and motherhood. On the other hand, if he were a feminist, he would, instead, focus upon her "healthy" rebellion against her husband's infantilization of her and would encourage her move out of the home as a laudable effort at self-realization. Still another alternative to these two extremes exists, however. One need not assume that motherhood and a fulfilling life in the outside world are incompatible, any more than fatherhood and such a life. In contrast to men, however, who are *expected* to combine these two aspects of life, women have alternatives now; they may or may not choose to combine them, and the choice is theirs. The task of the analyst is to help them make this choice, freely, without guilt, and in relationship to the realities of their specific life situations.

RUTH MOULTON

A LEADING ANALYST and teacher, Ruth Moulton is assistant
clinical professor of psychiatry at Columbia University
and a member of the faculty of the William Alanson White
Institute, the New York school of psychoanalysis based
on the teachings of Harry Stack Sullivan. She is probably
the only psychoanalyst who has presented a modern review of the concept of penis envy that encompasses the
ideas of both its supporters and critics. In so doing, she
has proceeded to evaluate these formulations against
present clinical and physiological knowledge, with material also drawn from her own practice. Because the latter will be of greater general interest, much of her more
detailed and scholarly review has been omitted here.

Dr. Moulton uses many biological terms in her own
formulations, but her use of them does not involve a re-
ductionist attempt to limit women to their biology. On
the contrary, her paper illustrates how an enlarged and
perceptive understanding of women can lead to a better
form of therapy.

A revised version of this paper will be incorporated into
a forthcoming book by Dr. Moulton from Quadrangle
Books.

A Survey and Reevaluation of the Concept of Penis Envy

MANY AUTHORS have commented on the inaccuracies that necessarily accompany a phallocentric view of women. It has become increasingly clear that the male sex cannot be used as a basic standard to understand the female; each sex has innate characteristics of its own which must be evaluated in their own terms. Recent developments in embryology, physiology, endocrinology, and child development make a reevaluation of psychological sexual differences possible.

Freud himself was not satisfied with his formulations about the psychology of women. In his later years, he turned to the women in his audience and suggested that further clarification might have to come from them, since they themselves were the riddle. Contributions from women analysts have differed widely and were often diametrically opposed. Marie Bonaparte seemed eager to agree that women had no libido of their own, and referred to the female's "belated and debilitated" orgasm as giving her no choice but to surrender to the superior power of the opposite sex and the masochistic enjoyment of pain. She labeled Karen Horney a feminist and apologist for the vagina when the latter first suggested that there were primary satisfactions in being a woman and doubted whether penis envy could so completely overshadow the unique qualities of the growing girl. On the other hand, even a close male follower of Freud, Ernest Jones, suggested very early in the controversy that there was more femininity in the young girl than most analysts liked to believe, and also suggested that the masculine phase through which she passed might be a reaction to her dread of femininity rather than something primary.

MISCONCEPTIONS ABOUT FEMALE SEXUALITY

Freud's phallocentric point of view is best understood in terms of his highly patriarchal Victorian culture. Erikson suggests that Freud tended to overemphasize the role of the father in the sexual maldevelopment of the young girl and did not fully appreciate the significance of her deep tie to the mother. Freud himself suggested that, as a male analyst, his ability to probe deeply into the early role of the mother might be limited so that he mainly evoked the paternal aspects of transference, with its love and fear, rivalry and competition. The preponderance of female hysterics in his early caseload may also have been reason for him to overemphasize the woman's preoccupation with man and caused him to underestimate her problem with her own sexual role.*

[Freud] believed that libido was identical in men and women; thus, the girl had nothing intrinsically her own to fall back on and could get satisfaction only vicariously by pleasing men and forgetting herself. When he observed how hard it was for women to do this, he decided that they were more narcissistic than men and, finally, he became quite pessimistic about successful treatment for them. Resignation to therapeutic failure seemed to be in order if women had to give up the original object, the mother, as well as their greatest source of sensory pleasure, the clitoris, for an organ seen primarily as one of service, the vagina. From a teleological point of view, this pessimism was acceptable, for man's pleasure is essential to reproduction whereas that of woman is not.

* Female "hysterics" were said to be typically coquettish and to seem preoccupied with relating to men. Most later psychoanalysts agreed that this flirtatiousness was a superficial cover for more deep-seated problems having little to do with true sexual interest in men.—ED.

One may question many steps in this sequence, beginning with the assumption that the vagina is not discovered until puberty.

Interest in bearing and mothering babies develops in both sexes. The little boy may show what Dooley has called uterus envy—a strong desire to make his own baby. This is so discouraged by the culture as "sissy" that he is apt to quickly repress it, although the wish may recur many years later in dreams when his wife is pregnant. All children are uncertain about their sexual role at first and each sex has a tendency to imitate the other. In other words, envy goes both ways. Now that nursery-age children are allowed more freedom of expression and are observed with less bias, normal little boys can be seen trying to sit down and urinate like girls, pretending to have babies and breasts, or envying girls some of their special privileges, such as the right to wear jewelry, to dress in a wide range of colors, and to be more protected. Such behavior and attitudes do not need to be interpreted as deep, instinctual bisexuality: they may be regarded as volatile and playful efforts at role experimentation.

Mary Jane Sherfey draws on newer advances in embryology to elucidate developmental problems. Genetic sex is established at fertilization but morphologically all embryos are females at the beginning. Maleness develops during the fifth to sixth weeks of fetal life, under the influence of fetal androgen. The inherent organizational pattern in the female primordium is "given," that of the male must be acquired. More males are conceived because they seem to be more rapidly destroyed. Thus, femaleness would seem to be the primary, as well as the more viable, sexual predisposition. A truly bisexual stage would be impossible to pinpoint, there being but a fleeting moment in time when female and male hormonal influences are equal. The masculine deviation is complete by the end of the third fetal month. Embryologically speaking, according to Sherfey, it would be correct to say that the penis is an exaggerated clitoris rather than the reverse. This would merely be a different example of the same fallacy, namely, that of trying to explain phenomena from one level of organization by inaccurate extrapolation from a totally separate system which is not truly analogous. (Sherfey herself warns against doing this.) However, it would seem permissible to use this data to underscore the strength and durability of innate femaleness, which precedes rather than being secondary to maleness.

There are multiple factors that may predispose a particular girl to suffer severe penis envy. Lack of awareness or appreciation for her own equipment, just mentioned, is one. This may be enhanced by environmental restrictions on early curiosity and exploration, by the unavailability of knowledge about, or contempt for, female function. A strong tendency toward envy and possessiveness due to deprivation or to an intense need for activity may also cause a girl to envy anything she does not possess, the penis being only one of many things coveted.

I am suggesting that an evanescent phase of penis envy is apt to occur when the little girl first becomes aware of the existence of a penis. This is in the nature of universal childhood curiosity and interest in anything new, and may be quite transitory if she is fairly satisfied with being a girl and has been allowed or encouraged to develop appropriate awareness of her own body function. This awareness is ultimately based on autonomous, internal sensations but consensual validation and affirmation are entailed in its realistic evaluation. If healthy growth ensues, this early, primary type of penis envy may easily pass, causing no significant conflict. It is neither malignant nor a ubiquitous obstacle. On the other hand, it may be secondarily reinforced under certain conditions so that it does become an important facet of a later neurotic problem. Even then, it is part of a process, not *the* cause.

Among the possible secondary reinforcing factors are the following:

1. *Sibling rivalry* may enhance a preexisting state of

envy based on general frustration of early childhood needs for parenting. This exacerbation of envy may occur with the birth of a new baby or the existence of a preferred child. If the rival is a male, of course, envy is apt to be focused on the penis as the reason for the preference. In some cases, the girl may simply envy the baby's access to mother but basically want the nipple rather than the penis.

2. *Deep, dependency needs for the mother* may be expressed in the wish for a penis not as an end in itself but as a way to win mother back or to attract her as father does. Lampl-de Groot has suggested that woman's jealousy is stronger than man's not because of deflected penis envy but because she can never possess the mother vicariously through a love relationship, as can the man. She believes that the castration complex in female children is a secondary formation, its precursor being the negative Oedipus situation; that is, the rage at the depriving mother and fear of her retaliation comes first. This attitude parallels that of Melanie Klein. Both differ with Freud, who felt that the castration complex in women came first and made possible the positive Oedipus situation.

3. Disappointment at the hands of a *rejecting or remote father*, in the oedipal stage or later in preadolescence, may also reinforce penis envy; the girl may feel she is sexually unattractive in herself and needs a penis to please father. She may also at this point renew her dependency on her mother with increased oral needs. She may want a penis in order to be self-sufficient rather than dependent on the man for her pleasure. If the father has been sadistic she may literally want a penis to protect herself, to get even, or via identification with the aggressor.

4. Any factor increasing the *dread of becoming a woman* is also apt to increase penis envy. If the girl's mother is ineffectual as a woman, resents the female role, and gets only contempt from her husband, the growing girl has no

positive model to identify with or learn from. She develops a deep fear about her ability to be sexually attractive, to make a home, and to bear and raise children. She may envy the man not for his penis but for his freedom from these anxiety-provoking responsibilities. As Ferenczi pointed out, a man can always vicariously get a mother through his wife, while the woman must *be* the mother— a role which, in many respects, is more difficult.

It is also necessary to reevaluate the assumption that an acceptance of passivity and masochism is essential to healthy femininity. Overt activity, visible and movement-producing, is more typically masculine, but the inner activity of the vagina, with its invisible smooth-muscle contractions and mucous secretions, although less tangible and more subjective, is not merely passive. *Receptive aims do not imply inertness:* the truly receptive vagina is grasping, secreting, and pleasure-giving through its own functions rather than just through the erotization of pain. Women may learn to bear certain types of internal pain more stoically than men do, but this adaptation to reality should be distinguished from clinical masochism—a pattern of accepting pain as a prerequisite to being loved or taken care of. Here, pain is exploited neurotically for an ulterior goal. This type of adjustment is not necessary to healthy femininity—in fact, precludes it, feeding a vicious circle of resentment, blame, and guilt. Masochistic women may always be available sexually but they get their satisfactions from having done a favor rather than from mutual exchange. Submission to get approval is not apt to lead to healthy, active participation on the woman's part; this ensues only when she plays her own unique role in lovemaking. The woman who feels free to be physically active in lovemaking usually makes a more exciting partner than one who never expresses her own erotic preferences or who takes no initiative, feeling that her role is merely to follow and please the man. This may be gratifying to some men initially, but it is apt to become stereotyped and lifeless to both partners. Active participation on the part of the woman may legitimately be resented if her goal is to take over, frustrate the man, or prove that he is sexually inadequate. The goal must be one of mutual facilitation of pleasure, which requires equal cooperation. Both the man and the woman need to freely observe and then exploit their physiological mechanisms, as well as their psychological reactions. Analytic theories such as the assumption that sexual activity is masculine may limit choice and cause inhibitions just as effectively as do cultural restrictions and taboos.

Another assumption to reevaluate is that concerning the need to *change erotic zones*. The concept that clitoral sensation is masculine, infantile, and must be relinquished for truly feminine, mature vaginal sensation is not tenable if vaginal sensation originates as early as clitoral and if both are seen as dual, intrinsic aspects of basic female physiology. A denser concentration of sensitive nerve endings exists in the clitoris than in the penis or in any other organ of the body, so that many now doubt that sensations from this area could ever stop.

However, this one-sided picture of vaginal function can now be questioned on the basis of the recent physiological observations of Masters and Johnson. They have shown that the clitoral apparatus extends deeply into the perineum, including much more extensive anatomical structures than just the shaft and glans of the clitoris. Vasocongestion and mytonia during sexual stimulation may originate in the clitoris, but they extend to the vaginal barrel, the uterus, and a wide area of the pelvis. During excitement, the inner two-thirds of the vagina distends, forming a receptacle for the seminal pool, whereas the outer third shows such marked vasocongestion that the lumen [i.e., opening] of the vaginal canal is narrowed to one-third of its previous opening. At orgasm there is a strong contraction of the bulbar vasocongestion around the introitus as well as uterine contractions, whose severity varies with the subjective degree of excitement.

In physiological terms, the vagina is involved in every orgasm, whether or not the woman is aware of it.

The functioning of the clitoris cannot be understood if it is considered to be merely a small penis. There are basic physiological differences, such as the fact that the penis functions much more as a separate organ; the clitoris does not. There can certainly be great variance in the quality and extent of orgasms in different women, or in the same woman at different times. A valid distinction can be made between a local, mainly external sensation restricted in area and strength, and the much deeper, more widespread, pervasive, and overwhelming sensation associated with full penetration and uninhibited participation. However, this difference is more accurately explained in terms of degree of relaxation and lack of inhibition than by attributing it to either vagina or clitoris acting alone. There is no anatomical reason for thinking of the clitoris and vagina as competitors; the clitoral shaft extends to the mouth of the vagina with the vestibular bulbs* encircling the entrance. Circumvaginal muscles also connect the two structures so that the movement of one pulls on the other. It would seem more logical to say that nature did her best to connect the two and transmit sensation inward.

In the female, wider areas are involved in erotic stimulation and vasocongestion is more extensive. Arousal may thus take longer and necessitate more imagination; resolution and return to a resting state may also be more lengthy. When these factors are taken into account, it may be possible for the woman to maintain arousal for long periods, thus putting her in the position of being more sexual than the man rather than less so, as has been commonly assumed.

* These are structures that lie in the superficial tissues alongside the opening of the vagina. They are composed of large venouslike chambers which fill with blood upon sexual stimulation; as such they are analogous to the chambers in the penis which fill with blood and thereby produce an erection.—Ed.

But such comparisons are useless. Women may achieve greater enjoyment of their own sexuality if they are encouraged to stop comparing their responses to those of men, and allow themselves a sensation that is uniquely their own. This experience is only hindered if the typical male response is regarded as standard.

CASE ILLUSTRATIONS

Illustrative case material was chosen from among a group of young professional women who would be expected to have considerable conflict about their femininity and much so-called penis envy. Surface façades varied from overt resentment and competition with men to passive masochism. Frigidity was a major problem in the three cases presented but is not dealt with here because it was the subject of an earlier report.

CASE 1   A thirty-year-old woman suffered from such severe vaginismus* that intromission had never been possible in eight years of an apparently happy and otherwise successful marriage. The patient described herself as experiencing frequent and intense sexual excitement with satisfying clitoral orgasm; she and her husband had settled on a pattern of arousing and relieving each other manually. Painful spasm made it impossible for her to let anything enter her introitus, whether her husband's finger or penis, her own finger in gentle exploration, or that of a gynecologist. Even the effort to insert a Tampax caused an anxiety panic and exacerbation of an inguinal neurodermatitis.† Her phobia included fear of penetration into any body opening, by otoscope, throat swab, rectal thermometer. She felt she was an anatomical freak who had only enough vaginal opening to permit menstrual flow.

This dramatic state of affairs, existing between two highly successful, well-educated professional people with no hint of psychotic processes, was partly explained by the fact that both came from bizarrely restricted, primitive communities

* Spasm of the muscles of the vagina.—ED.
† A skin rash in the area around the genitalia with no obvious external cause.—ED.

with strict moral standards and had been virgins at marriage. An interview with the husband showed him to have deep affection for his wife; although he was not very sexually assertive, he seemed to have no potency problems, achieving erection and ejaculation with her. She had a deep fear of pregnancy and he was willing to forgo children as their active teaching life would have made raising a family difficult.

She originally blamed her phobia on a fall occurring at age six when, after straddling a sharp board, she suffered severe pain and perineal bleeding. The mother was so suspicious and fearful of doctors that she did not have the child examined but merely kept her in bed. The mother was a submissive recluse who was disgusted at all sexual functioning, was herself terrified of pain, and tried to restrict her daughter from any physical activity that involved the slightest danger, such as bicycling and swimming. The patient's sadistic, teasing brother, fourteen years older, was allowed much more physical freedom. The household was dominated by a cruel, sadistic grandfather who successfully tyrannized four generations of passive and masochistic women. The patient, until she was seven, slept in her parents' bedroom, tied down in a crib jammed between their bed and the wall. She often awoke in panic, with choking sensations, nausea, and vomiting. To her father, the most outgoing and positive person in her life, she owed her education, and she attributed to his leadership whatever freedom she enjoyed. However, he tended to remove himself from the confining restraints of the household, leaving her in her mother's care, so that she felt disappointed and deserted by him.

After several months of treatment, she recovered memories about exciting sexual play at the age of five with a boy of the same age of whom she was very fond. She was surprised to recall that she enjoyed having him put wads of paper in her vagina; obviously, its opening was originally ample enough so that penetration was pleasurable rather than painful. They were discovered by his father and scolded. The patient's fall, shortly after that incident, was undoubtedly experienced as punishment, especially since she had been disobeying her mother's prohibitions about climbing when it occurred. Subsequently, she repressed all knowledge of her vagina and developed phobias about penetration, fear of knives, cuts, and blood. Her denial of femininity was so strong that she was convinced she would never menstruate, and was horrified when it happened. She was repulsed by the passive, masochistic women around her, saw them as trapped by marriage and children, and decided she would never have any. At age six or seven, she had a fleeting wish to be a boy, as boys were freer, stronger, could fight, and were thus less vulnerable. The pattern she adopted was that of the naïve, flirtatious little girl, whom older men and teachers would protect. She married a kind, nonassertive man, who makes no adult sexual demands on her and gives her much more warmth and mothering than she ever got at home.

The physiological observations of Masters and Johnson have been useful with this patient in that adequate questioning established the fact that she had uterine contractions following her so-called clitoral orgasm; in fact, sometimes she has awakened intermittently during the night with pelvic sensations like cramps, which would indicate incomplete resolution of excitement. It becomes clear through body language, which can be more convincing than words, that although she may arbitrarily stop stimulation at the entrance to her vagina, sensations and vascular congestion proceed inward without her consent. She makes a false distinction based on intellectual concepts to which her body does not submit. In order to be reunited with her body, as she has craved, she will have to learn from observing how it works rather than trying to control it.

Multiple aspects of this case can be discussed, such as the obsessive façade and avoidance techniques of the "untouchable anal character," hysterical symptoms of cardiospasm, vaginal spasm, choking sensations, and much evidence of oedipal taboos. Underlying these manifestations was a deep layer of resentment and fear of women due to early oral deprivation. The patient, fearing male aggression and fleeing from the female role (as she pictured it), sought solace in a world of orality. She had dreams of being choked rather than raped. She kept her sexual play at the level of the high school girl who merely "pets," and obtained from her husband, who also mothered her, the protection she wanted from her father.

Her dreams were replete with fears of bodily injury at the hands of men, as well as of dangerous menacing women who accused her of stealing; she had sexual freedom without paying the price. The penis was seen as attacking, oversized, and cutting; when it was represented as small and disgusting, like blood worms, the unconscious impulse was to step on it or chew it up. Thus, the penis was feared as the essence of male destructive power: it can injure and impregnate. There was no evidence of penis envy, except what one can read into an episode about playing with the handle of the refrigerator door, which was more apt to have related to the craving to be fed than to the need for a penis.

CASE 2 An unsuccessful actress who had always resented being a woman came to treatment very depressed and anxious at having allowed herself to become pregnant. Her husband had recently become extremely successful, and her envy and competition with him were enormous, especially since she was blocked in her own professional development. She felt that the best way to "show up" her husband was to do the one thing he could not do—bear a child.

She expressed only hatred and contempt for her mother, who had been a dependent, ineffectual housebound woman. This resentment seemed to have started at the birth of her sister, three years younger, at which time the patient hid herself and refused to talk for days. The mother, a masochistic woman dependent on her own mother, was hospitalized for depression when the patient was fifteen. The father was an unsuccessful actor, an exciting, talented person whom the patient adored. She turned away from her mother and spent the next ten years of her life trying to be her father's son. He encouraged her acting and took her to performances, partly to get away from the mother. However, he was very inconsistent and bitter, given to terrifying rages; he would alternate between leading her on and slapping her down. Her fantasy of being like a boy was brutally crushed at a time when she was preparing for a bas mitzvah; she thought she would be allowed to have one "as good as a boy's" but was suddenly humiliated publicly at puberty and sent home from the synagogue on the Sabbath because it was decided that she was now a woman and could no longer stay and compete with the men and boys. Menarche intensified her resentment of female functions but she compensated with fantasies of having a son and traveling around the world with him—self-sufficient, no longer needing her family or her father. While in Europe on a scholarship, she fell in love and, while petting the boy, had the only orgasm she has ever experienced. She feared his increasing power over her, experienced a resurgence of dependency needs and fled home, presumably because her father was ill. She felt she had spent her life trying to win her father's approval. But when she finally "made" Broadway, he taunted her, "Why not give it up, go home, and make babies?"

After his death and her professional failure, she became increasingly depressed. At the age of thirty, she decided to get pregnant—after having been married four years. (She had previously been phobic about pregnancy and remained a virgin until her marriage.) She felt that her baby was conceived out of emptiness, not fullness, and then feared that the child would take her life from her, would deplete rather than fulfill her. Having a baby trapped her, she felt; she could no longer try to be like a man. It was as though she had had a fantasy penis which she finally had to relinquish.

She resented bitterly taking care of her child and also over-identified with it. She discovered she hated being a mother because she so much wanted to be the baby; this aroused much guilt, which she fought against through fanatic breast-feeding. She would not leave the house for fear that the baby would be mistreated if entrusted to the nursemaid or others in the household. Meanwhile, even the planning of meals became too much for her, and she tried to get her husband to cook and care for herself and the baby. When she found herself trying to force him to mother both of them, she realized for the first time how deep were her own dependency needs. She also feared that motherhood would transform her into a person like her own mother—a fate desperately to be avoided. She found herself unconsciously imitating many of her mother's patterns, which aggravated her self-contempt and depression.

There was plenty of evidence of typical penis envy in this case. As a girl, the patient even tried to compete with boys in urinary contests, and was furious because she always lost. She first associated her bedwetting with rage at not having a penis, but finally viewed it as a way to punish mother for turning to sister, and as an effort to recover the maternal solicitude she had lost. She envied, and was attracted to, men who had powerful drives for achievement and were free to pursue them. The penis was for her as a symbol of such drives; to possess it would also save her from being like her mother. In one sense, she wanted a baby as a substitute for not having a penis; but she also had a burning wish to be a good mother—to prove her own validity as well as to "undo" her past. Her difficulty in achieving this wish forced her to work through her relationship with her mother, which she had contemptuously shelved, finding competition with men more exciting and less anxiety provoking.

In the process of becoming an adequate mother and getting more and more satisfaction from caring for her child, she became less resentful of, and freer from, her unconscious identification with her own mother. Functioning more capably in her household, she blamed her husband less, demanded less of him, and began to enjoy living with him. Her fears of being taken over by him, or of being submerged in domestic minutiae, diminished. She began to perform better in auditions and to work herself out of her depression. Her household was running fairly well with her part-time attention; neither husband nor baby was holding her back. At this point, she got a contract for an acting role that both frightened and encouraged her. While performing it, she began to experience real vaginal sensitivity and greater enjoyment of intercourse than she had ever before attained. Petulance began to give way under an upsurge of a more primitive and passionate sexuality, which she could now integrate and enjoy. Rage at father and husband and child then began to resolve. Being more successful as a woman enabled her to enjoy men.

It would have been easy in the beginning to have interpreted her professional aspirations as mere "penis envy" causing a secondary flight from womanhood. Had the primary problem been seen as a need to relinquish the fantasy of having a penis, she might have given up acting and resigned herself to being a housewife and mother, which would have increased her frustration and depression. She needed to work through what blocked her from being a good wife and mother, in order to prove herself first in these capacities. On that firmer foundation, she was able to continue her acting career. Actually, the roles she plays best require great understanding of feminine problems. Her increasing ability to perform them is an expression of her womanhood, not of her masculinity. She is an infinitely better wife and mother than when she felt trapped at home—an experience that enhanced the deep resentment of the female role that preceded her problem with men. After that resentment was worked out, she was free to move ahead to a new level of self-expression.

CASE 3 Another woman entered treatment complaining that, despite her many affairs, she could not have vaginal orgasm or develop any long-term relationships with men. Her early masochistic relationships with a sadistic older brother and a rejecting father were relieved in her affairs. She would frequently go to bed on a first date out of fear of losing the man. Her hostile submission filled her with rage and led to fantasies of magical revenge. She imagined herself as a succubus draining the man of all strength and filling him with poisonous milk. She could not "give in" and let him "give" her orgasm; she had to keep the upper hand in order to de-ennervate the man, and to prevent a dangerous blending that would mean loss of her identity, the dissolution of her ego boundaries. However, the underlying, earlier conflict was a deep hostile dependency on her mother, who had infantilized and undermined her. Her rage was expressed in bouts of mild asthma. She tried to get away from her mother to join father and brothers, who were freer, stronger, and more aggressive; but they pushed her back to mother with ridicule.

The most anxiety-provoking aspect of intercourse for this patient was that it evoked her wish to fall asleep while sucking at her mother's breast in utter helplessness. She protected herself from this ultimate threat by brandishing a "hate penis" —in revenge against mother and men, and to prevent herself from giving in to her dependency needs for them. Masochistic sexual submission allowed some sense of closeness and made her feel free to make demands instead of asking for affection; it would be owed to her.

In this case too, the primary problem was hostile dependency on the mother, for which the "penis envy" served as a camouflage and a defense.

The cases just presented illustrate my main point: penis envy should not be taken literally; it should be studied first in terms of its preoedipal underpinnings, and secondly through deciphering of the later reinforcing factors. The predisposing problems are mainly hostile dependency on the mother and the dread of becoming a woman.

In each of the cases reported, the fear of male domination was ultimately traced back to maternal deprivation, the helpless rage associated with this experience being reenacted with a man. If the marital battle is primarily a reenactment of the battle with the mother, with an underlying need to be taken care of, this dependency must be analyzed before real change can occur.

The patient may have more resistance to this approach; usually it is easier on her self-esteem to talk about her competition with men than to acknowledge her fear of helplessness and her wish to be mothered. The mothers of the three patients discussed were themselves clinging, dependent women; two of them still lived with and relied on their own mothers as well as being masochistically dependent on their husbands. Having no sense of their own value as women, they could give their daughters none; instead, the mothers transmitted their fear of men. The patients, blocked from access to feminine pride and competence, fled from womanhood as undesirable and dangerous, feeling that the male role would be safer and easier.

A father who respected and enjoyed women rather than having fear and/or contempt for them, might help a daughter work out of this trap. However, the fathers of these patients, although often seductive with their daughters, had such negative relations with their wives, for whom they had both resentment and contempt, that their warmth and support of their daughters were given inconsistently and mixed with hostility, thus reinforcing the girls' fears of men and male rejection. From early childhood, because of her contempt for her mother as well as the guilt about it, each of these patients felt herself to be unattractive and inadequate as a woman. Thus she initially approached a man with the expectation of being rejected. Rather than getting the extra reassurance she needed from him, she got very little because of her distrustful attitude. The lack of constructive fathering as a factor reinforcing penis envy was well illustrated. Another secondary factor, the influence of the sadistic, envied brother, also figured in this material.

THERAPEUTIC CONSIDERATIONS

Theoretical concepts can have an important influence on therapy. If the analyst assumes that woman's basic problem is envy of man, the patient is encouraged to project her anxiety about being a woman onto man's equipment and privileges as though these were the main source of her conflict rather than a secondary, reinforcing factor. Attention is then deflected from problems inherent in her own sexual role; there may be insufficient analytic work on intrapsychic obstacles to the development of feminine competence. Intrapsychic and extrapsychic factors are not mutually exclusive; rather, they coexist and assume unique proportions in each case. These factors need to be explored without preconceptions, so that each will be given its just due, instead of being allowed to reinforce one another.

Another danger in taking penis envy as a biological "given" is that it can be cited as justification for male aggression against the patient, which in turn exacerbates her feelings of being victimized. Negative attitudes toward men, such as hostility, envy, or competitiveness, certainly must be dealt with, but attributing them to biological inadequacy, which must be accepted as inevitable, perpetuates a vicious circle by enhancing woman's rage at man, whose superiority is thus confirmed. The patient is then encouraged to see herself as a victim—an amputee, with an inescapable compensation neurosis. This stimulates unhealthy masochism, which encourages projection and breeds resentment. Attention needs to be directed away from comparisons with men so there may be more focus on the development of woman's inner resources.

If activity is linked exclusively with masculinity, woman is deprived of access to appropriate self-assertion, and made to feel unfeminine when she tries to express herself, which further increases her frustration and lessens her self-esteem. The patient may get caught in the trap of assuming that all men dislike competence and strength in women, and fail to see that the real problem is her tendency to use her strength against a man rather than for constructive and mutually beneficial goals. She may mistake the neurotic nature of her fear of male disapproval for a realistic attitude. Behind the saying "Men are all alike," there usually lurks some male figure, who was influential in the patient's early life and whom she has come to regard as prototypical. She may set up a false dichotomy between her marriage and outside interests, feeling that she must give *them* up for *him*.

Some men marry professional women because they prefer an active woman, one who is less clinging and more stimulating than the traditional hausfrau. The husband's irritability is often provoked, not by his wife's career as such, but at her inability to handle it with satisfaction; he wants her to have some enthusiasm left over to share with him rather than projecting onto him her complaints, guilts, and conflict about her career. This was especially true of the husband of the actress; he placed little value on a serene and conventional domestic life, and preferred a balance allowing mutual freedom. He found his wife less interesting when she remained at home and, although she did so because of her own guilt and resentment about being a mother, she then blamed him for her dilemma. Her increasing ability to be an adequate mother led to her being a better wife, a better actress, and finally a better sexual partner—in that order.

This case recalls Josine Muller's observation that women with full vaginal capacity seem more successful in their careers than genitally inhibited ones. Frigid women often cannot get satisfaction either from so-called feminine gratifications or from the outside world. Thus, whatever penis envy they have becomes increasingly reinforced by their frustration.

Many women achieve a sense of complete fulfillment

257

when they are actively investing their intelligence and talents in pursuits that were formerly regarded as masculine prerogatives. The acceptance of narrow concepts of normal sexual function unnecessarily limits the development of individual activity patterns and may cause women to forfeit a great deal of what might become valuable and attractive feminine effectiveness. Activity has primary satisfactions apart from competition with men. To some extent, every woman yearns to find pleasure in her own femininity and to find ways to fulfill her role with dignity; but she may need active help in overcoming the negative concept of womanhood that she brings from her past. The therapist who would help her work toward an ideal she can respect must believe in woman's positive potential.

ROBERT J. STOLLER

BECAUSE OF his wealth of experience on the interrelationships between biology and psychology, Robert Stoller is in an eminent position to present an authoritative assessment of the current state of knowledge of those biological factors that may play a role in determining sexual differences in psychology and behavior.

A member of the classic psychoanalytic group, Stoller is affiliated with the Los Angeles Psychoanalytic Society/Institute and is a professor of psychiatry at the University of California at Los Angeles. His research concerns the nature and development of masculinity and femininity, about which he has written many papers. His work is also represented in his book *Sex and Gender*.

The Sense of Femaleness

In 1965 I suggested that in normal boys the sense of maleness comes from the attitudes of parents, siblings, and peers toward the child's sex, from the anatomy and physiology of his genitalia, and from a biological force that can more or less modify the effects of the attitudes of others. Some of the data I presented, however, indicated that even boys born without penises do not doubt that they are males if their parents also believe this without question. Such a defect may cause many problems in the later development of their masculinity, yet they take for granted that they are males. In the present paper I shall show that the conclusions apply equally well to the development of the sense of femaleness.

Boys born without penises but recognized at birth to be males have their equivalent in girls who are genetically, anatomically, and physiologically normal except for being born without vaginas. Discovery of such a defect may cause a girl or woman great pain, but I have not seen or heard of any such woman who had a disturbance in core gender identity (that is, a fundamental uncertainty whether she was female or male). Gynecologists, with much more extensive experience with such women, concur; they do not see severe gender defects.

The anatomical defect may make a woman feel flawed; she may question whether she is feminine enough, or she may wonder whether the vagina the surgeons gave her is not the real thing, but she does not think she is a male and she does not wish to be converted into a male.* It may

---

* If Freud had treated a woman without a vagina, I think he would have seen that the only thing a woman wants more than a penis is a vagina. It is only when a woman has normal genitalia that she can afford the luxury of wishing she had a penis.

be taken as evidence that they feel themselves females that these women seek to have a vagina constructed and then can use it enthusiastically; Masters and Johnson report that in such women a surgically constructed vagina is not only physiologically and biochemically essentially normal, despite the fact that its "mucosa" is created from a skin graft, but they have demonstrable evidence of orgasms that are physiologically indistinguishable from those of women with natural vaginas. I think it can be shown that the sense of being a female develops out of the same roots (parental attitudes and ascription of sex, genitalia, and a biological force) as does the sense of being a male and that this core gender identity persists throughout life as unalterably in women as in men.

If this is correct, there is good reason to question Freud's remark about women: "Their sexual life is regularly divided into two phases, of which the first has a masculine character, while only the second is specifically feminine." In fact, an important purpose of this paper is to support those who believe that Freud may have distorted his whole description of the development of "sexuality" in both boys and girls by his insistence on beginning the story (in certain regards) only after the onset of the phallic phase. He gradually came to see the tremendous significance of preoedipal relationships and especially the great importance of mothers for their developing children; yet his discussion of sexuality (by which he seems to have meant both development of the capacity for erotism and that related but still rather different quality—gender) is distorted; for there is evidence that what he considers the first phase of gender development in a little girl is in fact a secondary phase, the result of a growing awareness that there are people whom the little girl thinks luckier than she, whom she recognizes as belonging to the classification "male."

This question was raised a long time ago, most clearly by [Karen] Horney and [Ernest] Jones in the 1920s and most movingly in 1944 by [Gregory] Zilboorg. These three led others in stating that Freud was influenced by personal bias in constructing his theory. In 1933, Jones said: ". . . in Freud's description of the phallic phase the essential feature common to both sexes was the belief that only one kind of genital organ exists in the world— a male one." Zilboorg, in agreement, says: "The point at issue at first appears rather trivial, and yet it is fundamental, for it involves the question of whether femininity is primary in the civilized human female or secondary and subsequent to the rudimentary masculinity."*

However, such issues are not resolved by setting up the authorities face to face against each other. Clinical data are less stirring but more helpful. Most recently [Mary Jane] Sherfey has given us an extensive review of the anatomical and physiological findings of Masters and Johnson.

CLINICAL EVIDENCE†

If we were to design an experiment to help us understand the development of the sense of femaleness, we should want to study several types of patients: (1) females without vaginas but otherwise biologically normal; (2) females who are biologically neuter but whose external genitalia at birth looked normal so that no doubt was raised in their parents' minds as to the sex of the infant; (3) females biologically normal except for masculinization of their external genitalia (but with vaginas) who were reared unequivocally as girls; (4) females who

* See Ernest Jones, "The Early Development of Female Sexuality," *International Journal of Psychoanalysis* 8 (1927): 459–72; and Gregory Zilboorg, "Masculine and Feminine: Some Biological and Cultural Aspects," excerpted in this volume.—ED.

† That the findings described do not come from women in analysis is a weakness that may be offset by the consistent femininity observed in these patients' behavior: speech, movements, dress, daydreams, and object choices, and in the appropriate affects accompanying these manifestations.

are biologically normal except for masculinization of their external genitalia (but with vaginas) who were reared unequivocally as boys; and (5) females who are biologically normal but without a clitoris.

The first category is familiar to gynecologists. Its outcome is a sense of femaleness with an accompanying femininity that leads as frequently as it does in anatomically normal women to women's tasks and pleasures, including marriage, vaginal intercourse (in the artificial vagina) with orgasm, childbearing (when a uterus is present), and appropriate mothering.

This is illustrated by a seventeen-year-old feminine, pretty, intelligent girl who appeared anatomically completely normal at birth although behind her external genitalia there was no vagina or uterus. Her parents, having no doubts, raised her as a girl, and female and feminine is what she feels she is. Breasts, pubic hair, and feminine subcutaneous fat distribution began developing at age ten (because she has normal, ovulating ovaries), but, although she had bouts of monthly abdominal pain, no menstruation occurred. At age fourteen, a routine physical examination—including for the first time examination of the genitalia—revealed that she had no vagina and subsequent studies demonstrated that the uterus was missing but the ovaries were present and functioning normally. She was told these findings. "What shocked me most was I wanted to have kids . . . and I wanted a vagina. I wanted to feel like everybody else. I wanted to use mine. I mean, when the time came around, I wanted to use it. I didn't want to feel different from anybody . . . which I did. . . ." When given the opportunity for a vaginoplasty, she insisted on it instantly. When asked how she felt about now having a vagina, she said, "It's different; it's better; it's a step further. I feel like anybody else now." This is not literally true; at another time she made it clear that she felt almost like other girls and that this was deeply gratifying, but she could not escape her awareness that her vagina is not one she was born with.

Her reaction was what we should expect of a female who has no question as to her sex and who has the desires and fantasies (hopes) of a feminine woman. The absence of vagina and uterus had not damaged her sense of being a female, though since age fourteen the knowledge of this absence had made her feel like a defective female. She never felt she was a boy nor ever wanted to be a male.

The second category can be represented by a biologically neuter girl (the syndrome of ovarian agenesis): chromosomally XO, without gonads or any physiologically significant levels of female hormones. She is feminine, wants to be and works at being attractive in the ways that other girls do; she wants marriage, intercourse, and babies. While she knows she is anatomically defective, as with the nonneuter girl in the first case, she does not question that she is female.

When this girl was first seen at age eighteen, she was unremarkably feminine in her behavior, dress, social and sexual desires, and fantasies, indistinguishable in this regard from other girls in the community. There was one troubling condition which made her less than average to herself. Her breasts had not begun to develop by the time she was eighteen, nor had menstruation started. She was found to have no vagina, though her external genitalia looked normally female; her clitoris was small. She had no uterus, no ovaries, no tubes, no testes.

Her first response on being told she was sterile was to weep. "I wonder what my kids would have looked like." Later, when asked if she could recall any dreams from any time in her life, she could remember only one, from a time a year or two before, when she was seriously concerned about not having grown breasts or started to menstruate: "I was getting married. I had to marry the fellow because I was pregnant."

When told she would need to have an artificial vagina created, she fought against all the efforts of her family to delay this until she was ready to marry, insisting that they permit the operation immediately. Since the operation she has remained grateful for it. (I presume the reader can only say at this point, "Of course.")

What about her feminine interests and role? Her oldest sister told us that the patient when a child was pretty, interested in dresses and dolls and in using cosmetics to play at being a grown-up. The patient reported that on her dates with young men she liked to go dancing, bowling, or to the movies. Her greatest interest had always been stylish clothes, on which she would spend all her spare money. When in her late adolescence she first went to work, she did so only to have extra money for clothes. She did little reading and that exclusively movie and romance magazines. Her daydreams had the same content —interest in feminine ways—as her reading. This is certainly not a list of activities that strikes one as unique, bizarre, carefully thought out to accomplish a plan, or especially worthy of report, were it not that it is my design to underline the unspecialness, the naturalness of her gender identity.

Subjects in the third category (masculinized females reared as girls) and fourth (masculinized females reared as boys) were of key importance in the work of [John] Money and [J. G. and J. L.] Hampson. They studied differences in gender identity that arose in infants with the adrenogenital syndrome. In this condition, the external genitalia of the otherwise normally sexed female infant have been masculinized in utero by excessive adrenal androgens. They describe two such children, both biologically normal females, genetically and in their internal sexual anatomy and physiology, but with masculinized external genitalia. The proper diagnosis having been made, one child was reared unequivocally as a female (category 3); she turned out to be as feminine as other little girls. The other, not recognized to be female, was reared without question as a male (category 4), and became an unremarkably masculine little boy.

In the fifth category is the female normal in all regards except for congenital absence of a clitoris. I have never seen such a case, but should guess that such a child would have no question that she is a female and so during infancy and childhood would develop an essentially intact sense of femaleness, although like a girl without a vagina the part of this sense that results from body sensations of that part of the anatomy would be missing. But we have a clue in regard to such people. It is the practice in certain parts of the Moslem world to excise the clitoris of every female, some in infancy and some not until years later. Despite the fact that there are today millions of such women, they do not fail to develop their sense of being females; they do not lose it; nor do they or their men report that their femininity is reduced.

DISCUSSION

Except in the very rare situation where they are uncertain from the birth of their child whether they have a boy or a girl, the parents of the infants we have described have not doubted that the child was a female. And barring some fanciful explanation, such as that she has an inherited racial unconscious awareness of creatures who have penises, the infant will unquestioningly develop her sense of the dimensions and sensations of her body from her own sensory experiences, which confirm for her the parents' conviction that she is female. In this way an unquestioned sense of belonging to the female sex develops. As with males, it is fixed in the first few years of life and is a piece of identity so firm that almost no vicissitudes of living can destroy it. Even a severe psychosis or the deterioration of organic brain disease will not loosen the core gender identity. Other aspects of gender identity may be severely distorted in the symptomatology of such illnesses, but the severe disruptions of gender identity we often see in psychotics (Schreber is an extreme example*) are not evidence that the sense of maleness or femaleness has been destroyed. The patient still knows

* Schreber was the subject of one of Freud's famous case studies. —ED.

his sex and in unguarded moments behaves appropriately
for his sex, though his delusions and hallucinations reveal the force of his *wish* to be a member of the opposite
sex.

It seems to be well established that the vagina is sensed,
though probably not erotized, in little girls, yet I believe
that it is not the essential source of femininity. Just as the
sense of maleness of little boys is augmented by the
presence of a penis, but exists even if there is no penis,
little girls without vaginas develop an unquestioned sense
of femaleness. They do so because their parents have no
doubt that they are females. Awareness of their biological
femaleness coursing below the surface of consciousness no
doubt augments this development, but, as we have seen
even in the neuter (XO) child who is not biologically female, a feminine gender identity develops if the infant is
unquestioningly assigned to the female sex.

By adhering to the faulty premise that little girls believe
themselves to be castrated boys, Freud deduced unwarranted conclusions. For instance, he says, "the first steps
toward definitive femininity" occur only after following a
"very circuitous path," by which he means that no *first*
definitive femininity has appeared before the phallic
stage, around age three or four, a statement which simple
observation contradicts. Elsewhere he states that working
out the rage produced by penis envy on one's first husband is the reason that "as a rule, second marriages turn
out much better," an opinion we should find hard put to
prove a rule. And Freud said, as everyone knows, that as
a result of the anatomical distinction between the sexes he
"cannot evade the notion (though I hesitate to give it
expression) that for women the level of what is ethically
normal is different from what it is in men. Their superego
is never so inexorable, so impersonal, so independent of
its emotional origins as we require it to be in men. Character traits which critics of every epoch have brought up
against women—that they show less sense of justice than
men, that they are less ready to submit to the great

exigencies of life, that they are more often influenced in their judgments by feelings of affection or hostility—all these would be amply accounted for by the modification in the formation of their superego which we have inferred above. We must not allow ourselves to be deflected from such conclusions by the denials of the feminists, who are anxious to force us to regard the two sexes as completely equal in position and worth. . . ."

One gets the impression from observing little girls— and I cannot believe that others have not seen the same— that they show definitive signs of femininity long before the phallic and oedipal phases and that one can trace these early traits of femininity from at least the first year or so of life, not ever seeing them disappear as the little girl grows up and becomes mature. If the observation is correct, then this fundamental building block in Freud's theory of the development of femininity—penis envy and castration complex—becomes only one aspect of the development rather than the origin of it, and opinions like those of Freud quoted above must stand or fall on demonstrable evidence, no longer buttressed by the theory that women are by nature inferior to men, their personalities simply variants on the theme of their being castrated males.

Before closing, let us return to our first case, biologically normal except for having no vagina and uterus. I am not alleging that the body ego of this girl is the same as that of an anatomically normal female, for she has not had that vaginal awareness dimly present in anatomically normal little girls. I suppose that the latter have a sense of space within, of indefinite dimensions but definite significance, produced especially by the vagina and more vaguely by the uterus, this sense being brought in time by use into the sensed body ego, in a way comparable to the building up of the infant's body ego by the felt use of the various parts of his body.

For this girl, however, such sensed representation of these parts could not exist even dimly, and therefore her sense of femaleness could not be exactly the same as that of anatomically normal girls.* Her own words indicate how, despite her femininity and her unquestioned sense of being female, that part of her core gender produced by body sensations was formed a bit differently from the anatomically normal girl.

"We were taught in school about menstruation [at age ten, four years before she was told she had no vagina or uterus]. I never understood it at all. I even read books, and I still didn't understand it. I just didn't figure . . . nothing fitted in. My mind was just a blank on it. Then in the eighth grade, I recognized more—that there was a vagina. Yet I still never knew what was intercourse. I didn't know I was different from other people." She was asked whether, after the school lectures describing the vagina and uterus, she became aware that she was lacking. "No, in fact you may think it a little ridiculous, but I'll tell you how I thought girls menstruated: from the breasts. But they *had* explained how menstruation really occurred. I don't know *how* I thought that."

She says she looked as normal as other girls she saw nude; however, when her girl friends began talking about their first sexual experiences in adolescence and she began picturing more clearly what a vagina is, she did not, as far as she could recall, explore for hers, although she was now masturbating.

Then, still speaking of the time before she was told that she had no vagina and before she had any conscious thought that she might not—"I'll tell you what happened the first time when I realized something must be wrong: this boy tried to rape me. He had me down and there was

* I am certainly not trying to say that all women have exactly the same sense of femaleness, but only that one anatomically normal girl whose parents do not question her sex assignment has much the same core gender identity as another, and that these girls have a very different core gender identity from those reared as boys or as hermaphrodites and not much different from those without vaginas but with sureness of sex assignment.

nothing I could do. He started to have intercourse with me—and he just stopped. I thought maybe he was just stopping because he felt bad. Then [much later] for some reason or another, I came out and told somebody I thought I was never going to have kids—and yet I still did not know anything [about the abnormality] and I've never been able to explain that. I felt I couldn't have kids and I wanted kids and I felt I couldn't and yet I don't know what gave me those feelings. *I did not know a thing.*"

In other words, a girl's conviction that she is a female comes from her parents' conviction, but that part of her awareness of being a female which comes from sensing her genitalia will vary according to the anatomy and physiology of these tissues (but will not vary to the degree that she does not believe herself female).

As with little boys, in time the increasingly complicated structure of the personality will overlay the core gender identity with complications and subtleties of gender that are not now to be our concern. (I refer to the varying degrees of masculinity that can be found in little girls; their identifications with their fathers and brothers and the development of masculine traits; fantasies of being like boys; envy of the masculine role and of the prized insignia of that role, a penis; disturbances in resolving the oedipal situation; and other traits.) As with the clearly masculine behavior of little boys, however, one can see evidences of gratifying, unquestioned femininity in little girls often by the time they begin to walk. These vary from culture to culture (and from family to family), but even though they are learned attitudes by this early age they are nonetheless already rather firm parts of the child's identity.

These ideas may have some relevance for treatment. It is possible that the analyst has an incorrect criterion for the success of an analysis if he believes he has reached the core of a woman's femininity when he is able to get her to share with equanimity his belief that she is really an inferior form of male.

CONCLUSION

Freud says, "We have found the same libidinal forces at work in it [female sexuality] as in the male child, and we have been able to convince ourselves that for a period of time these forces follow the same course and have the same outcome in each. Biological factors subsequently deflect those libidinal forces [in the girl's case] from their original aims and conduct even active and in every sense masculine trends into feminine channels." Strangely, in the face of what they must have observed daily in their own small children, there are still analysts who are committed to Freud's supposition. Yet it is hard to conceive that such an observer as Freud really believed that the development of masculinity and femininity is the same in boys as in girls until the phallic phase. It may be that having committed himself to this theory ("We have been able to convince ourselves"), Freud tended to ignore his observations. There are hints that he was aware of an earlier phase before the little girl discovers penises, a phase before femaleness has been depreciated: "*When* the little girl discovers her own deficiency, from seeing a male genital, *it is only with hesitation and reluctance that she accepts the unwelcome knowledge.* As we have seen, she clings obstinately to the expectation of one day having a genital of the same kind too, and her wish for it survives long after her hope has expired. The child invariably regards castration in the first instance as a misfortune peculiar to herself; only later does she realize that it extends to certain other children and lastly to certain grown-ups. When she comes to understand the general nature of this characteristic, it follows that femaleness—and with it, of course, her mother—suffers a great *depreciation* in her eyes." I have italicized parts of this quotation, for therein Freud hints at the earlier phase of primary femininity. "When" means that that time has already passed and that there was a time before "the little girl discovers her own deficiency"; the word "depreciation" indicates a process that started at a happier point and then retreated.

Therefore, I think that Freud also knew of a time in the little girl's life when she did not feel depreciated but rather accepted herself unquestioningly as a female.

It is possible that Freud's view of the development of femininity in women is incorrect. He looked upon femininity as a secondary, reparative stage always following upon an earlier awareness of genital inferiority and penis envy. It is suggested, however, that the earliest phase of women's femininity—the core gender identity—is the simple acceptance of body ego, "I am female." Only later will this be covered over by penis envy, identification with males, and the other signs of femininity in disrepair with which analysts are so familiar.

This core of femininity develops regardless of chromosomal state or anatomy of the genitalia so long as the parents have no doubt their infant is a female. To explore this thesis, several types of patients are described: (1) females without vaginas but otherwise biologically normal; (2) females who are biologically neuter but whose external genitalia at birth looked normal so that no doubt was raised in their parents' minds as to the sex of the infant; (3) females, biologically normal except for masculinization of their external genitalia (but with vaginas), who were reared unequivocally as girls; (4) females who are biologically normal except for masculinization of their external genitalia (but with vaginas) who were reared unequivocally as boys. Some speculations and anthropological data are presented with regard to a fifth category, females who are biologically normal but without a clitoris.

In the first three types, those unequivocally thought to be females developed a female core gender identity— "I am a female." Evidence suggests that type 4 regard themselves as boys. Females of the first three types continued to regard themselves as female even after learning that they were anatomically defective.

ROBERT J. STOLLER*

The "Bedrock" of Masculinity and Femininity: Bisexuality

From his first psychoanalytic writings to his last, Freud was concerned about the relationship of biological forces, which he called the "bedrock," to human psychology. No such theme was more constant than constitutional bisexuality, which he always believed influenced object choice and the degree of a person's masculinity and femininity. In analysis, one could not penetrate the wish for a penis in females or the repudiation (fear of) femininity in males, because they are the "bedrock," ultimately determined by constitutional bisexuality. This paper suggests that, recent work showing how biological forces can change gender behavior in animals notwithstanding, these fundamental qualities in men and women can be caused by quite nonbiological forces—the family psychodynamics that help shape gender identity in infancy.

Freud, the biologist, hungry and impatient for sound laboratory data on which to hang the most profound speculations on human behavior, reached the end of that known world early in his studies. When he then set off upon the search that was to be psychoanalysis, he had to end his direct involvement with the laboratory, deferring to future experimenters discoveries of the physiology that underlies human behavior. Of the several fundamental biological questions he found crucial, none

---

* A biographical sketch of the author appears on page 259.

played a more central—or fascinating—role for him than that of biological bisexuality.* It is worth our tracing his thinking in this regard now, over seventy years later, not only to review his beliefs but to see how they accord with recent studies in neurophysiology.

We start back at the origins of psychoanalysis and Freud's relationship with Fliess.† Impressed by recent findings that the sexual apparatuses start with undifferentiated fetal anlagen [precursors] which, even after adult differentiation, retain vestiges of the other sex, Freud was captivated with his friend's speculations. [In a short section omitted here, Dr. Stoller concisely but thoroughly traces Freud's use of the concept of bisexuality.—ED.]

In "Psychoanalysis Terminable and Interminable" Freud summed up this lifetime of thought on biological forces underlying masculinity and femininity: "We often have the impression that with the wish for a penis [in females] and the masculine protest [in males] we have penetrated through all the psychological strata and have reached bedrock, and that thus our activities are at an end. This is probably true, since, for the psychical field, the biological field does in fact play the part of the underlying bedrock."

Tracing Freud's thinking regarding this "bedrock" (bisexuality) from the time of his relationship with Fliess to "Psychoanalysis Terminable and Interminable," you may see the following: (1) from beginning to end biological bisexuality is an essential building block for theory—fixed and unchanging in his mind; (2) he recognized

* "Bisexuality" is used several ways in the literature: overt homosexuality; pleasure in both homosexual and heterosexual intercourse; identification with aspects of the opposite sex; cross-gender nonintercourse behavior, such as effeminacy; the capacity of certain cells and tissues to shift appearance or function, or both, from that typical of one sex to the other; embryological undifferentiation; vestigial tissues of the opposite sex in the adult; an innate "force" that can influence behavior toward that of the opposite sex. In this paper, I shall use the term with only biological connotations.

† Fliess was a close friend and associate of Freud during the early period of Freud's work.—ED.

that the evidence for this bisexuality was sparse and that little new was being added in the over forty years he used this crucial concept; (3) it was not a very fruitful concept in the sense that it led to great new insights. (This is decidedly *not* to say that it was therefore unimportant to him—or to us.)

Freud, then, always believed in a constitutional bisexuality which influenced object choice and the degree of a person's masculinity and femininity. (It would be appropriate here to define "masculinity and femininity," to separate them from other behavior called sexual, and to consider the problem of the "evolutionary explanation"— [whether] what exists in lower animals does so in man; or doesn't; or how does it; or how much does it—but there is no time; so let us share our common-sense notions and put aside that discussion.) This bisexuality produced a resistance in each sex that was ultimately beyond the reach of analysis because of its biological origin.

Now let us consider this possibility: What Freud thought was an elemental quality, "masculine protest" or "repudiation of femininity" in men, rather than reflecting a biological force, is a quite nonbiological defensive maneuver against an earlier stage: closeness and *primitive identification with mother*. Comparably in females, earlier than penis envy in little girls is a stage of *primary femininity*. The biological lies deeper still.

Actually, Freud gives us no evidence that repudiation of femininity in males or the wish for a penis in females has a biological origin. It is rather a belief based on his finding these conditions ubiquitous and on his difficulty in removing them by analysis. (Often, when confronted with a ubiquitous or unanalyzable quality in humans, he fell back on the "metabiological," e.g., Lamarckian genetic residues of the ice age as a cause of the "biphasic" nature of sexual development—entropy and death instinct explain negative therapeutic reaction or masochism; masculine equals active and feminine equals passive because sperm are active and ova wait.) By now, we may suspect that important aspects of character structure are permanently fixed very early in life, not by innate factors but by the impingement of one's fellow creatures, as Freud showed in his psychological work in contrast to his "biological" theories. The evidence for this is overwhelming in lower animals: remember Harlow's monkeys, the work of ethologists, or the multitude of conditioning experiments. But more specifically, it is likely that in humans, masculinity and femininity can be permanently established in earliest life by psychological forces in opposition to biological state. The following findings suggest this:

1. Infants noted at birth to be hermaphroditic go on to develop a "hermaphroditic identity" (believing throughout their lives that they are neither male nor female or that they are both), whenever their parents are uncertain about the sex to which the child should be assigned. However, when the parents do not have this doubt, even in the face of ambiguous genitals, the child has no question he is a male, if the assignment was to the male sex, or a female, if the assignment was to the female sex. This occurs regardless of the biological abnormalities present, even hidden chromosomal, gonadal, or hormonal defects (an exception to this finding is noted briefly below: certain congenitally hypogonadal males).

2. Transsexual males, as the result of postnatal events —a specific family constellation—have an almost complete reversal of masculinity and femininity, acting like normal women and requesting that their bodies be changed to female; yet, they are without biological abnormality.

3. Fetishistic cross-dressers and certain effeminate homosexuals, as a result of specific attitudes and behavior in their mothers and fathers, develop mixtures of masculine and feminine or effeminate behavior as defensive maneuvers to protect their threatened masculinity (castration anxiety).

These cases are all examples of what Freud called "the

accidental factor." Regression based on futility, it seems to me, made him decide accidental factors could not sufficiently account for those almost universal conditions: repudiation of femininity and the wish for a penis. Might not the former also result from, for instance, the need to escape from primal identification with mother's body and feminine behavior and the latter from lessons in inadequacy taught by mother (adopting her sense of feeling inferior) and society (see [Kate] Millet for a recent and extensive criticism of Freud's views on femininity)? If boys, in the intimacy of the normal infant-mother symbiosis, identify with their mothers, and if excessive and prolonged blissful closeness produces extreme femininity in boys, the boy who is to become masculine will have to repudiate that femininity. But then the femininity (feminine identification) is there not because it is part of mankind's biological inheritance but rather because all boys have females for mothers.

In addition, observation of children just does not reveal that "both sexes seem to pass through the early phases of libidinal development in the same manner. . . . We are now obliged to recognize that the little girl is a little man." Instead, we all have seen girls already feminine between the ages of one and two years.

THE NEW PHYSIOLOGY OF MASCULINE AND FEMININE BEHAVIOR

Few new physiological data have been incorporated into analytic writings since Freud's death—only agreements or disagreements with or permutations on his theory. Especially in the last decade, however, controlled experiments on animals and "natural experiments" in humans have suggested that we shall soon know more about biological influences on masculinity and femininity. (The upsurge had its precursors among brain researchers, observers of bisexual manifestations in natural behavior, discovery of the chemical similarities between male and female hormones, and the endocrinologists' knowledge that many male tissues respond to female hormones [e.g., breasts, skin, hair, fat] and that many female tissues respond to male hormones.)

Controlled Experiments on Laboratory Animals

Now, after all these years, the studies Freud awaited are underway. Brain physiologists are beginning to find the central mechanisms of behavior in animals, including those of masculinity and femininity. This, it seems, is the breakthrough; formerly mysterious forces are found to be made up of hierarchies from components in the brain, influenced by hormones, internal and external perceptual inputs, other brain centers, chains of releasing mechanisms, "engrams" of previous experience, and new—psychological—experiences. Here, at this beginning, is a fascinating finding: it appears that, as it is with the anlagen for the sexual organs and their related apparatuses,* *the resting state for the central mechanisms of gender* (i.e., masculine and feminine behavior as contrasted to "sex") *is female. Only if the fetal brain (hypothalamus) is organized by androgen does masculine behavior result.* And, if normally occurring androgens are blocked in the male, then, once again, femininity appears. Apparently the brain makes do with one type of anatomic system: if it is activated with androgens, it is the "bedrock" of masculinity; without activation, it will subserve femininity.

The genital anatomic fact is that, embryologically speaking, the penis is a masculinized clitoris; the neurophysiological fact is that the male brain is an androgenized female brain. (Women's Liberation activists and other metapsychological romantics can make of this what they like, but what they make is, as I believe was true of Freud when he came to the opposite conclusion that women are innately inferior to men, related to science as daydreams are to reality.)

---

* Possibly even the chromosomes—some suggest that the Y chromosome, the so-called male chromosome, is simply a defective X chromosome, a late mutant in evolutionary history.

There are critical (sensitive) periods when the brain is most susceptible to the influences of fetal sex hormones which organize subsequent tendencies toward masculine or feminine (not just reproductive) behavior. The period of greatest sensitivity to such hormones varies from species to species, some just after and some just before birth, but is rather invariant for individuals of both sexes within the species. The power of the critical period is so great that a single pulse of hormone in the laboratory may set for life the gender behavior as masculine or feminine (without there being any anatomic change in the body, for by this time the development of the reproductive anatomy is complete).

"Natural Experiments" in Humans

In the past I have used the vague term "biological force" to indicate a belief in biological mechanisms that might influence the development and control of masculinity and femininity. We can demonstrate that such an influence has its final common pathway in the brain, at least in lower animals; here is where electrochemical impulse becomes drive and action. But what of humans?

The following categories, for which we are indebted to [John] Money and his colleagues in particular, are "natural experiments" which suggest similar forces at work in humans.

[The following abnormalities which occur, fortunately, quite rarely, are complicated. Essentially, they suggest that some of the same forces studied in animals may be at work in humans. Brief additional explanations have been added to some of the terminology.—ED.]

FEMINIZATION—CHROMOSOMAL ABNORMALITY XO (Turner's Syndrome [In this abnormality the individual has only one chromosome and that is the female chromosome. The individual also has no ovaries or testes. Normally each person has two chromosomes: females have two X chromosomes and males have one X and one Y. The letter designations are derived from the shape of chromosomes as seen under a microscope.—ED.]): Although these individuals are missing a second chromosome and have no gonads to produce sex hormones, anatomic development is nonetheless in the female direction. In addition, such patients grow up feminine in behavior and heterosexual in object choice.

TESTICULAR FEMINIZATION SYNDROME With male (XY) chromosomes, the subject nonetheless develops to adulthood as a normal-appearing female. It is probable that the hormonal defect is in the target organs (the extragonadal tissues) which, abnormally, fail to respond to circulating androgens. Subjects are feminine and heterosexual. [This situation is not well understood. Since both the X and Y chromosomes are present and there appears to be an appropriate amount of male hormones circulating in the body, it is presently suspected that the tissues of the body are just not responding to these masculinizing influences as they usually do. The reason for this occurrence is not known.—ED.]

(These two categories are not as yet highly suggestive. We need more information before we can decide if the adult femininity in these patients is related to their unandrogenized brains or simply to their having been raised from birth unequivocally as girls—see above, hermaphroditic identity.)

CONSTITUTIONAL MALE HYPOGONADISM These males, who appeared physically normal at birth, are discovered in adolescence or later to have had testes markedly deficient in androgen production since fetal life. An unusually large number from early childhood on are feminine and state in words and behavior that they believe they really should be girls.

TEMPORAL LOBE DISORDER A number of reports implicate paroxysmal temporal lobe disorder in cross-gender behavior, oddly enough, only in males. The behavior (usually dressing in clothes of the opposite sex) comes on with the paroxysmal electrical burst; remission of the disorder with treatment leads to immediate loss of the bisexual behavior. [Those who work on the problem report that there is a concomitant burst of abnormal electrical impulses that can be recorded from the temporal lobe of the brain in the manifestation of this disorder. The phenomenon described here appears similar to other forms of unusual episodic behavior of a nonsexual nature, which are known to be accompanied by abnormal electrical impulses from the temporal lobe. They can be reduced or relieved by drugs known to act on such brain abnormalities.—ED.]

MASCULINIZATION—PROGESTERONE EFFECT Otherwise normal human females were masculinized in utero by large doses of progesterone given to their mothers to prevent spontaneous abortions. In addition to masculinized genitals (hermaphroditism) these little girls have developed into tomboys (masculine in behavior but heterosexual in object choice) more than a control series.

ANDROGENITAL SYNDROME [The adrenal glands, which secrete several types of hormones, also secrete a small amount of androgen, i.e., male sex hormone. This is the source of the small amount of androgen which is found in normal females. In this disorder, an excess activity of the adrenal glands occurs and an excess amount of androgen is produced. It can occur in the fetus, before birth. This is the syndrome described here.—ED.]: Fetal hyperadrenalism causes masculinization of the external genitals in females. [John] Money, who has always reported these girls to be normally feminine if properly diagnosed and raised as females, now thinks they are "tomboyish," though heterosexual.

DISCUSSION

These human "experiments" are much weaker in convincing one of a biological bisexuality that can guide behavior than is the animal work. They are suggestive, but they do not as yet refute the evidence that postnatal effects in humans can quite overturn the biological (except, again, with hypogonadal males). Similarly, a body of work on genetics has tried to link overt homosexuality with in-herited factors. These studies cannot be evaluated ade-quately.

If, in males, biological bisexuality can be ascribed to the masculinization of an otherwise female brain by andro-gens, should we then say that females do not have a "bi-sexual" brain? (I am not seriously suggesting this; it is for biological experimentalists to answer such questions. We analysts would do best in this realm only to ask questions, not also to give "answers." For instance, the physiologist may some day tell us to discard the term "bisexual" for the kinds of reasons he tells us to avoid the word "in-stinct"; or he may show that in the female minute amounts of fetal androgens from the adrenals are enough to give just a "touch" of masculinization to the female hypothalamus.) The possibility that the original embryo-logical status of the male is to have a female brain and female body might arouse some to speculate that women are innately superior, and then those who, with Freud, assert that women are innately inferior will have to muster up still more imagination to tip the balance back to the male-innate-superiority position. . . . Or perhaps the new physiology will simply teach caution.

For myself, I wish we could declare a moratorium on such speculation.

I believe Freud was wrong in saying that the etiology of both repudiation of femininity and the wish for a penis was biological. But his conviction that there were physio-logical mechanisms that could influence either masculine or feminine behavior in the same person has support in hundreds of studies in animals, though the necessary studies in humans are as yet only weakly supportive.

The details of physiology certainly make for more so-phisticated discussion now than in Freud's time (although the future will show the present to be naïve enough). They also suggest errors by Freud. His insistence, beyond lip service, on taking the biological into account has not, however, been proven wrong. In the case of bisexuality,

282

THE "BEDROCK" OF MASCULINITY AND FEMININITY

we can see that the brain is not the tabula rasa some allege. While the newborn presents a most malleable central nervous system upon which the environment writes, we cannot say that the central nervous system is neutral or neuter. Rather, we can say that the effects of these biological systems, organized prenatally in a masculine or feminine direction, are almost always (with the exception of hypogonadal males) too gentle in humans to withstand the more powerful forces of environment in human development, the first and most profound of which is mothering.

I wish to close by bearing down on an area where I am uneasy: the dangers of biologizing. Freud recognized these dangers and, in sober moments, his own propensities therein: "I regard it as a methodological error to seize upon a phylogenetic explanation before the ontogenetic possibilities have been exhausted."*

Anyone who can set up experiments that demonstrate scientifically what Freud and Jung take for granted—phylogenetic memory of psychological events—will be quite a sensational genius. Even Fliess's excesses, how-

---

* The full paragraph is worth noting. It biologizes: "All that we find in the prehistory of neuroses is that a child catches hold of this phylogenetic experience where his own experience fails him. He fills in the gaps in individual truth with prehistoric truth; he replaces occurrences in his own life by occurrences in the life of his ancestors. I fully agree with Jung in recognizing the existence of phylogenetic heritage; but I regard it as a methodological error to seize upon a phylogenetic explanation before the ontogenetic possibilities have been exhausted. I cannot see any reason for obstinately disputing the importance of infantile prehistory, while at the same time freely acknowledging the importance of ancestral prehistory. Nor can I overlook the fact that phylogenetic motives and productions themselves stand in need of elucidation, and that in quite a number of instances this is afforded by factors in the childhood of the individual. And, finally, I cannot feel surprised that what was originally produced by certain circumstances in prehistoric times and was then transmitted in the shape of a predisposition to its re-acquirement should, since the same circumstances persist, emerge once more as a concrete event in the experience of the individual." In Sigmund Freud, "From the History of an Infantile Neurosis," *Standard Edition* (London: Hogarth Press, 1955), vol. 17.

ever, could not quite cool his own similar tendency (as we see in the quoted paragraph), probably just as much a contribution to their friendship early in the relationship as to their breaking off later. It is so often around biological words that battles in psychoanalysis have been fought, e.g., the stages of libidinal development as the origins of specific neuroses, the death instinct; Lamarckian inheritance, libido vs. a neutral psychic energy.

But each example is only a particular case, as is bisexuality, of one of his main philosophic concerns: the relation between the biological and psychological. A great pitfall, so seductive for many of us, is the premature linkage of the two. There not being enough facts yet, one is tempted to bridge the gap with grand theories or words that concretize concepts into "facts." Freud recognized this and was constantly struggling against his (repudiated) enthusiasm to be a philosopher, so as, in Kris's words, to "succeed in establishing the distance between the physiological and psychological approaches." Happily, unlike his colleagues-become-enemies, he never quite succumbed to the seduction of the one grand answer. Always after the flight, he backed off, expressed his uncertainty, softened his syntax, and declared the necessary data were still missing. That is why he contrasts markedly with the pyrotechnicians who have been so attracted to him.

The last words of "Three Essays on Sexuality," still valid, reveal Freud's admirable sense: "The unsatisfactory conclusion, however, that emerges from these investigations of the disturbances of sexual life is that we know far too little of the biological processes constituting the essence of sexuality to be able to construct from our fragmentary information a theory adequate to the understanding alike of normal and of pathological conditions."

PART III

Present Problems
and Some Future Possibilities

ALEXANDRA SYMONDS is an analyst, member of the faculty of the American Institute of Psychoanalysis and the Karen Horney Clinic in New York City, and assistant clinical professor of psychiatry at the New York University School of Medicine. In recent years Symonds has devoted special attention to stimulating psychoanalytic discussion of new ideas on the psychology of women. In this direction she has also written papers on the psychological aspects of the Women's Liberation movement.

Phobias after Marriage

WOMEN'S DECLARATION OF DEPENDENCE

FOR MANY YEARS I have been interested in a specific clinical problem which occurs when a young woman, who was apparently independent, self-sufficient, and capable, changes after marriage, and develops phobias or other signs of constriction of self. These changes invariably cause her to become excessively dependent and helpless. This sometimes occurs suddenly and dramatically, as in the development of phobias, or it may occur gradually and insidiously over a period of years. Either way, her entire way of life is changed. Where before marriage she was an active, apparently self-sufficient young girl who traveled, drove a car, had many interests, held a responsible job, and went many places alone, now all these activities are sharply curtailed, or completely impossible. She becomes fearful of traveling, especially by plane or subway. She may be afraid to be alone even for a moment. She usually can no longer drive a car herself, and in extreme cases may not be able to travel in a car at all, even as a passenger. In the less dramatic cases where this change occurs without specific phobias, she becomes fearful of making any decision or of taking any sort of responsibility on her own. She clings to her husband for constant support, apparently changing from a capable, "strong" person into a classically "helpless female."

Many of these women give up all their previous interests and activities which had represented independence of action, or expression of self, such as in the field of creativity. One of my patients who had gone to art school and had done excellent paintings as a young woman, gave up art entirely. Another young woman who had begun to develop a promising career in the opera dropped singing and never sang at all, even for pleasure.

These changes do not necessarily occur suddenly. Often it is a gradual process, and it takes place without conscious decision. In fact, these patients do not usually mention their former interests, enthusiasms, or involvements and may refer to them only in passing as though they were not important. References to their life of activity and responsibility before marriage are often elicited by me in the course of treatment and seem to represent no contradiction to the patient.

I want to make it clear that I am not referring to those young women who shift their interests and energies after getting married, from outside activities to the home and family as many young women do. These women continue to grow and develop, although in a different sphere. I am referring to the small but significant number who seem to shrivel up after getting married, who seem to lose all interest and involvements, who constrict their inner life, and who become depressed, anxious, and excessively dependent. Very often these patients have psychosomatic problems, and make the rounds of internists and gynecologists. I had one patient of this type who had glaucoma, and another had a thyroidectomy. Several suffer from various gastrointestinal symptoms, insomnia, and other evidences of chronic unresolved conflict. Phobias are only one of the psychiatric symptoms that may develop, and are likely to attract attention because they are dramatic. However, we also see many other signs of this process. All these patients are depressed to some degree, sometimes severely.

While phobias and other signs of constriction are not remarkable in themselves, what attracted my interest was the fact that they occurred after marriage. Instead of marriage representing a broadening and enriching experience, it caused the reverse effect. Incidentally, these patients do not usually complain about their husbands nor do they feel they have made a bad marriage. On the contrary, they portray their husbands as kind and helpful and they earnestly desire to stay married to them.

I have wondered about this apparent paradox ever since I first came across it about twenty years ago. At that time I saw a very successful professional woman in her thirties who seemed to be quite accomplished, yet she suffered from intense fear of traveling and of being alone. It seemed such a contradiction to me. She told me that these fears had developed suddenly about a year after she had gotten married, eight years previously. She was very ashamed of her "weakness" as she called it, and tried to master it by will power. Unfortunately, I saw her only briefly and I was not able to learn more about her personal dynamics, but it remained in back of my mind for many years as a puzzle which interested me. Since that time, however, I have had the opportunity to work with similar patients in greater detail, and I have found that it is not an unusual syndrome. It is frequently reported in the literature on phobias. For example, [Frederick C.] Redlich and [Daniel X.] Freedman, in their chapter on phobias [in *The Theory and Practice of Psychiatry*], give a lengthy case report of a professional woman who fits into the same category as I am describing.

In preparing my material for this presentation, I went over my records for the past twenty years. I have seen ten to twelve patients who fall into this category, some for consultation only, and others for prolonged treatment. I treated four of these patients in analysis for several years at least two or three times a week. I have also had contact with many others of similar type through my work with various hospitals and agencies as a consultant, and on occasion I have met such women socially. I have selected three patients who will be described in some detail to bring out the features they have in common. (Names and identities have been disguised.)

Mrs. A. was a woman of about thirty-eight who was referred to me by an internist to whom she had gone because she felt weak and rundown. The internist recognized that she was quite depressed and sent her for psychiatric treatment. She was a tall, thin woman who looked malnourished, neglected in her appearance, and was seriously depressed. She cried profusely during our sessions.

There were certain marked discrepancies in her manner which were quite apparent. She was a well-educated woman, who spoke with authority when discussing impersonal matters. However, when talking of more personal things, such as her feelings and her life at home, she became uncertain, wispy, and vague. Her appearance also showed marked contrasts. She was rather tall and gangly and she appeared her age or older, yet she wore the clothing of a schoolgirl, with knee-high socks, skirt, or jumper, and had a plain straight haircut with bangs. It was obvious that there were tremendous extremes in her personality. Intellectually she was developed and mature, while emotionally she was still childlike.

She stated in the very first session that her marriage was a failure because she felt that she was a total failure as a wife and mother. She was married for eight years and had two children. Since getting married, she had sex very rarely, perhaps once or twice a year, because her husband was usually impotent. However, he had convinced her that this was her fault, although he would never tell her just what she was doing that was at fault. He told her repeatedly that she was an aggressive, castrating woman and all their difficulties were because of her. They did not argue often. She accepted his accusations and was overwhelmed with feelings of guilt and hopelessness.

Mrs. A.'s accepting all the blame and her lack of criticism of her husband are characteristic of these patients. On the conscious level they express no resentment, or even the ordinary griping typical of most married people. They never complain openly about their husbands (or anyone else for that matter). However, they are involved in the special sort of interpersonal dynamic which is characteristic of the dependent personality with the "appeal of helplessness" as described by [Karen] Horney. While these individuals do not allow themselves to express any open hostility or criticism, they describe to the analyst or listener such outrageously provocative behavior on the part of their husbands that the listener may be impelled to come to their defense and even to become angry at the husband. For example, the material I have just presented about this patient's husband may have made you annoyed at the husband. In this type of communication, the analyst or the observer becomes more upset about the partner's behavior than the patient seems to be. They describe outlandish and extreme behavior on the part of their husbands with no effect—and with no visible protest, presenting a picture of a weak, helpless woman being pushed around at home by an inconsiderate and aggressive husband. This particular message, the appeal of helplessness in a woman, often comes across as seductiveness. In therapy or in analysis, a male analyst is especially vulnerable to this and may be drawn into a very sticky and confusing countertransference where he finds himself constantly coming to the aid of his patient against the husband. As a woman, I am not affected in the same way by these patients.

Superficial therapy, such as marriage counseling or direct intervention, is also a frequent occurrence because the patient externalizes to such an extent that it appears as though all her troubles would be over if only she had a different husband or if only someone else would get her husband to change. It may be tempting, but it does not usually bring any lasting benefit, since the problem lies not in the marriage, nor in the husband, but within the patient herself. I think we have all seen instances where people get a divorce, and then remarry the same sort of individual as before. We must recognize that these women are caught in a state of chronic, unresolved conflict of a profound nature which paralyzes them, and it may take years of analysis before they develop enough of a sense of self to handle their lives effectively. However, unless they do it themselves, it will not work out.

The need to avoid criticism of their husbands often leads to outlandish situations at home, since the husband goes blithely about his business doing as he pleases, while the wife builds up an explosive rage, all unknown to both of them. The many psychosomatic symptoms are an expression of this repressed anger. Mrs. S., for example, only mentioned in passing that her husband's hobby was collecting antique automobiles. He insisted on keeping an automobile motor disassembled on the living room floor for months while he tinkered with it. At other times he would bring in all sorts of assorted junk and clutter up the entire house with it. Mrs. S. said that occasionally she felt annoyed, but she never complained because she felt that she should be more understanding.

A few words about the third patient, Mrs. M. She also came into treatment by way of a medical referral. She had been suffering from severe anxiety for three or four years, with headaches, palpitations, insomnia, gastrointestinal distress, and tremendous feelings of tension. These symptoms were becoming so severe that she was afraid she was losing her mind. She was in her thirties, had been married for ten years, and had a child of two. She expressed no criticism or dissatisfaction with her husband, stating that he was extremely helpful and sympathetic to her distress. He did all he could to help out. In the course of the first few sessions, however, she gave numerous examples that described him as an extremely difficult man to live with. He had a fear of germs, and had insisted that they wear masks until the baby was eighteen months. He would not allow anyone to baby-sit for the child, so they were forced to take him everywhere. He did not trust restaurants and would never eat out, or allow the child to. However, in spite of many, many peculiarities on his part which differed from her point of view, Mrs. M. said that she deferred to his opinion because she felt he was very thorough, and he must know. And besides, if she insisted on her way, and anything happened to the child, she would not be able to endure it.

In each case, the patient tries to build up rationalizations for herself so that she can avoid direct confrontation with her husband's peculiarities, and thus avoid awareness of her own hostile or aggressive feelings. It is not that the husbands are so peculiar or different (although in certain instances this may be true) but the problem is rather in the wives' inability to handle even the ordinary friction which occurs between two people who live together.

The attempt to avoid open friction by retreating results in an enormous personal restriction in their lives. For example, Mrs. A.'s phobias developed gradually, within the last few years. She did not recall any abrupt event or sudden onset (this is frequently the case). However, she could not use an elevator, subway, drive a car, or travel by plane. Any attempt to do so produced panic and unbearable anxiety. When she was single she had her own car, and had enjoyed traveling. She often flew to distant places on her vacations. However, now she had become practically housebound. Interestingly, while the inability to use the subways and elevators hampered her activities, she did not give it any special emphasis in telling me about it, and it wasn't mentioned in the first few sessions. She also seemed untroubled by other evidences of this constriction which had occurred since getting married. Her husband did not particularly like to socialize or to go out, so they rarely did. They seemed to have few friends and few interests in common, and they spent most of their time at home, reading or listening to music (in separate rooms) because this was his preference. All this she apparently accepted as natural because she was married, reiterating that she loved her husband and had always wanted to be married and have a family. While this may sound on the surface like an ordinary, contented domestic scene, keep in mind that there was very little display of affection or love between them. Mr. A. frequently spent the entire evening alone in his room, and Mrs. A. felt miserably neglected by him most of the time that they were together. If she ever tried to approach him affectionately he would freeze up.

Mrs. M. also had many phobias which restricted her; however, she was more overtly troubled by them. She was angry at herself for being so "stupid," as she called it, and she desperately tried to get to the bottom of them by direct assault. Occasionally she would force herself to travel even though it made her have vomiting spells. She would frequently come into the sessions and start the hour with a very precise statement such as, "I still can't think of any reason why I should be afraid of subways." She was a highly intelligent woman, a college graduate (as were all three patients), and was exceptionally intellectualized. She stressed the control of feelings, and talked of "arranging her feelings" so that they would not betray her. She had many dreams where people wore masks—usually the mask was benign and friendly while, underneath, the real face was frightening. She was terrified of her own hostility, and it was only with great difficulty that she came to accept some of it. Of these three patients, Mrs. M. had the most subjective anxiety and the most distressing physical symptoms. Sleep was very difficult for her—often she would awake in a panic, without remembering her dreams or having any clue as to what was disturbing her. When she did recall her dreams, they were filled with emotion—usually rage, anger, anxiety, and apprehension. There were also many sexual dreams. In telling them she seemed disconnected from the feeling, but her face showed the extreme tension and inner pressure she was under.

Mrs. M. was the only one of the three who remembered a sudden onset of her phobias. They had occurred about eight years ago while she and her husband were on a tour. She recalled the details of this with great difficulty, only after many years of treatment. The essential factor was that Mrs. M. had insisted on the trip over her husband's reluctance. To her this represented a very aggressive act, and when he expressed some dissatisfaction with the trip, she remembers only a mild feeling that he was dampening her enthusiasm. The next day, she was frightened of the plane they took and the remainder of the trip was a nightmare. Insisting on the trip in the first place had a special significance to Mrs. M. It was one of the only times that she can remember where she persisted in actualizing a very personal desire of hers. She had always yearned to travel and especially looked forward to this after getting married. The awareness that her husband did not share her enthusiasm was catastrophic for her, although she only realized that after years of therapy.

All three patients had the same sort of relationship with their husbands. Whenever any area of difference developed which would ordinarily have caused friction between man and wife, they avoided it at all costs. Rather than differ, and perhaps fight, or at least argue, they would automatically and unconsciously drop their point of view, their need or their desire—and go along with the husband's. The phobias were one of the ways to handle their repressed feeling. It seemed to immobilize them and prevent them from any act that might be interpreted as aggressive or self-assertive; in fact, it was a statement to the very contrary, since it made them helpless and harmless.

I was always struck by the price these patients were willing to pay in order to avoid the faintest possibility of expressing anger or hostility openly. And they were doing all of this silently and without their husbands' being aware of what was happening. Thus they became more like villains as time went on. Part of the problem is their inability to communicate clearly to their partner. To do this would require a stronger sense of self and a willingness to accept the consequences of their acts. They would have to consider their wishes worth fighting for. However, since these are people who consider ordinary assertion to be the equivalent of hostility, they have an exaggerated fear of this type of encounter. They do not express their needs directly, yet they feel angry and hurt because the partner does not perceive it. All of these feelings are pushed out of awareness. One of the patients had a dream where she was hanging outside a fifth-floor window, just barely holding on, and her husband passed by without seeing her. She was only able to whisper in a very low voice—"help."

This is what interested me from the very beginning. Why do certain women respond to marriage with such extreme suppression of self, especially when it occurs in those who seemed to have been so different in their life before marriage? Without making a conscious decision, ruthlessly they choke off their inner self; in terms of Horney, they give up their real self. One of these patients expressed this brutal deadening of self in a dream which she had when she thought she was pregnant. In the dream she strangled several baby birds. She often dreamed of birds as a symbol of herself, sometimes as a canary in a cage. The canary was especially significant since Mrs. S. had a particular joy in singing and when she was a young girl she had been quite involved in it.

We must come to the conclusion that people who so readily give up their own genuine growth are either desperately in need of what they get in return, or value themselves so little that it does not seem to matter—or both. If this is true, then what sustained them earlier in life? And what was happening in marriage which triggered such a negative reaction?

As I got to know these patients, I began to understand more about them. They all had some similar experiences in their background. All came from families where self-reliance, independence, and control of feelings were necessary, either because they were highly prized and encouraged (as with the first two) or because they were necessary for survival. Not only was control of feelings necessary, but in their background there was very little respect for childlike interests. As a result, they had to grow up in a hurry. For example, Mrs. S.'s parents would not allow any conversation at the dinner table unless it was of interest to the adults. The children could not speak to each other. She recalls that most of her meals were spent in silence. Mrs. M.'s parents were totally ineffectual and immature, and unable to respond to their children's needs. Mrs. M. was the eldest and had to take care of the younger children as well as herself. She felt from an early age that she could not trust her parents if she needed their help.

This early need for control of feelings and self-reliance was important in understanding their later predicament. From early childhood they developed skills and qualities that gave the illusion of strength. They all chose work or education that seemed to bear out the illusion, and that gave others the feeling that they were strong and self-sufficient. They repressed their healthy needs to be taken care of and repressed the child in them as well. They only did "important" things. For example, when Mrs. A. was a child she loved gardening but she recalls that she raised only vegetables because these were useful and she could sell them whereas flowers were only to look at. As teenagers and young women all these patients acted cool, capable, and self-reliant. They remember themselves as fearless, and several were known as tomboys or daredevils. Mrs. A. said that she had always loved the ocean and had been an active swimmer as a young girl, although now she was afraid to swim anywhere except in a pool. They had no conscious plan to be different after getting married, yet each of them underwent a profound change. Mrs. M. had been a nurse before she was married. She had been in charge of a large ward in a busy hospital and had no difficulties in handling her job. It was only in analysis that she realized that she had been secretly yearning for marriage so that she would no longer have to be a responsible person and maintain the façade of strength. Then she would be able to put down a tremendous burden which she had been carrying all her life, and be the dependent little girl she had never been before. But she would only allow herself this luxury in marriage, because there it was socially acceptable and no one could criticize her for it.

Many women freely admit their dependency needs, and they are not ashamed to say that they are looking forward to marriage so they can quit work and be taken care of. Healthy needs are not insatiable and do not cause difficulties. On the other hand, those who deny these needs all their life, who repress and feel ashamed of these feelings, and who have not had their ordinary needs gratified as they are growing up, often have secret expectations of marriage which make them vulnerable and cause them many difficulties. Marriage for them represents their opportunity to be dependent without self-criticism and self-hate. Marriage then becomes their "declaration of dependence." If for any reason this is questioned, or the marriage does not seem to be all they expected, they are in a panic and they cling even more. Their rage at being frustrated is immediately suppressed and cannot be acknowledged by them since it seems so destructive.

We often see the first stages of this process when an apparently capable, highly educated young woman—perhaps even a professional such as a doctor—gives up her work and her education as soon as she marries, and seems to settle for very little other than the mere structure of a marriage. This may be the first indication that she is trying to utilize the marriage relationship to fulfill an enormous neurotic need to be taken care of. Marriage for these girls reveals an aspect of themselves that was not obvious before. They have exaggerated and idealized expectations of what marriage is to be, and what a strong man will be. No matter how sophisticated or broadminded they were before marriage as to the role of men and women, they tend to become the paragons of Victorian femininity—helpless, housebound, and ineffectual.

I borrowed the term "declaration of dependence" from

Dr. Carl Binger who used it in an article on "Emotional Disturbances among College Women." In the college population he found that many girls' reaction to any crisis was a tendency to become depressed, apathetic, and excessively dependent, suddenly losing their former self-sufficiency. He does not mention this, but I have found that girls often get married as an alternative to continued growth, and as a retreat from life. When they are faced with a difficult problem in their own development, they may seek marriage as a refuge.

Many women, and men too, equate morbid dependency and helplessness with femininity. My patients all had some confusion and uncertainty about their femininity and saw marriage as a confirmation of their feminine identity. This proved that they were really women. They were willing, in fact eager, to avoid any evidence of self-assertion since they consider such impulses as masculine. Healthy impulses and feelings of growth and self-assertion were rejected by them as too aggressive, and too masculine. When they were single, they could develop expansively to some extent since they were not attached to a man, and there would be no question of coming into conflict with a man, and perhaps winning out. However, once they become involved with men, they tend to suppress all their assertive impulses for fear it would endanger their much needed partnership.

Treatment for these patients is painstakingly slow and prolonged. Underlying the anger, the frustration, and the fear of conflict is a profound resignation. I found that marriage had represented to them the only acceptable way for them to have significance, and for the deeply repressed and denied self to have an opportunity to live. They tenaciously refuse to accept the concept of separateness. For example, one patient who liked art and theater at first would not consider going anywhere alone or with another woman even though she had done this often when she was single. She felt that she would be pitied or ridiculed as unmarried. As treatment progressed, she did begin to go places without her husband, and to enjoy things on her own. She even went on a few vacations with her children.

It is not too difficult for these patients to recognize that they are angry, and this awareness relieves much of the depression. However, though they are less depressed, for a long period of time there may be no essential change in their life. They have so successfully compartmentalized their feelings that they often achieve intellectual understanding without true insight. We know that phobias represent isolation and compartmentalization of feeling, and are of necessity difficult to treat. Perhaps the prolonged analysis which all three of these patients had was necessary so that by way of the analytic relationship they could allow themselves to be taken care of by the analyst. This was brought out in one of the first dreams of Mrs. A. where she saw me as a pediatrician.

A word about the significance of the phobias in these patients. They expressed the typical fears which patients have who fear closed spaces or who fear travel. They described their fears as fear of being closed in, a fear of being trapped, a fear that they would not be able to leave any time they wanted to (as on a turnpike or in a plane). Mrs. M. said that once she was in a plane she would have to give control over to the pilot. Mrs. S. could not drive a car anymore (although she did at one time) because she feared that the car would do something that she did not want it to do. One patient became terrified if she had the slightest stuffiness of her nose because she was afraid she might not be able to breathe, and she would die. All these fears which the patients described, the fear of being closed in, trapped, helpless, and without control, are symbolic expressions of how the individual closes herself in, keeps down her impulses and imprisons herself. However, direct interpretation of this nature is usually not understood early in therapy.

The traditional explanation for phobias is related to the fear of loss of control. Freud felt it was loss of control of sexual or aggressive impulses. Others, such as Leon Salzman in his book *The Obsessive Personality*, broaden it to be a fear of loss of control of any impulses that would be considered a threat to the integrity of the personality, or as Horney would say, to the pride system. This would include tender impulses, power drives, needs for detachment or closeness, and so on. The fear of humiliation is closely tied up to the anxiety involved.

I would like to add another dimension to the understanding of the function that these phobias played in this type of patient. These women were actually afraid to be *in* control. They feared the consequences of taking their life into their own hands, of setting their own direction (as driving a car), of movement on their own, of exploring, of enjoying, of discovering. They feared dealing with the unknown, they feared the ordinary aggression and assertiveness that accompanies growth and involvement. Many years ago, Otto Rank referred to this when he said that more people have a "fear of life" than a "fear of death." The existentialists call it fear of being. Kierkegaard stated in speaking of anxiety "the alarming possibility of being able causes dizziness."

This problem has nothing to do with femininity or masculinity. These are only convenient catchwords for the people I am describing. They may attach their anxiety to these concepts, and may find ready acceptance in others. But their problem is a deeper and more basic one. It is a fear that many people have who are unable to actualize their own growth and development. Unfortunately, many women suffer from this because of ancient cultural prejudices that have barred them from full participation and growth, and which makes it easy for them to defer their own development, and to live vicariously in others. Such people express their fears of self-realization in terms of fear that by their growth they will hurt others. Thus it comes easy for them to accept any accusation such as being "a castrating female" or "too aggressive."

In my therapy with such patients I focus on themselves

—not on the marriage or the husbands. Slowly and pains-takingly they discover islands in themselves that they have ignored, discarded, and minimized. Gradually they acquire enough feeling of self to make their needs known to themselves and their husbands, to stand behind them-selves and not abandon themselves (as they accuse others of doing). This requires prolonged treatment, often with only partial success.

In conclusion, what sort of people have I been talking about? These are women who came from an atmosphere where they had to grow up in a hurry. They had little opportunity for genuine self-expression, especially of warmer feelings. They may have had great compassion for the suffering of others, but very little sympathy for their own. As girls they were capable and self-reliant, but were not really whole. They saw marriage as an absolute ne-cessity for them to achieve status and significance, and minimized or completely ignored any achievements or interests prior to marriage. Once married, then all their unexpressed needs would be allowable. When faced with the ordinary difficulties in marriage, when faced with the necessity for friction and for self-expression, they reacted with enormous rage, and underlying this, a profound de-spair. For these women, the phobias and other signs of constriction of self were the end result of the tremendous emotional turmoil which lies within.

ROBERT SEIDENBERG

A PSYCHOANALYST of classical background, Robert Seidenberg is currently active in presenting far-reaching and original material for a reevaluation of the significant forces operating on and within women. He has extensively reported on the implications of his findings for his daily clinical work. To his many writings Seidenberg has brought his wide knowledge of mythology, classical civilization, and literature. He uses the insights gained from these realms to focus on specific problems in the therapeutic arena.

The first two selections are condensed from his book *Marriage in Life and Literature,* from which I have omitted some literary and clinical illustrations. The third selection demonstrates how his understanding of a woman's problem has led to a reorientation of basic psychological constructs, such as the theory of anxiety. This discussion will be of great interest to the professional, although some of it has been omitted here because of the technicalities involved; the basic concepts are, however, intact.

Dr. Seidenberg is currently clinical professor of psychiatry at Upstate Medical Center in Syracuse, New York, and president of the Western New York Psychoanalytic Society.

Is Anatomy Destiny?

> Women are the universal depressed minority group,
> which is why they are looked down upon, exploited,
> patronized, and resented. I thought everyone knew
> that.
>
> —Emile Capouya

THE PSYCHOANALYST must turn to Mill, not Freud, for the heuristic statement about the problems of women in our civilization. The disappointment with Freud in this matter is all the more distressing since psychoanalysis cut its eye teeth on the psychic illnesses of women patients. Preoccupied with psychosexual matters, [Freud] missed the opportunity to illuminate the psychosocial factors which as [Erik] Erikson was to point out later in the Dora case, were more consequential. This error of psychoanalysis, unfortunately, has resisted correction in the mainstream of orthodoxy. How one would have welcomed in Freud something similar to the opening statement of John Stuart Mill in his essay, "The Subjection of Women": "That the principle which regulates the existing social relations between the two sexes—the legal subordination of one sex to the other—is wrong in itself, and now one of the chief hindrances to human improvement; and that it ought to be replaced by a principle of perfect equality, admitting no power or privilege on the one side, nor disability on the other."

Woman's status in the world today, even in the United States, where it is better than most places, is grossly unequal to that of her sexual counterpart. Most women, apparently succumbing to the euphuistic prose and poetry about sweet femininity and domesticity, do not seem to know or care about the grossly inferior place to which they have been relegated. As a matter of irony, women themselves, in a form of self-hate, generally condemn members of their own sex who strive for something better.

It is the old story that, once they have gained it, men and institutions rarely give up power without pressure to do so. In the case of women, the pressures have been minimal because they have dutifully "known their place" and made virtues out of submission, docility, and inferiority. They become ecstatic over the niggardly crumbs handed to them. The difficulty here is that all those tasks and roles assigned to women are principally in the realm of biology, the having and feeding of children, the care of the lean-to, and a variety of things that a self-respecting male would consider demeaning and would stalk off the job if asked to do. According to statistics, in 1969 there were 26 million working women. But the vast majority were working at very menial jobs. When the *Harvard Business Review* attempted to make a survey of women's executive opportunities, they gave up in despair, the barriers being so great that there was scarcely anything to study. The percentage of women in the professions has actually declined since the 1930s.

There is tragic irony in the generally held belief that women are strongly "narcissistic." This term is applied to them because of their well-known habits of preening and other self-attending activities. The importance they place on their clothes, mannerisms, and other attention-getting devices as well as their so-called propensity for hypochondriasis and psychosomatic disorders have led many erroneously to feel and write that women have a high level of narcissism in them. The opposite, of course, is the case. It has been observed that self-love, as far as the female is concerned, is grossly wanting. It is both scarce in women and poorly tolerated by society when it exists.

Freud recognized this absence or diminution of self-love in women. However, he characteristically attributes this quality to anatomy rather than to society. Clara Thompson wisely pointed out that the girl's envy of the boy could be adequately explained in the gross cultural inequities that do exist. Unfortunately her voice has not received the attention it deserves. By demonstrating the frustrations and renunciations that generally held for the female in the patriarchal society, she eclipsed Freud's anatomical theory. Similarly, Karen Horney was in the forefront of exposing the social aspects of woman's plight. Her treatment at the hands of mainstream psychoanalysis is a sad chapter in the history of that science.* Freud's was a hard act to follow.

It is generally agreed that one has to search far and wide for female geniuses in science or in the arts. This has been used as evidence of cerebral inferiority or at least psychological inhibition or inadequacy. Psychoanalysis, following Freud, tends to explain the woman's seeming lack of creativity on the nature of her being and on psychological ontogeny. [Phyllis] Greenacre postulates that the woman's creativity becomes absorbed in her bio-

* There is, however, ample evidence that mainstream psycho-analysis continues to view women as an inferior breed. Here are the written words of an eminent analyst, Dr. Judith S. Kestenberg: "Feminine integration is completed when woman learns to adjust to her role as wife and mother. In this she can succeed only if she is teachable and can accept her husband and children as organizers of her femininity" (page 485). Again, she explains: "Women who are teachable, but unsuccessful in meeting and attracting men able to teach and assume domination [sic] in a relationship, frequently adapt to habits, neurotic attitudes, and unconscious fantasies of the men they do find" (page 479, in the *Journal of the American Psychoanalytic Association,* July 1968). From what Dr. Kestenberg says, not only is a woman to be dominated, she will be made neu-rotic if she is not! I can think of no other instance in human rela-tionships or social or political life, outside of brutal totalitarian societies, where domination becomes an imperative for "health"— a proud goal to be sought after, a sine qua non for the good life, a described condition for survival. Dr. Kestenberg herself leads an active professional life and is, from all reports, an excellent teacher of men and women in psychiatry and psychoanalysis.

logical function of producing children. And in a strange twist of values, she seems to indicate that because a woman creates children, she would therefore have no need to express herself creatively in other ways. And there are those in psychoanalysis who hold that man's creativity results from his frustration at not being able to become pregnant, i.e., he is reduced to having brain children. Although quite poetic, this simplistic formulation regarding creativity in the male and female is unconvincing.

On the contrary there is evidence to indicate that the factors of opportunity and salutary climate play decisive roles. The most pertinent and perceptive statements on the subject seem to come from those outside of psychology and psychoanalysis. For instance, in the matter of woman writers, Madeline Chapsal finds the dearth of women novelists is due primarily to cultural restraints. She states [in the *New York Times* Magazine, 12 March 1967]: "The act of writing, a hyperindividualistic act, would seem to be incontestably linked to social condition, that is, to the degree of individual freedom with respect to the group and to the society as a whole—the society itself having to be not only free, but economically 'developed.' " She also writes: "For centuries, and especially in the nineteenth century, the one thing forbidden to girls above all, just as it was to married women, was freedom of speech, which was suspected of leading—and we see how right they were—to freedom of thought, then of action."

The above statements appear to be more logical in their explanation of the woman's lack of artistic production than the focus on her biology. Without in the least knocking the value and delights of having babies, writing books would seem to be another thing again. The picture might be quite different if her spiritual freedom went hand in hand with her child-producing license.

It has been observed that although we have outstandingly talented actresses, very few playwrights write substantial parts or plays for them. Harold Clurman, in an article called "Our Neglected Women," writes in this regard:

Women today are free but the stage neglects them. We are all crazy about them, but do we love them? They are rarely seen for and in themselves. They are seen as babies or brides who need protection, monsters from whom we must protect ourselves, martyred saints, mothers who stifle us, thorns in the flesh, solace to broken men. Even as the cause or excuse for outrageous passion they have become almost obsolete. Ibsen's *A Doll's House* is now held to be outmoded. And it is: Nora doesn't have to leave the house and slam the door; she is virtually pushed out. But once she's out, where, humanly considered, does she go?

One statement of Mr. Clurman warrants emphasis and is applicable to areas of involvement other than the stage. He indicates the training, willingness, and freedom of the woman today but the lack of *opportunity*. There is no place for her to go. She is shut out by design or bias from all but the menial and routine jobs. Unfair to those already in the market, the real damage is done to the will and hope of the young who are deprived of models to emulate. Thus a malignant constraining force is produced which diminishes the options and alternatives for the young girl. This may account for the stampede toward marriage and the relinquishing of educational opportunities.

Mr. Clurman says that there are no villains here. There do not have to be, for as in other instances of prejudice and persecution, the dirty work is done by the institutions, the silent coalescence of man-made and man-dominated systems of education, religion, business, government, and "psychology" which effectively does the job of exclusion and diminution. So effective has this work of attrition been that chastity belts need no longer be applied—women have been reduced to ensuring their own modesty.

It is this depreciatory attitude toward their daughters

that largely accounts for the hostility that daughters feel toward their parents—especially their mothers. The mother, characteristically looking to her son for the fulfillment of her own frustrations, relegates the member of her own sex, her daughter, to second-class status. This is felt by the daughter as a horrible betrayal and disloyalty. Psychoanalysis, routinely finding this rage in daughters toward their mothers, has attributed it to the sexual rivalry between women for the father's love, the classical Oedipus triangle. In addition, the concept of the castration complex has been invoked to explain further this antagonism. This complex in women is derived from the daughter's alleged fantasy that mother *had* taken her penis away when she was an infant, i.e., has castrated her. On this basis, the daughter's rage against the mother is irrational—a figment of her imagination and a derivative of her "unreasonable" penis envy.

Professor Andrew Hacker at Cornell writes:

It is the fate of . . . girls not to be taken seriously by their parents. After teaching young women for a dozen years, I never cease to be depressed over the low level of expectations that most parents . . . set for their daughters. Even the most up-to-date mothers and fathers persist in thinking of Judy and Carol as sweet, scatterbrained young things to be dutifully raised and ultimately married off in a white gown at the neighborhood church.

These anatomical and biosexual explanations have proved to be oversimplifications. For as Hacker points out above, "the castration" of the girl in her childhood and adolescence does in fact take place via the lack of serious consideration that is afforded her. Therefore the daughter's fantasy of "being cut off" is not an irrational fantasy —but a social reality. She is in fact cut off from the world that we have always defined as being most meaningful and relevant. The castration complex is no myth as psychoanalysis would have it.

Yet much of the injury to women is self-inflicted. They

have succumbed to the culturally directed penis awe and fully cooperate in the apotheosis of the male. Ask a woman for whom she would rather work and most often she will say "for a man." In seeking out a physician or a lawyer, most women would say they would have more trust in a male regardless of matters of training, competence, skill, etc. Just as many Negroes are "Uncle Toms" in the civil rights movement, most American women would rather be docile and cooperative than fight for their self-respect. In this process, they hate women who do seek out other than the traditional destinies. It is most difficult for them to understand that they indulge in self-hate when they heap ridicule or scorn upon those of their own sex who may attempt to break through some of the male-female shibboleths.

Because women are traditionally bossy around the home, permitted a great say in inconsequential matters, there has arisen in America the mythology of the matriarchy. Everybody seems to know and remember that Mother appeared to run everything; nothing is further from the truth. (In the so-called American matriarchy, seven states do not give mothers equal control with fathers over their children.)

In reality the consequential and crucial decisions of the destiny of Americans are in the hands of the males. There are no women in the National Security Council, rarely in the President's cabinet, and never in significant numbers in legislative positions. Women are given a say in their families perhaps as a compensation for their almost total exclusion from influence in public matters. And this compensatory authority in the home (and we know in life and clinically) is often less than salutary to powerless children. Mothers often "identify with the aggressor" and bludgeon the children to degrees of their own exploitation as people. That boys grow up feeling that their mothers have castrated them comes as no surprise. Similarly, girls, who find their mothers inadequate models for themselves, feel that they have been betrayed. For them the bossy and overbearing mother is not somebody whom one could profitably and honorably emulate. This is if anything a pseudo-matriarchy system—with all the ill effects of responses that accompany chronic subjugation, hypocritically called equality and even dominance.

The concept of "equal but separate" roles for male and female is to a degree a necessary one and a sine qua non for the merger known as marriage. There must be a division of work and responsibilities, and this dichotomy must be responsive to the all-important biological needs served by women. Theirs is to bear and nurture and there can be no adequate substitute for this—nor should one be sought. Childbearing and the rearing of children do not take second place in importance to anything the husband accomplishes. Granting these irreducibles, one must then carefully examine whether womanhood has been encumbered by many labors of unlove which are the result of the male-dominant society. The dictum separate and equal too often suffers pejoration wherein those with power take unto themselves more and more, to the attrition of the other.

The male has always been and must be more than a husband or a father. If that is all he aspires to, we know that he is destined to fail, for one can be nothing before there is identity as a person with goals of personal development and achievement. Unless he has such goals and some measure of success with them, he will fail miserably as a husband or a parent because he will expect his wife and children to provide the gratification that should come, must come, from his own achievements. Furthermore, unless he has some modicum of creativity, he brings very little of enrichment to the family other than his biological presence.

What of the woman? Strangely enough, she may be censured if she aspires to anything more than mother and wife. Being witness to comparative results in the academic world, she finds it difficult to remain in the house watching the division of work and roles evolve in which her husband just *happens* to be able to use his education effectively and participate in worldly affairs, to be stimulated by contacts with other minds, and on the other hand finds herself immersed in activities about 180 degrees opposite. Instead of having stimulation, opportunity, rewards, etc., she is witness to her lack of opportunity, inability to use her skills (which are gradually lost through disuse), and sees herself reduced to the menial labors of the day which she is told are feminine.

It is said that being a wife and a mother are full-time jobs and of inestimable importance. A mother before she is anything else must be a person with self-respect, assured of her own worth, and, more importantly, must feel that she has not paid an inordinate price for motherhood in terms of her personal striving and aspirations. If she has, her motherhood will produce sour milk and the offspring will know there is something horribly wrong.

If, as we are told, love is not enough for children, it is equally true for parents. For a woman, as for a man, to be loved by husband, by children, by family, is not enough in the quest to be whole. Meeting the biological needs of one's self and of others, as important and as basic as these are, cannot alone sustain either man or woman. Being a decent model for a child is a most worthy objective, but one can become a worthwhile model for a child only if one feels himself worthwhile. And there must be some confirmation of "worthiness" from other people than those who love you or who depend upon you. This entails performance, use of skills, professional confrontations, and varying degrees of competition in the marketplace of talents not found at the supermarket.

When a woman is able to find the formula that successfully combines personal and family fulfillment, her comfortable level of self-esteem makes family life actually easier. For one thing, she does not feel "gypped" and does not look upon her husband and children as burdens or persecutors. She can also enrich the family with the example of achievement that she sets and the worldly knowledge that she can bring back with her. But finding that formula, striking that happy balance, is a most difficult task, attained only after agonizing appraisals and prodigious soul-probing. It is a task that a man has simplified for him in that he rarely has to make a decision between being a father and making a livelihood; he has a built-in stimulus and opportunity for personal achievement.

Is work a cure? If it is used as one, beware! Women who get married or have babies to solve deep intrapsychic problems are destined for disappointment or worse. Similarly, "going to work" as a solution for long-standing personal conflicts will be found a weak reed for both men and women. "Going to work" should never be considered a cure for neurosis, or a usually good thing, or a submission to a contemporary fad, or some heaven-directed categorical imperative, but rather a derivative of one's own truth. Yet Freud indicated that work has a greater effect than any other technique of living in the direction of binding the individual more closely to reality; in his work, at least, he is securely attached to a part of reality, the human community. However, did he have only men in mind when he made this statement? Or are women to look elsewhere for reality-finding devices? It would be consistent with truth for a dependent and aimless person to seek shelter and not meddle with situations too fearful and too complex for his capacities. So, too, those who have goals within the realm of achievement, by reason of training, skill, and personal investment, would be untrue to themselves if they turned their back on, or were blocked from, pursuit of them. Therefore a "back-to-work" movement as a cure for unhappy or discontented women has a built-in self-destroying mechanism. No one can or should work unless adequately prepared and honestly motivated.

This motivation has to do with the ego ideals—those internalized images of worthwhile goals, which we value highly and think worthy of our own maximum efforts. These internalized ideals give direction as well as stimuli.

The ideals of many women in their own development are not solely homemaking. They often share the goals of their fathers and brothers. These ideals which may be commonly shared with their brothers should not be labeled "masculine" or "feminine," but perhaps "family" truths. Whether the one sex or the other succeeds in the propagation of this inheritance depends on a myriad of complex circumstances, including luck, opportunity, and social tolerance.

Anatomy may be destiny, just as skin color or religious background play an overwhelming force in determining one's destiny, but it must be remembered that these circumstances of anatomy or destiny loom as large or small as the social rules of society make them. There is a great tendency in humanity to fear differences, and an equally great tendency to find excuses to relegate the subjugated to inferior roles. Women have been the subjects of men and have been badly exploited. They have been, paradoxically, victims of cultivated inequalities. They have never made a real protest because they have been sold a bill of goods that their "assigned" role was a "natural" one and to protest was to go against nature. The words of Goethe seem quite appropriate: "No one is a greater slave than he who imagines himself free when he is not free."

Women have been called the defeated sex probably from the time when men learned that women could not produce children by themselves. Stripped of this magic, woman was thereafter placed in a secondary role in human society. To keep her subjugated, she was "endowed" by men with unfavorable and demeaning characteristics. Erich Fromm writes: "The war between the sexes has been going on for several thousand years, and men's propaganda about it is just as silly as war propaganda. Men say women are less courageous; it's notorious that they are *more* courageous. That they are less realistic; it's notorious that they are more realistic. Women are more concerned with the question of war and peace than men are."

Let her strive for excellence in almost any field and she will be called "masculine." The doctrine of natural law has had an infamous history of being invoked to vindicate all types of subjugations and suppressions, but nowhere more flagrantly than in the treatment of women. Separate-but-equalism has worked as badly here as in race relations, because the power to give or withhold and to balance is reserved to the dominant group. It results operationally in the accretion of the one and the attrition of the other.

The woman who seeks a professional identity in the world is faced with many hazards. They arise not only from a hostile and resentful environment, but also from her own inner doubts about what she is doing. Even when she reassures herself or is given support that her stand is proper and justified, she frequently manifests a feeling of guilt about not being in her proper place—the home.

It is all new for women, and they often succumb to the onslaughts of a hostile environment as well as inner distortions. These failures become living ammunition for those who preach that such roles are unnatural for women; much is always made of the mess they make in any but their divinely directed life of domesticity. For the patient observer, these instances, far from proving feminine inferiority, or biological or divine determinism, point up inherent problems of *transition* which will eventually be resolved, as both sexes accommodate to new and more equitable modes of behavior.

Many women who sincerely possess strong convictions about the value of their professional work find that married life and the pursuit of traditional feminine expectations are quite impossible for them. Dr. Alice S. Rossi, at an assembly of women at Cambridge, Massachusetts, adroitly observed: "Hence women who enter the more demanding professions may remain unmarried, not simply because they are not chosen by men but because they find fewer men worth accepting, and because marriage is not an exclusive life goal. It is also the case that marriages among professional women are slightly less apt to 'succeed' in the conventional demographic sense of persistence."

If a girl in her development has no other than the image of a woman in the domestic role, this image will be internalized and become her principal knowledge of what a woman is and does. It forms the basis of her morality, and behaving differently sets up a moral conflict. In spite of later worldly education, the earliest lessons come from all-powerful, life-giving, and sustaining giants—parents— and they stick. This learning is, then, the education of how to please, how to be loved, how to survive. These earliest lessons from kin take priority and can be overcome only by vigorous self-purging efforts. The little girl who sees her own mother and aunts and grandmothers invested completely in household matters and disdainful of women who are active in the world will feel that any but the attitudes and roles of her female relatives are unnatural and immoral. She is getting her definition of femininity, and will thereafter "know" what a woman should properly do. Contrary to the expectations and demands of reformers, human growth is never acrogenic.

Even though it is very high sounding and presently popular to claim that the chief goal of living is to be or become "a person," very few individuals have the strength to overlook or transcend their sexual identities. No woman will treasure any fame or glory she may achieve at the price of being called "unfeminine." This below-the-belt blow sends most women into despair. Therefore, we see that the doubt cast on sexual identity is another great deterrent to worldliness.

The problem of sexual identity, never absent in everyday living, may become particularly acute and distressing because of personal developmental experiences. One woman in her childhood had the misfortune of losing her mother through an acute illness. She, along with three brothers, was thereafter raised by her father and transient housekeepers. There was no woman with whom she could identify. She was exposed to a masculine world and for a while enjoyed being "one of the boys." In her late adolescence, however, she became acutely conscious of her different attitudes and modes of behavior. Now the youths shunned her even as they had played with her earlier in her life. She wasn't feminine! However, she would do something about it. In college she asked for help from her roommate about how to dress, how to use cosmetics, how to behave on dates. Yet it all came to her with great effort and unnaturalness. She did begin to date but continued to have grave doubts about what she really felt and who she really was. In her conscious effort to be feminine, she rushed into marriage, forfeiting her educational goals. She married a man with two children by a previous marriage. This, she felt, would keep her feminine and motherly. She became a good mother, endured financial hardships that plagued her husband, and was generally successful except for recurrent periods of mental depression. She felt, however, that she would have to stick it out to prove that she was feminine after all. She raised "his" children and had "two of her own."

In later life, when her children were grown, she resumed her education. She did very well in her studies and was faced with the issue of working at her interest. She now had severe misgivings about going out into the world, even though both her home situation and outside opportunities were conducive to her doing so. She was faced with her old dilemma of identity. Was she now to risk the emergence of her old "masculine" ways if she were to work and compete with men? She had spent years proving that she was feminine and now was on the threshold of placing her "acquisition" in jeopardy. At this point in life, on the threshold of achieving worldly goals, she began to have obsessive thoughts that her body was changing, turning into a man. If she were to work, it would mean to her that this was what she had wanted all along—that her motherhood was a sham, that she was really one of her brothers all along. She was beset not only by the external problems of a middle-aged woman seeking a place in the world, but also by the internal issue of identity that was a recurrent source of anxiety for her. As it turned out, she could not risk the doubts of her femininity that working might bring, and she relinquished her ambitions.

As if serving the expiatory needs of a male-dominant society, physicians are now telling American women that the distress of their lonely and alienated middle years is due mainly to an internal hormonal imbalance to which all women are allegedly heir—no less than 85 percent of them—the other 15 percent miraculously escaping by dint of a fortuitous and still unknown biological factor. Furthermore, the women have been told that both the imbalance and resultant distress are readily cured by proper medication. Although the cause and the cure are subject to question, the proportions of women's agony are here acknowledged and documented. We cannot fully trust the gynecologist's eye view of the world in these matters and must ponder about forces other than internal biological ones that may be consequential in the destiny of American women. There may indeed be an imbalance— one that the physicians care not to see, for it might entail healing themselves, not their patients.

Whether or not psychoanalysis, used in a doctrinaire fashion, has also contributed to modern woman's dilemma, as Betty Friedan suggests, is an interesting issue.* The argument is that psychoanalysis, by stressing the importance of motherhood and the early infant-mother relationship, has kept woman in the home for fear of imparting mortal damage to her offspring. Allusion has also been made to psychoanalysts' loosely used male and fe-

* One cannot deny that psychoanalysis has been no friend o feminists. O'Neill writes: "The jargon of psychoanalysis gave the old charge that feminists were 'unnatural' a more sophisticated appearance. Of course, it is also true. When society decrees that a woman's place is in the home, the woman who leaves it is by definition aberrant." William J. O'Neill, *Everyone Was Brave* (Chicago: Quadrangle Books, 1969), p. 290.

male character classifications, and their purported jubilance when an analysand marries, a woman's acceptance of her "feminine" role, etc. Psychoanalysts are indeed responsive to conventional expectations (although less so than most).

The psychoanalyst in theory does not tamper with the ego ideal of the analysand. This is strictly his or her business. Admission for therapy requires that the ego ideal be reasonable, be within the frame of reality. However, the analyst never seeks to interfere with—much less destroy—the convictions and aspirations of the fellow human being before him. It is instead the analyst's job to help an individual pursue his goals more effectively. Whether these goals are "masculine" or "feminine," as convention sees them, should not concern either analyst or analysand.

The success or failure of therapy is based mainly on whether an individual is able to reaffirm and act effectively on those inner truths which he deems most valuable and important to himself. The issue in analysis is whether the analysand can free himself of the doubts and ambivalences wrought of experiences throughout his life. If a woman wants to become an atomic physicist like her father, the analyst does not seek to change her mind. Nor is the analyst apt to extol the virtues of marriage and motherhood to her, as some critics have intimated. He is more likely to hear her aspirations with the attitude of one who would fiercely resent any tampering with his own.

We have seen that the ego ideal of the male is generally a confluence of breadwinner, husband, parent, and achiever, and that these are more or less compatible. On the other hand, for the female the ego ideal as achiever may sharply clash with ideals connected with her womanhood. She cannot easily be a "good" wife, mother, and homemaker and at the same time aspire to "soul-satisfying" goals. There is set up for this more complex woman a conflict of goals or ego ideals which she somehow must integrate. Today it is past saying that women ought to be brought up or educated with only the one ego ideal, that

for which she was biologically built. Her task is most difficult because she is made to feel guilty if her other aspirations impinge on her role as a mother. Therefore she
needs help not only from an exceptional mate who genuinely understands her struggle and provides a proper
milieu and opportunity for her fulfillment, but from
society, which needs a reorientation on the male-female
question similar to the one it is attempting in the racial
issue. It is not a question of educating women; they take
to that themselves and usually outperform the men here.
They must be given full opportunity for the expression
and use of their skills without discrimination and condemnation. The idea of masculine professions and female
jobs should be done away with. In this there might have to
be legal protection—stronger laws and a bit of militancy
on the part of those who are oppressed. Change of attitude
would be nice, but unfortunately, as the Negroes have
learned, this is unlikely. Human nature being what it is, a
group does not relinquish its power unless forced to.
Contrary to the euphuisms of some "realistic" politicians,
morality generally has to be legislated.

If a woman is allowed to accomplish the more difficult
task, her shame about loss of identity will be lessened, and
she will be more apt to accept her children as developing
human beings rather than despising them as burdens, or
clinging to them as toys or as parts of her own body. If
ever there is a schizophrenogenic mother, it is the one
whose aimlessness causes her to cling to her children with
the desperation of a drowning person. The child is never
allowed to test reality on his own, never learns his own
boundaries, often fails to distinguish between the animate
and inanimate. He treats the world as a "thing," just as
he has been treated by a mother who has no thing. A
mother who has something is apt to behave quite differently. Although it is a vast oversimplification to attribute
mental illness to one cause, we are becoming aware of
social forces that filter down to the family and mother-
child unit. The effects of a male-dominant society on

"mothering" cannot be overlooked as potentially and actually disintegrative. Justice and equality for women may pay the dividend of more stable male offspring and females with a more hopeful model to emulate.

Men have never wanted to compete with women, whether on a tennis court or in a court of law. The prospect of being bested is altogether beyond toleration. Misogyny throughout history is well documented. The historical phenomenon of the witch and witchcraft, perhaps the all-time low point in man's intellection, bears evidence of the hatred and depreciation that the male was capable of toward woman whom he purportedly loved and loved to protect. He simply placed the blame and burden for his impotency on her. The irony of this blackness is that to this very day the word witch is used to characterize a bad female; there is no word at all for bullies whose delusioned creations they were. Some very serious psychiatric historians have come up with a new fantasy, diagnosing these women as mentally ill. In their scientism and misogyny they seem to overlook the fact that witches were pure delusions in the minds of men. If mental illness was involved (and if it was then we must indict all of humanity for periods of hundreds of years including the writers of the Bible, where witches are floridly described), it was the illness of those harboring the delusions, rather than the victims of this projection.

If all this was in the past and over with, if it was just an object lesson in foibles of which man is capable, then we should content ourselves with being happy historians and leave it at that. In the dark years of each man in the desperation of facing his inadequacies, whether moral, political, ethical, economic, social, or sexual impotence, he can even today find it within himself to place the blame on his wife. This is not to say that women are incapable of bitchery, and they have done their share of harm in the subtle and circuitous ways open to them. They too share the heritage with their sexual counterpart of aggression, demonolatry, and destructiveness. Yet the sexual imbalance, blatantly evident today, is the responsibility of the power structure which prefers to maintain it that way. A great deal of the ignoble in women can be viewed as an excretion caused by the pressures directed against them.

Marya Mannes adroitly observed: "Most men of our society, although they claim to be interested in women, are not interested in Woman. What concerns them is not what a woman is but what she is to *them*. Their interest even their affection is still relative rather than absolute."

To achieve sexual balance in quotations, the following is offered. Jules Feiffer, who can be listened to with great advantage on most social issues, under the rubric "Men Really Don't Like Women," wrote in a popular magazine: "The American woman is a victim. She is unique, as far as victims go, in that she has been trained to be ill at ease admitting it. Her trouble is that she is doing comparatively well as a victim—making a buck, running a family: and then, too, there are so many more *imposing* victims around."

Freud reveals the typical attitude of his day toward women, that they should be there for the needs of man.* They have to be meek, docile, weak, dependent, not because these qualities are good for them, or necessarily

---

* Freud's statement on the importance of *work* for a person has been widely quoted by social scientists. Freud wrote: "It is not possible within the limits of a short survey to discuss adequately the significance of work for the economics of the libido. No other technique for the conduct of life attaches the individual so firmly to reality as laying emphasis on work; for his work at least gives him a secure place in a portion of reality, in the human community. The possibility it offers of displacing a large amount of libidinal components, whether narcissistic, aggressive or even erotic, on to professional work and on to the human relations connected with it lends it a value by no means second to what it enjoys as something indispensable to the preservation and justification of existence in society." S. Freud, *Civilization and Its Discontents* (New York: W. W. Norton, 1962), p. 27. Does this apply to women as well? How is the housewife to "test reality in the human community?" And unto whom is she to displace *libidinal components?* Freud's statement adroitly defines the role of work (professional, he says) in keeping one's identity, integrity, yes, sanity. It is a valid and salutary prescription, if not an imperative, for both sexes.

promote their own feelings of worth and identity, but because all of these serve "our ideal of womanhood." This is the rhetoric of the Southern racists in our own times who cannot give education and suffrage to Negroes because it will take away their carefree, irresponsible nature and possibly their love of folk singing, and shatter the social-comforting ideal of white supremacy.

In fairness to Freud, with the wisdom that, hopefully, comes with maturity and being witness to the circumstances that women, including his own beloved daughter Anna (and none of his sons), contributed to the new science of psychoanalysis disproportionately to their number, he wrote quite differently in later scientific papers.

In 1932 Freud recanted and advised against equating any particular psychological trait or characteristic with either masculinity or femininity, even such opposites as activity and passivity, which had been solidly ensconced in all psychoanalysis as male "nature" and female "nature" respectively. Then, in a concession that may become an all-time paradigm for niggardliness, he wrote: "It is true that influence [sexual function] extends very far; but we do not overlook the fact that an individual woman may be a human being in other respects as well." Finally Freud succumbed to the wisdom of the inadequacy of his own appraisal, and perhaps the invincibility of his own prejudices, and advised: "If you want to know more about femininity, enquire from your own experiences of life, or turn to the poets, or wait until science can give you deeper and more coherent information."

Psychoanalysis continues to drag its feet in understanding the plight of women. Even our "liberal" psychoanalysts have an inaccurate understanding of how it really is. The sad reality is that women do not have a choice—they are *given* a choice but a choice so weighed with inequities that they stay home. Today women are allowed into the world only if they do not take what they do *seriously*. That is, in no even trifling way jeopardize their marriage and/or their image as a wife or mother. She is tolerated as a working person only if she is ambitionless and steers clear of decision-making areas. After all, who likes a woman who is not "feminine"?

The job by the male on the woman has been so well done, using every important social institution—religions, schools, law, medicine, psychology—in his own behalf, that he has been successful in extinguishing even the *wish* of women to have equality with the male in those matters which stamp the value of a human being. She has bought the bill of goods about the determining effects of her biological nature. "Anatomy is destiny; anatomy is destiny," they repeat until there is no room for the examination of any other dimension. Thankfully, the female is different, but because she is different, she should not be hated and despised and deprived of those opportunities for self-development and accretion which men have always considered their God-given and "natural" rights. Men have not shown proper respect for differences—sexual, academic, racial, or religious.

Man's fear of differences has made him reluctant to extend opportunity to those who are different. In the unconscious of men as found in psychoanalysis, there is a deep-seated fear and loathing of women. All the songs of love do not dispel this underlying contempt for those "unfortunates" with gaping wounds where a penis ought to be. It is the loathing of differences that encourages and maintains the male homosexual culture from which females are regularly excluded. Men's preference for their own is seen in any gathering and in most living rooms where people may come together for sociability and conversation. It is not only the church or the army, as Freud alleged, that are homosexual institutions, but also big business, science, law, and almost everything else of importance. Men just are not comfortable with women unless some degree of flirtation is involved. The issue of intellection and even passion between the sexes is largely dismissed. It is an old story. Kenneth Rexroth writes: "To judge by primitive song, legend and epic, romantic love has commonly existed between members of the same sex, and seldom in the institutionalized relations between men and women until those institutions pass through formalization to etherialization, as in the court circle of *The Tale of Genji.*"*

In a treatise, surprisingly late in coming for something so obvious, sociologist [Lionel] Tiger confirms the strong affinity (and bonding) men have for one another in both public and private endeavors.† No argument against this verity. However, Tiger reaches the conclusion that this is quite salutary and attributes civilization's major advances to it. For those (women) who are automatically excluded from the most creative and exciting aspects of their community and must experience these vicariously, if at all, such successes might seem pyrrhic, just as black people might not be particularly enthralled by white America's progress. There are many who justify white racism because "our way of life" has achieved so much. But for whom? Some might consider Tiger's conclusions as derived more from self-serving male chauvinism than from "science."

Our present society, based on male dominance as it is, most reluctantly accepts women for positions of authority and/or possible leadership. Women are different, but most of their purported differences are cultivated in the minds of men in order to justify oppressing them. Then, men have interpreted women's aimlessness, which results from this oppression, as intrinsic and natural to them. Women, then, must be kept down because they are not trustworthy. They must then be loved and protected because they are too stupid to fend for themselves. Unfortunately, we cannot turn to most women for statements confirming this oppression, for, as indicated above, for the most part women have fully succumbed to the propaganda against themselves. Yet they do not know why they

---

* Kenneth Rexroth, "Sappho–Poet and Legend," *Saturday Review*, 27 November 1965, p. 27.

† Lionel Tiger, *Men in Groups* (New York: Random House, 1969).

are so bored, restless, hysterical, hypochondriacal, and too often mentally stunted.

The corroding effects of the unfair use of power at each level of existence from interpersonal to international, is the theme of a recent book by R. V. Sampson. We know of the corrupting as well as self-blinding effects of power and its disabling effects on the person in subjection. We have recognized these in international and political spheres but have been reluctant to see them in the structure of family life. Sampson's words are most instructive:

To the extent that the forces of power prevail over the forces of love, domination and subjection characterize human relations. The former is good and leads to human well-being; the latter is bad and leads to human suffering and strife. The struggle between these dialectical forces is always the same. No one may contract out of it, however much he may wish to do so. For of necessity, everyone at all times and in all positions stands on a relation with other men which will be predominantly of one category or the other. In this sense, what happens in the world, what happens in history, inevitably reflects the contribution, active or passive, of everybody who participates in the vast web of human interrelations. There are not diverse planes of reality to be judged by different stands. There are no separate, insulated planes of the cloister and the Chancellory Office. Jesus Christ and Adolf Hitler belong together to the common plane of our single human experience. It is merely that they represent extreme polarized positions within our common moral spectrum.*

It may be argued that the quest for equality is utopian and that, as Freud purportedly said, there must be a leader in every social unit. If this is indeed so, that marriage can be based on no other than a dominance-submission model, then let us at least face the reality to which our sisters, wives, and daughters are to be subjected instead of invoking the euphemisms of love and devotion

* R. V. Sampson, *The Psychology of Power* (New York: Pantheon Books, 1966), p. 2.

to cover up what is nothing else but servility. Then, if servility is all that is wanted or can be hoped for, so be it. At least women will not have to bear the burden of guilt when, as is happening in ever increasing instances, they rebel against their assigned role of inferiority and subjugation. Furthermore, if their basically unjust treatment is recognized, men will no longer be puzzled and dismayed by the atrophy of mind and emotions that befalls their daughters and wives that inferior status inevitably brings. Men will then be able to understand the zombie-type apathy of those who have totally submitted and the Medea-like frenzy of those women who have nothing remaining but intransigent desires for revenge.

Love conquers all, we are told. Yet if it does, there must be concern for protecting the vanquished. Until now, the defeated party in love and marriage has been the woman. Therefore, if love is to have the transcendent meaning we purportedly hope for, [Martin] Buber's "I and Thou" must prevail. Can we reach the level of human relations wherein loving the other includes concern for her well-being apart from the pleasure and services she can provide? Let us not ignore "Love's Body" but, hopefully, therein can also be tolerated an intact soul.

For the Future—Equity?

AFTER THE SO-CALLED expert presents his cases and clinical data on the vagaries and vicissitudes of marriage as he has seen them in his consultation room and in life, the legitimate question is asked of him, "What of the future for marriage?" The nihilist can of course indulge in all sorts of hyperbolic pronouncements, such as "It is altogether rotten to the core and will destroy all those who enter into it"; or, in the same tone but opposite vein, "There is nothing wrong with marriage. It is the participation of 'sick' people who ruin it."

Marriage as the predominant way of living will be with us long after 1984. Socialist countries in our time have not eliminated it nor do they anticipate doing so. Capitalistic countries find that the marital state is consonant, perhaps all too consonant, with the ideology of personal possession.

It is the author's hope that the marriage of the future be perceived in a way quite different from that of the present. First, it will become dissociated from divine sanctity and be placed in the hands of the participants. It will become a worldly compact, an open covenant openly arrived at. (Monarchs no longer rule by divine right, but all too often today husbands [occasionally wives] appear to be doing just that in their marital provinces.)

[The inequities of the marriage contract] have a dele-

---

* A biographical sketch of the author appears on page 305.

terious effect on men also. But for the moment the urgency of the oppressed must preempt the plight of the oppressor. Men ultimately suffer the corruption of unearned victories and ascendancy. Their personalities become warped by the myth of their own dominance and superiority. It places them in a position of having to be the literal oppressors of those they profess to love. They decorticate their own sisters, wives, and daughters, fulfilling a vow no less ruthless than that against Jephthah's daughter. This "heroic" Judge of Israel immolated his own daughter in exchange for winning a battle. Agamemnon did the same with Iphigenia to get his ships moving. Unfortunately these inglorious deeds of our heritage continue to the present day in more sophisticated and malignant forms. Wives and daughters are sacrificed today for men's ambitions. These go largely unreported. There are no modern-day chroniclers. There are an articulate few who can communicate their feelings in words rather than symptoms. One is Caroline Meline, of Philadelphia, Pennsylvania, who wrote to the *New York Times* (Magazine Section, 12 November 1967) as follows under the rubric "Alienation: Housewife Dept."

To the Editor:

Steven Kelman makes the point in "These Are Three of the Alienated," Oct. 22, that alienation today takes many forms. This corps of the alienated may be larger than he or many people suspect, because I have the feeling that many of America's most stable group, the housewives, are included.

I am the wife of a promising young businessman, the mother of two small boys, and I work at home as a freelance copy editor. I have been out of college almost five years. The college is Smith. At 25, I am faced with the crisis of finding some meaning in life or, if that proves impossible, finding a satisfactory way of living and functioning despite it.

No, my family is not enough. Yes, I want to make their lives as happy and problem-free as possible, and I will, no matter what, go through all the necessary motions. But I really do want to be more than a smiling zombie. The more I think the less real enthusiasm I can muster, and unfortunately I can't stop thinking.

The question is, how do you find something to look forward to? And how do you achieve that sense of purpose in what you are doing that will end this questioning? Like Bill in Mr. Kelman's article, I wonder how you go about feeling committed. What difference does it make whether I go back to school and get more educated or just read or go to painting classes or try to make a career out of something? Basically, what good are goals of any kind in the face of death? Yet how is it possible to be happy in the present, forgetting goals, if there is no sense of accomplishing anything?

The trouble is that I, probably like many of the other alienated, can't get out of myself. I think deeply mainly of me, and I am isolated in my thoughts. To be able to communicate in this impersonal way, that is, write a letter to The Times, is a pleasant relief, but still very self-oriented and of course very temporary.

What is the answer? Keep busier? See lots of people and communicate like mad? See a psychiatrist? Drugs?

These sentiments can no longer go ignored or discredited as the products of a "sick" mind or a spoiled, maladjusted adolescent. They are in fact the laments of one who takes neither her life nor her "voluntary" servitude lightly or cavalierly as the "alienists" (sic) have up to now been prone to do.

Something is terribly wrong with a social contract that results in such real deprivation. It is ludicrous to say, as some do, "Well, she didn't have to get married. If she wanted to pursue a career, why didn't she stay single?" The reasonable rejoinders should be apparent. No man is ever asked to make such a choice. He is expected to have both. Furthermore, in life today, marriage is a woman's only *acceptable* destiny. She really has no choice but to get married. Yet the understanding "humanist" who is appalled when the man-in-the street says, "If the Negro doesn't like the Ghetto, let him come out," is as likely to ask his own wife, "Why didn't you stay single if you wanted a career?"

The inherent inequities of the customary contract blind and corrupt the male. His often accurate vision of broad social issues and problems stops at his own doorstep, invariably skips the one he "loves." The corruption of the male usually shows its effects on both sides of his own doorstep. John Stuart Mill in 1869 was able to write:

All the selfish propensities, the self-worship, the unjust self-preference, which exist among mankind, have their source and root in, and derive their principal nourishment from, the present constitution of the relation between men and women. Think what it is to be a boy, to grow up to manhood in the belief that without any merit or any exertion of his own, though he may be the most frivolous and empty or the most ignorant and stolid of mankind, by the mere fact of being born a male he is by right the superior of all and every one of an entire half of the human race: including probably some whose real superiority to himself he has daily or hourly occasion to feel; but even if in his whole conduct he habitually follows a woman's guidance, still, if he is a fool, she thinks that of course she is not, and cannot be, equal in ability and judgment to himself; and if he is not a fool, he does worse—he sees that she is superior to him, and believes that, notwithstanding her superiority, he is entitled to command and she is bound to obey. What must be the effect on his character, of this lesson?*

It would be pleasant to report progress in the hundred years since then, but that is unfortunately not possible. There is little or no progress to report either on the domestic scene or in man's general ability to inhibit his "aggressive drives" in dealing with diverse political and social problems. In the latter he is constantly driven by his insatiable need to be superior to his neighbor, to save face, and to be a winner in war.

Does this corruption start in his relationship with women as John Stuart Mill and R. V. Sampson seem to

* John Stuart Mill, "The Subjection of Women," *Three Essays* (London: Oxford University Press, 1966), pp. 522-23.

think? Perhaps there is a need now for a massive reappraisal. In the idiom of the day, might not we now leave "love" aside for a while and wonder about redistribution of power in the marital contract? This will be no simple task, for, as minority groups have painfully learned, power is not readily relinquished by those who comfortably and traditionally possess it. The problem becomes even more complex because maleness itself has become identified with the possession of power and the innate superiority that it brings. Any step in the direction of equity between the sexes must then be unfairly called emasculation. The woman then is placed in the hapless position of "emasculating" her brother, husband, and son. It is probably this particular mythology which has deterred her from either effectively resisting or rebelling against her voluntary servitude which is part and parcel of most marriage contracts. The tragic aspect is that the servitude indeed is voluntary—she has internalized her role of inferiority; the chastity belt is now unneeded. *The Story of O* tells of a woman who has to be beaten into submission, then submits, without being beaten; having lost her identity, all she wants is death.

The magic word in psychiatry today is "identity." It can be defined in many ways. It encompasses having some uniqueness and distinguishing features in a world of three billion people. It means standing for something. It also means being what you are supposed to be and, more than that, *doing* what you're supposed to do. It is being an engineer and as Ralph Nader might say, "Being allowed to build a well-engineered car." It is being a lawyer and being able to defend clients instead of routinely pleading indigents guilty. In the idiom of Arthur Miller's *The Crucible,* it is having and defending one's name.

We soon realize that these are fine-sounding ideals which apply almost exclusively to the male. Perhaps it is picayune to discuss, but in the marriage contract in the United States the woman is automatically deprived of her very name, and she is glad to lose it, without a whimper.

But one suspects that the "repression" of the woman's name is the message of how things are and what they are to be. That she had better forget her own search for identity in the meaningful world. Can this "custom" be modified? Simple and as innocuous as such a move is? Probably not, because this is but one of the many ways that our cultural misogyny has been institutionalized. Who wants to pull one fiber in the fabric?

It may be that there has been too much emphasis placed here on the oppression of women in the marital situation. Ironically, it is quite probable that men become victims of their own advantages. An unearned superiority is thrust upon them. This places a constant burden of proof upon them which causes distortions of character and personality which are tragic to behold. The man is placed, often through no personal need or desire of his own, in a position of proving why he, of two people, should automatically be the standard bearer for the family. Often to prove his doubtful superiority, he must resort to pseudo self-enhancement such as uncalled-for bravery, bravado, cunning, tricks, and outmoded feats of courage. On the other hand he must assume an often unneeded executive role with his wife. This entails both a dictatorial attitude and at the same time a subtle campaign of depreciation of her talents, ability, and intelligence. Authority must often be exerted, as upon children, to prove and maintain dominance.

In other words, the male is expected to wear the "emperor's clothes" even though he risks pneumonia. Even though psychoanalysis has labeled the female as the narcissist, it is in fact the male who is forced consistently to show and prove himself, leading to the "hangups" of eternal competition and inevitable oneupmanship. Albert Camus [in his *Notebooks 1935–1942*] recognized and hated this distorting compulsion in men: "Every time a man (or I myself) gives way to vanity, every time he thinks and lives in order to show off, this is a betrayal. Every time, it has always been the great misfortune of wanting to show off which has lessened me in the presence of truth. We do not need to reveal ourselves to others, but only to those we love."

He must be superior whether he is or not. Whether this man-woman supremacy myth has led to or encouraged concepts such as racial supremacy, chosen people, and master race is an interesting speculation, but one which must be seriously considered, given the serious social and political problems that such concepts have created. In entertaining such speculations one does risk the sin of global extrapolations; we must concede it has been the male sex that has controlled governments, and has brought the world to the very edge of disaster. Women have had little say in the inner councils of high-level decision making. R. V. Sampson asks about the price we pay, politically and morally, when we allow urges to dominate and to submit to control our lives.

As the inequities of marriage were enforced by "Divine Will" the marital status quo has been reified by modern sociology and psychology in their theories of roles, role playing, and role taking. Marital partners then are not dominant or submissive in marriage but play proper dominant or submissive *roles*. Problems of equity need not arise. Then the unction of "instinctual" drives are applied to prove that it is natural enough for the male to dominate and the female to submit. To complete the male self-serving mythopoeism, evidence is gathered from lower animals to show predetermined patterns. Ergo, if a man dominates and a woman follows, they are correctly following their biological givens. Therefore, accusations of exploitation as well as hopes for correction of inequities become irrelevant. These types of justifications have successfully kept people enslaved for centuries. The problem of autonomy inherent in "assigning" roles to the male or female, to black people or white people, is that the roles *are* assigned. Perhaps justified in a play on Broadway, the reader in his self-preservative wisdom would like to have a say about the role in life he is to play—even if that say turns out to be pitifully small. At least there is the hope that everything about one's destiny is not preordained by mythologies of the past and present. If the concept of role foredooms, the addition of the word "natural" condemns. Nature is by and large neutral in social and political matters. The history of the word "natural" is not a happy one. It has too often been applied as a self-serving demiurge amongst individuals, nations, and races. Even though everyone glibly speaks of them, inherent sex-linked character traits are products of pseudo science and more often than not are used to create differences for purposes of prejudice or self-justification. But character is indeed formed through both training and role imposition. With the assigned role of dominance and superiority inevitably come arrogance, feelings of self-love, favored access to opportunities, a right to decision making, and expectations of leadership. Pejoratively, the role of dominance too often means the right to exploit, to prevail, and to show off. The role of submission has little to commend itself for in the context of the "good life." It is a condition that a man might endure as the price of failure or ineptness. Yet society generally recommends submission on the part of women as both virtuous and beautiful. Above all it allows fully for the quality of humility. It leads to character traits which, although often allowing for good adjustment to the dominant counterpart, stymie genuine expressiveness, discourage noetic functioning, and promote abdication of personal responsibility. Secondary consequences are malaise and retreat to biological preoccupations, including hypochondriasis and self-hate. The clinical ramification of this self-hate is involutional melancholia—the woman's menopausal syndrome—the outcome of twenty years of submission.

As everyone knows, nothing succeeds like failure. Lederer and Jackson speak of "the stable—unsuccessful marriage." Historically, marriage worked best when it was the "sickest." Dreikurs correctly observes:

It was much easier to maintain marriage and to find peace in one's home as long as the man was dominant. (There was no conflict about sex; women considered their sexual role merely as one of satisfying the needs of their husband.) . . . As soon as one wants more than the other, the relationship is disturbed. The one who wants less feels imposed upon. . . . These difficulties, which discourage and demoralize husbands and wives alike, are partly due to this new relationship of equality, which developed as part of the democratic evolution. There is no tradition that teaches us how to live with each other as equals, in mutual respect and trust.*

Is there an alternative to the dominance-submission model for marriage? A majority of people will not admit that marriage today is based on this model; this reality offends the egalitarian image. They admit to a difference of roles but with equally important functions. Their argument does not hold up under close scrutiny. They ultimately must fall back on the argument of what is "natural." Other people admit the dominance-submission model and praise it. They talk of the dominant role as a heavy responsibility, almost as a yoke, and submission as a manifestation, or as an intrinsic necessity of love and devotion. They ultimately invoke Divine evidence as the authority for ordering the man-woman relationship in this manner. In answer to them, the cynic might reply with Camus, "Do not confuse sanctity with idiocy."

In suggesting alternatives for personal conduct in marital relations, one need not fear now the accusation of utopianism, simply because time may be running out for the human community. It may be the changes at the "precinct level" that will give impetus to the reordering of social and normal values of our foundering society. And the alternatives carry with them no guarantees of happiness, elimination of mental illness, or the elimination of war. They are proposed in the simplistic and naïve framework of doing what is right. This may betray a

* Rudolph Dreikurs, "Determinants of Changing Attitudes," in *The Marriage Relationship. Psychoanalytic Perspectives,* ed. Salo Rosenbaum and Ian Alger (New York: Basic Books, 1968), pp. 83–103.

personal arrogance on the part of the writer but here again the alternatives that are to be proposed are not original but have been a neglected moral theme of the liberal humanistic tradition of Spinoza, John Stuart Mill, and Martin Buber. It was Spinoza who exposed the hoax of humility—the keystone on which most bias leans. John Stuart Mill, a hundred years ago, wrote of "The Subjection of Women" in which he carefully explained the corrupting effects of the dominance-submission model. Martin Buber more recently doubted whether there could be love at all if it were not on a basis of equality. This writer, lacking originality, compensates for this deficiency by placing himself in good company and taking a job that will be, in Irving Howe's idiom, "steady work."

It is probably impossible to change the marital contract without demythologizing the traditional images of maleness and femininity. This will probably have to start in primary education in the content and illustrations depicting the roles of the sexes. Children might see a woman doctor treating patients and women in the church pulpits. They might at least see them in textbook illustrations if not in real life. Small boys might be allowed to play with dolls, as so many long to do, instead of being directed toward toy tanks and gun sets complete with Russian cosmonauts as targets. These are but a few examples of the type of patterning that the educational establishment actively promotes in "forming character." It is an ironic joke to say that the school system omits "sex" education.

It is indeed preoccupied with sex education, actively creating artificial differences to fit the male and female children for the dominance-submission yoke which is to come. There is rarely an attempt to educate the young girl to think that she is just as good as anyone else, but just the opposite. She is too often discouraged from serious subjects such as science and mathematics "because girls really don't need that." Boys are quickly directed toward athletic games which exclude females to impart to them the message that this physical superiority

339

is meaningful, indicative of a "natural" superiority which can be spread to everything else. For in terms of the scholarly curricular pursuits, no such superiority for boys is evident; often the evidence is to the contrary.

There are many who say that a drive for equality breeds a new form of bitterness and frustration. A new competition is nurtured which augments and unleashes aggression. Thus "love" and "peace" along with harmony are destroyed. Here the world continues to be a vast hunting ground—now with everyone fully armed. Mr. John Wilson, the British philosopher, writes as follows: "A belief in equality is no real improvement over a belief in privilege or meritocracy: people still continue to compete, to measure themselves—only this time they measure to see that they are equal, rather than to see that they are getting what they deserve or what they are privileged to get. *We need to get away from the notion of achievement and competition altogether.*" (Italics mine.)*

Mr. Wilson's point must be taken seriously because it is utopian. Yet it may be discouraging to those affected to find that fair play is no longer relevant when they finally get a turn at bat. It is like the chagrin of the black person in America who, after finally being allowed in the white man's church, is told from the pulpit that God is dead! Similarly, the woman is to be told that the fight for equality is now spurious and that achievement as well as competition are to be immoral. Perhaps in some millennium this may prove to be so, but it seems to this writer that achievement in its authentic sense is something that can be preserved. The issue of competitiveness as it is too often practiced in our society is a legitimate one for reappraisal. Here there has been an overemphasis; it has become a way of life rather than a necessity for achievement or even survival. One can agree with Mr. Wilson that achievement has often been obscured by the inordinate need of the male to show off. There is no need to discredit achievement; instead there is a need to sharpen our dis-

* John Wilson, *Logic and Sexual Morality* (Baltimore, Md.: Penguin Books, 1965), p. 144.

criminatory abilities. We must desist from calling everything that gets attention an achievement. But if not achievement, what? Is man destined to spend his years in "Peyton Place" preoccupations? But then in all fairness, Mr. Wilson, in wishing to eliminate what he considers a scourge, is under no obligation to supply an alternative. On the other hand, he can leave us naked but not skinned. Even though much can be said for the life of pure contemplation, this has proved inadequate for modern man. Camus' modification of Socrates reflects this: "To know yourself you must act."

Can one then at this point prescribe action for women? One would think that they can lay claim to our heritage too. But tradition, as well as text books in psychology, tell us that to be feminine is to be *passive*. Thereby women are all too effectively eliminated from seeking those values in living that philosophers espouse and recommend.

The passivity of women, like the purported laziness of the Negro, is another instance of male self-serving mythopoeism. Even Freud, no patron saint of women, had to recant on this score. Yet the discrediting continues unabated. The male has sold this idea and the female has, outwardly at least, accepted it, or at best her rebellion against it has largely been indirect and circuitous—to be understood only by the casuist.

Both male and female might be reeducated about alternatives to the dominance-submission model—in lieu of indoctrination, which now prevails. In this reeducation, there might be included the "sinfulness" of powerlessness. Matters of power especially in the romance of relationships are never brought to conscious awareness. How can one mention power to people in love—a state of being wherein for a short time intrusive worldly matters are denied? "Power" is a dirty word—abhorred especially by those who possess it.

The wholesale repression of the subject of power (and its distribution) as it affects human relations is scandalous. Freud, who unlocked the subject matter of sex, never mentioned power as a determining factor in marital relations. Here again the interest was centered on *impotence* of a physical (sexual) nature, as if sexual power was the principal demiurge of relations. The term "power" is herein used, not in the sense of the physicist as a neutral force or energy, but as Lord Acton saw it. Differing from influence, it functions through coercion rather than reason; it operates to prevail and dominate rather than to cooperate. It worries little about equality, justice, or fair play. Mr. R. V. Sampson defines it as follows: "By power is meant the production of desired consequences in the behavior or belief of another, where the intent to exercise personal ascendancy is present in the one producing the effects. Motive is all important, although the motive may be unconscious. Usually the victim of another's power will be aware of at least some sense of psychic constraint. But this is not necessarily the case. The victim may have long since come to accept his position and regard it as natural."*

The elimination of "power" in this sense in international relations or in marriages should have highest priority. However, before it is reached, there must be some defensive stances to discourage the use of power and to protect against its effects. One might for purposes of expediency talk in terms of corrective action to create a "balance of power" or a system of "checks and balances" in the idiom of the political scientist. We do not live in a pristine world in which we can fully rely on the "powerful" to relinquish their easy advantage. A profession of love has been used as a justification for many unfair tactics. Yet love is the answer but only when the heart becomes informed.

The black man in the ghetto cannot lift himself one inch out of his destiny with all his purported or fancied sexual strength. He has now offended the sensibilities of the classes of people who have the significant power of

* R. V. Sampson, *The Psychology of Power* (New York: Pantheon Books, 1966), p. 233.

living, economic and social, by bringing forth power as a subject of discussion. Black power, practically nonexistent as it is, has become a major threat to the white community. The black power leader has offended because he has attempted to undo a repression; he has called attention to the reality that power, and principally economic power, gives people control, allows them to dominate, to exclude, and to exploit. This same power may control relationships between father and son and husband and wife. It may even determine one's state of sanity.

Love hates to discuss money. Yet in most marriages the woman is expected to give up her economic independence, to relinquish her own earning capacity. While it may be true that most husbands are generous and considerate as providers, control remains with them and more often than not they see themselves as both responsible and generous. Furthermore, among the sophisticated at least, the withholding of money punitively is rare. Generally it is the male's great pride that he can "give" his wife and children more than the next fellow does. Yet there is always an overhanging "terror in reserve"—the potential for the male's self-righteous nastiness about being ruined or being run into bankruptcy. And the wife, with her children, all euphemisms aside, is placed in the role of recipient and dependent. Using Kierkegaard's formula, the woman loses doubly. He writes: ". . . it is better to give than to receive. . . . It is far more difficult to receive than to give."

A sort of economic independence is being reached by many wives. In 1969, 34 percent of them were in the labor market. They work allegedly to supplement the "family" income, to finance houses, cars, boats, educations, and other needs which characterize an affluent society. They have jobs—not careers. Rarely are they able to reach high incomes or decision-making levels. Wives who are trained professionals do badly. They are less in evidence in the world today than twenty-five years ago. They are hopelessly incapacitated by their lack of acceptance in the world and by their inner panic about competing with (thereby castrating, they are told) their husbands.

Coming into marriage with economic reserves of her own (e.g., inheritance) gives a woman more leverage, and is to be highly recommended. This unfortunately is still a rarity. To obtain an economic balance of influence it would seem mandatory that the woman never relinquish her earning capacity—even when it is not "needed." The main obstacles here are the shibboleths of society rather than rational considerations. With minimal ingenuity arrangements can be made to run an office and a home, providing the spirit is willing. Husbands will have to help in the menial work—no biological factor precludes him from such tasks. Only inequality will be castrated. Day-care centers for children may become as highly recommended for the middle class as they now are for the poor. Why must only low-income or welfare mothers be "liberated"?

It is this writer's contention that behind the façade of love, devotion, and compassion, the specter of power looms to take its toll in marriage. The toll that is taken is really not measurable in terms of divorces or separations, for power can create inescapable traps in which all that are left are resignation and apathy. These, ironically enough, because there is no movement or resistance in them, are often called happiness and contentment. Here there may operate a relentless spirit-destroying machine that leaves the body intact but spineless without an apparent wound.

The power that each of the mates can use on the other might be described simply in terms of positive and negative—each can be destructive. The male has the power that has been institutionalized and supported by tradition. This comes from earning power, religious authority, and social approval of the male's dominant role. He has advantages of education and access to worldly opportunities. The woman generally lacks these or gets them through union with her husband. With this power, the male can keep the woman from fulfillment of goals and can effectively bind her to his needs and directions. The woman's power is negative in that she can act as an impediment, slow up progress, cause embarrassment, and great expense. She may overspend and bankrupt her husband. She may cuckold him, discrediting him before all. She may turn to alcoholism or drugs to frustrate his ambition, and there are hysteria, psychosis, and suicide. This is not to suggest that these latter are purely linear to the husband's behavior, but often enough they are. This is negative power which damages the husband but is also self-defeating. It is Medea, Salome, and Turandot; it is also Samson, who suffers self-destruction as he pulls down the temple. The woman's negative power has the shortcoming of lacking much disguise or subtlety. The positive power of the male, derived from generations of experience and practice, has become incorporated into what is "natural"—ironically consciously accepted even by the victim. And, it is often the case that a man is despised and ridiculed if he does not use power.

It then becomes unmanly not to oppress. It makes one almost agree with Sartre that most marriages are exercises in sadomasochism. (Some investigators have found an association between the occurrence of psychoneurosis in husbands and wives who have been married many years. They attribute this to "contagion." Are we being told of the dangers of prolonged marriages?) This represents the malignancy of positive and negative power. If the use of power in interpersonal relations is inevitable, the confrontation of power with counter power would seem preferable. Hopefully, this confrontation too may eventually become vestigial for human affairs.

Can we afford to become optimistic in this direction? We may if people become educated to human rights as they pertain to themselves and others. There must be the recognition that the days of ownership and possession of human beings are over. That the time of adults asking "permission" should be at an end as well as the postures of the generous donor and grateful recipient. People must make social contracts such as marriage both out of passion and strength, the passion derived from a wish to cooperate and build, and strength that comes from equality. People in marriage need not be either authoritarian or dependent; both may be autonomous.* Autonomy and passion are not antithetic. One would hate to think that the price of love is the sacrifice of dignity and identity.

All of our humanistic words have become so overused as to vitiate their meaning. One such is "cooperation." Marriage might be based on the basis of cooperation rather than the dominance-subjection paradigm. This would obviate the need for or use of power. It would, however, mean that our culture would have to become accustomed to the manliness of cooperation and give credit to women for independence. In a union of self—as well as other—loving, autonomous persons, there would be the expectation that the destiny of one is congruent but not fused with the other. Personal as well as family goals will coexist.

Autonomous persons cannot be chattels; the conjugal contract cannot include ownership of bodies or "free access." Similarly, a person's worthiness must be loosened from his sexual behavior. Sex must undergo demoralization. To consider a person moral solely on the basis of one's sexual impeccability cheapens virtue.

Under the guise of the expectation of sexual fidelity is the covert demand for possession of the body and soul of the other. To insure this "fidelity," liberties and human rights which normally would prevail in society are abrogated. Demands for sexual fidelity, a generally expected

---

* For the woman to adjust to marriage and in the process to acquire those attributes which endear her to the world, that is, to be the good or beloved wife, she most often accepts, or has to appear to accept, the role of an inferior person. Of one of his female characters, the British novelist William Golding writes: "She was beginning to look up, to belong, to depend, to cling, *to be an inferior in fact*, however the marriage service may gloss it." (Italics mine.)

accompaniment of love and devotion, have too often taken on the force of total ownership of the mate.

The British philosopher, John Wilson, made sense when he wrote:

"Fidelity" means keeping a sexual contract, analogous to an economic contract, whereby both partners agree not to spend money except on each other: this, for us, is the basis of "marriage." "Love," in a sexual sense, is supposed to imply a similar situation: the concept is so used that if one is "in love" with someone, or even if one "loves" him or her it is supposed to follow that one can have no proper sexual interest in anyone else. Even more obsessive is the concept of specifically "romantic" love; this too implies sexual fidelity, and "romantic" is thereby contrasted with "promiscuous," "animal," and other unfashionable concepts. Without discussing these and cognate concepts at length, we need only contrast our attitude to sexual relationships with our attitude to the ordinary relationship of friendship; although friendship too can be possessive, it is generally recognized that this is abnormal and undesirable, whereas in sexual relationships we accept it as the norm.*

We must respect a high degree of sexual fidelity in marriage if it can be separated from exclusivity and possessiveness with the attendant jealousy which they promote. Few of us now have "nervous systems" strong enough to withstand the total sexual freedom of our mates. However, we should strive to worry more about fidelity in other areas in our living. We might more profitably be concerned with *fidelity* in our work, and with our ideals in the conduct of our public as well as personal affairs. This, in short, means being faithful to one's own identity —that is, being what you are supposed to be and doing what you are supposed to do. This writer suspects that the morbid and obsessive preoccupation with the faithfulness of the other represents a compensatory projection of the corrosion of one's own integrity—the doubts that

* Wilson, p. 67.

exist about one's own real worthiness in areas other than sexual.

Sexual fidelity must be kept in perspective; it is not the ultimate virtue, nor does it make a person moral. Fidelity to a mate, a friend, or a client encompasses a sincere concern for his fate and a respect for his human rights. One can be sexually faithful to a mate and deceive him or her in a myriad of ways both subtler and more vital.

Another issue that is most significant to marriage is the respectability of the alternatives to it. Society might make it a great deal easier for the single person to exist. This acceptance may come sooner than expected because of the population explosion and the imminence of "standing room only" for the human race. Tax advantages for the married person will disappear. Staying single may become an act of patriotism; necessity is frequently the mother of morality.

Today the opposite exists. The male who prefers bachelorhood is charitably considered "a mother's boy" and more frequently someone with homosexual tendencies. Our psychologists are happy to confirm these views. The girl who finds herself a spinster is in far worse shape; she is accused of being unwanted, deemed not valuable to the least of males. Whatever she does or attains in life is looked upon as a poor substitute for the real success that passed her by—namely, marriage. She is an object of pity to all except some housewives who have found themselves marooned and forgotten in a plush suburb. Today for the young woman the only real success or proof of one's worth is via marriage. One-half of all women who enter college leave before graduation for marriage, and, for a short time at least, feel wonderful about it! They are never considered to be dropouts; they rarely, if ever, are sent to psychiatrists to uncover psychological reasons for their intellectual failures. No papers are written about this "dropout" problem, for in this situation nothing succeeds like failure. Here the woman who completes her college work, and is not married, is apt to be an object of concern by now nervous parents and relatives.

The stampede to marriage can be viewed as a rigidity of our times. Society, with an unhealthy assist from psychiatry, has been the cause of this. The frantic attitude does a tragic disservice both to the young people and the institution of marriage.* It prevents adequate experimentation and deadens adventuresomeness. Only a few are able to declare a moratorium and properly examine themselves and the world around them; the hippies are the exceptions which prove the rule. Conformity is still the role for young people—long hair and street demonstrations notwithstanding.

If, hopefully, the single state does gain respectability, marriage will cease to be the unalterable imperative that it now is. With that pressure relieved, better and more equitable social contracts may evolve. The frenzy may disappear and there would be more time to read the fine print or change the wording. The hope for our times and the future is a climate of understanding that may allow young people to work out their destinies *with passion* but also with autonomy which demands the elimination of power as an interpersonal demiurge, and with love which has an authentic concern for the identity of the other and self.

---

* Margaret Mead, drawing on her knowledge of how other peoples live, has recommended a dual marriage system. She writes: "I have recommended that we have different kinds of marriages. An *individual* marriage in which young people who are not ready to have children can legally live together. . . . Thereafter a couple knows they can get on together. There could be a second kind of marriage involving parental *responsibility*. I propose it because the only alternative today seems to be getting married and getting divorced and getting remarried and getting divorced. . . . We live in this unreal world where people still assume in spite of the divorce rate that marriage is going to be different." M. Mead, *Life,* 23 August 1968, p. 34.

ROBERT SEIDENBERG*

The Trauma of Eventlessness

To fear the worst oft cures the worse.
—*Troilus and Cressida* (III, 2)

THE PATIENT who is the subject of this article, a twenty-eight-year-old housewife, was perhaps, in the interpretation of the author, afraid of the street as representing "the world" from which she had been systematically and traditionally barred.

Waelder's† psychoanalytic interpretation of agoraphobia oversimplifies the problem. While language origins are not to be used as ultimate definitions, it is nonetheless instructive to remember that the Greek word *agora* mainly referred to the popular political assemblage of a community. We also know that "proper" women were excluded from this public domain; courtesans were the only women seen in this environment. Today, the term "agoraphobia" connotes the fear of open spaces and is a symptom most commonly, although not exclusively, found among women. One then is faced with the paradox of a woman who was originally prohibited by law and custom from entering "public areas" of activity, now diagnosed as "phobic" when she becomes anxious there!

It may be useful to examine the temptations in addition

---

* A biographical sketch of the author appears on page 305.
† At the outset of this paper Seidenberg reviews Freud's early and later theories of anxiety and the theory which is currently accepted by most psychoanalysts; he quotes Robert Waelder on the dominant theory of anxiety.—ED.

THE TRAUMA OF EVENTLESSNESS

THE TRAUMA OF EVENTLESSNESS

to sexual ones, even if the patient, as is often the case, expresses her agonies in the rhetoric of sex.

Today, a woman's desire for a public life is burdened by many frustrations as well as social and psychological penalties, in addition to gross inequalities of actual opportunity. Traditionally, hers has been the *private* sector; the *agora* was never a place where she was expected to be, or expected to feel comfortable. She is often faced with the dilemma of being a "private person" who is excited and stimulated by public affairs. As we know, the Greek word for "private person" is *idiotes,* from which we have derived "idiot." (Identifying with such a word in itself might cause alarm.)

It is hoped that the aim of psychoanalysis is not to reduce its clients to the level of the average person's perception of what a dangerous situation is. Waelder's suggestion that a fear is "neurotic" because it is a response to a situation in "which average people can neither detect danger at all or no danger great enough to justify the intensity of the wrong" sets out low goals indeed for the psychoanalyst. Of course the issue is not whether the particular street is dangerous or not but the gestalt of the individual's life situation, its restrictiveness or autonomy, its oppressiveness or freedom. In this context a restriction of freedom, an impingement upon one's legitimate rights might be very worrisome to sensitive individuals and a matter of indifference to average people.

These are facts of contemporary life as well as the lessons of history. It is not only a fallacy but it betrays a naïveté (where it certainly should not exist) to say that because the *average* person does not *feel* external dangers, they do not exist. If the dangers are not external, as defined by the populace, they must, according to Waelder, be internal. And finally, Waelder's further proof that the anxiety must be "neurotic" because "of its intensity, its refractoriness to ordinary explanations of fact and probability, and its omnipotence" may betray the rigid thinking of the therapist more than the neurosis of the patient.

Of greater significance is the reaction of alarm to help-lessness in determining the future course of one's life. This type of anxiety response might appear irrational to Waelder's "average" observer. Finally, Freud fully real-ized that the distinction between real (outer) and neu-rotic (inner) danger was untenable. There are indeed many real external dangers which are not apparent (sic) and one cannot assume that because such dangers are not perceived by the average person they are products solely of inner threats.

To demonstrate how helpful to this writer is Freud's modified theory, the following case is presented. The reader will note the evolving story of frustration and deprivation of human rights which characterized this woman's life. A person who might be described as having "absence d'esprit" proved to have the opposite. The reader may also contrast the interpretations herein given with the libidinal ones usually "assigned" to the anxious and agoraphobic patient. Missing also is the reductionistic tendency of infinite regression, a concept which is grow-ing in popularity as an explanation for human behavior.

A CASE OF EXISTENTIAL AGORAPHOBIA

This protocol concerns a timid twenty-eight-year-old housewife. She was referred to the author for psycho-therapy by her family physician after she failed to respond to a variety of tranquilizers and other "psychotropic" drugs. Her presenting symptoms were fear of losing her mind, episodes of severe apprehension in the street and in stores, and fear that she might harm her three-year-old daughter. She was a plain-looking woman, uneducated, showing all the signs of social bewilderment and inept-ness. The theory that she was beset with imaginary dan-gers stemming from drives and affects from within was only part of the story. She related that she was the elder of two children, having a brother five years younger than she. Her parents were immigrants from Eastern Europe, of the Russian-Orthodox religion. Her father had advanced to a semimanagerial position in a small paternalistic company. Her mother worked periodically to supplement the family income. The patient was brought up under strict discipline. She was a docile child and adolescent, having proper obedience and respect for her parents. Her father worried about her outside activities and fretted about some of her girl friends. He often followed her to school and met her on her return to see that she did not stray into corrupting circles of teen-agers. Her social life was therefore restricted, but she managed to have some friends of both sexes. She never evidenced any rebelliousness.

After high school, no mention was made of further education although she had done fairly well in her courses. Instead, her father got her a job as a stenographer in the same company where he was employed. (Nepotism went along with the paternalism of this concern.) The father prided himself on being able to place his daughter in a secure setting, where he could keep an eye on her. She was not consulted as to where she would like to work, or at what; it was assumed that any girl would be grateful for such a job.

At her job, again through her father, she was introduced to a young college student who worked there during the summer while preparing to become an engineer. This was thought of as a fine match by her father, who did everything to encourage the relationship. The French say: *Marie ton fils quand tu voudras, mais ta fille quand tu pourras.* (Marry your son when you will, but your daughter when you can.) The young man completed college and they were married; he returned to this same company as a full-time employee. After her marriage, she left her job. A daughter was born soon thereafter. The external circumstances of her life appeared ideal—she had a husband who was good to her and who had a bright future, satisfied parents, a nice home, and a healthy baby.

Concurrently her younger brother was approaching

manhood. The course of his life, however, contrasted sharply with hers. An inferior student in high school, he was nonetheless encouraged to go to college. He was fully supported financially, and even given a car when transportation became a problem. With some continuing academic difficulties, he completed college and was immediately hired by an architectural firm at a good starting salary. There was no suggestion that he join the father's company, which was thought to give inadequate opportunity for his talents.

Three years after the birth of her daughter, the patient responded to her seemingly ideal external conditions with the symptoms mentioned above. This was a puzzle to everyone and a source of rage to her father, who did not want his daughter to be a burden to his son-in-law. The patient found no friendly listener among her relatives—they interpreted her sadness and fearfulness as signs of selfishness and ingratitude. "Doesn't she have everything? What more does she want?" Yet she was beset with attacks of anxiety.

"I'm afraid something is going to happen but I don't know what it is." As her life story unfolded, it became apparent that her timidity and docility had naturally deprived her of adventuresomeness, choice making, and even minimal self-determination. She had not become pregnant out of wedlock, as her father feared she might. Her present and her future were reasonably assured.

What had she to fear? She was well adjusted, accepted by her friends and family, loved by her husband, fulfilled as a woman and mother—there were certainly no external dangers—she had probably more security than the average person. Internal dangers, of course, might include fear of sexual feelings, long repressed or contaminated by earlier parental threats and warnings. Then there was fear of harming her daughter, an obsessive thought that might too readily be interpreted as sadistic in quality. Clearly, her anxiety could be interpreted as a reaction to danger from within—deductively there being none from without.

However, the hypothesis that proved to be more logical and heuristic was Freud's statement of anxiety, as a response of anticipation to future dangers *which were as much outside of herself as within her*. This encompassed her life style which would be set for the next thirty or forty years—one in which she would continue to be dutiful and obedient, now to her husband instead of to parents, and one in which there would appear neither choices nor challenges—an uninterrupted continuation of the first twenty years of her life. We soon became aware that in her apprehensive exclamation, "something is going to happen, but I don't know what it is," she was secretly lamenting the danger that the *opposite* would be true, that in her life "nothing would happen"! She had been caught in a secure trap with the courage neither to complain directly nor to extricate herself. Her life at home and in the streets and in the stores was devoid of deprivation, predatory human beings, or ferocious animals! The absence of challenge, of decision making, of problem solving would instead be her destiny. Even her daughter at the age of three appeared self-sufficient, engaging only a small part of her time and attention.

A trauma, in psychoanalysis, generally has been difficult to define. Broadly speaking, it is thought to be "a startling experience, a shock, with lasting effects." The *Glossary of Psychoanalytic Terms and Concepts* published by the American Psychoanalytic Association defines trauma as follows:

A stimulus, arising from an external situation or from a massive inner sexual and aggressive excitement, which is experienced as overwhelming the ego's capacity to mediate between the various forces making demands on it. Such stimuli are usually sudden and disruptive, and produce a state of helplessness ranging from apathetic inactivity to emotional storm. Traumatic events are usually followed by marked regressive phenomena, severe inhibitions, and physical symptoms reflecting autonomic dysfunction.

This traditionally held view of trauma has as its chief distinguishing components a *stimulus* from without or within which overwhelms the ego leading to various symptoms and incapacitation of the person.

This writer contends that the very opposite—namely, *the absence of stimuli*—can have the same effects. A lack of external events and appropriate internal responses can constitute a trauma no less than the "dramatic" assaults against the ego. More than that, the anticipation of more and more eventlessness may similarly constitute a danger of severe proportions to one's well-being. The case of the woman under discussion is explained by this hypothesis. Her "breakdown" occurred at the point when she painfully realized that without some change or correction, her future life would be a continuum of a past which was characterized by submission to authority, absence of choice, and a general exclusion and isolation from the significant stimuli of life. Consistent with psychoanalytic theory, her anxiety contained the anticipatory repetition of the "traumas" of the past. Was she irrational in fearing that her future life would be as intellectually and emotionally constricted as her past?

The contrasting fate of her brother proved to be a precipitating factor in this woman's belated rebellion. This was no "neurotic" sibling rivalry but a realistic, objective appraisal of the inequities attending the raising of a son and a daughter in a family of these socioeconomic circumstances, where the son is held to be a dividend, the daughter a mortgage—as the ancient Greeks might tell us. Credit for intelligence, judgment, and choice making, and self-determination that was lavished on the son never was accorded the daughter. Not one to complain, she nonetheless felt the inequity and responded to it with her cryptic alarm and protest.

There are similarities between this life situation and that of Freud's "Dora," of whom Erikson writes: "Dora needed to act as she did not only to vent the childish rage of one victimized but also in order to set straight the his-

356

torical *past so that she could envisage a sexual and social future of her choice*" (italics added). And Erikson finds the turning of the father away from the daughter to the son as the crucial wound; "a vital identity fragment of her young life was that of the *woman intellectual* which had been encouraged by her father's delight in her previous intelligence, but discouraged by her brother's superior example as favored by the times. . . . The negative identity of the "déclassée" woman (so prominent in her era), she tried to ward off with her sickness. . . ."*

Although the woman in this protocol had none of Dora's intellectual pretensions, the fall from importance and significance in the family was quite similar. The contrasting destinies of brother and sister in each instance became crucial in determining the attitude of pessimism and hopelessness of the overlooked ones. Apparently for Dora and this woman their struggle for equality and their sense of injustice foredoomed a graceful acquiescence to a role of passivity and (for them) inferiority.

Similarly her untoward thoughts about her daughter originated not so much from pent-up sexualized or deneutralized aggression, but as a component of the chagrin over the fate of the female. Was her daughter to be destroyed as she thought herself to be? Would destiny impel her to foist upon her daughter the inequities she herself felt?

These are *real* dangers and they are *external* but may not be apparent except to the observer who has thought about them. One is not justified in declaring these dangers either unreal or internal because they are not universally perceived or acknowledged. Often the therapist is still listening with the "third" ear when the times call for a fourth.

The course of psychotherapy was in large measure predictable. For a long period, she both affirmed and disclaimed her boredom, her dissatisfaction and her own

* E. H. Erikson, "Reality and Actuality," *Journal of the American Psychoanalytic Association* 10 (1962): 459–60.

insignificance. She asked the questions put to her by her husband, her parents, and her own superego—to wit— why her? Why was everyone else in her circumstances contented with their lives? No one else had to go to a doctor! And when would she stop going? Was she really indulging herself in receiving a "talking" treatment? And was she in truth going through an infatuation with the doctor when she should have her mind on her family and household chores?

The area of greatest suspicion was the absence of medication in the therapy. There are now miracle drugs that bring contentment. The doctor seemed to be agitating rather than relieving. The husband began contemplating what might happen to the marriage. Yet with new insights she began observing and noting that all was not so tranquil with others "in her circumstances." It became a source of pride for her to recognize new aspects of living and forces that were acting on her and others. Her husband, predictably, felt that she must "change her attitude" and then all would be well. In this, there was inordinate pressure for chemical tranquilization so that she would no longer be a disrupting factor. When she finally became aware of her legitimate struggle against "disappearance," her physical symptoms largely abated and her energies were channeled into areas that might change her plight. This eventually was encouraging to the husband who earlier in the "illness" had felt he was at the end of his rope in dealing with her, and had wondered whether or not she should be hospitalized.

Was her past disturbing? Yes. In her early years her parents were in the throes of elevating themselves from the poverty level of existence. Both parents worked hard, and there was always anxiety lest the fragile progress be impeded. The children had to be well disciplined and separated from the temptations and exposures that bring social disaster to all. The father was a hard and determined worker, never departing from the proper behavior and decorum his boss demanded. At times it was touch and go but gradually he became a member of the team and felt a modicum of security. Overhanging his existence, however, was his lack of formal education; he felt the pressure of the new employees, now almost entirely college trained. Here he was confronted with his ambivalence toward education. On the one hand determined that his own son receive "the best education possible," he was conscious of his own deficiencies and inadequacies vis-à-vis the upcoming young men "who could write a decent letter when they had to." Yet if he reluctantly and painfully saw the necessity of education for his son, his pride could not allow his daughter to have more education than he. In this time of life, as if learning from Lear, he would not have a daughter lording it over him. His frustrations were unevenly distributed, landing on the female, as typifies worldly priorities. For him, a girl was a success if she caused no trouble or disgrace, as well a girl might through "becoming a bum" or getting pregnant out of wedlock. He had heard that girls who go off to college are apt to "go wild," losing respect for parents and bringing shame to the family name. It would not do for the son to have a sister who was a "tramp." Elevation to the middle class had come hard enough, no need for experimentation.

She became "daddy's girl" and frequently was the only one in the family who could talk back to him, but only in inconsequential areas. She was very solicitous of her brother and sought to protect him from the wrath of their father on the infrequent occasions of his rebelliousness. Toward her mother she was similarly solicitous but felt neither awe nor affection. It was the father who appeared as the ultimate figure of authority who would determine her destiny.

In her teens the sexual threat, the specter of "going wrong," was constant and made sex loathsome, mysterious, and intriguing. Her one great power was to undo; her father made her aware of this. At times his very preoccupation with sex appeared to her as a command. She related that she felt that he was almost disappointed that she was not adventuresome in this area. Sexual adjustment in marriage, after the initial shock, was satisfactory to both partners and remained that way.

Similarly, her "object relationships" by all conventional standards were adequate. The family, particularly the father, breathed a sigh of relief; the ordeal of carrying a daughter through the pitfalls of adolescence ended in success. That the father's preoccupation was a manifestation of the *repressed sexual problem of fathers and daughters* is a given but the augmentation wrought by social pressures as well as class prejudices were determining factors in his attitude and behavior. Her obeisance was more apparent than real. Unexpectedly, she became aware that she was paying too high a price for the needs, real or fancied, of others. Her neurosis, developing as it did, was her rebellion. She was not "spoiled by success" as some would say. Instead she sought to save herself from complete annihilation by a self-preserving negativism, a refusal to become the possession and vassal of still another man (her husband) who would take her for granted. She could not, with her training and timidity, become a "bad woman" to show her protest. What was left to her was more of the same, to exaggerate her timidity to a fault, literally to become afraid of her own shadow (how much more feminine and passive can one get?).

In all, the dilemma of this woman was summed up in a statement which came in the context of a request for an assessment of her own struggle: "I don't want to be forgotten."

Attuned as we are to the threats of untoward nefarious drives from within, and catastrophic events from without, we may forget the despair that comes from the prospect of a passionless and unchallenging existence. The trauma *of nothing at all ever happening*, of eventlessness as far as involvement or engagement are concerned, can be a catastrophe of major proportions. Thomas Carlyle observed: "The tragedy of life is not so much what men suffer, but rather what they miss."

Stein, in an essay entitled "Fear of Death and Neurosis" [in the *Journal of the American Psychiatric Association*], points out that the anticipation of one's death, the knowledge of the ultimate biological defeat to which all the living are heir, is an intrinsic part of the neurotic and psychotic process which has not received adequate emphasis in psychoanalysis. He writes: "Whereas neurotic anxiety contains anticipatory repetition of the biotraumas of the past, the affective state of depression, which originates in the separation from the object, seems to be maintained by the anticipation of the future inevitable loss of self." Stein's reminder is a welcome one in that it points in the direction of man's concern about his existence, but his conceptualization falls short of dealing with problems of existence which are not primarily biological but perhaps are more relevant to identity, sense of worth, and personal goals.

Deaths can be many, the biological is but one. People worry about their survival: professional, social, and political, as well as biological. It has been this writer's professional experience that loss of self encompasses matters of quality of living, accomplishments or the lack of them, meeting or falling short of one's ego ideals, and, to be sure, success in object relations. Failure at these are as relevant and crucial in fostering hopelessness as the knowledge of one's inevitable demise. We hold with Kierkegaard that we are always well aware of the loss of a limb, a wife, or a five dollar bill. However, the loss of self in its many subtle manifestations and forms is not well understood. The self slips away and only the fortunate get a warning signal.

In the case of this woman, one gained the insight that she was anticipating, or perhaps reporting, her own social and psychological "death." Luckily, she was anxious about her destiny and cried out against what might seem its inevitability. Her anxiety was salutary and self-preservative; she would "not go gentle into that good night."

This woman's symptoms allowed her to separate herself from the fate of the young women with whom she grew up and who now surrounded her in the suburbs. In the other world, she withdrew from the role of shopper and hair-dryer captive. In her home, she held her ground in having but one child, no small feat in light of the persistent pressures of husband (don't you love me?), relatives, friends, and the church. If not for having children, why women?

Limited by lack of education and worldly experience, her positive accomplishments were modest. She was able to work part-time as a door-to-door canvasser for a research corporation. This was surely not world-shaking but nonetheless puzzling and dismaying to her relatives who deemed such work dangerous for a woman, especially since it brought her into "inner city" districts. Plagued by anxiety in supermarkets and beauty salons, she suffered no fear in this "outside" work, only exhilaration, giving evidence once again that the overriding danger to her existence lay in the "safety" of the housewife's role. The hostile elements of her environment were not the people of the street but her "loved" ones who saw her as pure biology.

Therapy encouraged the *actualization* of her worldly aspirations. A woman's destiny might indeed be broadened. As a result she began to feel human and rational. Until then in her milieu she had been perceived as insane at best, misanthropic at worst. Incidentally, there was a fortuitous assist from the fast-moving events of the world, to wit, with the new urgency for population control, her insistence on not having more children now appeared as not entirely nonsensical and selfish to some around her.

Freud's modification of his earlier theory of anxiety in which the temporal (anticipatory) dimension is emphasized proved heuristic in explaining the problem of a young married woman who sought therapy. In her life situation, it was the anticipation of "more of the same obscurity" that proved to be the frightening factor.

362

LESTER A. GELB

LESTER GELB stands with the group of psychoanalysts who reject the traditional concept that characterizes psychological structures as derivations of biological transactions. Gelb finds instead that psychological structures can be understood in the context of the interactions which individuals experience. The quality of these interactions is, in turn, determined by the societal values that prevail and that permeate all the early and current experience of the individual. In this context Gelb views the societal devaluation of women.

A psychoanalyst who is involved in a developing community mental health program, Gelb has written on topics ranging from the relationship between biological and social evolution to the problems of psychotherapy in a corrupt society. He is presently associate and clinical director of the Maimonides Community Health Center, Brooklyn, New York.

Masculinity-Femininity

A Study in Imposed Inequality

It has always been hard for me to understand why women, a deprived and exploited majority, have not, as a group, rebelled more strongly before this. We are now beginning to see evidence of organized agitation by women for life as full human beings.

Before the current woman's movement there were signs of a quiet but firm deemphasizing of sex in dress and in general appearance. Even names were becoming blurred. (A study of a large sample of given names reported in birth announcements in the *New York Times* from 1948 to 1963 concluded that almost one-fifth of them were not gender specific, for example, Leslie, Robin, Tracy, Dana, Lynn—although the 1923–38 period had few such names.) This "neutrality" may have been an expression of an attempt to escape the imposed pressures of maleness and femaleness. Although this role blurring may have been part of an expression of a wish for equality of women, it did not in itself guarantee equality or represent a direct struggle for it.

Equality and, in some ways, a superiority of women in sexual functioning has been proven on a physiological level by Masters and Johnson in their book *Human Sexual Response,* but this does not guarantee an acceptance of this sexual equality on the part of present-day society.

Very few early psychoanalysts, except for Alfred Adler, clearly and directly challenged the gender role that has been forced on women. Most psychoanalysts have felt the need to be apologetic about the Freudian view of women, claiming that Freud only pointed to certain difficulties which were bound to arise for little girls because of their unavoidable penis envy. A careful reading of Freud's writings, including his "Three Essays on the Theory of Sexuality" (1905), his "Some Psychological Consequences of the Anatomical Distinction between the Sexes" (1925), and his lecture "Femininity" (1938), reveals that he thoroughly rejected women as full human beings. He saw women as "castrated," and he insisted that all women were doomed, for biological reasons, to feel inferior and to have contempt for themselves. He viewed woman as a "mutilated creature," weaker in her social interests and having less capacity for sublimating her instincts.

Because Freud and his followers were subjects of an autocratic authoritarian social milieu, they reflected and accepted the institutionalized role of women in their time. However, there was available to them a historical body of knowledge and literature which they could have used to rise above their narrow and fixed positions. The "woman's movement," decrying women's deprived status, was well established and documented in the literature long before Freud began his work. Now we are witnessing a flood of articles and books for popular consumption by many politically active women and some men. More recently there is a small number of psychoanalysts who also have rejected the psychoanalytic concept of inequality of women or the stereotyping of either men or women (Bernard Robbins, Natalie Shainess, Judd Marmor, Leon Salzman, Leonard Gold, Jean Miller).

Bernard Robbins was the first of the modern psychoanalysts firmly to reject the theory of the nature of femininity as biologically determined. He believed that psychoanalysis has and will continue to profit from the revolt of women against a view of masculine priority with its dominance and supremacy and the corresponding emphasis on feminine weakness, passivity, envy, and bitterness. Although Robbins rejected the theory of biological determinism of characterological differences between the sexes, he did believe that a feminine psychology exists. Robbins believed that it would be a mistake, in rebelling against the "weaker sex" principle of Freud, necessarily to erase women as such. He felt that for women to become pale images of men would prove nothing other than the assumption that masculinity per se is superior and is, therefore, to be copied.

Any person, man or woman, who is aggressive, controlling, or dominating is destructive. Yet, if a woman is this way she is usually referred to as "masculine." I suggest that we stop imposing aggressive-passive labels on men and women respectively, and move toward helping people, regardless of sex, to be able to develop and use their resources actively and effectively, in order to reach their full potential as human beings.

By calling for equality I do not, thereby, suggest sameness. I certainly do not intend to depreciate the importance of the physical differences between the sexes. Nor do I deny that there is room for a study of the psychology of women in our society. What I am objecting to is the assumption that because specific personality features are discovered to make up the present-day "psychology" of the American woman, we are then justified in assuming that these personality features are in fact intrinsic to woman, and that any substantial deviation from this is a denial of womanhood or a moving toward "masculinity." The so-called basic characteristics making up the psychology of women are not basic at all. Certain positive characteristics, such as being more gentle and less warlike, exist in contrast to men but may be related to the child-rearing responsibilities of women and the war-making practices of men. Passivity, however, has been produced by coercive social institutions. In different lands and in different times varied social institutions have produced different "psychologies" of women and of men.

What psychological test can differentiate a woman from a man? There is really very little difference in psychological testing in terms of sexual differentiation. What about the cultural institutions which make up our civilization? Is there feminine art? or music? or literature? Can science be divided into feminine or masculine? In sum, is there such a thing, specifically, as woman's mind? The essential feature of the human being is human consciousness. I do not believe that the workings of woman's mind is different from that of man's except that each may have been specialized, distorted, or limited by social impositions.

The present role of the sexes in our society has a complicated early history. Basic, however, is that man historically took advantage of woman's physically weaker and biologically dependent status and imposed economic controls over women, making them semislaves or chattels. As time went on the role of men and women became institutionalized and both men and women became accepting of these roles. Mothers as well as fathers impose a distorted value system on their offspring. Thus both sexes are deprived of a full life. Today, many sons and daughters are rebelling against the system.

Since I am addressing myself to psychiatrists and psychoanalysts, perhaps the most useful point I can make is to accuse many of us not only of being passive in the face of the continued denial to women of full participation in human life, but of embracing a decaying value system and of actually promoting deprivation.

I believe that many in the field of psychoanalysis have been guilty of contributing heavily to the coercive institutionalization of male and female roles which have little to do with sexual identity. Psychoanalysts have contributed to the view of women as weak, inferior, passive, fragile, soft, vacillating, dependent, unreliable, intuitive rather than rational, castrated, and handicapped. Men have been polarized as aggressive, controlling, strong, superior, proud, independent, venturesome, competitive, hard, and athletic. Psychoanalysts have tended to lag far behind other workers in the field of human relations in regard to the position of women in our society. While women have been trying to escape from economic and psychological enslavement, many psychoanalysts have continued to discourage the full freedom of women by talking all-knowingly about their feminine role and even about the glory of passivity (e.g., Helene Deutsch). Also we promote polarization of our male patients by talking about "reestablishing masculine identity" rather than moving toward full capacity as human beings.

Men often lose opportunity for full human existence by being socially coerced into the mythical masculine stereotype for fear of not being "manly." They are deprived of the full freedom to express their feelings and to be gentle. Their expression of love is warped because of this myth, leading to a one-sidedness and nonmutuality of the man-woman relationship.

Kenneth Clark years ago taught us that children cannot grow up mentally sound in a society that segregates some of them as inferior. White children cannot be mentally healthy if they grow up seeing their fellow black children so treated. Both suffer the mental distortion that comes from destructive and dehumanizing social practices and stereotypes.

The same cause for mental distortion applies to the segregation and dehumanizing of men and women. Just as the poor white is encouraged to feel that he is at least superior to a black, so the man, buffeted by our competitive society, is encouraged to feel superior to "his" woman. Women are expected to accept lower wages for equal work. They have been segregated in schools, segregated and degraded in most religions, forced to accept roles with demeaning sexual stereotype in television, the theater, clothing fashions, and advertisements. They are expected as wives to accept the role of being legal and sexual property of the husband—more an object than a fellow human. Recent laws do not abolish their status as property but merely prevent excessive exploitation. For example, the lack of guaranteed economic security and guaranteed care for children, should the husband for whatever reason not remain with the family, is a major source of conflict, fear, and actual suffering. Can we as psychotherapists really expect that we can help women to reach their human potential with such restrictions? The shameful truth is that too many of us, without being fully aware, have actually encouraged women to accept their alloted role. With anything less than social and economic freedom for women there is only the dreaded "accept-ance" and "adjustment"—the phony peacefulness of a person who is resigned to "circumstance" and the phony superiority of a man who lives with an acquiescent prop-erty rather than a true partner.

As a young psychiatrist, when working with women patients, single or married, I felt under the pressure of a pervasive obligation, often promoted by the women themselves, but mostly derived from early professional training, to help them "adjust" to their difficult situa-tions. In the case of single women the goal was to help them find "happiness" through finding a man with whom they could "get along"—despite their often having to place themselves in a most humiliating role of playing up to the whims of men who were often exploitative and competitive. If they could not find the right man this was to be considered a "resistance" or an unresolved "com-plex."

It took me many years to realize that when a woman de-scribed many of the men who wanted to take her out as "no damn good," she was likely to be right. It became necessary for me to reexamine my theoretical bias which ascribed the difficulties that the women presented to their own psychopathology. I gradually began to accept the fact that their painful failure to adapt was often an unsuc-cessful protest against impersonal social forces deriving from the larger social system in which they were helpless victims. I began to realize that much of women's suffering was not derived from "intrapsychic" pathology origi-nating in the early adaptive failure, but that many of their symptoms were an ineffectual reaction against their distorted and oppressive sexual-social existence. They could not maintain healthy functioning in such a cruel milieu. Finally it became clear that social change, and involvement in the struggle for social change, may be a most meaningful therapeutic experience and goal and, therefore, must be a real part of our professional concern. Since change of social experience is the most important factor in changing human consciousness, social oppression, by the same token, must be of professional concern to us as an important cause of the deterioration of an individual's mental health.

My concern as a member of the psychiatric and psychoanalytic profession is that we often impose our own bias on our patients so that they may "get along" in our society; we have even rationalized sexual role as "human nature."

It is true that the realities of the biological differences and special needs of women contribute to some of the many problems with which women have to cope in our society. But many women look upon the opportunity for pregnancy, childbirth, and child care as a very special pleasure. This should not be contaminated by the anxieties of economic insecurity or, as is often the case in city living away from the "homestead," the threat of twenty-four-hour-a-day isolation in her home. It is true that most women, if they are to contribute to society, are faced with the problem of either choosing a career or a family—or, if they wish both, to suffer, during their most productive years, with the multiple roles of child rearing, family, and home responsibilities in addition to career development, with the added work, schooling, mental energy, and time required. Women who, despite these difficulties, manage to clear the hurdles, do so at a tremendous cost to themselves. Solutions for this dilemma, while being sought, may not be immediately at hand, but certainly the solution is not to insist that women accept their assigned "feminine role." Women are beginning to rebel against an assigned role as a slave to their assumed bodily functions.

Society must provide solutions for their dilemma, otherwise it will continue to lose the full resources of half its members.

We are beginning to see some trials at a solution of the problem. Now that large-family homesteads have already all but disappeared, families are smaller, and both men and women are working, day-care centers are forced to take on the early educational and acculturating role that families once held exclusively. In some countries (Israel, for example) child rearing is occasionally becoming more a responsibility of the community and less exclusively that of the family. Sex role in child rearing is now not everywhere as fixed as it used to be. There is no doubt that modern society, even in socialist countries, has not yet provided the opportunity for the father to be equally involved in child rearing. In capitalist society the man almost always has to maintain the economic base while the wife cares for the child. The problem of child rearing is not so easily solved by day-care centers since they, unless carefully and creatively programmed, are only mass baby-sitting factories with insufficient opportunity for creative individual growth. Furthermore, in socialist countries where many day-care centers are reported to be of good quality, the mother is usually expected to take on the second job of homemaking activities after the workday. This is true in both the Soviet Union and China.

But even in the traditional family pattern in child rearing, once children are born and on their way to school, does the mother's role have to be so restricted? If the mother can be freed to participate in the social, economic, and cultural life of the community, certainly she will be able to develop herself and also contribute more to the enrichment of the developing children in the home. But she must have preparation for this. At this period of time, the mother's and father's roles need have much less differentiation. The mother and father can *both* be appropriately available, loving and kind, friends and teachers to their children. If, in our present state of social development, the requirements for being the manager of the home dictate that the woman can devote only part of her time to work or study, does this require a special "psychology of women"?—or does it require new social institutions to allow both men and women to participate both inside and outside the home!

And what of the later years? Women can be expected to have a long life after menopause, both now and increasingly so in the future. Certainly there is no reason to assume that this life must continue to be especially different for a woman than it is for a man. The specific biological role of childbearing and nursing is over. There is no reason why there should be a special "psychology of women" to limit her at this time. Actually, however, we know full well that most women are not prepared for life after the childbearing years. It is especially urgent that we ensure that women can assume a full role as creative contributing members of society.

It might be well to consider what part men now play in perpetuating the special coercive and limiting "psychology of women" that we are concerned with today. Perhaps (like many whites who are threatened by the coming equality of blacks for full participation in the life of the community) men are being threatened by the increasing signs that women are able to participate fully in the adult world. Men often react to this in a competitive way. Many of them try to "prove their masculinity" by asserting dominance or, in a sulking way, refusing to accept the responsibility of the partnership of marriage; or they may seek dependent relationships, rather than cooperative shared ones.

There is no absolute femininity or masculinity. The psychology of women, as well as of men, is very minimally dependent on biological differences and more dependent on the restricted position of both men and women in our society. Psychoanalysts have long provided rationalization for this state. The social milieu has detracted from, rather than enhanced, the potential for a full and satisfying development of life for both men and women in our society. Our psychotherapy must help each person to approach optimum healthy living by enabling the person to participate in the struggle against character-distorting forces not only inside himself but also outside himself. We should especially be ready to help women struggle toward the achievement of a life that is unfettered by coercive social and psychological restrictions, including the restrictions so ignominiously promulgated by some leaders in our own field of psychiatry and psycho-analysis.

CONCLUSION

New Issues, New Approaches

AFTER READING these papers, it is clear that much new information on the psychology of women is available to advance the discussion well beyond past debates in over-simplified terms. It is then apparent that while certain topics can be laid to rest (e.g., penis envy, innate bio-logical passivity, submissiveness, and masochism require no further comment here), other issues are arising. The *seeming* passivity, submissiveness, dependency, and lack of direct assertiveness on the part of many women may still bear discussion. Similarly, women's development of their own individual personalities, sexuality, childbear-ing, and an evaluation of their strengths, another very ne-glected topic, also merit further examination. It now seems perfectly apparent that women can and should try to be and do whatever they wish, as Judd Marmor and Leon Salzman have indicated in their papers, but many obstacles to such full growth still remain.

Women have always grown in certain ways despite whatever obstructions were in the path. Several of the present papers elucidate the realities of that growth and the fact that it has gone largely unrecognized and un-acknowledged. What is new today is the conscious and explicit search for even further growth by large numbers of women, not only the great or the gifted. These women are now asking about the prospects and processes of self-development, and for explanations that can apply to the specifics of *their* existence.

What is the next step? What are the costs? Obviously not all women are at the same stage in this process. Some have recently experienced new levels of keen intellectual, artistic, or political insight and activity. Others have a newly acquired sense of personal worth and productivity; and still others, a new feeling of emotional resolution and equanimity. But not all. Many women seek help in the search for both greater personal effectiveness and a larger inner sense of well-being and spontaneity. They also seek bases for meaningful, authentic, and honest relationships with other people. (One immediately hears oneself echo internally, "So do men." The search here, however, is specifically about women. That concentration *is* the new phenomenon.)

These issues obviously arise in many different forms. Specifics vary for the working woman, the artist, the intellectual, or the woman who has not yet found a particular focus for her life: the married woman, the mother, the younger woman who now seriously questions the value of marriage, or the older unmarried woman. The recognition of this phenomenon is also new. Psychology in the past presumed essentially one model of woman, that of helpmate and mother. Other life patterns seemed almost to lie in the realm of "deviations" rather than chosen ways of living.

Within these pages the contributors have pointed to a new and specifically feminine framework for dealing with these many issues. Karen Horney, at the very outset, exemplified this concentration on a feminine view, seeing this not as a secondary, but as a fully valued endeavor. She brilliantly demonstrated the productive results to be achieved from this approach. By studying women as women, Clara Thompson reoriented psychological understanding of such major issues as dependency, intimacy, and authenticity. Likewise, the papers that followed demonstrated the understanding to be gained from this orientation and the errors that can ensue from its neglect. Witness their insights into the consequences of the in-

ability to allow authenticity in women, the seeming simplicity of this need, and the great complexities that follow
its disavowal.

We have recently learned much about the forces that
influence women's overall development. Some are social;
some biological. Both influence and articulate with psychological forces but are not identical to them. Our new
knowledge increases our ability to unravel confusion in
these realms. Several of the present writers have demonstrated that many factors thought to be immutably determined by biology are instead artifacts, results of social
conditions. They are therefore susceptible to change.
Actual change in the conditions affecting women is, of
course, another matter. But this knowledge revises the
whole understanding of the psychic economy.

In similar fashion truly biological forces were often seen
as psychological factors when the specifics of women's
biology were not fully acknowledged. The full study of
women's sexual functioning, for example, reveals that
much that was called frigidity can be explained on a
straightforward biological basis. In some instances the
problem is no longer why a woman "is frigid" but why the
male partner is not providing the stimulation that we now
know is biologically necessary. Such problems are of
course complicated, but they were even more so in a climate in which women did not feel able to explore the facts
of their own sexuality and wherein science neither concentrated on those facts nor saw them in independent
terms as they differed from male biology. Psychological
factors are still intimately entwined in such issues, but
due to recent researches the emphasis of the problem
should undergo a marked shift. Many of the specifics of
the psychological processes themselves, however, have
still to be filled in. Meanwhile, the knowledge offered here
suggests that the psychological elements in any given
problem may be weighed quite differently than they were
in the past.

One seeks to move even beyond these valuable insights

to gather them into a coherent and unified overall theory of the psychology of women. These writings do not yet fulfill this goal but they do move us further ahead. Some outlines of such a theoretical outlook can be perceived even now.

The work of Sherfey, Zilboorg, and Stoller jolt long-accepted assumptions about necessary and natural sexual priorities. In large sweeps they overturn the biological and historical premises on which most thinking was tacitly based. One may take issue with certain portions of the evidence presented, but one is also stimulated by their suggestion for a major reordering of past theory on the great global issues of mankind's—now, more appropriately, humankind's—relation to all of civilization. They thereby confront us with major dilemmas. Both theoretically and practically, the question becomes how shall we proceed with the knowledge they have elucidated for us? All is certainly not clear, but the implications of their work lead to major questions about our most basic institutions.

These dilemmas can perhaps best be approached by starting with certain simple and practical points. Today, many people ask openly and/or indirectly: if women aspire to enlarge their own lives and to focus directly on their own needs, will they violate some inborn or natural psychological rules which psychoanalysts presumably know? And, if so, will these women misguidedly pursue destruction of themselves, men, or children? The great weight of the evidence presented here demonstrates that this is a misconception. Although this point may seem a simple one, it has not been a minor misconception. It has been deeply absorbed by most people and still manifests itself in many ways, large and small. It underlies much of the thinking in psychology, especially when it is not so openly posited.

In marked contrast, the bulk of the psychoanalytic data in this book indicates that misinformation about women's nature and the prevalent conception that women should not attend directly to their own needs have been major causes of their problems—and concomitantly, but by a different route, of the problems of men and children.

This issue leads to the next basic proposition: women have developed thus far within a milieu that fosters and reflects a distorted conception about their essential nature. This occurs not to an obvious "minority group," for whom we have learned to acknowledge this process, but to one of the two main bodies of all humankind. Almost all authors agree that this "reality principle" has been badly skewed for women. Moreover, it has been weighted toward a profound underestimation of women's attributes, since their strengths go unrecognized and their troubles are ascribed to causes other than the real ones. The new definitions of reality presented here range from an illumination of the psychological value of women's valid qualities to totally new formulations of women's biological strengths.

When we recognize how ignorant we have been we find a new basis for optimism. We also find a new basis for a theoretical approach to both the basic nature of women and the sources of psychological troubles. The problem is not that women do not have these strengths but that they have been encouraged to transform them into something else. Thus, the therapeutic exploration becomes centered on how woman's attempt to transform herself into something inappropriate has led to her problems. The crucial issue here is that the inappropriate transformation has been the prescribed one.

Laing, in his way, deals with this question on a universal scale. To be crazy is the appropriate response to a crazy world. He does not, however, clearly delineate, as the present writers have, the specific inappropriateness prescribed for women as it differs from that for men. Nor does he emphasize the specific strengths of women which may save some women from craziness and may illuminate those aspects of the present world that drive men to madness. Men, too, are led to inappropriate transformations of themselves but in different ways, which are not simple opposites of those of women; each takes on its own particular momentum and builds up complexities on the basic misconceptions.

Freud was concerned with this issue too. He thought that society could not countenance recognition of one's basic and essential nature: the unrecognized sexual (and later aggressive) drives of *man*. Man's essential nature was in conflict with civilization, inevitably and for all time and place; but woman's essential nature was harmonious and, it seems, "tailored" to fit in with man's civilization, e.g., essential passivity, the need to be guided by men, and the like. If we agree that Freud was not a misogynist, perhaps he ultimately hoped, despite all the work he did on the sufferings of women, that they could be spared the anguish he perceived as the lot of men. Some of his writings about his wife and the history of his mother suggest this.

What, then, is the basic nature of women? Papers as divergent as those of Stoller and Salzman indicate that this question can now be approached in a much more sophisticated manner than that of the past. They perhaps come closest to an answer when they indicate that the nature of women will change because it is a reflection of changing social structures. If women take a hand in the process, their nature will change in a different direction and at a different speed than if they do not. Femininity will take on new qualities and encounter new problems and then change again.

There is a basic biology, to be sure, and it is very different from what most of us believed until recently. Stoller brings us the most up-to-date biological knowledge. There are complicated interactions between brain and hormones with complicated timing mechanisms that make for differences between male and female animals. As yet these are minimally verified in human beings, and we know that the huge cortical-conceptual system of humans has a way of overriding and modifying the operation of lower systems of brain activity. We now know that such lower systems of chemical and neural activity cannot be equated with innate drives and instincts, and that they are vastly different from psychological processes. After examining our present knowledge about these physiological mechanisms, Stoller concludes that all evidence indicates that what we call femininity and masculinity is overwhelmingly determined by social and familial interactions.

Biology certainly poses no inherent limitations to women's development. Quite the reverse. Sherfey, Salzman, and others demonstrate that women's biology has unacknowledged power and flexibility. One may not agree with every one of Sherfey's conclusions, but the major evidence from modern observers certainly suggests that the problem is not weakness but strength in a milieu that has obviously sought to curb that strength.

These papers make clear that the belief that women could or should accept and adjust to the stereotyped role has been a cause, not the cure, of their problems. From this new perspective, they then suggest many exciting reorientations for therapy. One permits all so-called symptoms to be seen in a new light—no longer merely as defenses, maneuvers, or other such tactics, but as struggles to preserve or express some deeply needed aspects of personal integrity in a milieu that will not allow for their direct expression. The task of a therapist then becomes the cooperative search for an understanding of those needs and an understanding of how they have been diverted or distorted. It is interesting that Adler suggested this formulation years ago and that Seidenberg has arrived at it by a different route. He illustrates it in his description of a woman who was freed from an immobilizing phobia. And what a new outlook on phobias he gives us! Its implications obviously extend to other problems and to such basic issues as the concept of anxiety itself.

Another overall view of women's symptoms emerges. Seidenberg describes them by a new psychological usage of the term "undoing." They are a disguised *protest*, an attempt to block participation in a prescribed way of life.

(Virgil said, "The only power left to the vanquished is to have no power.") The most common problems in women tend to be the powerless "undoing" or "refusing" kind—as in depression, phobias, so-called frigidity.

Although variations can be seen among the therapeutic views presented here, for instance, the obvious difference in Symonds' and Seidenberg's approach to phobias, it is striking to note that both authors sense a similar theme—the fear of grasping and directing one's life and a concurrent protest against a life of lost identity. Seidenberg quotes Carlyle, who relates the problem "not so much to what men [sic] suffer but what they miss." Symonds refers to Rank's statements that most people have a fear of life rather than a fear of death, and also to Kierkegaard's description of anxiety as "the dizzying possibility of being able." Symonds' view that some women have been led to develop the unconscious assumption that their own growth and self-realization will be equivalent to hurting others articulates with Matina Horner's studies which appeared in *Psychology Today* (November 1969). Horner demonstrates that a similar equation exists not in a small number of women "patients" but as a predominant characteristic in the female population. Women have deeply incorporated the conception that their personal effectiveness will lead to destruction—self-destruction and the destruction of others.

In these and other papers new theory and practice on some of the most common problems of women begin. All of the leads require development, but new pathways are open. It is apparent that the terminology which has formed the basis of our working conceptions requires re-examination. States such as dependency, passivity, submissiveness, and masochism are not ideals, and certainly are not goals to be sought. Nor are they even necessary human traits that we must reluctantly admit into the domain of the "normal." They are destructive whenever they occur. The attempt to inflict these traits on anybody, adult or child, precipitates a reaction, an attempt to fight back. If the reaction cannot be an open one, it will occur nonetheless, but in disguised form, often destructive to self and others. (We are not discussing here the differences in cultural or temperamental style which have also been described by these terms, but the more technical psychological usage of the past. These usages are, however, usually confused.)

This point can be taken one step further, for example, with reference to the frequent prescription for passive behavior in women. Clearly the essence of animate life is activity. No one is passive—certainly not babies, with whom the term is usually linked in psychological circles. Every psychiatrist knows that beneath the most extreme forms of passivity observed in human beings great activity seethes, but it has lost a path for direct expression. So it is with all these terms. A great deal of confusion has grown up around them and a large amount of this confusion may not be unrelated to the fact that they have all been sex-linked.

GROWTH

The terms that have been employed have importance beyond mere words. They are used as if to portray *processes,* complex sequences of events. As with the terminology, we now have a new outlook on some of the processes, most of them basic to all psychological theory, such as the conception of growth. Psychoanalysis, in essence, has always dealt with this topic, but a point here—an obvious point—seems to have been overlooked. We have all grown up in a world within which one-half of the people have been portrayed as a lesser breed. Thus growth for men has tended to be conceptualized as movement away from those attributes identified with women. From the material presented in this collection, it becomes apparent that when we think of growth, we have conceptualized the image of a man. Psychoanalysts have said that a boy must first renounce early identification with the mother and then, later, renounce sexual attraction to her. He must renounce not only the person but the processes in which she is engaged as well. Thus, our conception of growth has become a complex mélange. A male baby is supposed to give up identifications with certain *ideas*. These are the sex-linked attributes, e.g., passivity, which women, in fact, do not exhibit or they could not take care of an infant. Simultaneously, he is encouraged to give up identifications with those *processes*, e.g., the care of human life, which women are doing. Yet this process would probably be salutary for everybody to identify with rather than renounce. The negative attributes are not good for anybody, and are ideas falsely linked to both women and babies. Underneath it all runs the interdiction of another, even more basic process, which, as demonstrated here, seems the most frightening prospect of all: close and direct emotional engagement with another human being who is different—and female. The boy is encouraged to turn to the world of men, where processes are structured to limit direct emotional involvement with anybody, male or female.

The ramifications of this are many. First, regarding the concept of growth itself: is this the prototypic pattern on which all later growth will model itself? A paradigm based on the renunciation of certain attributes, rather than on a process of taking in and creating?

There is no inherent reason that closeness to women— or men—should inhibit a boy's growth or produce a confused sexual identification. Surely the reverse is true. Only from direct and emotional engagement does growth proceed. It is when such engagement is thwarted or distorted that problems occur and that people are forced into devious routes in their attempts to grow. How does this initial renunciation affect one's capacity for direct emotional engagement with all that one subsequently encounters?

The child's and man's difficulty in confronting that which is new and different, the essential feature of growth, may relate to the unrealistic suppression since infancy of direct, close engagement with those different and omnipresent people—women. In this first encounter with difference, the child is taught to fear and master it rather than welcome and embrace it. Tasks set for boys may have led us to an unnecessarily tortuous view of growth and may have served to obscure the more obvious yet strangely neglected observation that psychological growth is a great gift as well as an inexorable fact of human life.

In our sex-linked model of growth we may have introduced unnecessary obstacles, obscuring the fact that growth may be easier and more straightforward, requiring much less renunciation and only the obvious thrust toward emotional engagement, which seems to be eminently "natural" in humans. Similarly, renunciations and suppressions have concerned us so much that we seem to have lost the explicit recognition that humans are basically creative. Carrying with us the sum total of our past conceptions and their emotional concomitants, we also constantly transform these conceptions. We copy no blueprint, either from our own past or from the experiences of others. But what sufficed in the last stage will not suffice in the next. The attempt to force past conceptions into immutable service renders them inappropriate and forces both the perception of self and of the new situation into an inaccurate image.

We readily perceive that the developing child is impelled toward growth, but we seem less able to acknowledge that the process continues throughout life. Perhaps we have allowed ourselves to recognize the fact of children's growth because it so obviously forces itself upon us. But we have obscured the process in relation to later life. (It appears that it is only recently in Western history that we recognize children's growth. Is that because we no longer needed them to join us in the serious business of work? Nevertheless, as our children have entered the labor market at progressively later ages, we have "discovered" that growth continues longer; witness the psychological recognition in recent years that growth no longer stops at adolescence. Now it goes on into the "identity crisis" almost to age 30, if you're male and have gone to college and graduate school.)

Another factor in the model of male growth is the notion of renunciation of the *processes* involved in human interactions, when one of the participants is female. In early life, as it has been structured, these processes, of course, involve mainly a woman and the child. Caretaking may be one description. Suppose men did not renounce identification with this process but instead incorporated it? Would it enlarge men's human capacities? Writers as different as Zilboorg, Erikson, and Bernard Robbins have suggested that men are backward in this area. Adult men have some notions of taking care of women and children—often more in the material than the emotional sense—but it is equated with taking care of lesser beings. What is rare is a man who has incorporated an image of himself as a person who takes care of his equals—both men and women—who feels this identification as a critical part of his inner sense of self, equal to or more important than other inner images, like that of being superior to his "equals," for example. So it seems to be with all of our past notions about the processes that include interaction with women—they lead to severe distortion and limitation of our conceptions of the total human experience.

Even "caretaking" is a great global term requiring more precise delineation. It does not describe the complex interaction in which both adult and child contribute and in which both learn and grow, although each proceeds from a very different level. The term still tends to reflect its origins in which women were seen as either fully formed "caretakers" or sex objects, a view based largely on the concept of women as the repository of "the desires and disappointments of men," as Horney said, and little related to the realities of women's lives.

Psychological thought has been diverted away from a

direct focus on the essential facts of growth and creativity. The source of psychological problems lies in those forces that militate against these seemingly intrinsic yet amazingly uncelebrated human needs. Perhaps the diversion of psychological thought into the belief that men must grow away from women has prevented us from fully recognizing that men and women must grow and create and that other things stand in the way.

And what of the growth of women? Here the conceptions have become even more confused. The attributes toward which women are still expected to aim are those that are linked with childish or infantile qualities, e.g., helplessness, dependency, and the like. Women are not expected to grow toward those attributes associated with men; to do so would be unfeminine. In fact, we seem to have no model for women's growth at all. Here, at least, the classical psychoanalytic model may have more accurately reflected processes occurring in most women, because it described women's development as the process of overcoming active forces within them and assuming a passive, dependent, masochistic role. It saw the active forces as masculine, remnants of a bisexuality that had to be overcome. Such a concept of bisexuality has now been superseded.

More seemingly modern psychoanalysts talk in terms of women's need for full development, but most do not seem to recognize that their own concept of full development is still generally tied to an image of men. They thus overlook the psychological value of those processes in which only (or especially) women have engaged. This also precludes their recognition of the specific difficulties that confront women as they try to grow and the realization that notions about women's growth have been limited conceptions derived from male notions of the meaning of maturity.

As some present writers have indicated, however, despite the foregoing women have grown in many ways, ways that may be more closely related to the necessities of human life but that have not been fully acknowledged as such. Women have grappled with many crucial aspects of living even as they have been prevented from full development by adhering to male values.

Sociologists speak of women as playing the expressive role in life while men play the instrumental. These terms may describe the realms assigned to each sex, but they are used as if this separation were optimal—as if all human activity did not have emotional meaning. Much current literature and philosophy by male authors seems to deplore this artificial split and to seek some path to fuse these two realms. What these writings do not do is recognize how much women already know about both realms. Because this split did predominate in the past, women in general tended to develop a keener sense of the meaning of all human activity. Their "work" tended to force them into an awareness of the intricate interstices of human relationships rather than the manipulation of things. It has also brought them into much closer interaction with the processes of human growth and development. Women are more attuned to the vicissitudes to which humans are inevitably subjected and can acknowledge human weaknesses or limitations as necessary aspects of current reality. Because most women were never part of the "race to the top," they did not concentrate as heavily on the development of the feeling that they must triumph over others. They more readily allowed themselves to experience the feeling that it is more gratifying to relate to others than to outdo them; to understand others than to outsmart them; to serve others than to master them. Serving others is not necessarily a bad thing, if it is equal and reciprocal.

The arena for these valuable assets has not been limited to home and family. Professional and other working women tend to choose fields in which they can serve others or relate to human needs. This choice is not explained solely by the fact that these fields are lower paying and/or easier for women to enter. Studies of teen-agers who are not even fully aware of such practicalities reveal a real difference in motivation between the sexes.

Women have, in addition, always functioned on the instrumental level. We know that women have often been the mainstay of families, organizations, and businesses. Women have exercised a high degree of executive and organizational ability. For some there has been a discontinuity here. They have felt able to utilize their abilities only in situations where the major responsibilities were nominally under someone else's aegis, e.g., the secretary who really runs the business but would never think in terms of being the company president, the efficient housewife who believes only her husband can accomplish anything valuable. Matina Horner's studies dramatically demonstrate the conflict produced in women by the open acknowledgment of their own abilities. Another study shows that even women doctors, women engaged in very rigorous work, tend to describe themselves in the old female stereotypic terms that their actions, in fact, disprove. Recognition of effectiveness or valid achievement provokes in women frightening visions of destruction. They fear that an admission of their abilities will result in loss of the only sense of self they have been allowed, the whole notion of the meaning of femininity they have acquired, the sole basis on which they have been accepted and allowed to relate to others.

We need not repeat here the great contributions women have made to social, political, and other issues, but many more are still to be fully revealed. Ellen Moers, the literary critic, has pointed out that there was a great flood of English women writers in the nineteenth century, many more than those who are well known. Moreover, they dealt with the great problems that most men left untouched: the brutalities of early industrialization; anti-Semitism; and, in the United States, slavery. The lists of such seemingly forgotten accomplishments are long.

These discontinuities in evaluating their abilities and strengths remain problems for many women today, but for the first time women are beginning to approach them without believing that they must cast aside the valuable facets of their heritage. That heritage can be openly cultivated rather than left unrecognized under the general relegation of feminine matters to secondary status.

Going beyond these assets, some women today are seeking to create something new, a new form of personhood which incorporates these strengths but seeks to expand and extend them. Until this essential is grasped, women's efforts will continue to be visualized in terms of the old models. There is still a great tendency to see women's growth as either masculine or in terms of an endeavor that seeks to destroy or surpass men. Clara Thompson made this point thirty years ago, and current women leaders have emphasized it. Many women writers have also carried this theme forward, to emphasize women's own set of values, but a large amount of work remains to be done in the psychological fields on this point.

In this area white people, and white women in particular, have much to learn from black women. Black women have long lived with the knowledge that black men have not been allowed to enter the heights of instrumental living in the white man's world. Black women have learned even more about combining the instrumental and the expressive roles. They have never been properly honored for the strengths they have developed; instead they are maligned for them (witness recent sociological and psychological writing), as if they are the cause of black men's troubles; this in the face of all the destructive forces which are known to act on black men. The fact to be remembered, however, is that destructive forces have acted against black women also.

The problems of black women differ in many ways from those of white women, and grow out of different circumstances and history. Many among them have expressed suspicion of the current women's movement dominated by white women for reasons which grow out of their experience with racism. Others are well aware that they have special interests and problems simply because they are women. But even those who are most aware of their problems as women tend to refuse to overlook the problems of the entire black community, and of course black men. That black women have survived is a great tribute. That they have in addition nourished, protected, and worked in slavery and afterward for their men and children; that they have refused to abandon this concern in face of all the extra deprivations and hardships; and that they have maintained a sense of strength and personhood —all this serves to underscore women's special strengths and values.

Mabel Blake Cohen has demonstrated that even when these factors were not so clearly seen, some women and men found a way to meet each other's needs by current standards. In general, they were found to have had emotional capabilities that have been labeled both masculine and feminine, characteristics that are more related to being human. The path to acquiring these characteristics has been tortuous, but different, for each sex and has tended to preclude advancement to fulfilling other needs which may be even more important. Thus, many authors speak of giving and getting satisfaction of one's dependency needs. We do not yet talk about how much we all are interdependent and *need* to relate to an equal, how challenging and beneficial that process can be, how often this need is thwarted, how little practice we get in it, and how much of our life is spent at the much more primitive level of learning how to be either one-up or one-down.

Perhaps modern attempts to talk in universals have obscured the specific problems and the specific possibilities for each sex. While we would like to think in terms of basic human needs and psychological processes, the time has not yet come when we can do so without first sorting out differences.

LIFE STAGES

The present writers give us some concrete starting points for the yet-to-be-created model of women's growth.

Growth tends to be discussed today as a series of life stages. (The commonly favored term is that the child must "master" the issues of each stage.) Several papers demonstrate that the current differential treatment of children interferes with optimal development in each sex. Clearly a new model for childhood is required, one which incorporates the idea of the development of some accurate sense of effective individuality as part of a process of interacting *equally* with others. Members of one sex need not be raised to believe that their ultimate goal is to assume a role in which they will be permitted to serve others. Members of the other sex need not be raised to believe that they are superior and are to be serviced by lesser human beings while they struggle to succeed in doing the important work in the world.

While the present conditions prevail, however, there exist specific complexities which the contributors have begun to unravel. In contrast to the male model touched upon above, the girl may be driven to disengage from the woman in the family for different reasons. Adler, Moulton, Seidenberg, and others show that she may be driven against her mother by her accurate recognition that her mother does not value her as much as she does a boy. Or she may adopt the general tendency to demean the female in the family, again reflecting the prevailing reality whether it is grossly or subtly expressed. She then may be immediately caught in conflict with the most significant person in her life who is also the figure from whom she builds an image of herself as a feminine being. Without a full assessment of the devaluation of women, we cannot grasp the nature of these and other conflicts specific to the girl.

Mabel Blake Cohen and Paul Chodoff have explored some of the aspects of this topic. Yet in the short time since the publication of their papers, we have seen an expanded number of sophisticated studies bearing on these issues, including longitudinal studies of children, of temperamental differences in children, of parent-child interaction. Even more recently some researchers have related this data to the problems of sexual stereotyping.

There is currently a great emphasis on adolescence. Some of the major characteristics of this period are said to be rebellion and expansion. Clara Thompson first pointed out that for girls it is the reverse, a period of restriction and greater conformity to a limited role. Furthermore, that major issue of late adolescence and early adulthood, the attainment of an inner sense of separate identity, so far concerns mainly men. Women have been led to believe that the development of an authentic, independent identity is not important. Symonds and others note that the achievement of a sense of worthwhile identity is a difficult task at best, and women are not even given the eighteen or so years of preparation that men receive for the job. Women can attempt to escape the anguish and anxiety of this period by fleeing into marriage. They can avoid the risks of determining their relationship to the world by focusing on their relationship to one man. For this escape women pay a high price. (Often so do the man and the children.) Marriage may provide some women with the opportunity for new forms of relating, to a husband and children. These relationships may truly enhance some facets of a woman's development. But for many women they do not. For others they may aid in some ways and yet suppress other aspects of their personalities. Cohen shows that mutual enhancement in marriage depends on the ability of each partner flexibly to meet the needs of the other. She demonstrates how the past sexual stereotypes militate against this for both partners. The prevailing masculine values and upbringing prevent many men from equaling women's ability to relate to the most important human needs. Because men have been less able to relate to these needs, and because men's values tend to dominate the structure of the family, these important needs are not fully recognized or fulfilled for anybody and tend to get lost in the family's pursuit of more spurious goals. This is another example of how the devaluation of qualities associated with women comes full circle and deprives everyone.

For some women the submission of self in marriage can be so disastrous that they suffer profoundly. Rather than prescribing marriage for all, we need more accurate analyses of the ways in which this relationship articulates with each person's particular history. Thompson, Seidenberg, and Moulton have begun such analyses.

Many problems inherent in the various stages of life may become manifest in psychic and somatic symptoms or may be attenuated in minor, chronic form only to explode at the time of the menopause. For women, this is almost the equivalent of a delayed "identity crisis." Women who may have avoided the task of building a valid sense of identity in adolescence and early adulthood now face even worse anguish at a time when they have much less chance of finding a successful solution. Society's devaluation of anyone past youth adds its fearful effect. This disparagement falls particularly heavily on women since they have been valued primarily for their physical attributes. Adler and Seidenberg have opened up this topic. Their brief words offer a marked contrast to the reams that have been written about hormones and drugs in the face of this *human* dilemma.

For women who do not marry, the problem has often been even greater, at least until recently. Regardless of their other accomplishments, most unmarried women carried within them a sense of second-class citizenship, feeling unworthy and unwanted. In contrast to this attitude, there have always been a few women who found their greatest personal growth and satisfaction without marrying. For these women, remaining single was a deliberate choice, not the generally assumed indication of undesirability. Today many more women are consciously weighing the benefits of marriage against its costs. In the current climate the frightened and compulsive rush into marriage has abated. In many circles people have learned to respect different kinds of relationships, allowing them-

394

selves and others the right to seek the form best suited to their needs and desires. Concomitantly, a great urge for a true sense of participation in a larger community has emerged, a turning from the narrow attachments of the nuclear family. For many people the choice is no longer between marriage or some second-class isolation. Other more varied relationships take on significance, whether or not they involve joint living arrangements. Some people are relating to others with the concern and devotion that once was considered appropriate only within a family. For some, these new ties have proved more gratifying and fulfilling. Who today can seriously study the situation of marriage and the problems of family breakdown and advocate this one form for all?

CHILD CARE

All the crucial issues touched upon briefly in the last few paragraphs call for much further study. The papers in this volume represent only the beginnings. Two other aspects of women's development require specific mention, not because they in fact are more important for women but because they have been made so. Indeed, they are the two areas toward which women's development has traditionally been pointed, the goals for which women are still groomed: child care and sex. They are, therefore, areas that women want particularly to understand today.

In both these areas, but especially in child care, it is almost as if women are now being challenged to provide the answers to some of our modern dilemmas. Obviously it is not a concern for women only. But obviously, too, if changes are made, they will very likely be initiated by women. Some already have been.

The whole topic of pregnancy and child rearing is still grossly misunderstood. The father's current abandonment of the mother and the child in the process of child rearing is a characteristic of our society so accepted that we hardly recognize its destructiveness. Instead of saying that men must do the important work and make the important decisions, while women raise the children, we might say that the most important work in the world is the participation in the care and growth of human life. We might provide first for women and men to develop as individuals and relate as equals and then to share equally in the important work of child rearing if they choose to do so. Those, either men or women, who do not choose to devote a large part of their lives to the heavy responsibilities entailed in raising children need not have them.

True, we have never had such arrangements. People have had to be preoccupied with physical and economic survival, and if men could do better in the marketplace, it seemed they had to be there. But we can recognize that in such arrangements the child is placed in a distorting environment. The child is led to believe that he or she has a father, and in essence, he or she does not. Rather, the child has a legal relative who says, in effect, "I am dominant and do the important things. I leave the major interaction in your development to your mother because it is a lesser matter." The inevitable conclusion is that dominance and important affairs do not include involvement in the growth of another human being. The message has come through, as now evidenced by the reaction against it in many of the themes of the youth culture.

Mabel Blake Cohen and her group provide one of the keynotes for understanding this. They found that the well-being of the mother during pregnancy and after was definitely related to the interaction with the father, whether or not the woman had her own previous problems. Yet this topic has not usually been seen in this light. If there were problems, they were the woman's, problems she carried with her and inflicted on the situation. Instead, the issue can be defined in terms of the quality of the interaction, one in which the man's contribution, or lack of it, weighs as heavily as the woman's. No doubt the same framework applies throughout the child's life. Here is a whole new realm of living from which traditional values have excluded men and in which they might find one source of the human connection and engagement that many seek desperately today.

Several writers have focused on this deficit in male development. The problem is not that women have taken care of children but that they have been forced to do so (or else feel deviant or deprived). Additionally, they have tried to do so with the expectation that men would offer equally committed emotional participation and devotion. Women have concentrated their attention on the attempt to foster growth of individuals within the context of a family distorted by the requirement to maintain a false situation of dominance. Even within this context, recent articles have begun to cast new light on past conceptions of the relationship between mothering and child development.

Along with the turning away from marriage, some people today are also envisioning different forms of child care. They think not only of child-care centers but of alternative forms by which people other than biological parents may form close and intimate relationships with children, may enrich and be enriched by them. They seek to enhance children's experience and to expand children's emotional ties beyond the limits imposed by the possessiveness and inequalities that the nuclear family tends to engender. In my experience, many women who are trying these forms do so only after serious thought. They are fully aware that this is a change from long-held patterns. They know that children need sustained intimate relationships, but they have also considered the deficiencies of the intimate relationships to which children have been limited or subjected in the past.

SEX AND CHILDBEARING

Despite their criticism of Freud and psychoanalysis, some women writers and some advocates of encounter and other group movements seem to have taken over various simplifications of Freudianism, in forms Freud never used. If women will only become sexually liberated, their pent-up energies will be freed, their life force released from its bonds, and they will find creativity, health, and happiness. Women's strength and hope lie in their real sexuality—not as "sex objects" but as a free, uninhibited, natural, sexual beings.

It is true that sexuality should constitute one of the most compelling and joyful forces to bring humans into more profound and rich contact with each other, to the great enhancement of both their independence and mutuality. It makes sense that civilizations which developed inequalities enforced by power, and which forced the vast majority of people to spend most of their lives doing work without pleasure, should also have evolved all manner of ways to separate and isolate people from pleasurable interaction with each other. It follows that sex, one force that impels people toward each other and provides so much pleasure, should suffer the most extreme distortions and limitations. It does not follow that sex, per se, is the road back to greater equality, mutuality, and satisfaction. Human beings now bring to sex all their other conceptions and feelings. These feelings either move toward love, respect, and trust in each other or move toward some degree of the opposite qualities. Sexuality, with its great force for driving people toward each other, can provide a powerful impetus for mutual human growth and communion. But many obstacles must be overcome. Understanding these obstacles allows us to recognize that sex can also undermine these goals.

Here psychoanalysts have experience to offer. After long attempts to free people's sexual blocks, almost all agree that this effort does not usually provide the solution to psychological problems. One after another, the major psychological syndromes which were presumably based on lack of full sexual function have given way. Psychoanalysts now tend to talk in terms of the "preoedipal

398

problem" involved in every one of them. Even in relation to "hysteria," the great classical example of inhibited sexuality, most psychoanalysts have long since taught that there is a deep preoedipal problem, usually described as a problem of dependency from the oral stage. When sexual problems were found to be an insufficient cause, psychoanalysts tended to look for the origin of the problem farther back in the individual's history. Alternatively, a less linear approach may be used to inquire whether the problem occurs as a result of the total quality of the interactions the individual experiences and the kinds of complicated inner transformations that follow when an individual suffers destructive treatment or distorted interactions at each stage of development. As indicated earlier, the total quality of interactions may be heavily distorted by, among other things, the notions of renunciation and disengagement inherent in the "masculine" growth model. Within this framework, when women, devalued by society, attempt to fight back, the only means that seem available to them appear distorted and covert. Some recent observers have gone on to a much more sophisticated view of the interrelationships between sexuality and psychological problems.

Of the psychoanalysts writing on this topic, Bernard Robbins was the first to note that the attempt to keep love and sex separate has been the traditional operation of men in our culture. Recent advocates of sexual freedom for women often prescribe a corresponding course for them. The obvious question arises: is it ever possible for human beings to maintain this separation? Even in cultures where sexual activity has been much freer than our own, it has always embodied human meanings. If these are not cooperative and constructive, they are degrading and destructive. Whatever the meaning of sexual activity in other societies or whatever it may come to mean ultimately in our town, no one born in our society can engage in sexual activity without experiencing meanings which he or she has learned from our culture, and these are mixed at best. If women can move toward changing the context in which sex occurs, then they can perhaps free sex from its past bondage. It is doubtful that the reverse process will occur, that is, that that sex will free women.

A number of observers have recently stressed the point that many of the so-called manifestations of "free sex" have rapidly become attempts to remove sex from human communion, leading to increased degradation of women and isolation of men. In this sense, men are neither more free nor more advanced than women.

Zilboorg's article raises a different but related theme, also somewhat akin to a thesis recently articulated by some women, which proposes that women are generally more in tune with nature than men, biologically more "primary" and "natural," sexually richer, more free and unrestricted. By contrast, men, in dominating all our civilization, have gone against nature. In attempting to conquer nature rather than live in harmony with it, men have developed a hypertrophied, aggressive, executive, and organizational ability that has become a Franken-stein. Their efforts to dominate nature and women have squeezed and distorted them into inhibited, robotlike creatures, yet militaristic and aggressive power seekers who have fouled and polluted a large part of nature and threaten to destroy it altogether.

Superficially there is much that appears obvious in this line of thinking. It seems oversimplified and assumes either a natural state which presumably existed in pre-recorded history or an ideal state which should or could exist. This natural state is equated with something that was right and good and which has been inhibited and twisted by civilization. These underlying assumptions are close to the Freudian model—that human beings are basically more animal-like; if they could be totally so and play out their instincts uninhibitedly, they would have no problem living in harmony with nature. Civilization, of necessity, intervenes. For Freud it was a two-edged development. Civilization required all manner of inhibition of man's natural tendencies—and for Sherfey, even more inhibition of women's—but it was necessary for the development of social cohesiveness and survival. People would otherwise have destroyed each other through the free exercise of their sexual and aggressive instincts. For some women's theorists, presumably not. Only because civilization became dominated by men has it led to aggressive destruction. If left to nature alone, everyone would have been totally satisfied sexually and otherwise happy, healthy, peaceful, and equal.

Other models are possible. There seems no reason inherent in biology that civilization should be incompatible with sexuality or that it should inevitably thwart other human necessities. Indeed, we fulfill humans' needs only by virtue of living in groups. Various societies provide for some aspects of human potentialities and suppress others. There probably was no natural idyllic state but more likely a harsh struggle to survive in a nature that was in part hostile and in part harmonious with human life. We have developed some measure of cooperative human existence. We have simultaneously, as a group, created forces that militate against the fullest cooperative living for all. These destructive forces can exist to varying extents and still be compatible with survival of the group, but within these limits they can produce many distorting effects on individuals. We have barely emerged from a state of struggle for physical survival. Psychologically we reflect these primitive conditions, though we have the fantastic conceptual-emotional apparatus of the human brain with which we keep trying to direct our lives. At some point it became advantageous to reduce women to an inferior status. A huge conceptual-emotional structure of rationalization and legitimation of that situation developed and is still with us.

It would seem that we could develop a form of cooperative human existence that would provide for more fulfillment. Admittedly the task of achieving this is still monumental. Until it is achieved, we will suffer from its absence, but realization of this source of suffering seems to be the framework in which one can begin to understand the psychological problems of human beings. At least it seems so for the majority of them—women.

Other aspects are closely related to the issue of sexuality. Horney's paper of 1926 attempts to counter Freud's belief in the primacy of penis envy by asserting that women experience a positive pleasure in childbearing. Frieda Fromm-Reichmann's paper of 1950 does the same. Their basic emphasis was important since it viewed women in their own right, not as pale images of men, and it is impressive to note how much of their thought has since been validated by later evidence, not only in relation to childbearing but also to all sexual functioning. This line of thinking, however, leaves a possibility that has since been utilized as a basis for a seemingly advanced but an equally restrictive view of women. In a sense, this has been the thrust of some modern psychoanalysts. The womb need not be put down as less than the penis. It can be valued and even esteemed in its own right. Only it should be the center of women's activity and the basis of their life plans. Thus women are still defined by their biology.

This raises a related, basic question: do human beings find full satisfaction and fulfillment in life in biological functions alone? Again, early Freudian theory was interpreted so as to imply this since all other important activities—and these were mainly those of men—could be seen as sublimations, that is, fulfillment of biological or sexual functions in other guises, those that the culture will allow. Since no culture seems to allow totally unrestricted, instant sexual activity of all sorts (the Freudian polymorphous perversity), the best men can do is develop "healthy" sublimation. (Again, Freud "spared" women this deflection. They could more directly fulfill their biological destiny and had to sublimate less.) In fact, later Freudian and non-Freudian analysts have emphasized many other aspects of man's development in what is called the newer ego psychology. Women, however, have been led to believe that they are to plan their lives around the functioning of the womb. This premise becomes even more untenable today in that the womb will be called upon to perform its reproductive function on the average of twice in a lifetime.

NEED FOR PSYCHOLOGY

Aside from the above line of argumentation, it has long been clear that human beings do not find their full development and satisfaction in biological function. Rather, to be human is by definition to be part of a group which operates by principles that interact with and thereby transcend, but need not suppress, biology. To be human is by definition to operate under the guidance of a conceptual system which takes primacy over and determines the meaning of all functioning. Here again the work of the most enlightened students of biology seems to confirm this process. Human activity does not exist without conceptual content and associated emotions. The individual psychological level of organization is in constant reciprocal interaction with the social and biological level. Out of this interaction psychological structures emerge which are neither social nor biological but something different from both. They bring their own momentum to the next immediate interaction with both the social and biological forces. We have not developed a full understanding of the psychic processes of women as they interrelate with the societal forces acting on them and the biological forces arising from within. We do not have such an understanding for anyone.

Many psychoanalysts now believe that psychological problems do not develop because of sexual suppression except if one stretches the meaning of sexuality to its broadest sense, but by that time there are probably better terms of discussion. People suffer from suppression and confusion of their psychological needs—for growth, for creativity, and for full communion with other people. Society provides for these even less than it provides for the expression of sexuality, or rather, suppression of sexuality is one part of the suppression of human communion.

When those needs are thwarted, humans develop complex psychological transformations in their attempts to grow and to relate to others. In the face of obstacles, they still use their inherent creativity to construct inner conceptions to attempt to deal with them; but if the obstacles are great and confusing, these inner conceptions tend to become more and more convoluted and remove them even further from the possibilities of growing and relating, and from the realities of their existence, from an accurate consciousness of what they are feeling and doing. We are now experiencing a climate that may encourage and stimulate more advanced study of these psychological factors in women.

These few paragraphs cannot possibly cover a full assessment of the complexities of the current situation of psychoanalysis. Nevertheless, they may indicate that the field has always been in a state of tension with the society in which it exists, and today it seems again to be at a turning point. The situation is influenced by a number of factors not elaborated here. Psychoanalysis, a unique historical phenomenon, has always been in a dual position, having the potential for promoting conformity to the established order and for creating conflict within it. This situation is illustrated by these contributions. If psychoanalysis is to play a role in the future development of women, or to seek to help women to help themselves, it may move again into more conflict with society. Will the field as a whole take on this role? A definitive answer is impossible, and it may be a two-part one. Psychoanalysts and other therapists may be able to help women only if women on the larger scale continue to create and strengthen an assertive force of their own. (If one reviews the dates of the papers presented here, one finds interesting evidence on this point. After the early controversy in the twenties, the next wave of papers appeared during and immediately after World War II, when changes occurred in women's participation in life. There were few papers again until the late sixties, when the current women's movement began.) Psychoanalysis surely needs this nourishment. With it the field may have greater possibilities of enlarging and developing a wide focus on this topic. Undoubtedly not all psychoanalysts will move in this direction for it involves moving against the values and rewards to which they too have been conditioned. In this, psychoanalysts are not a great deal more virtuous or flexible than anyone else, despite hopes to the contrary. Some, however, have seen beyond virtue to a deeper grasp of where their own most satisfying work and gratifying human connections lie.

All this discourse may not help to answer a pressing and serious question for a woman seeking help. Perhaps the best answer is to point to the writings here and add that many other psychoanalysts also share an openness and a desire to expand their consciousness. In recent months, several national and local psychoanalytic groupings have initiated ongoing study groups on women and numerous meetings have been held dealing with newer formulations on women.

It is also important to recognize that psychoanalysis gave us the first theory and methodology by which people themselves could investigate and change some of the forms of suffering that had previously been so inexplicable and immutable. Neither social theory nor biology suffices in these realms. Psychoanalysis has also placed a value on the individual and on individual expression. This value has been a fragile one, difficult to honor both because it is hard to extend to large numbers of people (although not as difficult as some have made it appear) and because the attempts to impose other values seem more easily accomplished. Without constant vigilance, this value can also be violated in psychoanalysis in an even more subtle manner than in those therapies which are more obviously controlling and directive. Psychoanalysis, has, at least, held out the goal of self-determination.

One pivotal point around which the issues in psychoanalytic therapy and theory have revolved is the delineation of the crucial variables that determine both the origin of psychological problems and the possibilities of psychological change. The nature and operation of these psychological forces can hardly be considered definitely known. Some people have been greatly helped by psychoanalysis; others have not. Our conceptions of the crucial determinants have been changing and will continue to change, possibly more decisively, now that women have made such a resounding impact. Perhaps women will provide the stimulus and be the main movers and participants in the next great advance.

Bibliography

The references here have been compiled into a general list of the most frequently used sources in the text, followed by a list of works of special interest drawn for each article.

Deutsch, Helene. *Psychology of Women,* vol. 1. New York: Grune & Stratton, 1944.

Freud, Sigmund. "Analysis Terminable and Interminable" (1937). In *The Standard Edition of the Complete Psychological Works of Sigmund Freud,* vol. 23. London: Hogarth Press, 1964. (Hereafter, this edition of Freud's work will be referred to simply as *Standard Edition.*)

————. "Female Sexuality" (1931). In *Standard Edition,* vol. 21. London: Hogarth Press, 1961.

————. *New Introductory Lectures in Psychoanalysis.* New York: W. W. Norton, 1933.

————. "The Taboo of Virginity" (1918). In *Standard Edition,* vol. 11. London: Hogarth Press, 1957.

————. "Three Essays on the Theory of Sexuality" (1905). In *Standard Edition,* vol. 7. London: Hogarth Press, 1953.

————. "Totem and Taboo" (1913). In *Standard Edition,* vol. 13. London: Hogarth Press, 1955.

Fromm-Reichmann, Frieda. "Notes on the Mother Role in the Family Group." *Bulletin of the Menninger Clinic* 4 (1940): 132–48.

————. *Principles of Intensive Psychotherapy.* Chicago: University of Chicago Press, 1950.

Horney, Karen. *Feminine Psychology,* edited by Harold Kelman. New York: W. W. Norton, 1967.

————. *New Ways in Psychoanalysis.* New York: W. W. Norton, 1959.

————. "On the Genesis of the Castration Complex in Women." *International Journal of Psycho-Analysis* 5 (1924): 50–65.

Jones, Ernest. "The Phallic Phase." *International Journal of Psycho-Analysis* 14 (1933): 1–33.

Masserman, Jules E., ed. *Science and Psychoanalysis*, vols. 10, 11, 13. New York: Grune & Stratton, 1966, 1967, 1968.

Masters, William, and Johnson, Virginia. *Human Sexual Response*. Boston: Little, Brown, 1966.

Sherfey, Mary Jane. *The Nature and Evolution of Female Sexuality*. New York: Random House, 1972.

Stoller, Robert J. *Sex and Gender*. New York: Science House, 1968.

Thompson, Clara. *Interpersonal Psychoanalysis*, edited by M. R. Green. New York: Basic Books, 1964.

————. "The Role of Women in This Culture." *Psychiatry* 4 (1941): 1–8.

THE FLIGHT FROM WOMANHOOD: THE MASCULINITY COMPLEX IN WOMEN AS VIEWED BY MEN AND BY WOMEN

Deutsch, Helene. *Psychoanalyse der Weiblichen Sexualfunktionen*. Vienna: Interrationaler Psychoanalytischer Verlag, 1925.

Freud, Sigmund. "The Infantile Genital Organization of the Libido" (1923). In *Standard Edition*, vol. 19. London: Hogarth Press, 1961.

————. "On the Transformation of Instincts with Special Reference to Anal Erotism" (1916). In *Standard Edition*, vol. 14. London: Hogarth Press, 1957.

Simmel, Georg. "*Philosophische Kultur*." In *Philosophischsoziologische Bucherei*, vol. 27. Leipzig: Kronet, 1919.

THE PROBLEM OF FEMININE MASOCHISM

Deutsch, Helene. "The Significance of Masochism in the Mental Life of Women" (Part 1: " 'Feminine' Masochism and Its Relation to Frigidity"). *International Journal of Psycho-Analysis* 11 (1930): 48–61.

Rado, Sandor. "Fear of Castration in Women." *Psychoanalytic Quarterly* 2, nos. 3–4 (1933): 425–75.

SOME EFFECTS OF THE DEROGATORY ATTITUDE TOWARD FEMALE SEXUALITY

Freud, Sigmund. "The Economic Problem of Masochism" (1924). In *Standard Edition*, vol. 19. London: Hogarth Press, 1961.

Fromm, Erich. "Sex and Character." *Psychiatry* 6, no. 1 (1943): 21–32.

ON THE DENIAL OF WOMEN'S SEXUAL PLEASURE: DISCUSSION OF DR. THOMPSON'S PAPER

Fromm, Erich. *Escape from Freedom*. New York and Toronto: Farrar & Rinehart, 1947.

Groddeck, George. *The Book of the It*. New York: Nervous and Mental Disease Publishing Co., 1928.

Marsh, Erle M.; Moore, William G.; and Vollmer, Albert. *Your Baby Is Born*. San Francisco: Accommodation Letter Shop, 1949.

Mead, Margaret. *Male and Female: A Study of the Sexes in a Changing World*. New York: William Morrow, 1949.

Read, Grantley D. *Childbirth Without Fear*. New York: Harper & Bros., 1944.

MASCULINE AND FEMININE: SOME BIOLOGICAL AND CULTURAL ASPECTS

Freud, Sigmund. "Some Psychological Consequences of the Anatomical Distinction between the Sexes" (1925). In *Standard Edition*, vol. 19. London: Hogarth Press, 1961.

Horney, Karen. "Denial of the Vagina." *International Journal of Psycho-Analysis* 14 (1933): 57–70.

Jones, Ernest. "Early Development of Female Sexuality." *International Journal of Psycho-Analysis* 8 (1927): 459–72.

Ward, Lester F. *Pure Sociology*. New York: Macmillan, 1914.

ON THE NATURE OF FEMALE SEXUALITY

Bachofen, J. J. *Das Mutterrecht* (1861). Basel: Benno Schwabe, 1948.

Beach, F. A. *Hormones and Behavior*. New York: Harper & Bros., 1948.

Dickinson, R. L. *Atlas of Human Sexual Anatomy*. Baltimore: Williams & Wilkins, 1949.

Ford, C. S., and Beach, F. A. *Patterns of Sexual Behavior*. New York: Harper & Bros., 1951.

PERSONAL IDENTITY AND SEXUAL IDENTITY

Bandura, A.; Ross, D.; and Ross, S. A. "A Comparative Test of the Status of Envy, Social Power and Secondary Reinforcement Theories of Identificatory Learning." *Journal of Abnormal and Social Psychology* 67 (1963): 527–34.

Bell, R. Q. "Activity, Arousal and Early Object Relations." Manuscript presented to the Washington Psychoanalytic Institute.

Erikson, Erik. *Childhood and Society.* New York: Norton, 1950.

Hartley, Ruth. "Children's Concepts of Male and Female Roles." *Merrill-Palmer Quarterly* 6 (1960): 83–91.

Kagan, J., and Moss, H. A. *Birth to Maturity: A Study in Psychological Development.* New York: John Wiley, 1962.

Schaefer, E., and Bayley, N. "Maternal Behavior, Child Behavior and their Intercorrelations." *Research in Child Development* 87 (1963).

FEMININE PSYCHOLOGY AND INFANTILE SEXUALITY

Aries, P. *Centuries of Childhood.* New York: Alfred A. Knopf, 1962.

Bornstein, Berta. "The Analysis of the Phobic Child." In *Psychoanalytic Study of the Child,* vols. 3–4. New York: International University Press, 1949.

Brody, Sylvia. *Patterns of Mothering.* New York: International University Press, 1956.

Escalona, Sybille, and Heider, Grace H. *Prediction and Outcome.* New York: Basic Books, 1959.

Gagnon, J. H. "Sexuality and Sexual Learning in the Child." *Psychiatry* 28 (1965): 212.

Goldstein, K. *The Organism.* New York: American Book, 1939.

Hampson, J. L., and Hampson, Joan G. "The Ontogenesis of Sexual Behavior in Man." In *Sex and Internal Secretions,* edited by William C. Young. 3rd ed. Baltimore: Williams and Wilkins Co., 1961.

Home, H. J. "The Concept of the Mind," *International Journal of Psycho-Analysis* 47 (1966): 43.

Miller, G. "Information and Memory," *Scientific American* (August, 1956): 42.

Money, J. "Sex Hormones and Other Variables in Human Eroticism." In *Sex and Internal Secretions,* edited by William C. Young. 3rd ed. Baltimore: Williams & Wilkins, 1961.

Rado, Sandor. "A Critical Examination of the Concept of Bisexuality." In *Sexual Inversion,* edited by Judd Marmor. New York: Basic Books, 1965.

Schachtel, E. *Metamorphosis.* New York: Basic Books, 1959.

Wolff, Peter. "Panel Report: Contributions of Longitudinal Studies to Psychoanalytic Theory." *Journal of the American Psychoanalytic Association* 13 (1965): 605.

PSYCHOLOGY OF THE FEMALE: A NEW LOOK

Beach, F. A., ed. *Sex and Behavior.* New York: John Wiley, 1965.

Chodoff, Paul. "A Critique of Freud's Theory of Infantile Sexuality." *American Journal of Psychiatry* 123 (1967): 507–18.

Money, J.; Hampson, J. G.; and Hampson, J. L. "Imprinting and the Establishment of Gender Role." *Archives of Neurology and Psychiatry* 77 (1957): 333–36.

Montagu, A. *The Natural Superiority of Women.* New York: Macmillan, 1953.

Salzman, L. "Memory and Psychoanalysis." *Journal of Medical Psychology* 39 (1966): 127.

CHANGING PATTERNS OF FEMININITY: PSYCHOANALYTIC IMPLICATIONS

Friedan, Betty. *The Feminine Mystique.* New York: W. W. Norton, 1963.

Maslow, A. H. "Self-Esteem (Dominance-Feeling) and Sexuality in Women." *Journal of Social Psychology* 16 (1942): 259–94.

Opler, M. "Anthropological and Cross-Cultural Aspects of Homosexuality." In *Sexual Inversion,* edited by Judd Marmor. New York: Basic Books, 1965.

Romm, May. "Sexuality and Homosexuality in Women." In *Sexual Inversion,* edited by Judd Marmor. New York: Basic Books, 1965.

A SURVEY AND REEVALUATION OF THE CONCEPT OF PENIS ENVY

Bonaparte, Marie. *Female Sexuality.* New York: International Universities Press, 1933.

Dooley, L. "The Genesis of Psychological Sex Differences." *Psychiatry* 1 (1938): 181–95.

Jones, Ernest. "Early Female Sexuality." In *Papers on Psychoanalysis*. Boston: Beacon Press, 1961.

Lampl-de Groot, J. "Problems of Femininity." *Psychoanalytic Quarterly* 2 (1933): 489–518.

Marmor, Judd. "Some Considerations Concerning Orgasm in the Female." *Psychosomatic Medicine* 16 (1954): 240–45.

Moore, B. "Frigidity in Women." *Journal of the American Psychoanalytic Association* 9 (1961): 571–84.

Moulton, Ruth. "Multiple Factors in Frigidity." In *Science and Psychoanalysis,* vol. 10, edited by J. Masserman. New York: Grune & Stratton, 1966.

Muller, J. "A Contribution to the Problem of Libidinal Development of the Genital Phase in Girls." *International Journal of Psycho-Analysis* 13 (1932): 362–68.

THE SENSE OF FEMALENESS

Bettelheim, Bruno. *Symbolic Wounds: Puberty Rites and the Envious Male.* Glencoe, Ill.: Free Press, 1954.

Freud, Sigmund. "Some Psychical Consequences of the Anatomical Distinction between the Sexes" (1925). In *Standard Edition,* vol. 19. London: Hogarth Press, 1961.

Jones, Ernest. "The Early Development of Female Sexuality." *International Journal of Psycho-Analysis* 8 (1927): 459–72.

Masters, William, and Johnson, Virginia E. "The Artificial Vagina: Anatomic, Physiologic, Psychosexual Function." *Western Journal of Surgery, Obstetrics and Gynecology* 69 (1961): 192–212.

Money, John; Hampson, J. G.; and Hampson, J. L. "Imprinting and the Establishment of Gender Role." *Archives of Neurology and Psychiatry* 77 (1957): 333–36.

Stoller, Robert. "The Sense of Maleness." *Psychoanalytic Quarterly* 34 (1965): 207–18.

THE "BEDROCK" OF MASCULINITY AND FEMININITY: BISEXUALITY

Beach, F. A. *Sex and Behavior.* New York: John Wiley, 1965.

Diamond, M. *Perspectives in Reproduction and Sexual Behavior.* Bloomington, Ind.: Indiana University Press, 1968.

Green, R., and Money, J., eds. *Transsexualism and Sex Reassignment*. Baltimore: Johns Hopkins Press, 1969.

Kleeman, J. A. "The Establishment of Core Gender Identity in Normal Girls." In *Archives of Sexual Behavior*. Forthcoming.

Marmor, Judd, ed. *Sexual Inversion*. New York: Basic Books, 1965.

Stoller, Robert J. *Sex and Gender*. New York: Science House, 1968.

PHOBIAS AFTER MARRIAGE: WOMEN'S DECLARATION OF DEPENDENCE

Binger, Carl A. L. "Emotional Disturbances among College Women." In *Emotional Problems of the Student,* edited by Graham B. Baline, Jr. New York: Doubleday, 1961.

Horney, Karen. *Neurosis and Human Growth*. New York: W. W. Norton, 1950.

———. *Our Inner Conflicts*. New York: W. W. Norton, 1945.

Redlich, Fredrick C., and Freedman, Daniel X. *The Theory and Practice of Psychiatry*. New York: Basic Books, 1966.

Salzman, Leon. *The Obsessive Personality*. New York: Science House, 1968.

IS ANATOMY DESTINY?

Chapsal, Madeline. "Feminine Plural, Present Tense." *New York Times Book Review,* 12 March 1967.

Clurman, Harold. "Our Neglected Women." *World Journal Tribune Magazine,* 12 March 1967.

Mannes, Marya. "What Every Male Should Know," *Sunday Herald Tribune Book Week,* 14 February 1965.

Mill, John Stuart. *Letters of Sigmund Freud*. Selected and edited by Ernst J. Freud. New York: Basic Books, 1960.

———. "The Subjection of Women." In *Three Essays*. London: Oxford University Press, 1912.

Sampson, R. V. *The Psychology of Power*. New York: Pantheon Books, 1966.

FOR THE FUTURE—EQUITY?

Mill, John Stuart. "The Subjection of Women." In *Three Essays*. London: Oxford University Press, 1966.

Sampson, R. V. *The Psychology of Power.* New York: Pantheon Books, 1966.

Seidenberg, Robert. "Sacrificing the First You See." *Psychoanalytic Review* 1 (Spring 1966).

———. "The Sexual Bias of Social Prejudice." *Psychoanalytic Review* 39, no. 1 (1952).

Wilson, John. *Logic and Sexual Morality.* Baltimore, Md.: Penguin Books, 1965.

THE TRAUMA OF EVENTLESSNESS

Deutsch, Helene. "The Genesis of Agoraphobia." *International Journal of Psycho-Analysis* 10 (1929).

Erikson, Erik H. "Reality and Actuality." *Journal of the American Psychoanalytic Association* 10 (1962): 459–60.

Feldman, S. "Anxiety and Orgasm." *Psychoanalytic Quarterly* 20 (1951): 528–49.

Gero, G. "Sadism, Masochism and Aggression: Their Role in Symptom Formation." *Psychoanalytic Quarterly* 31 (1962).

Miller, M. "On Street Fear." *International Journal of Psycho-Analysis* 34 (1953): 232–40.

Ruddick, B. "Agoraphobia." *International Journal of Psycho-Analysis* 42 (1962): 537–43.

Stein, M. M. "Fear of Death and Neurosis." *Journal of the American Psychoanalytic Association* 16 (1968): 3–31.

Waelder, R. "Inhibitions, Symptoms and Anxiety: Forty Years Later." *Psychoanalytic Quarterly* 36 (1967).

MASCULINITY-FEMININITY: A STUDY IN IMPOSED INEQUALITY

Mill, John Stuart. "The Subjection of Women." In *Three Essays.* London: Oxford University Press, 1966.

Thompson, William. *Appeal of One Half of the Human Race, Women, Against the Pretensions of the Other Half, Men, to Retain them in Political, and thence in Civil and Domestic Slavery* (1825). New York: Source Book Press, 1970.

Winick, Charles. *The New People: Desexualization in American Life.* New York: Pegasus, 1968.

Wollstonecraft, Mary. *A Vindication of the Rights of Women* (1792). New York: Source Book Press, 1970.

CONCLUSION: NEW ISSUES, NEW APPROACHES

Block, J. H. "Conceptions of Sex Role: Some Cross-Cultural and Longitudinal Perspectives." Institute of Human Development, University of California, Berkeley. Bernard Moses Memorial Lecture, 1972.

Broverman, I., Broverman, D., et al. "Sex Role Stereotypes and Clinical Judgements of Mental Health." *Journal of Consulting and Clinical Psychology* 34 (1970): 1–7.

Gelfman, Morris. "A Post-Freudian Comment on Sexuality." *American Journal of Psychiatry* 126 (1969): 651–57.

Miller, Jean B. "Sexual Inequality: Men's Dilemma. A Note on Paranoia, the Oedipus Complex and Other Concepts." *American Journal of Psychoanalysis* 32, no. 2 (1972): 147–55.

———, and Mothner, Ira. "Psychological Consequences of Sexual Inequality." *American Journal of Orthopsychiatry* 41, no. 5 (1971): 767–75.

Robbins, Bernard. "The Nature of Femininity." Proceedings of the Feminine Psychology Symposium. New York: Psychoanalytic Division, Department of Psychiatry, New York Medical College, 1950.

Seidenberg, Robert. "Does Misogyny Sell Mind Drugs?" Paper presented at the New York State District Branch Meeting, American Psychiatric Association, November 1971.

———. "Is Sex without Sexism Possible?" *Sexual Behavior* (January 1972): 47–62.

———. "Older Women and Younger Men." *Sexual Behavior* (April 1972): 9–17.

Wortis, Rochelle P. "The Acceptance of the Concept of the Maternal Role by Behavioral Scientists: Its Effects on Women." *American Journal of Orthopsychiatry* 41, no. 5 (1971): 733–46.